THE CIVILIZATION OF THE AMERICAN INDIAN SERIES

HALF–SUN ON THE COLUMBIA

HALF-SUN
ON THE
COLUMBIA

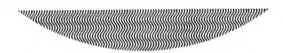

A Biography of Chief Moses

By ROBERT H. RUBY

AND

JOHN A. BROWN

FOREWORD BY
ANGIE DEBO

INTRODUCTION BY
DEWARD E. WALKER, JR.

UNIVERSITY OF OKLAHOMA PRESS
NORMAN AND LONDON

Dedicated to
Jessica and Joey
and Kay

Library of Congress Cataloging-in-Publication Data

Ruby, Robert H.
   Half-Sun on the Columbia : a biography of Chief Moses / by Robert
H. Ruby and John A. Brown ; foreword by Angie Debo ; introduction
by Deward E. Walker, Jr.
      p.   cm. — (The civilization of the American Indian series ; v. 80)
   Includes bibliographical references and index.
   ISBN 0-8061-2738-4 (pbk.)
      1. Moses, Chief, ca 1829–1899.   2. Sinkiuse-Columbia Indians—
Biography.   3. Sinkiuse-Columbia Indians—Government relations.
I. Brown, John Arthur.   II. Title.   III. Series.
E99.S55M677   1995
979.7'03'092—dc20   94-37092
[B]   CIP

3   4   5   6   7   8   9   10   11   12

Foreword

BY ANGIE DEBO

IT IS AXIOMATIC to say that the American Indians have exerted an influence all out of proportion to their numbers upon the history of the United States. This is true whether it was a Squanto showing the Pilgrims the New World techniques, which alone enabled them to survive; a Tecumseh allied with the enemy in wartime in a threat to push back the boundaries of the young Republic; or a rush to Indian lands—in Georgia, Dakota, California, Oklahoma, wherever the tide of settlement flowed—involving local populations and national leaders in wholesale corruption and exploitation.

This story has been often told, but usually from the standpoint of what it did to the white people who encountered the Indians, whether these white people were helped or hindered in their progress, even how their moral standards were affected. True, scholarly books have been written showing the bad faith, the cruelty, the greed of which the Indians were often the victims, but this is still the white man's history. How the Indians felt and what all this did to them have been largely untold.

Even from this standpoint the name of Chief Moses (Sulktalthscosum or Half-Sun) of the Salish-speaking people of the mid-Columbia is written large upon the history of the Pacific Northwest. Unlike the Popés, the Tecumsehs, the Sitting Bulls, the Satantas, he held his united tribes at peace in spite of an almost unendurable pressure that would have swept the entire area with fire and death. The history of that frontier is very different from what it would have been except for him. This is the white man's story. Dr. Ruby and Mr. Brown understand it well, and it is always the background of their biography. It forms a case study of the vitality and savage strength of the white frontier, and the accommodation of public officials to its onward sweep.

vii

But this is background only. Their central story is the life of Moses, and they have been able to break the barriers of language and culture and present it from the inside looking out. His one life span (1829–99) bridged the transition from native to white society. In his childhood he knew the ordered confusion of the Indian camp, the jogging movement on the trail, the hunts and the fights with enemy tribes on the buffalo plains, and the seeking after Power to guide the warrior's life. Even then the white man's presence was apparent, for his chieftain father sent him to a mission school; but he mounted his horse and rode away relatively untouched by its religion or its learning. As a fledgling warrior he killed a Blackfoot foe, and soon he won a name for himself opposing the white man by stealthy attacks on lone travelers and in open battle with avenging soldiers.

Then with maturity and the responsibilities of chieftainship, he became a statesman, ambitious to extend his authority, concerned for the welfare of his people, convinced of the futility of resisting the mounting white encroachment. But although regardless of provocation and injustice he held the peace, as long as adroit diplomacy would serve he maintained his independence from government control. Eventually he lost this contest, too, and became a reservation Indian, exposed to "civilizing" influences, instructed in farming, and urged to educate his children.

He always remained an Indian. He dismissed the missionaries' religion as absurd: if hell was hot, why didn't the water boil in the white man's well? The mention of monogamy incensed him; it would cause the "breaking up of families." He had a mystical reverence for the Great Father at Washington, but he saw through the schemes of his underlings and thwarted them so far as possible. Industrious and thrifty in the old way of living by the rhythm of salmon fishing, root-gathering, planting, and hunting, he rejected the white man's more serious economic efforts. "We do not want to work and don't know how. Indians are too old to learn that when five years old." As his power and influence declined and his responsibilities fell away in the stagnation of reservation life, he sought pleasure in uninhibited eating and drinking, racing his horses and joining the celebrations in the booming new towns, and visiting white friends now settled in the familiar haunts of his childhood.

One significant experience of those years was his relationship to Chief Joseph of the Nez Percés. Joseph has always had a romantic interest for historians of Indian wars because of his masterly retreat, his tragic defeat and surrender, and his banishment to the Indian Territory; but only in this biography of Moses have the remaining twenty years of his life been told. The two had long been friends, and when the Nez Percés went to war it had been difficult for Moses to resist his appeal for aid. Even during his exile he had managed to communicate with Moses, and when he and his people were finally permitted to return to the Northwest, he joined Moses on the reservation. For years the two were inseparable, sharing their frustrations and uniting their voices in complaint. Then perhaps because of the deadly monotony of their lives, their relationship was marred for a time by petty jealousy and mistrust.

Joseph is only the most well known of Moses' associates. Many others are there—chiefs, prophets, renegades, wives, youthful protégés, even young children—and all appear as distinct personalities. Here is not only Moses' life, but tribal and family relationships and participation in joy and sorrow.

Moses never relaxed his care for his family and his people—his "children," as he called the members of his band—but tragedy struck down the ones nearest to him. "He was made an old man too soon and too sad," said one of his people. But his spirit was sunny and his humor never left him. On his deathbed he joked feebly about the old Indian custom of marrying widows to the brothers of the deceased—"Of course I am the homeliest of my family," he said. When he died, the white man's probate laws gave way to the biggest potlatch ever held in the Northwest.

Thus the biography of Chief Moses gives a graphic picture of what the confrontation of an advanced and a primitive race meant to the one that had to yield. Through the skill of its authors, who combine extensive research with sensitive perception, it is even more than that. It is an important human document, and its meaning is universal.

Introduction

BY DEWARD E. WALKER, JR.

THROUGH THEIR MANY WRITINGS, Robert H. Ruby and John A. Brown have deepened our understanding of the interaction of Indian and non-Indian peoples of the Northwest. Their work has brought to light and documented neglected topics, events, and personalities often ignored by academic writers. Much of their writing focuses on the lives of influential but little-known Indian leaders, and this book is no exception. In *Half-Sun on the Columbia* the authors portray the life of an important and heretofore largely ignored Indian leader, Chief Moses of the Columbia Indians. They deliver an even-handed biography of Moses drawn especially from official documents, and they reveal Moses to be one of the great leaders who helped shape the early history of the Columbia Basin into its present social and political form. The approach taken by the authors reveals the importance of Moses' interaction with federal officials, such as Gen. Oliver Howard, and demonstrates how their relationship helped create the reservation system now operating in the Columbia Basin.

Ruby and Brown also document the federal practice of attributing extraordinary powers to a few Indian leaders in order to gain their support for agreements that might otherwise have been rejected by rank-and-file tribal members. The authors demonstrate that the federal bureaucracy rewarded Indian leaders who cooperated with their programs of land cessions, concentration of tribal populations on reservations, and other actions necessary to open tribal lands for non-Indian settlement. Moses and other Indian leaders became pawns in games played by governors, generals, and federal officials, in which the various Indian tribes increasingly were viewed as obstacles to non-Indian settlement of the Northwest. Ruby and Brown make a major contribution in reveal-

xi

ing that Moses was able to negotiate favorable agreements with such officials, showing his awareness of these federal practices and his diplomatic skill and sophistication in overcoming them.

Ruby and Brown continue to demonstrate the value of official records as source material for ethnohistory and ethnohistorical biography. Their efforts have opened new areas for research into the complex events surrounding the confrontation of Indians and non-Indians in the settlement of the Columbia Basin. We are indebted considerably to these two tireless writers who have spent most of their lives developing a history of the Northwest.

Preface to the Paperback Edition

IN THE FOLLOWING PAGES we present the story of Moses, the Columbia chief who futilely resisted the encroaching white man and then made peace with him as others of his race were making what has been popularly called the red man's last stand. Leaders in that struggle—Geronimo, Cochise, Crazy Horse, Sitting Bull, and others are well known. The peacemaking of our subject assured him a place not among the blazoned, but among the blessed, yet this assured him no immunity from persecution and misunderstanding which trailed him beyond the grave. Nor did it insure him from sadness as he watched the victorious white man choke the trail which had been his way of life.

The gathering and piecing together of information preparatory to narrating the story of such an unheralded, misunderstood, and saddened life have been a stimulating experience for us. In preparing the story, we have drawn on the white man's record—largely printed—and that of the Indian—largely verbal. Despite our caution in the use of the latter we have found that in most cases it paralleled the former. For example, the Chief's great-granddaughter told us that the stagecoach in which he was riding was robbed as it wheeled toward the home of the Great Father in Washington City in 1883. As the narrative unfolded, two reasonably intelligent white men knew the story was poppycock, for the Northern Pacific Railroad on which Moses traveled east had been completed—or so we believed until we discovered that there remained unspanned a short, robber-infested distance traversed by stagecoaches in western Montana. Our researches in the white man's record have as yet yielded no definite proof of the robbery, but in time the story may be proved true.

Since this volume first was published we have confirmed our judgment that eloquence in discourse and elegance in apparel were very important to Moses, especially in his adult years. Through both he expressed his statesmanship when dealing with the increasing numbers of whites entering the interior of the Pacific Northwest, particularly his Columbia Plateau homeland. We remember the words of one Indian informant: "Moses should have been an actor."

In 1877, through his eloquence Moses persuaded his restless young warriors not to join his friend Chief Joseph and the Nez Percé in their flight from the U.S. Army. Again, in 1878, he restrained his warriors from allying themselves with the Bannock-Paiutes against American forces. But in 1879, speaking with Gen. O. O. Howard's emissary Edward ("Ned") Chambreau, Moses disclosed his remorse at the loss of his lands to whites and his fear both of their aggressions against Indians and of Indian reprisals against whites:

You know the Nez Perces were always the friends of the whites. You know at the time of the Whitman murder that one white man ran to the Nez Perces for protection and got it. You know they gloried in never having spilled a white man's blood. Now, while General Howard was fighting Joseph and his people [1877], I did not take a bad heart and make the ground red. When the Piutes and Bannacks [sic] were fighting we kept out of it.

A long time ago (1854) Gen. [Joel] Palmer called all the Indians together and he told me and my people that I could always stay all around from White Bluffs, Moses Lake, Priest's Rapids, Moses Coolie [sic], Grand Coolie [sic] and Wenatchee. We were strong then, and there were few Bostons (white settlers). They were poor and afraid of me. Now the Bostons are strong and they don't want the Indians to live. What shall we do? We look upon this land as we do on the sun. This land is our father and mother. I take a bad heart in my dreams because of my land and my people. Strongly I tell you, to part with my land is like parting with my flesh. It is now two moons since Gen. Howard and I spoke together. Has he talked crooked to me or has he talked straight? My people say to me:

Moses, you are an old woman; you will never get any other land. You have taken bad medicine. Gen. Howard and all the Bostons are laughing at you. The white men all around me have taken bad hearts because of the Indians. They are coming here to kill my people. The Indians have no friend to talk strong to the great father at Washington. Does the great father at Washington know we need to be pitied? Is not the white man's blood red, the Indian's blood red? Do we not all turn our faces towards the sun? Oh, Frenchman! my heart is heavy and sick. The old men and the old women cry to Moses. The mothers are looking for places to hide the little ones. The young men have lost their senses, and they have become as wolves. They want to tear the white man's flesh and drink his blood. Help me to talk strong to my people, that they may take the right road. I am done. (*Oregonian*, February 23, 1881)

Following the capture of Joseph and his people and defeat of the Bannock-Paiutes in 1878, Moses journeyed to Washington, D.C., to present his people's plight to Department of Interior officials and to President Rutherford B. Hayes. Promised a reservation for his people, and having seen the great numbers of white people in the capital, he was fortified in his resolve to maintain peaceful relations with the whites.

While Lewis O. Saum, professor of history at the University of Washington, was researching the life of Bill Nye, the humorist, he uncovered an interesting reference to Moses' visit in Washington. The visit of Moses and his party to Cheyenne, on their way to Washington, served as an excuse for the *Cheyenne Daily Sun* (Wyoming) to disparage the *Laramie Leader* (Wyoming). Nye, a writer for the *Sun*, succeeded in talking with Moses and other chiefs in the party, and wrote: "I talked with several of the chiefs, but their conversational powers were all out of order, so I excused them."

In the interview, published April 6, 1879, Nye did nearly all the talking, ending his column with this comment: "I don't know when I have enjoyed a little social interchange of ideas as I did this one. These Indians, of course, as any one will see by the remarks which I have quoted above, are a little reserved and non-committal, and are resolved to go to Washington un-pledged, but at the same time their quiet, unassuming ways and ladylike behavior will not fail to win them bests of friends wherever they may go."

Not to be outdone, the *Leader* correspondent attempted to "scoop" his rival, Nye, by interviewing Moses on his return from Washington. His attempt proved unsuccessful because an Indi-an agent, A. N. Cornoyer, barred the correspondent from enter-ing the train car in which Moses was eating dinner. In the April 30, 1879, edition of the *Sun*, Nye made much of the *Leader* correspondent's failure. No doubt exaggerating, Nye reported that after "a brief scuffle . . . the next instant a plug hat, cane, note-book and some other dilapidated rubbish [belonging to the *Leader* correspondent] was observed scattered on the track on the opposite side of the train. . . . It was the quickest and qui-etest grand bounce ever witnessed in Wyoming."

As for Moses' sartorial correctness, what might be termed "The Saga of Chief Moses' Clothing" began nearly a decade ago when a copy of *Half-Sun* found its way to New Zealand, where anthropologist G. S. Park of Dunedin's Otago Museum told us that his institution held the chief's clothing. We feared the items were those that had been stolen from his body in the grave by two renegade white men, who subsequently fled to Canada. We journeyed to Sydney to meet with Wendy Harsant, Otago's curator, who was vacationing in Australia. From there we went to Dunedin, where anthropologist Dimitri Anson displayed for us "Moses' clothing." On it were celestial insignia such as Moses wore. At this point we were certain the clothing was not that from the grave. At his death the portly (over two hundred pound) Moses could not have been dressed in these smaller Otago garments. Furthermore there were no spoiled areas on the leather that would suggest a burial.

Our journey to New Zealand, which sparked considerable interest back home in Washington, became the subject of news-paper interviews and "letters to the editor." It was also the subject of an article we wrote: "In Search of Chief Moses's Lost Possessions" (*Columbia: The Magazine of Northwest History* 1, no. 3 [fall 1987], 21–28). The board of Seattle's Burke Museum considered bringing the clothing to the Pacific Northwest to display in the "Time of Gathering" exhibit, which featured Washington's American Indian artifacts for the state's centennial celebration in 1989. The board decided, however, that the taint of the grave robbery was reason not to return the materials to America.

The matter did not rest. Wendy Harsant wrote an article on Moses' clothing in *American Art* 13, no. 2 (spring 1988). Anthropologists Anson and Moria White then wrote the lead article on the clothing for a new Australian magazine, *Coastal Observer Peoples Magazine* 1, no. 1 (July 1993). Pieces of the puzzling connection between the Columbia Plateau and New Zealand's South Island finally were put together. During hop-picking time in Washington's Yakima Valley, Indians had traded the clothing to a merchant for his goods. The clothing then was taken to Portland's Lewis and Clark Centennial and from there across the Pacific Ocean, thousands of miles from the home of its original wearer.

Stories about Moses' penchant for clothes crop up repeatedly. He maintained his reputation as a clothes horse by wearing flashy Indian attire or clothes similar to those of tasteful white men. He frequently attended celebrations of whites, where his sartorial splendor was highly visible. One such event was a July 4 celebration in the Big Bend town of Sherman, south across the Columbia River from the Colville Indian Reservation. According to the *Sprague Journal*, July 9, 1886: "Chiefs Moses and Joseph rode up. Moses was fantastically attired in a superb white buckskin suit." Further comments on the two dealt exclusively with Moses' betting on his favorite horse and rider. The account, which we recently discovered, reveals the close relationship between Moses and the Nez Percé chief, despite Moses' isolationist posture during the so-called Nez Percé War.

Reviewing a number of books on American Indians in an article entitled "Will the Indians Get Whitey?" in the March 11,

1969, issue of the *National Review,* anthropologist John Greenway referred to "guilt-ridden, history distorting" writers of such books as *Half-Sun,* challenging our depiction of Moses as a peace chief. In his early years, as we point out in the book, Moses followed the restless young warrior syndrome. His later, mature years, however, were devoted to peacekeeping. We stand by this contention and are pleased that Moses for his stance was included among a hundred Washingtonians in the state's 1989 Bicentennial Hall of Honor.

Robert H. Ruby, Moses Lake
John A. Brown, Wenatchee

Contents

Foreword *by Angie Debo*   *page* vii

Introduction *by Deward E. Walker, Jr.*   xi

Preface to the Paperback Edition   xiii

I.   Loolowkin the Child   3

II.   Quetalican the Warrior   21

III.   Terra Infirma   43

IV.   War Drums or Peace Pipes?   64

V.   Paddle Wheels and Deals   86

VI.   Reds, Whites, and the Blues   98

VII.   Forked Tongues and Twisted Trails   120

VIII.   Down from Camp to Father   141

IX.   Hail Columbia—Promised Land   156

X.   Ill-Fated Illihee   167

XI.   White Giver   191

XII.   Farmers in the Dell   214

XIII.   Prophets and Losses   244

XIV.   Reading, Writing, and Wrangling   265

XV.   Double Trouble   278

XVI.   Tempest in a Tipi   297

XVII.   Vanity and the Fair   321

XVIII.   One Wide River   347

Bibliography   351

Index   365

Illustrations

Chief Moses, 1897   *opposite page* 76
Chief Joseph of the Nez Percés   77
General Oliver Otis Howard   108
Francis Streamer, Editor of the Omaha *Herald*   109
Washington, D.C., Delegation, 1879   172
Chief Sarsopkin of the Okanogans   173
Chief Lot of the Spokanes   204
Skolaskin, Self-appointed Leader of the San Poil Indians   205
Chief Moses in a Coat Made by His Wife Mary   300
Father Stephen deRouge, S. J.   301
Mary, Chief Moses' Wife   332
Chief Moses in the Clothes of the White Man   333

MAPS

Land of the Half-Sun   *pages* 12–13
Yakama [Yakima] Treaty Cession, Ratified March 8, 1859   31
Moses' Reservation Requests of 1877 and 1878   95
Moses Posse Sites   117
Moses (Columbia) Reservation by Executive Orders of
    April 19, 1879, and March 6, 1880   153
Colville Reservation by Executive Order of July 2, 1872   209

HALF–SUN ON THE COLUMBIA

I. Loolowkin the Child

"My parents gave birth to me here, and I fancy that this is my Country."—Moses to Indian agent, Okanogan River, June 30, 1870.

MIDWAY IN ITS JOURNEY from the glacial streams of the Canadian icefields to the misty Pacific, the Columbia River (Enbotquatqua) makes a sweeping bend like the arc of an ellipse. Here lived the Columbia Sinkiuse,[1] usually known as the Columbias, an interior Salish-speaking people, with their chieftain, Sulktalthscosum (Piece Split from the Sun), the Half-Sun or Scarred-Sun. Sulktalthscosum was a son of Slukpostaglanna (Wolf with Chain of Hearts), named for the headgear he wore for stalking game.[2] It is believed that Sulktalthscosum was born at the time of an eclipse about 1800 in the Coulee Chuckahmiahpast (Moses Coulee), which gashes westward through the basalt of the Columbia Plateau to the lower end of the bend of the Columbia River. For a time he bore the name Sqoolalthscosum, the Half-Moon, but after assuming the chieftaincy, he changed it to the Half-Sun to fit his rising power better. His ascendancy was not based on heredity alone, but on exploits in war, the chase, and diplomacy and on the acquisition of horses, goods, and wives.

For the Half-Sun the acquisition of horses was a slow process, involving many trips east across the Plateau to the Spokane

1 White traders and other white men called them the Sinkiuse, Sincayuse, or Columbia Cayuse to distinguish them from the Cayuse (Waiilatpaun), who were sometimes called the Nez Percé Cayuse. Sometimes they were called the Priest Rapids and Rock Island Peoples (Isles de Pierres). They were also called the Kawahchen, their native word for Rock Island. For a background on these people, see James H. Teit, "The Middle Columbia Salish," University of Washington *Publications in Anthropology*, II (1928), 83–128.

2 The early nineteenth-century fur trader, Alexander Ross, wrote: "The royal insignia of an Indian King or Chief is simple, and is always known in camp. . . . It is suspended from a pole in a conspicuous place near the Chief's lodge." See *Adventures of the First Settlers on the Oregon or Columbia River*, 291.

country and south to the Chelohan root grounds overlooking the Kittitas Valley. There, he annually joined hundreds of natives from the vast area between the Rocky and Cascade Mountains in temporary villages bursting with the din of their trafficking, politicking, gaming, and particularly horse racing.[3] From these and other aboriginal fairs beyond the Plateau, he brought his horses home to feed on the nutritious bunch grass of that high land, where his young men watched them closely to prevent their being stolen by nearby bands, particularly the Yakimas and the Cayuses from the south. Sulktalthscosum and his men became as capable as any horsemen in history. The horse gave the chieftain not only his royalty, but his mobility; it enabled the tall, agile, ambidextrous huntsman to range eastward across the Rockies through the treacherous lands of the Blackfeet (Stqueequeno) and far down the Missouri, even to the edge of white settlement.

Perhaps the first white man the Half-Sun met in his Columbia River homeland was the North West Company trader, David Thompson, in 1811 near Rock Island (below Wenatchee, Wash.). Nor'Westers occupied Fort Okanogan, near the confluence of the Columbia and Okanogan rivers, from 1813 until 1821, when the Hudson's Bay Company took over. From that company's main post, Fort Vancouver, the Half-Sun returned with many new things: chickens—"strange grouse," which would roost in their lodge-poles and crow each morning—and potatoes—"strange camas," which were much larger and yet less tasty than their own. He instructed them to till the soil of the flat with their mattocks and fashion tools from limbs and trunks of hawthorne bushes to beat the clods for planting the tubers. Subirrigation in the flat and cool breezes blowing across it from the broad Columbia kept the plants from withering during the summer, and the Columbias harvested their first crop in the fall. Once Sulktalthscosum re-turned from the fort with a large number of hogs, which he turned loose in a canyon west of the Columbia where they soon became a nuisance, uprooting the grass and edible roots of the

3 For a description of this tipi city in 1814, see Alexander Ross, *The Fur Hunters of the Far West*, 22–24.

4

area. On his final trip he acquired a small herd of six cattle of the "Spanish breed," previously driven overland from Mexican settlements in California to the fort. He turned these slim, hardy, long-horned, rather vicious animals loose on the plains east of the Columbia where they multiplied rapidly. After 1833 he drove horses to Fort Nisqually of the Hudson's Bay Company to exchange for more cattle for his home ranges.

When he distributed his cackling chickens, banging hardware, and lowing cattle to his goods-hungry people, their eyes opened in wonder as did his own in pride. Now that they had chickens they might not have to hunt sagehens. Now they could cook their chickens and other food in the iron kettles rather than in those laboriously fashioned from wood and stone. Now that they had guns they would not have to kill deer by stampeding them over basalt cliffs. With cattle they might not have to depend so much on deer for food. The white man was good.

The Half-Sun was also a man of diplomacy, maintaining his leadership between the Cascade and Rocky Mountains to a great extent by marrying women throughout that area. Since they often chose to remain in their far-flung villages, he contented himself with occasional visits to them. His many marital ties and journeys to hunt buffalo—"to buffalo," as they called it—kept him away from the Columbia for increasingly longer periods of time. Occasionally, he returned to the river to prepare for dangerous trips into the Plains.[4]

In his Columbia villages, like the one at Wenatchee Flat, he joined old friends who had come from far and near to play and palaver around driftwood fires and to snare the salmon flashing their way up the two streams. It may have been on one of these occasions that Karneetsa (Between the Robes), the chief's favorite

[4] An account of Sulktalthscosum's early travels is given in Harold Weaver's "A Tour of the Old Indian Camp Grounds of Central Washington." See also A. J. Splawn, *Ka-Mi-akin, the Last Hero of the Yakimas*, 281–82. Further information on the exploits of Sulktalthscosum was derived from interviews with Emily Peone at Auburn, Washington, May 1 and May 6, 1962, and May 4, 1963. These and other interviews with Mrs. Peone are hereafter referred to as Peone Interviews and an interview with Moses George, of Wenatchee, Washington, June 8, 1963, as Moses George Interview.

wife, a half-Spokane who had been pledged to him from child-hood, awaited the birth of her child. That the birth occurred about 1829 on the Flat, we learn only from the child, who when an old man presented this meager information for the printed record.[5] It was customary among peoples along the mid-Columbia for expectant mothers, accompanied by attendants, to repair to simple oblong shelters framed with cross poles and covered with reeds to give birth to their children. Then, according to ancient custom, relatives of the newly born held informal feasts in the babies' honor at which they passed them around, greeting them warmly.

Although the baby had older brothers who could one day assume the chieftaincy on Sulktalthscosum's death, the child's father must have rejoiced that the Half-Sun royalty had gained a new member, because the threat of extinction hung over those he was so carefully grooming for the task. Tradition has it that his people once numbered ten thousand and occupied lands stretch-ing from the Cascade Ridge (Kenkempkin) on the west to the San Poil and Spokane rivers on the north and east, and south to the valley of the Umatilla and across the Plateau to the bound-aries of the great Nez Percé nations.[6] Disease had been the chief agent in reducing the band to but a few hundred souls.[7] Shortly before Sulktalthscosum's birth, smallpox had been carried over-land from the East to the Columbia, where it had finally burned itself out only to come again with other diseases on ships by way of the Pacific, transforming the lower river into a valley of death. Pitted faces warned that it might return, and at the time of the

[5] Interview, *Seattle Post-Intelligencer* (Seattle, Washington), October 23, 1895, p. 2. A few days before this interview, in a brief autobiography given in Yakima, he claimed his birthplace to be the Moses Coulee country (Chief Moses "Autobiog-raphy," Spokane Public Library). Since the Wenatchee River is but a few miles from Moses Coulee, his word is perhaps correct. However, some present-day Indians maintain that he was born neither at the mouth of the Wenatchee nor in Moses Coulee, but on the buffalo ranges.

[6] Teit, "Middle Columbia Salish," University of Washington *Publications in Anthropology*, II (1928), 102.

[7] James Mooney, "The Aboriginal Populations of America North of Mexico," *Smithsonian Miscellaneous Collections*, Vol. LXXX, No. 7 (1928), 16.

child's birth, the "intermittent fever," probably malaria, was taking a heavy toll of life on the lower Columbia.

About the time the child had eaten his first solid food, he received the name Loolowkin (the Head Band). A white explorer in their country gave the following explanation of the Indians' nomenclature: "Their adoption of names is arbitrary, and a fortuitous circumstance is frequently seized upon to gratify the passion for a change. The first name they bear is generally taken from some circumstance at the child's birth, and in after life, others are added to the first, and there are few individuals but are well supplied with them."[8]

Being a child of the traveling Half-Sun, Loolowkin spent his early years not only in the Columbia watershed, but also in that of the Missouri. Crossing the Plateau, the lad jogged along cayuseback with a motley group—his parents, brothers, sisters, other relatives, and members of the band, including servants. They sought security in the company of other buffalo-bound Salishans—Spokanes, Coeur d'Alenes, Pend Oreilles, and Kalispells, the latter met at Clark Fork, which they leisurely followed, packing and unpacking along the way. As one white member of a similar party observed, "for wherever they are, that place is their home."[9] After several suns they came to Hell Gate, present-day Missoula, lying before them with a beauty betraying the sinister name derived from the many Blackfoot raids on this gathering place of many streams and peoples.

Near Hell Gate they were usually joined by another Salish people, the Flatheads, their staunchest allies on their buffalo trips and their best buffer against the Blackfoot raiders. In the previous century, the Blackfeet had driven the Flatheads out of the Plains into the Bitter Root Valley just west of the Divide, where their closeness to the buffalo herds had been offset by their closeness to the fierce plainsmen who had nearly annihilated them. The Blackfeet had even raided Salish territory as far west as the

[8] Charles Wilkes, U.S.N., *Narrative of the United States Exploring Expedition,* IV, 456.
[9] Samuel Parker, *Journal of an Exploring Tour Beyond the Rocky Mountains,* 106.

7

Columbia, plundering salmon stores and killing the old ones and children while their men were away. The Flatheads attempted to hold off the attackers with guns given them by white traders, and with these new weapons they had become somewhat less dependent on other Salishans although they continued to welcome them as allies in a common cause.

The travelers from the West often depended upon the Flatheads to tell them the location of the buffalo herds and to point out the best of the several routes across the Rockies to find them. Following this advice, they sometimes went up the pleasant country to the Jocko or up the Hell Gate River where they would break off at the Little Blackfeet River, a well-traveled path to buffalo that was open and well watered, with ample grass and fuel, through the passes to the arteries of the Missouri. Sometimes they traveled the valley of the Bitter Root swinging east to the Missouri tributaries flowing north of the Yellowstone. Reaching the Missouri, Loolowkin and his people exchanged the jogging of their cayuses for the dangerous ride to the opposite shore with their *bundles*, strange-looking craft covered with tipi hides. As horses towed the *bundles*, containing camp gear and personal belongings, the Columbians had themselves towed by holding on to the tipi ropes for dear life.[10]

After the Columbians had settled in the buffalo camps, Loolowkin tested his feet on the curly buffalograss of the Plains. While Karneetsa performed her chores and her husband hunted buffalo, the boy, taking advantage of the absence of the old ones, who had remained near the Columbia, played boisterously in camp. Sometimes he led his young friends into the braves' tipi sheltering the sacred eagle feathers earned by the warriors for courage in battle. Karneetsa, knowing that any disturbance to the trophies would bring ill fortune to their owners, would chase the "invaders" out of the tipi; but the children only retreated to more mischief in the forbidden bow and arrow or

10 Peone Interviews. Mrs. Peone's description of these *bundles* corresponds to information in Gregory Mengarini's narrative (*Mengarini's Narrative of the Rockies*, 16–17).

maternity tipis. Sometimes, the boy led his playmates in throwing dirt on buffalo meat slowly curing over a smoking fire or in dropping sticks into the wooden bowls in which Karneetsa was stirring buffalo broth. Karneetsa would then give the ringleader a few light blows of a switch. If this were ineffective, she tied his hands and feet as did her chieftain husband with errant adult members of his band. Loolowkin, a strong-willed child, resented his mother's discipline, and Karneetsa sometimes had to confine her young prisoner for several hours before releasing him with the warning that if he did not behave, the "Old Man from up the River" would carry him away. Sometimes she turned him over to the "Whipper," a man of the band who disciplined the children by administering blows of willow withes tied in a bundle.

As the children grew older, they carried their games and mischief-making outside of camp, sometimes steam-cooking wild rose berries and gorging themselves on the delicacy to baffle Karneetsa with their loss of appetite. Once a poor old woman died and was carried on a mat litter to her grave. On the way, her patched and torn moccasins protruded, evoking much laughter from Loolowkin and his playmates, who were quite unaware that she was dead. After the burial Sulktalthscosum placed a stick in Loolowkin's mouth to keep him from screaming and then administered five blows with the willow withes.

The return of the men from the hunts was an exciting time for Loolowkin, especially when they brought horses and scalps from Blackfeet encounters. On these occasions they danced the victory scalp dance, followed by a less exciting time of processing the shaggy hides of the big beasts.[11]

It was not unusual for the parties to remain on the Plains for a year or longer. On long winter nights by buffalo campfires Loolowkin heard stories of the old days—perhaps of how his ancestors used to meet with the Spokanes to fire the Plateau toward Grand Coulee (Inches) to stampede and kill antelopes, or of snows (the *Skiniramun*) along the Columbia, when gray bands encircled the sun and moon, and the sun shone coldly in a sky,

11 Peone Interviews.

9

icy blue on the evening horizon, and a million stars shivered in silence at night. Then the dreaded wolves stalked down from the north and forced people to huddle on the floors of their pit houses some four feet below the surface of the ground. Overhead, hides stretched over frameworks of wood poles were poor baffles to keep out the noise of the beasts wailing all night in the hills. In the mornings the Indians crept up the ladders of their semi-subterranean dwellings to the corrals to find their horses killed or badly clawed by the marauders. And, of course, there were the always popular stories of the legendary Coyote, the intermediary between the animals, yet a great trickster who, along with Gray Squirrel, was responsible for the absence of buffalo in the Coulee Chuckahmiahpast.[12]

The return to the Columbia did not end the travels of the young nomad. Sometimes, he would ride with his people to visit the Chelans, whose glacial-fed lake penetrated arrow-like into the craggy Cascades. In contrast were visits to the warm waters of Soap Lake (Smoqueem), "The Healing Waters, where the Great Spirit Doctor Lives." There his ailing people would seek relief for their stiff and rheumatic bodies. From there, perhaps, they would ride south a short distance to Howaph (a Willow), now Moses Lake, for fishing and egg-gathering along its marshy shores or for hunting sagehens and deer on the nearby plain. Oftentimes, they would swing north again to rest and play at the campground by the large rock at the camp, Entepasneut (Rocky Ford), on Crab Creek, and then would move on to Tahtahitan, present-day Ephrata, to cultivate potatoes in one of Sulktalthscosum's many gardens. From there they would sometimes return to the Columbia by way of its ancient bed, the Grand Coulee, and rest at the campground Squaquint near Dry Falls, where the river, after rushing out of the Coulee, once spilled its waters in a Niagara-dwarfing cascade four hundred feet high and nearly three miles wide. Moving up the Coulee, they would come to one

12 L. V. McWhorter, "How Gray Squirrel Drove the Buffalo from Moses Coulee," McWhorter Papers, No. 6, MS 1512 (Holland Library, Washington State University, Pullman, Washington).

of their ancient landmarks, Steamboat Rock (Chakawah, "Something Set Down in the Open"), Coyote's cooking pot of legendary times, where trails ran west to the bend of the Columbia and north to the San Poil country and Kettle Falls (La Chaudière of the French fur traders). Upon reaching Steamboat Rock, they would sometimes alter their course to the big river and follow it to the Spokane to trap salmon in intricate weirs stretched across that stream. When they moved north on the Columbia to Kettle Falls, they would catch salmon in nets and baskets as they did also at The Dalles on the lower Columbia, where, after visiting root grounds at Badger Mountain, Chelohan, and Rock Creek below the Spokane, they fished and traded horses for pemmican. Often, they would fish at Rock Island (Kawahchen), on the Columbia near the mouth of Moses Coulee, or up the Wenatchee, where Salishans met hundreds of Shahaptian neighbors from the south to play and work in bilingual harmony. Here they would pull salmon onto the rocks and dry them on racks exposed to the sun. Beyond the Wenatchee Fisheries they could gather berries in the Cascade Mountains, a frightening land of streams thundering down from granite peaks thrust skyward in jagged confusion, where according to the legends lived a wild race of men who used to snatch people from their homes. After hurriedly gathering their purple harvest before marauding bears or early snows claimed them, the migrants returned to their river villages to mix their fruit with salmon caught in the fall runs to make a highly nutritious food for winter.[13]

During winters along the Columbia, as on the Plains, Loolowkin learned about spirit power as he observed the winter dances, where young adults, who had received their power as children, danced and sang their power songs and where dancers gyrated around poles in the long house to hasten chinook winds.[14] During

13 An excellent description of how these people lived may be found in Grace Christiansen Gardner, "Life Among North Central Washington First Families," *Wenatchee Daily World* (Wenatchee, Washington), May 31–December 20, 1935.

14 For an explanation of the spirit dance, see Verne F. Ray, "The Bluejay Character in the Plateau Spirit Dance," *American Anthropologist*, Vol. XXXIX, No. 4 (October–December, 1937), 593–601.

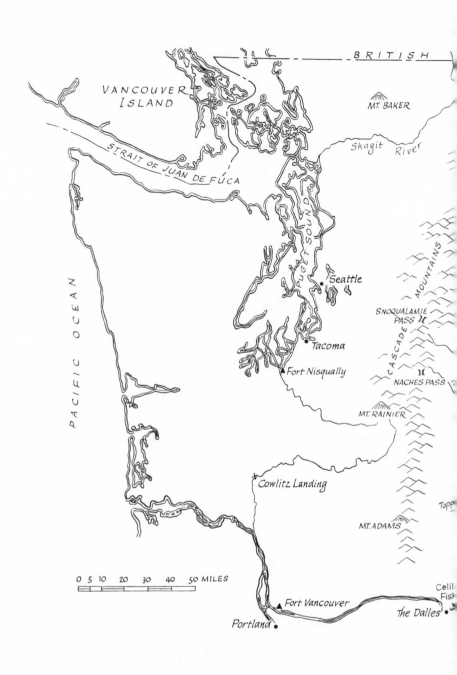

LAND OF THE HALF-SUN

times of sickness he saw the shamans, older men, who, as the fur trader Alexander Ross observed, were "grave and sedate, with a certain shyness and cunning about them" blowing, massaging, and sucking evil-spirit darts from fever-racked bodies. At the beginning of fish, root, and berry harvests, he saw his elders perform the first fruit ceremonies, and, when the harvests were over, the Thanksgiving Dance at which they thanked the Great Spirit, Shomak, for a successful season.[15]

Like a zealous novitiate, Loolowkin heeded his father's admonition to seek his powers early in life. One summer when encamped with his people at Tahtahitan, where the spring issues from the Plateau, he accepted the claws and cluster of feathers from his father's power bird, Magpie, and went to a nearby hill. There, in a sleep, dream, or trance, he was visited by a person who faded from his vision in a rushing of wind. It was Sagehen, who gave him powers of cunning and fleetness to aid him in hunting and war. Seeking more power gifts, he went to Howaph, where White Swan interrupted her flight to bestow upon him her healing power to be employed by merely placing his hands on affected parts of bodies. Seeking still more powers, he went to the edge of a marshy lake to receive the gift of bravery from Turtle, and later to the rim of Chuckahmiahpast to receive strength from Horse, augmented with especially potent gifts from Wolf and Grizzly, whose claws he wore around his neck.[16]

As Loolowkin was making his pilgrimages to lakes and mountaintops, another spiritual power, Christianity, was beginning to stir the land with a force no young pagan could escape. The natives had caught glimpses of it when it broke through the hard commercialism of the fur traders. One trader, Ross Cox, viewing the idolatrous practices of his pagan clientele, looked forward to the day when missionaries would "meet on the Rocky Mountains, and from their ice-covered summits proclaim to the

[15] Spier, Leslie (ed.), *The Sinkaietk or Southern Okanogan of Washington* (written by Walter Cline and others), 172.
[16] Peone Interviews. See also June Randolph, "Witness of Indian Religion," *Pacific Northwest Quarterly*, Vol. XLVIII, No. 4 (October, 1957), 139–45.

benighted savages 'Glory to God in the highest, and on earth peace and good-will towards men.' "[17]

In one of Sulktalthscosum's travels, he had met French or Spanish traders who showed him several papers containing printed messages. He resolved that one of his sons should be taught to read the magic words. In his close association with the Spokanes, he could not have failed to learn of Spokane Garry, one of their number who returned in 1829 from an Anglican mission school with the ability to speak and read the English language, and with a religious zeal which prompted him to build a little tule-mat sanctuary and to preach to his people. Nor could Sulktalthscosum have failed to learn from the Spokanes of a white missionary, the Reverend Henry H. Spalding of the American Board of Commissioners for Foreign Missions, who had come to them in 1836 and 1837. He may have been the chief from near the mid-Columbia who sent runners to Spalding's Nez Percé mission at Lapwai near the Clearwater, a Snake River tributary, to ask the missionary to come to his people, only to be told that he could not grant their request even though their "hearts broke."[18]

Since no white prophet came to his mountain, he vowed to send one of his sons to the mission. He ruled out the older ones, Patshewyah and Quiltenenock, whom he needed to fight the Blackfeet, and chose, instead, Loolowkin, the next in the line of succession—a boy of about "ten snows" and "about three feet tall," as the lad later put it.[19]

In his zeal Spalding had proclaimed at his mission, "May we count souls flocking to Jesus as doves to their windows." Loolowkin, under Sulktalthscosum's fatherly eye, rode there quite unlike a dove flocking to a window, for the child of nature was repelled at the thought of exchanging the freedom of swimming, hunting, and riding for the confinement of a schoolhouse. His reading, having ranged from watching signs in the heavens to signs in the

[17] Ross Cox, *Adventures on the Columbia River*, I, 311.

[18] American Board of Commissioners for Foreign Missions, *Annual Reports* (1839), 143–45.

[19] *Seattle Post Intelligencer*, October 23, 1895, p. 2.

dust of the earth, left him uninspired at the strange methods of teaching employed by Mrs. Spalding, a zealous teacher, but one whose difficulty with the Nez Percé tongue did little to improve an awkward situation. In contrast, Loolowkin learned that language easily. Several times he was scolded for his laggardness, and several mornings, when heads were counted, the wilderness child was missing. At daybreak he had crept to the field, unstaked his Appaloosa pony, and ridden it into the lonely hills, where his only shelter was his buffalo-robe blanket and his only food was the berries he gathered at the place of his vigil. Food and shelter were not as important to him as the power visitations from which he sought consolation for his confinement and revelation of a means of escape. When searchers found him, he may have felt the chastening sting of the whip which Spalding frequently used. If so, the little truant held no resentment against the whipper, whom he admired for his bold stand against Nez Percé chieftains, who, on threatening the missionary, found themselves under an interdict until they came seeking his pardon. This "Mission Chief" must have reminded him of his father, whose strong arm also disciplined his people or anyone else standing in his way. Following his absences, Loolowkin returned and stumbled through the mechanics of reading and writing exercises that were happily augmented by illustrated Bible stories. (He never forgot the Bible stories.)

He developed an attachment to Spalding, whom he saw as a devoted spirit working under difficult conditions, his slender means supplemented by occasional gifts from "the States" of clothing and other items. (Some of the latter were distributed to the Indian children, much to the disgust of the Reverend A. B. Smith, a Spalding critic who also had a mission among the Nez Percés at nearby Kamiah.) In return, Spalding showed affection for the boy and instructed him in such manner that one day he might exert a temporal and spiritual influence on his own people for good. Spalding named him "Moses," a name chosen from the Bible with a prayer for its bearer's eventual leadership.[20]

20 Francis Streamer, Miscellaneous Notebooks, Folder No. 2 (Washington State Historical Society).

In their talks Spalding expressed hopes for the mission, such as the plan of establishing a boarding school so that native children might remain there for longer periods of time. This made such an impression on the boy that many years later he doggedly sought a boarding school for his children on his reservation. Spalding also taught his pupil about the white men in the East, as numerous as leaves on the trees. Knowing that whites would one day invade Loolowkin's homeland, the missionary instructed him in their treaties and laws, a subject of peculiar fascination for the boy and the knowledge of which he would have occasion to use later in life.[21] Spalding also taught him the rudiments of geography, to build and mend fences, to prepare the soil for planting, and to care for the cattle, the contemptible manure-smeared *molops*, a task in which a horse lover found little pleasure. Although he perhaps knew little of the personality and policy conflicts among missionaries of the American Board in Oregon, the boy would have agreed with the blunt statement of the Reverend A. B. Smith concerning the introduction of cattle among the natives: "I have no hope of converting them in this way." Yet, when Spalding seated his young pupil on a rail of one of the enclosures, he taught him far more than could any of his critics.

During these intimate talks, the missionary must have found time to speak to Loolowkin about his spiritual progress. The boy's response in these matters is not known; most likely he was not among those of whom Spalding joyously exclaimed, "We might as well hold back the sun in its course, as hold back the minds of this people from religious inquiry." There is no official record that he was ever baptized; indeed, when he was at the mission, there were fewer than twenty souls, red or white, who had been.[22] Spalding warned all of his pupils to forsake the sins

21 When Dr. E. White visited the Spalding Mission in 1843, he observed of the native children that "none but the law interest them." Dr. E. White, *Ten Years in Oregon: Travels and Adventures of Doctor E. White and Lady West of the Rocky Mountains,* 205.

22 Rev. Henry H. Spalding and Dr. Marcus Whitman, *A True Copy of the Records of the First Presbyterian Church in the Territory of Oregon, Organized in 1838.*

common to red men: idolatry, polygamy, gambling, and drinking, the last an evil that the white man had thrown in for bad measure. He also instilled in them a bitterness towards Roman Catholics (Sulktalthscosum had resented their attacks on his polygamous practices), whose entrance into the Oregon mission field the American Board viewed with alarm. At the very time Spalding was exhorting his pupil, Father Modeste Demers was ascending the Columbia, visiting Hudson's Bay Company posts, Forts Walla Walla, Okanogan, and Colville, and baptizing the children whom he had missed the previous year on his way from the East to Fort Vancouver. For Loolowkin, he had come too late.

Spalding feared that every talk he had with the boy would be their last, for the pull of aboriginal life drew the natives from the mission as fast as they came. Smith, who approved of the hunting proclivities of the Indians, observed that over half of the nearly five hundred people living within fifteen miles of his mission at Kamiah had gone to buffalo and to the Snake and Blackfoot wars, and that few men returned from the wars. Spalding, unlike Smith, pleaded with the natives to give up the chase and grieved when he heard of his red parishioners lying dead on the Plains.

One morning the Indian Moses was missing. Heavy with homesickness, he had ridden out on a spirit quest to quiet his soul. In a dream trance the spirit had told him to return to his mother's tipi. Since this was the revelation he was seeking, he mounted his Appaloosa and rode home to his people without going back to the mission for the formality of farewells.[23]

Soon after his return, the lad found his people preparing to journey to buffalo even though each trip to the Plains was becoming more hazardous. The Blackfeet increasingly resented

23 Information on Moses' sojourn at the Spalding mission is largely from Peone Interviews. References from American Board sources are sketchy. Spalding mentions Moses in his diary. Henry H. Spalding and Asa B. Smith, *The Diaries and Letters of Henry H. Spalding and Asa Bowen Smith Relating to the Nez Percé Mission* (ed. by Clifford Merrill Drury), 265. The Moses mentioned elsewhere in the *Diaries* was a half-blood, Moses Lair. Forty-four years later, when Spalding returned to the Nez Percé and Spokane mission fields, he tells of Moses' attendance at the mission. See Presbyterian Historical Society, *The Spalding-Lowrie Correspondence, Journal of the Department of History, the Presbyterian Church in the U.S.A.*, Vol. XX, Nos. 1, 2, 3 (March, June, September, 1942), 47–54, 75.

encroachment on their lands, particularly since the buffalo were being driven farther west. Also, the Blackfeet had a personal score to settle with Sulktalthscosum for killing one of their number when he had visited a Blackfoot camp to trade. On that occasion, through a misunderstanding, he had been attacked but had escaped by means of a clever ruse. He had let his horse run around in circles at the end of a long hair-rope which sent his attackers reeling in confusion. When they had regained their balance, they discovered that his horse had killed one of their number and that he had escaped, his red shirt riddled with bullets.[24]

Aware of Blackfoot hostility, Loolowkin's people carefully prepared for their buffalo trips, readying their packing and riding gear and their bows and arrows supplemented by Hudson's Bay Company trade guns. Ceremonial preparations were not neglected, particularly the buffalo dance and the *Kaseesum,* a three-day ceremony of soul-searching when each brave made his decision to go on what easily could become a one-way trip.[25] Since the Salishans were always outnumbered on the Plains, all hands were needed for the venture, and Loolowkin, whose mission experience had matured him considerably, was expected to perform useful chores in the hunts or in battles.

Crossing the Rockies, the Salishans moved cautiously down the Plains past scattered mounds containing the remains of their fellow warriors whose journey to the buffalo grounds had become, instead, a journey to the happy hunting grounds. No time now to mourn the dead. There was much to do. When they spotted buffalo herds like cloud shadows creeping across the plain, they singled targets from the moving mass, wheeled, charged, and fired muzzle-loaded and arrow volleys into a rampart of thick hides. As they pursued remnants of the herds, the women moved in to process the kill and to move it to camp.

24 Spier, *The Sinkaietk,* 156.
25 For a description of their buffalo dance, see Edward S. Curtis, *The North American Indian,* VII, 90. In the *Kaseesum* ceremony each brave sealed his decision by stepping to a blanket held by four of his fellows and pounding on it with a stick. This gave him powers to search out and kill the buffalo or the enemy.

Sometimes parties of mounted Blackfeet approached the Salishan camp under a flag of truce, expressing a desire to smoke and trade. This invitation was usually accepted when Blackfoot parties were small. Sometimes when larger contingents were trading, an argument would erupt, and blows would be exchanged across the trading strip. After one of these stormy trading sessions, the Blackfeet challenged the Salishans to battle.[26] During the encounter Loolowkin shuttled back and forth between the battleground and camp carrying water and ammunition to the warriors. On one of these trips to camp while he was gathering another round of supplies for the front, he was attacked by a tall, bronzed, fully-grown Blackfoot. When the surprised youth recognized his knife-wielding adversary as one of a party of traders who had been in camp, he summoned his power spirits and grappled his attacker. With a supernatural burst of strength, he sent the contemptible Stqueequeno and his buffalo knife spinning to the ground; then before his stunned adversary could recover, the young Columbia was upon him, plunging a knife into his heart. Loolowkin had killed his first man. In later years on more peaceful occasions, a pair of black hands sewn on the red of his horse's hood would commemorate the encounter. Then, he would recall, "It was his life or mine."[27]

The Salishan camp feasted and rejoiced the night that Loolowkin the youth had killed a Blackfoot. Shortly a crier went from lodge to lodge broadcasting his exploit. Some of the warriors in the Council of Braves proposed that the young hero be permitted to daub ochre on his face and body, wear an eagle feather instead of his simple fur headpiece, and join their number. Others did not take so kindly to the proposal. A mere boy entering their proud council? Unthinkable!

The decision rested with the Council of Braves.

---

26 White observers testified to the ferocity of the Salishan buffalo hunters in their encounters with the highly vaunted Blackfeet. See Father DeSmet, *Life, Letters, and Travels of Father Pierre-Jean DeSmet, S. J., 1801–1873*, II, 572–80, and Samuel Parker, *Journal of an Exploring Tour Beyond the Rocky Mountains*, 240–41.

27 Peone Interviews. See also June Randolph, "Witness of Indian Religion," 141.

II. Quetalican the Warrior

"I . . . have been in blood up to my elbows"—Moses to Adjutant General, Department of the Columbia, February 11, 1888.

TALK OF LOOLOWKIN'S BRAVERY eclipsed talk of his limited years. The Society of Braves gained a new member. The honor was well earned. Yet, not unimportant in the Society's decision to admit him to their number was its quest for new blood to replace that spilled on the Plains.[1] This problem also prompted Sulktalthscosum on his return to the Columbia to attempt to unite bands of that area against the Blackfeet. In a four-day council at the confluence of the Yakima and Columbia rivers, he scolded his Salishan and Shahaptian hearers in fluent, angry words for raiding and pillaging one another's villages and those of small unprotected bands. Ironically, the techniques and trappings of warfare acquired from Plains Indians had intensified their hostile activities.[2] Later, Loolowkin, seeking to enhance his warrior status, was wounded in these encounters—a matter of grave concern to his father, who sought to preserve his royal line.

To perpetuate that royalty as well as intertribal unity, Sulktalthscosum encouraged his sons to consummate frequent and early unions with aristocratic women of the intermountain West. Loolowkin's first marriages of which we have knowledge were to women living in the far confines of that area. From the Flatheads on the east he chose the maiden, Silpe, and courted her in the traditional manner by doing her favors. She joined her

---

[1] Peone Interviews.

[2] Descendants of Sulktalthscosum say he introduced the war bonnet of the Plains among Indians of the Okanogan area. For instances of intertribal raids see James H. Teit, "The Salishan Tribes of the Western Plateaus," *B. A. E., Forty-fifth Annual Report* (1930); Clara Hughes Moore Interview, Belvedere, Washington, June 30, 1961; Spier, *The Sinkaietk*, 80; Chief Moses, "Autobiography."

young warrior husband in the buffalo hunts and returned with him to the Columbia; but then, suffering from homesickness, she rode back to her people.

In the Cascade foothills at the very western edge of the intermountain West lived the Shahaptian Upper Yakimas (Kittitas) ruled by two chieftain brothers—Teias and Owhi of the house of Weowikt. Sulktalthscosum had long sought closer ties between that house and his. His followers mingled freely with the Upper Yakimas, and marriages between the two peoples were common. Now with Silpe gone, Loolowkin sought to marry Chief Owhi's favorite daughter, the frail, delicate Quemollah. Owhi did not wish to give her up. He protected her in a sort of regal isolation by surrounding her with ladies in waiting to perform her domestic tasks, leaving her free to decorate costumes, saddlebags, and bridles. Her artistry as much as her beauty attracted the restless Loolowkin, who had an eye for fancy clothes and trappings as well as for a pretty girl.

One day he stealthily rode to the outskirts of her camp at Selah near the mid-Yakima, where he hid near a spring waiting for her to come for water. When she appeared, he swept her onto his horse and rode pell-mell for the Columbia River. There he drove his mount into the cold water and commanded the frightened maiden to hang to his neck as he clung to his horse's tail until they were safely across. The impetuous brave gave little thought to the kidnaping; after all, his father had urged intertribal marriages and now another tie had been forged between the Weowikt and Half-Sun houses. About that time, Loolowkin took another wife—a Columbia girl about whom little is known, which leaves one to surmise that she did not have the royal blood of her lodge mate, Quemollah.[3]

Sulktalthscosum's plan of knitting the western tribes more closely to face the Blackfeet was not as successful as he had hoped. The measles raging along the lower Columbia in 1847, purposely spawned there by white men to reduce the native population, the Indians believed, caused the Indians to shatter the

3 Peone Interviews.

hoped-for peace in the West by massacring the American Board missionaries, the Marcus Whitmans and a dozen other residents of their Waiilatpu Mission. The troubles would continue as the Oregon provisional government tracked down their Cayuse Indian killers.

The American Board missionary to the Spokanes, Cushing Eells, relates that in a council after the massacre he had Sulktalthscosum promise, with hand on a New Testament, to refrain from hostilities.[4] Thus detached from affairs in the West, Sulktalthscosum prepared for his trek to the Plains. His preparations, however, were not enthusiastic because with increasing age he found each successive trip to buffalo more difficult. Soon he would have to join the aged ones sitting in the villages recalling the past. Karneetsa, too, was finding the trips arduous. She refused to accompany her husband eastward and urged him to find a young wife to take her place. Sulktalthscosum then took a young woman of the band, giddy and inexperienced.[5]

The chief, his new wife, his sons, braves, their women, and servants, accompanied by a band of Kalispells, rode into the buffalo ranges of the Upper Missouri country.[6] On previous trips to this dangerous land, Karneetsa's uncanny intuition had more than once saved her people from annihilation. On this occasion the party killed many buffalo and were preparing to start home when they ran into a large Blackfoot band. A savage two-day battle ensued. (Later, some participants remembered that it lasted seven days, and at least it was much longer than the usual Indian engagement of a few hours.) It consisted of a series of unorganized attacks by the Blackfeet, which were repulsed in vicious hand-to-hand combat by the outnumbered Salishans. In one of these encounters Sulktalthscosum and a nephew were cut off from their fellow warriors and ran into a Blackfoot party. A bullet crashed into Sulktalthscosum's body. His nephew shouted to him to withdraw, but, with an indifference to life not unusual among

4 Cushing Eells, "Reminiscences," typescript copy No. 5, p. 6, Holland Library, Washington State University, Pullman, Washington.
5 Peone Interviews.
6 "Mary Moses' statement," August 1, 1918, Brown Papers.

older braves, he rushed out to meet the enemy. His leg was broken by a bullet and his ammunition was spent. Soon another bullet found its mark, and the great Half-Sun fell dead. His men took no time to pursue the enemy or to observe the customary obsequies; they laid his body in a scooped-out grave, covered it with dirt and grass, and rode over it to make it look as though horses had been kept there.[7]

The hunters limped home to the Columbia. Their buffalo trip had become a catastrophe. To add to their grief, they received word that their enemies had exhumed and disemboweled the chief's body, had torn out his heart, had cut off his limbs, and, worst of all, had taken the late leader's proud head across the border to the agency in Canada. As Loolowkin listened to this report, a bitterness burned within him towards "King George Men" (Englishmen).[8]

Sulktalthscosum's death did not deter his sons from again going to buffalo. Although they would not pass up an opportunity for revenge, still with inferior numbers, they wished as always to avoid a showdown with the Blackfeet. They even hoped the Roman Catholic priests on the Plains would instill among the enemy a desire for peace.[9] But the Blackfeet, proving more war-like than ever, drove the vicious Snakes off the Plains and resumed their raids into the Bitter Root Valley.[10] The year following the Half-Sun's death, Loolowkin's eldest brother, the brave Patshewyah, owner of eagle feather regalia sweeping to the ground, was killed by the treacherous Blackfeet. In company with a Nez Percé, he carelessly traveled ahead of the main body of hunters and under a flag of truce was enticed by a Blackfoot party to "have a smoke." After smoking what was apparently a noxious substance, he became dizzy and was easily dispatched.

Patshewyah's death only intensified the revenge cycle. On

7 *Ibid.* See also Teit, "The Salishan Tribes of the Western Plateaus," *B. A. E., Forty-fifth Annual Report* (1930), 363.

8 Francis Streamer to General O. O. Howard, September 11, 1889. Streamer, *Miscellaneous Notebooks,* Folder No. 1.

9 George B. McClellan, "Papers—Engineering Notebook and Memoranda 1853 *et al.,* Journal, May 20–December 16," microcopy.

10 Mengarini, *Mengarini's Narrative of the Rockies,* 8.

several buffalo trips Loolowkin's people, by their own account, killed several of the enemy with considerably smaller losses to themselves. In winter they won silent victories, creeping to the Blackfoot camps, untethering and driving horses away, and praying the power spirits to cover them with blankets of fog. The Blackfeet retaliated by stealing to the Salish camps where they attempted to steal Salish horses; but the westerners corralled the horses within the protective circle of their camps under strong guard until they could drive them back across the Rockies.

Tragedy at home continued to plague the house of the Half-Sun. Loolowkin's sister, Sinsinqt, who had managed her peoples' affairs while they were to buffalo, died, leaving a baby boy, Chillileetsah. Karneetsa assumed the care of the child, for every heir of Sulktalthscosum was now regarded more than ever a potential leader of his people. To help meet the problem of the dying aristocracy and to assist in the work of the lodge, Loolowkin's ailing wife, Quemollah, brought her younger sister, Shantlahow (Mali or Mary), into her lodge as an additional wife to the rising warrior. The girl, barely in her teens, shrank from the marriage, but gave way to the insistence of her family.[11]

Little is known of Loolowkin just before the Indian wars of the 1850's. Theodore Winthrop wrote, in *The Canoe and the Saddle*, that Loolowkin, son of Owhi, was his guide in 1853 on the first leg of his journey to the East from Fort Nisqually across the Cascade Mountains to The Dalles. Although Loolowkin was the "son" of Owhi through marriage, a natural son of Owhi's also called Loolowkin claimed to have guided the "Boston Man." By coincidence, the latter Loolowkin, who was, of course, a brother-in-law of the son of Sulktalthscosum, had the same physical and personality traits. The story of the journey bears repeating since the two Loolowkins must have discussed it often. It also reveals how white men were breaking the isolation of the country east of the Cascades, a situation soon to involve the two young men in war. "My future comrade," wrote Winthrop, "was a tallish stripling of twenty, dusky-hued and low-browed" with "a

11 Peone Interviews.

proud uncleanliness. . . . I saw that there was no danger of our becoming friends."

In Chinook—used obviously for Winthrop's benefit—Owhi explained to Loolowkin his responsibilities: "Great chief go to Dalles. Want to go fast. Six days. Good pay. S'pose want fresh horses other side of mountains,—you get 'em. Get everything. Look sharp. No fear bad Indian at Dalles; great chief not let 'em beat you. Be good boy! Good-bye!"

The strange traveling companions—the scion of the old Puritan family and the western "savage"—mounted their horses at three o'clock the afternoon of August 24 to begin their long journey. The disdain Winthrop felt for the young Indian—for all Indians, in fact—is apparent throughout his account of the trip, but even from this unfriendly characterization Loolowkin emerges as a distinct personality. He was completely self-centered ("his real deity, Number One"), said Winthrop. At the very least he must have been self-assured. He was vain of his personal appearance and possessed of coolness, "caution more highly developed than any quadruped I have met," and—his one virtue in Winthrop's eyes—great "ability in guidance. He has memory and observation unerring; not once in all our intricate journey have I found him at fault in any fact of space and time." His guardian spirit, his *tamanoüs*, the "link between himself and the rude, dangerous forces of nature," was the Wolf. Winthrop was uncertain whether the young brave had "chosen his protector according to the law of likeness, or, choosing it by chance, has assimilated to its characteristics." In either case he was a "Wolfish youth . . . an unfaithful, sinister, cannibal-looking son of a horsethief. Wolfish likewise is his appetite" and his manner of eating. This last, incidentally, was to be commented upon by white observers throughout Loolowkin's life.

On the second day out, another Indian joined them, to the obvious relief of Loolowkin, who could not have failed to sense Winthrop's hostility. At night the two Indians found amusement together "in everything that was or that happened,—in their raggedness, in the holes in their moccasins, in their overstuffed proportions after dinner, in the little skirmishes of the horses, when a grasshopper chirped or a cricket sang." They traveled through the densely wooded Cascade foothills and soon came to the "Boston Road," a wilderness ribbon being laid out by Puget Sounders across the mountains; and they spent one night with the road builders, who made the guide feel their prejudice against redskins. Descending the eastern slopes of the Cascades on the twenty-eighth, they met young Captain George B. McClellan, who was in charge of a survey party searching for a route across the mountains for a transcontinental railroad.

The next day, approaching the Wenas in the Yakima country, Winthrop observed that Loolowkin's feelings were stirred by the familiar surroundings. Shortly they met an Indian—dubbed the "Shabbiest" by Winthrop—who urged Loolowkin to turn back. "No good Loolowkin go Dalles. Bad Indian there. Smallpox there. Very much all bad." Soon they reached a native camp— "Stenchville" was Winthrop's name for it—where they tried to get fresh horses. The Indians refused to furnish any, because they were afraid that if Loolowkin continued his trip to The Dalles, he would bring back the contagion. Winthrop believed that they were ready to use force to stop the guide. At all events, Loolowkin refused to go farther.

When he asked pay for his services, Winthrop informed him, "No go, no pay."

Loolowkin replied, *"Wake nika memloose"* ("I do not die for lack of it"). With rifle and Colt ready for action, Winthrop spurred his horse and rode on alone, leaving Loolowkin in the obscurity of his native background.[12]

12 Theodore Winthrop, *The Canoe and the Saddle* (ed. by John H. Williams), appendix, "Who Loolowcan Was," 241–42. Winthrop gave the name of his guide as Loolowcan, the son of Owhi. Williams, basing his opinion largely on the word of Edward Huggins, a manager of the Fort Nisqually post, believed that Loolowkin must have been Owhi's son, Qualchan. The clerk's record for August 24 stated that Winthrop acquired three horses and an Indian guide and left for The Dalles. Years later, Huggins interpolated in brackets the name of the guide as "[Qualchan, son of Owhi]." But the authors have found no evidence that Qualchan ever bore the name "Loolowkin." Also the physical description does not fit; Winthrop's guide was "tallish," while Qualchan was of medium stature. Winthrop's guide was "dusky-hued"; Qualchan's complexion was lighter than that of his fellow tribes-

Loolowkin's elder brother by six years, the well-built, handsome, ambitious Quiltenenock (Something Warm in the Distance) or Louis, stood to inherit the Half-Sun leadership after Patshewyah's death on the Plains. He had sought unsuccessfully to strengthen his position among the mid-Columbia bands; then sensing their lack of support, he made special trips across the Cascades to Puget Sound and down the Columbia to the Willamette Valley to get an endorsement in writing from government agents there. In the late summer of 1853, he learned that McClellan was in the Kittitas, where he had been greeted by Owhi, all togged out in a white man's suit. Quiltenenock hurried over the Wenatchee Mountains to the Kittitas to greet McClellan and curried his favor by guiding him back across the mountains to the Columbia and by showing him important landmarks like the two women whom the Great Spirit had turned to stone for luring men to their deaths. On the Wenatchee Flat, McClellan told the natives to join their neighbors in selecting a head chief to talk with the white chief, Isaac I. Stevens. Stevens had just been appointed governor of the newly established Washington Territory and its superintendent of Indian affairs, and had been charged with the additional duty of heading the railroad survey. At that very time, September 21, 1853, he was on the Plains pleading with the Blackfeet to cease their wars.[13]

Assuming Quiltenenock would win the election, McClellan gave him the lion's share of the cloth and tobacco which he was dispensing to insure native good will; but the ambitious contender lost out to another whose name McClellan failed to record, possibly his father-in-law, Tecolekun of the Wenatchees. Undaunted, Quiltenenock continued to act as spokesman for the bands along the Columbia near the Wenatchee, responding negatively to the Captain's questions about the feasibility of

---

men. The Loolowkin who claimed to have been Winthrop's guide revealed this fact to the pioneer A. J. Splawn. During the Indian wars he went under the name of Lokout. Splawn, *Ka-Mi-akin*, 126–27.

13 McClellan, "Papers," microcopy; Isaac I. Stevens, "Narrative of 1853–1855," *Pacific Railroad Report of Explorations and Surveys*, XII, 115.

railroads across the Cascades to the coast, for the Captain concluded, "There can be no pass at its head for a road." (Forty years later, the Great Northern Railroad would follow this route.) Quiltenenock was equally pessimistic of routes between the Okanogan and Mount Baker, relating the story of an early-day pack train destroyed in attempting to cross there. There was a man in the village, he said, who had been over this route, but he lay ill with the smallpox then sweeping the Columbia, where, as a member of the survey party observed, "Several villages had been nearly cut off . . . the dead left unburied on the surface of the ground."

McClellan remained at the camp a few more days making compilations and buying potatoes grown perhaps, as a member of the earlier Wilkes expedition had noted, in enclosures surrounded by turf walls. He also examined "colors" in the Wenatchee and Columbia rivers and stayed for an Indian horse race, after which he gave a yard of red cloth to the winner.

Quiltenenock continued to guide the party over the treacherous trail up the Columbia. Near the river's junction with the placid Okanogan, by the decaying Hudson's Bay Company post, McClellan repeated the process of coalescing the tribes before continuing on with his command.

The natives had been impressed by the survey party's wonderful gifts and magic instruments, quite unaware that it was an advance guard of white civilization. Their security was short lived. The following year Owhi, in McClellan's words "a man of very considerable understanding and policy," told them that an agent, A. J. Bolon, of the white chief Stevens had been in their country talking with head men and laying the groundwork for a council which his superior wished to hold in the Walla Walla Valley the following year. Owhi warned that the proposed council would involve treaties and reservations presaging the end of their freedom. He also alerted an important chieftain whom Bolon had missed—Kamiakin, a Lower Yakima chief of Palouse descent living nearer the path of white immigration along the lower Columbia, who would soon be thrust logically, yet unwillingly, into a place of leadership among the interior tribes against the whites in what became known as the Yakima War.

Kamiakin requested Owhi to bring Quiltenenock and Loolowkin to his village on the Ahtanum for a strategy meeting. When the brothers got there, they found Kamiakin back from what he described as a very successful trip presenting to various tribes his plan of confederating the natives from Canada to Oregon. As soon as Kamiakin finished reporting his activities, Qualchan (Loolowkin's brother-in-law, the son of Owhi), a fiery small-limbed, yet powerful brave, hurried to the coast to inform its chieftains of the proposed council, and Kamiakin and Owhi went east to coalesce those tribes; Quiltenenock and Loolowkin went north to the Canadian border for the same purpose, using persuasive powers inherited from their father to bring various chiefs of that area to their standard.

Shortly, an intertribal council was held in the valley of the Grande Ronde River, a Snake River tributary, to map out strategy for their inevitable clash with the white man. The mid-Columbia bands were represented by Tecolekun. Apparently Kamiakin absented himself from the council and sent his more peaceably disposed brother, Skloom. No definite decision was reached at the council concerning war or peace with the invader, but the vast Indian country of the interior was divided into definite bounded areas so that when the Walla Walla council convened, the bands could hold out for reservations corresponding to the areas marked out. This maneuver was calculated to complicate, if not to wreck, the forthcoming Stevens Council.[14]

But at that council, held in May, 1855, their plans were to no avail. Although they knew that Stevens wanted their heartlands, not "their hearts," they sat before him immobilized by his pressures and promises. The sons of Sulktalthscosum deferred to Tecolekun and Lahoom, chief of the Entiats. These chiefs, in opposition to the angry Quetalican, signed away with twelve other chiefs under the Yakima standard an empire of nearly ten million acres—from the Cascade ridge on the west to the Chelan-Methow

14 Splawn, *Ka-Mi-akin*, 22–23.

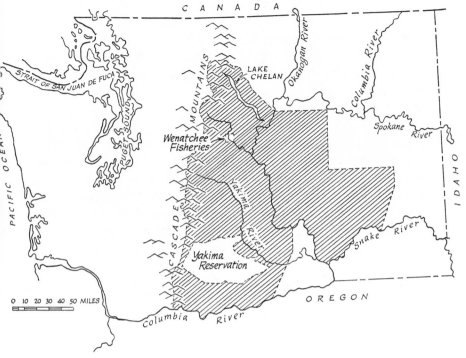

YAKAMA [YAKIMA] TREATY CESSION, RATIFIED MARCH 8, 1859

Cascade ridge to the north, to the Palouse and Snake rivers on the southeast, and back to the Columbia. Within the vast treaty area there were reserved two pinpoints on the map—the vital, ancient, six-square-mile Wenatchee Fisheries and the larger Yakima Reservation.[15]

Before the treaties were signed, let alone before the ink on them was dry, miners probing for gold crisscrossed the Indian lands. Loolowkin and Quiltenenock burned at this violation of the treaty.

[15] *Portland Daily Standard*, March 23, 1879; and Charles J. Kappler (ed.), *Indian Affairs: Laws and Treaties*, II, 698–702. See also Hazard Stevens, *The Life of Isaac Ingalls Stevens*, II, 34–65; James Doty, "A True Copy of the Record of the Official Proceedings at the Council in the Walla Walla Valley," McWhorter Papers, 201; and Curtis, *The North American Indian*, VII, 67.

About this time, Loolowkin adopted a new name—a warrior name, "Quetalican" (One Blue Horn). The name of his child-hood and youth had served him well in his dealings with his fellow red men. Now, for the first time, he was confronted with a new enemy—the white man—numerous, cunning, possessor of great medicine. With a new powerful name, the Columbia brave prepared himself to fight the trespasser.

During the summer of 1855, the new Quetalican roamed the country from the Spokane River north to the Colville stalking the intruders, rushing on them, and "choking" (killing) them, as Chief Big Star (called by white men the Elder Lot to distin-guish him from his son of the same name) explained the young Columbia's actions to Stevens. In spite of the pleas of the factor at Fort Colville and of Big Star, who said he was "crying all the time" since the attacks, the restless and embittered Quetalican would not stop his aggressions.[16]

Emboldened by his success and thirsty for more blood, Queta-lican returned to the Yakima country. There Kamiakin, growing increasingly remorseful for having signed the treaty, sought to repudiate it, knowing full well that to do so meant war. Taking advantage of the cautious Owhi's absence in the buffalo country, Kamiakin made contact with the chief's son, Qualchan, and his fellow warriors, Quetalican and Quiltenenock, for their support. After several hours of haggling, the three consented to help him in exchange for blankets, guns, ammunition, and four horses apiece.[17] With this backing, he called an emergency meeting to discuss the possibility of going to war. The older Yakimas argued for peace, but Quetalican and his firebrand cohorts overruled them. As the council broke up, each promised to go among his people to seek support in the anticipated war and agreed to form

16 Stevens, *The Life of Isaac Ingalls Stevens*, II, 188–89. For another translation of Big Star's speech, see Isaac Stevens, "Journal of Governor Isaac Ingalls Stevens" (ed. by William S. Lewis), typescript copy. A letter from C. H. Mason, acting governor of Washington Territory, to Major G. J. Rains, September 22, 1855, tells of the murder of a Pacific Coast resident by four of Quetalican's people. Virgil F. Field (ed.), *The Official History of the Washington National Guard*, II, 42.

17 Peone Interviews.

a defense line between Rock Island on the Columbia and the Wenas in the Yakima country.[18]

Near the latter point of the defense line, Qualchan and his braves killed six intruding miners. Shortly, Agent Bolon while attempting to ferret out thé killers was himself slain by the angry natives. After this incident, Major Granville O. Haller with one hundred regulars and a howitzer was sent to punish the killers of Bolon. The war was on.

Early in October Quetalican and his braves disputed Haller's passage at Toppenish Creek, a lower Yakima tributary, in a three-day seesaw battle, which broke up with the timely arrival of Qualchan and his Yakima braves. Haller, writing later of the encounter, implied that Kamiakin was late arriving at the scene of action. Quetalican's later terse description of the fight belied its intensity: "Then we started a war here and we whipped most of the soldiers; we kept fighting the soldiers right here at Toppenish on the little river that runs into the big river. We kept fighting the soldiers and drove them to The Dalles and then we quit and came back."[19] Had Quetalican and his allies been better supplied with guns and had they not fought in their traditional small detachments, their assault on the command could have wiped it out. As it was, Qualchan helped save the day, but not Haller's mules, which Quetalican safely corralled for his own people. Kamiakin, who had lost horses to Quetalican to entice him into the war and now the mules, was embittered, but the affair did not sever the relations between the two, only strained them.[20]

Haller's defeat and receipt of word that Major G. J. Rains with a force of several hundred volunteers was moving north toward Kamiakin caused that chief to close ranks temporarily with Owhi, Qualchan, and the sons of Sulktalthscosum. At Selah, Quetalican and Qualchan showed their unity by the old custom of riding double on a horse about the tipis warning their tribes-

18 Splawn, *Ka-Mi-akin*, 415–20.
19 Chief Moses, "Autobiography."
20 Major Granville O. Haller, "Kamiakin in History," manuscript.

men of the approaching enemy, inciting them to action.[21] After speech-making and dancing, the fired-up warriors rode down the Yakima to Union Gap (old town of Yakima), a narrow place along the river where breastworks had been thrown up on the west bank. Stationing themselves behind the breastworks and rocks in the underbrush and on a flat on the east bank, they waited. On November 9, a silence-shattering bugle call sent a howitzer into action, scattering breastworks and natives in all directions. A spent bullet struck Quetalican, but failed to break his skin, proof to him that Turtle's protective shell had saved his life. Sagehen's fleetness helped him race across the Columbia to safety.[22]

From headquarters he established on the Ahtanum, the victorious Rains sent Kamiakin and his warriors a message from his pen (since he could not reach them with his sword) that was calculated to upset what security they had left: "You, a few people, we can see with our glasses a long way off, while the whites are as the stars in the heavens, or leaves of the trees in summer time. Our warriors in the field are many, as you must see; but if not enough, a thousand for every one man will be sent to hunt you, and to kill you; and my kind advice to you, as you will see, is to scatter yourselves among the Indian tribes more peaceable and there forget you ever were Yakimas."[23]

Gradually, the natives filed back to their homes along the Columbia and Yakima, where Stevens, hoping to contain them, sent Colonel George Wright from The Dalles with five companies. Wright's approach threw the hostiles into confusion, with Kamiakin urging war against the intruders, and the Quetalican-Owhi bloc advocating peace, at least for the moment, in a dis-

---

[21] William D. Lyman, *History of the Yakima Valley*, I, 917.

[22] Curtis, *The North American Indian*, VII, 67. On July 4, 1916, the Daughters of the American Revolution erected a monument at Union Gap to commemorate the victory by U.S. troops over the Indians. Shortly, the Indians erected a monument there in memory of Towtownahhnee, a noncombatant, who, they claimed, was the only person killed in the encounter. Lyman, *History of the Yakima Valley*, I, 904.

[23] Secretary of War, *Annual Report*, 1856 (34 Cong., 3 sess., *House Exec. Doc. No. 76*), II, 195.

agreement splitting wide open the long-standing rift between the two factions. Rains had warned Kamiakin to forget he was a Yakima; now the Quetalican-Owhi faction reminded him that with Palouse blood, he was not truly a full blood Yakima. The miffed warrior thereupon left with his men for the Spokane country, where he unsuccessfully attempted to get its natives to enter the war.

In the meantime, Wright made camp on the Naches, a mid-Yakima tributary, nervously waiting for the remaining chiefs to come in. Several small bands from the Yakima and from as far north as the Canadian border trickled in to assure him of their peaceful intent, but where were the leaders of the Half-Sun–Weowikt bloc? One day the answer came when Quetalican, Quiltenenock, and Owhi entered his camp and assured him in council that they would gather their men to surrender.[24] After returning to their people, they changed their minds and failed to yield their warriors. Wright's fear that the bands would harbor the "renegade" leaders sent him across the Wenatchee Mountains early in July to the Wenatchee Fisheries to warn the throngs there to keep clear of their "bad chiefs." Wishing to quarantine them from these leaders, Wright moved them bag and baggage from the fisheries to the Kittitas Valley in a procession strung out for a distance of five miles. His mission completed, he triumphantly exclaimed, "His [Kamiakin's] career on this side of the Columbia is ended."[25]

Several Wenatchee and Columbia River chiefs, believing that further resistance was futile, came in with assurances of peace to Major Haller, who was still wary from his recent defeat as he kept guard on the Indian country from a camp he had established on Nanum Creek in the Kittitas Valley. In the meantime, Quetalican, Quiltenenock, Qualchan, and their braves hid out—in all probability near the Columbia's east bank—and depended on scouts to keep them informed of the military's moves. Near the

24 Curtis, *The North American Indian*, VII, 67.
25 Secretary of War, *Annual Report*, 1856 (34 Cong., 3 sess., *Sen. Exec. Doc. No. 5*), II, 175–77.

first of September the group, now a truly renegade band, decided to visit Kamiakin, but whether or not with the intention of joining him in some hostile action is not clear. They literally got off on the wrong foot. Awaking one morning near Priest Rapids on the lower mid-Columbia, they found that their horse tender, Kiyuya (David), a spy in the employ of Major Robert Garnett of the newly built Fort Simcoe, had stolen their horses. Quetalican rounded up an old horse and rode it to Simcoe, where he appealed to Garnett to return their mounts. After a great deal of haggling and over the protests of Kiyuya, the Major gave him the horses, and he rode to rejoin his friends on their way east.[26]

Their talks with Kamiakin concerned a second council about to begin that September in the Walla Walla Valley. Quiltenenock was anxious to attend the council to show Stevens an endorsement Wright had given him on the Naches. When he presented it in council, however, Stevens showed no interest in the letter. Quiltenenock's anger at this rebuff did not blind him to the fact that Stevens and his territorials occupied a separate camp from Colonel E. J. Steptoe, who had just arrived with four companies of regulars. Hurrying back to his fellows, he urged them to join the Nez Percés, Walla Wallas, Umatillas, Palouses, and Yakimas encamped nearby in an attack on the divided whites. The natives burned the grass where Steptoe's horses were grazing and attacked Stevens as he retreated toward The Dalles, his mission a failure. The harassed Stevens quickly formed a wagon corral and fought the elusive attackers into the night. The stubbornness of the Indian attack forced Stevens and Steptoe to make common cause and gave them greater respect for their adversary—particularly Quiltenenock, who had two horses shot from beneath him during the fighting.[27]

The natives returned from the encounter to their homes, where they spent the remainder of the year and the next, 1857, in tense watchful waiting. It was suddenly broken by gold dis-

[26] Splawn, *Ka-Mi-akin*, 62.
[27] William Compton Brown, *The Indian Side of the Story*, 170–71; Stevens, *The Life of Isaac Ingalls Stevens*, II, 221–23.

coveries on the Fraser River in Canada, which sent miners hell-bent through the Indian country in formidable numbers often organized in military fashion. One party of seventy-nine men and ninety-four pack animals, which set out from The Dalles in June, 1858, started a chain of events that opened Quetalican's path to the chieftaincy. Just north of the Wenatchee, the natives attacked the miners in what would have been a rout had not peaceful, crippled Chief Skamow come to their assistance. Having received from Wright a paper (later lost when his canoe upset) guaranteeing his people an eight-square-mile tract of land on the Wenatchee River, Skamow felt obligated to escort the whites safely past the hostiles. Not wishing to risk further hostilities, the miners crossed to the east bank of the Columbia and began a retreat down stream.

As Quiltenenock rested in camp, a taunting brave called him a coward for not pursuing the trespassers. Immediately, he called for his chestnut war horse and started out on a one-man war against them. He crossed the Columbia to the east bank and trailed the miners down river for about five miles. The miners then recrossed the stream to the west bank with Quiltenenock still in pursuit. He carelessly exposed himself by a large rock, and a miner killed him. Some natives say that Tecolekun was killed by the miners; others say by soldiers in the Palouse. The fiery Qualchan, trailing the miners further down river to avenge these deaths, was shot and might also have died had Quetalican not combined Swan Spirit with clever surgery to heal his friend's wounds.[28] Quetalican thus found himself the eldest male heir of the Half-Sun; and with Tecolekun's death and Skamow's appeasement of the whites, he sought the role of leadership along the river.

[28] Government reports vary widely regarding the miners' casualties in the Wenatchee fight: one killed and five wounded, or fifty killed, the latter being closer to the Indian claim. See Commissioner of Indian Affairs, *Annual Report,* 1858 (35 Cong., 2 sess., *Sen. Exec. Doc. No. 1*), I, 620; and R. H. Lansdale to J. W. Nesmith, June 30, 1858 (Washington Superintendency Records, 1853–74, No. 5, Roll 20). To the Indians the miners appeared to be wearing soldier uniforms (Peone Interviews).

A month after the Wenatchee engagement, another large caravan of miners, traders, and packers, known as the McLoughlin party, set out from the lower Columbia near where it receives the Walla Walla and followed the Columbia-Okanogan route to the Fraser. The Palouses, under Red Jacket, followed the train and made several attempts to break it up. At Moses Coulee they killed one of its members and wounded several pack animals before withdrawing to leave the responsibility for wrecking it to the northern bands. Quetalican later would be accused of the murder.[29] Now he hurried north to the Chelan country to alert Chief Innomoseecha Bill, who in turn warned Chief Sarsopkin in the mid-Okanogan. These two with Kekehtumnouse (Pierre), chief of the Lower Okanogans, gathered their men at the site of the old Fort Okanogan, near the confluence of the Okanogan and Columbia rivers (just above the point where the latter makes its big bend to the south), and waited for the trespassers to appear.

When the train, traveling up the east side of the Columbia, neared the rivers, two men, trader Francis Wolff and an interpreter, paddled across the Columbia to its north bank for a parley with the Indians. The two dragged their craft onto the beach and started toward the fort. On the way, they saw a native dressed in white man's clothes, possibly those of the victim of the Red Jacket attack—a warning to Wolff that the natives were hostile. Quetalican and the other chiefs gave the trader the courtesy of an audience, lasting the better part of the night, and sent him back across the river with the warning that, if the party recrossed, they would be attacked.

The next day, not heeding the warning, the party borrowed two canoes from an old Hudson's Bay trapper and shuttled their supplies and horses across the broad stream. Quetalican held a hurried conference with his chiefs, who decided not to take a stand against the intruders in open country around the fort, but to attack from a more strategic position. The decision was prompted not by lack of bravery but of firepower; the natives had old Hudson's Bay flintlock rifles, obtained previously from

[29] See below, p. 166.

38

Napoleon's defeated armies, which were no match in range and accuracy for the Mexican War muskets of the "Boston Man." They hurried some forty miles up the Okanogan to a rock-terraced oval (McLoughlin Canyon), a perfect spot for an ambuscade. The train's advance guard inched suspiciously into the canyon. Suddenly the defile exploded in a Pandemonium of yells and gunfire. The whites fell back carrying their dead (which vary in the accounts from two to six). After regrouping and burying their dead, they continued northward to the gold fields.[30]

Quetalican was unable to return to his camp near the mouth of the Wenatchee, for a military expedition commanded by Major Garnett left Fort Simcoe on August 10 to punish the Indians for their attacks on the miners. A few days out, a detail captured a number of Indians and shot three who were recognized as "murderers." The expedition then struck the Columbia and followed it up to the mouth of the Wenatchee. From that place Garnett sent Lieutenant George Crook (later to become the well-known Indian fighter) with a company of infantry to run the hostiles down. On the upper Wenatchee, five suspects were lured into the army camp through the efforts of a friendly chief and pinioned for execution. Crook delegated the command of the shooting detail to a second lieutenant, because "This whole business was exceedingly distasteful to me" and the subordinate "rather enjoyed that kind of thing."[31]

Garnett failed in his prime objective, the capture of Quetalican, Qualchan, and their followers, but he blocked their escape west to the mountains. All hope of gathering the numerous Yakimas to the Half-Sun—Weowikt cause was gone, for the military occupation held them in check. While Quetalican and his braves were still harassing the miners' train on its way to Canada, their tribesmen retreated to the east bank of the Columbia. Here

30 R. D. Gwydir, "In Early Days," *Spokane Falls Review* (Spokane Falls, Washington Territory), May 24, 1891, p. 1. See also Francis Wolff, "Reminiscenses," Winans Collection, No. 20; Splawn, *Ka-Mi-akin*, 108–11.

31 General George Crook, *General George Crook: His Autobiography* (ed. by Martin F. Schmitt), 59–68.

they found temporary refuge, for a shortage of boats, canoes, horses, mules, and experienced drivers prevented Garnett from pursuing them further. In desperation, Teias and Owhi hurried to Canada to investigate the possibility of taking the band there. Several Canadian Indians urged them to bring their people there until the trouble should blow over, after which they could drift back to their homes. The two quickly returned to report this invitation. According to Yakima sources, they were preparing to accept it when Quetalican's wife, Shantlahow, and one of Qualchan's four wives warned them not to. As women were believed to possess special powers of divination, their protestations were heeded. The alternative was to retreat to the east, where the Spokanes, Coeur d'Alenes, and Palouses were at war with the army.

Qualchan and Lokout (see pages 27–28n.), who had gone there to investigate, urged their people to throw in their lot with these tribes.[32] The decision was made, and the band headed across the Columbia's Big Bend by way of Grand Coulee and on to an ancient camp they had on the Spokane River near where it enters the Columbia. They arrived there about the first of September as Wright, with seven hundred troops using howitzers and Sharps percussion carbines, was defeating the natives at Four Lakes (southwest of the present city of Spokane). Four days later, after again defeating the hostiles at nearby Spokane Plains, Wright and his command moved eastwardly along the Spokane to encamp above the falls of that river. Near this point on September 7, the Anglican mission-trained Spokane Chief Garry crossed the river with expressions of peace to the Colonel.

After impressing the chief with the hopelessness of the native cause, Wright ordered him to bring his people in and to send messengers carrying the same order to Moses, as he called Quetalican, and to Big Star. That same day, the son of Big Star came in to ask for peace on behalf of his father.[33] Quetalican,

[32] L. V. McWhorter, "A Tragedy of the Yakima War, 1855," McWhorter Papers, MS 1531.

[33] Lawrence Kip, *Army Life on the Pacific*, 68.

however, having retreated in all likelihood to his camp on the lower Spokane, was nowhere to be found. Here he no doubt received word of the army's slaughter of nearly one thousand native horses near the falls of the Spokane.

Thus immobilized, the various chiefs came in to make peace with Wright, now encamped on Latah (Hangman) Creek (just south of present-day Spokane) after his victorious swing east through the Coeur d'Alene country. As senior chieftain of the Half-Sun–Weowikt band, Owhi went to Wright's camp, arriving with one or two of his men on the evening of September 23. There he met Wright, whom he had not seen since their meeting at the council in the Yakima country two years before. His failure to surrender his people at that time and the subsequent depredations of his son, Qualchan, whom Wright believed to have been Agent Bolon's killer, ruffled the Colonel greatly. He interrogated Owhi concerning Qualchan's whereabouts, and he learned that he was at the mouth of the Spokane. Now at the boiling point against the two, Wright clapped Owhi in irons and sent a messenger for Qualchan to come in.

About this time, Quetalican with a Spokane and some younger men entered the camp unrecognized and approached one of the officers, who asked him for his buckskin war horse. Quetalican was about to hand it over when his Spokane friend whispered to him not to surrender the animal. A few minutes later, Quetalican learned through this same friend that Owhi was in chains. Calling on Sispilh Kalch (Seven Shirts), one of his many power spirits, to help him escape and, if possible, to warn his friend, Qualchan, of his father's plight, he dashed for his horse, mounted it, and rode pell-mell out of camp.[34]

Qualchan missed the warning and rode into Wright's camp to a death by treachery, which Wright tersely described: "Qualchew came to me at 9 o'clock this morning, and at 9¼ A.M. he was hung." It took six soldiers the best of those fifteen minutes to subdue the powerful brave, who fought savagely for life in spite

[34] Peone Interviews.

of wounds recently received on the Columbia.[35] Native sources claim the hanging rope broke twice. Some of these accounts have it that Qualchan's power, Otter, failed him—others, that Quetalican stole it, preventing the rope from breaking a third time.[36]

Quetalican remained in hiding on the lower Spokane until the soldiers were gone. Then Quemollah and a sister, Sahmesahpan, went near the army camp, found Qualchan's nude body protruding from a grave partially covered with dust, grass, and sticks, wrapped it in a blanket, put moccasins on the feet, and reinterred it.[37] As they completed this sad task, their father, Owhi, was killed in an attempt to escape from the soldiers. Quetalican bade farewell to a broken and sorrowful remnant of the band and sent them on their way to the Kittitas, while he took his wives down to the San Poil country to a year's hiding near Keller Mountain. This proved to be a wise move, as Captain James Archer sent soldiers and "friendly Indian" parties to the Wenatchee and Okanogan rivers in November to search out and kill the Indians Garnett had missed on his expedition. One of these native raider bands, captained by one Josiskin, captured and killed Quetalican's half brother, Keelpucken, whom Archer claimed had killed one of Garnett's command.[38]

In exile, Quetalican had ample time to contemplate his own survival, the deaths of his loved ones, and the near extinction of the Half-Sun–Weowikt families. It would be many years before the babies born to his wives near Keller Mountain could carry on the ebbing aristocracy. That responsibility now rested with him. As he prepared to face a new world destined to become the white man's, his own world trembled with uncertainty beneath his feet.

35 For a description of Qualchan's death, see E. D. Keyes, *Fifty Years' Observation of Men and Events Civil and Military*, 277–78.

36 L. V. McWhorter, "A Tragedy of the Yakima War, 1855," MS 1531.

37 "Mary Moses' statement."

38 Captain James J. Archer to Captain Alfred Pleasonton, January 1, 1859. Fort Dalles Papers, No. 248–51.

III. Terra Infirma

"I fear the ruin of my people is coming."—Moses to Indian agent, Okanogan River, June 30, 1870.

WHEN THE SOLDIERS HAD LEFT the mid-Columbia, the young warrior Quetalican returned there in 1859. Shortly one of his wives, the delicate Quemollah, died. Grief for her kept him from his lodge and his young wife, Shantlahow, for long periods of time. He remained away for another reason—to gather war-scattered remnants of Columbia bands to his standard to escape confinement on a reservation by the white man. To symbolize his new mission, he assumed his father's name—Sulktalthscosum, the Half-Sun.[1]

The white man was coming. Already unwelcome wagons were creaking north from White Bluffs, the last white outpost on the lower Columbia, across the Plateau on finger-like trails pointing to the Okanogan and Colville Valleys. In the latter, the United States Army in 1859 established Fort Colville (some fifteen miles east of the Columbia and the Hudson's Bay Company fort of the same name) on the heels of the war, to protect white settlers soon to occupy its fertile lands.[2]

[1] Peone Interviews.

[2] One traveler in the interior during 1860 was Edward Huggins, manager of the Puget Sound Agricultural Company, a subsidiary of the Hudson's Bay Company. In the fall of that year, he drove a band of the company's horses and mules over Naches Pass in the Cascades, north to old Fort Okanogan, and on to Canada (Letter from R. A. Reynolds to authors, January 15, 1962). That winter, William Gray built a fifty-ton sloop with a ninety-foot keel and a twelve-foot beam at Lake Osoyoos on the Canadian border. He sailed it down the Okanogan and the Columbia, to Celilo on the lower reaches of the latter river (Elwood Evans, *History of the Pacific Northwest: Oregon and Washington*, II, 349; Lyman, *History of the Yakima Valley*, I, 333). The wagons belonged to freighters like Joel Palmer, who with about thirty-five other men formed a company to promote the overland route to the Canadian mines to help the Portland area, which was being by-passed by sea routes to Canada. With nine ox teams of three or four yoke apiece, carrying about three thousand pounds to the wagon, they first left The Dalles, July, 1858. They

To hasten their settlement Edward R. Geary, superintendent of Indian affairs in Portland, Oregon, on September 1, 1859, recommended to A. B. Greenwood, commissioner of Indian affairs in Washington, D. C., that "outside" or "nontreaty" Indians of the Columbia—so called because they refused to be bound by the treaty signed at Walla Walla in 1855—and the Okanogans, with whom no treaty had been made, be placed on the Yakima (Simcoe) Reservation.[3] During the lull (1857) in the recent war, an agent of the Indian Office, Ben F. Yantis, traveling with his young son, had visited the Half-Sun people in the fishing camps on the lower Spokane; he recommended that four young men be sent to assist them in using hoes and spades issued to their families, something in the fashion of the modern Peace Corps.[4] Under the strengthening leadership of the new Half-Sun, the "In Between People," so called because they lived between northern and southern Columbia bands, showed little interest in the proffered gifts. The new Indian leader cautiously promised Fort Colville's commandant, Major Pinkney Lugenbeel, to report trouble among the tribes, but this apparently was as far as he wished to go with his dealings with white men.

Then came the Civil War. Troops were drawn from the western commands, and it appeared that the Great White Father at Washington had something else to do than tie Indians down on reservations. The war, however, gave natives of the Columbia no respite from white men. Driving their herds through stirrup-high bunchgrass to furnish beef at the Canadian mines, cattlemen now moved on to interior ranges. On the way they discovered something the red man had known all along—that each tiny clump of parched bunchgrass contained every nutrient

---

traveled north by way of Wallula near the mouth of the Snake River to Priest Rapids, old Fort Okanogan, and north along the Okanogan River to the Thompson River in British Columbia (Phillip H. Lewis, "Coal Discoveries in Washington Territory," manuscript, 13–15). Subsequent trips in the sixties were made by debarking at White Bluffs.

3 *Annual Report,* 1859 (36 Cong., 1 sess., *Sen. Exec. Doc. No. 2*), I, 759.

4 Ben F. Yantis to Superintendent of Indian Affairs, July 20, 1857. Washington Superintendency of Indian Affairs Records, No. 234, Roll 918 (Referred to hereafter as Washington Superintendency Records, 1853–80).

needed to raise fat, sleek cattle and horses. "The bunch-grass country is the best and finest country on earth," one white man exuberated; "bunch-grass cattle and horses are the sweetest, fleetest, and strongest in the world and a bunch-grass man is the most superb being in the universe."[5]

Some of those "superb beings," the Half-Sun braves, restless and revengeful since their recent war with the white man, would have attacked the trespassers had not their new chieftain restrained them. Sensing this hostility, the drovers tried to ingratiate themselves with the natives and rewarded them with beef every time Indian buckaroos, riding canoes as well as horses, helped wrangle stubborn cattle across the Columbia. On September 1, 1861, as the Half-Sun Chief and his band were camped on the east side of the river between Rock Island and the Wenatchee Flat, a Canada-bound party with cattle appeared on the other side of the river. The camp buzzed with excitement. The Chief, now a large, powerful man in his thirties, untethered the blue roan staked by his lodge, plunged into the river, and rode "like a centaur" to meet the strangers. Any crossing of the Columbia on horseback was dangerous, but in the low water of late summer he accomplished the feat quite easily; had there been high water, he would have swum, holding his horse's mane on the downstream side, keeping his body from the animal so as not to impede its movement. Coming out of the river, he rode across the rocky beach to a group of white cattlemen and some Indians, including Nanamkin of the nearby Entiats, who had met them on the trail and offered his services as guide. Not least among the party was a sixteen-year-old drover, Jack (A. J.) Splawn, who would never forget this meeting. The Chief asked him to whom the cattle belonged, and the lad pointed out a tall cattleman, Major John Thorp. As the big Indian turned his roan toward the Major, Splawn interrupted to ask his name. Looking down at his young interrogator, he replied, "Sulk-talth-scosum, but better known to white men as Chief Moses." "*Nika Moses*" ("I am Moses"), the

5 Thomas W. Symons, *Report of an Examination of the Upper Columbia River and the Territory in its Vicinity* . . . (47 Cong., 1 sess., *Sen. Exec. Doc. No. 186*), 111.

tribal leader would say many times thereafter to introduce himself to white men.

After speaking with Thorp, Moses, as he would have the white
man call him, rode back to the east side of the river. He was at
his lodge only a short time when Nanamkin appeared to tell him
that he had overheard some braves plotting to massacre the party
and steal its cattle. The Indian Moses had come to respect Thorp
in their brief meeting, and the thought of his men's killing the
cattleman and his towheaded helper filled him with anger.
Quickly, he and Nanamkin rode across the river to the party's
camp at the mouth of the Wenatchee. By then, night had fallen.
A full moon revealed to them the plumed-and-painted braves on
a hill preparing to rush the little group. Immediately, the Chief
rode between the hostiles and the party and waved the attackers
back until the hill was cleared. Moses had saved the lives of the
little group and, because of his dramatic action, had strengthened
his leadership among his own people as well.[6]

The boy, Splawn, shook hands with the big Indian, Moses, and
the two went their separate ways. A few months later, they met
under circumstances not so friendly. Splawn had taken a job
freighting supplies from The Dalles to Rock Island, where two
trading posts had been established, one on the east side of the
Columbia, run by the Chinaman Mr. Wing. These "Pigtail
Braids" (to the Indians, the *Kaspellelpsh*) were part of an Oriental
invasion which swarmed to the Columbia and its tributaries in
the wake of white miners, catching gold by diverting ditch water
into sluice boxes or by dipping water from tin cans into crude
cradles. After toiling far into the night by the light of pitch
torches, they fell exhausted into their river-bank dugouts, awaking early to resume their labors in enigmatic silence.[7]

On the west side of the Columbia near Rock Island, a large
camp of over a hundred of these "Celestials" worked a ditch

6 Splawn, *Ka-Mi-akin*, 160–62.
7 Sometimes the Chinese combined agriculture with mining. To insure water
for mining and gardening near present-day Brewster, Washington (on the Columbia), they dug ditches into and out of a lake. U. E. Fries, *From Copenhagen to
Okanogan*, 215–16.

abandoned by white miners, patiently sluicing out a fortune which Splawn took to Portland to deposit in the banks for them. On one of his return trips he was accompanied by two Chinamen. On reaching the Columbia near the "China Camp," he was confronted by Moses and another Indian. Moses' friend began beating one of the Chinese with the elkhorn handle of his riding whip. The angered towhead stopped the fracas at gunpoint and continued toward camp with his Oriental companion howling with pain.[8] Possibly the Chief's friend shared the bitterness of natives who attacked and killed the Chinese near the mouths of the Cheland and Methow rivers. Sometimes the Chinese took Indian women to their camps. The Indians, however, depended on the Chinese for gold. In 1877 Moses, complaining that Chinese were taking that metal out of the country, would condone Indians driving these Orientals from Rock Island.[9]

Generally the Chinese attended to their own business and posed no obstacle to Moses as he went about his, gathering his tribes. He opened his villages to natives wishing to escape the white man. Accepting his hospitality were those from the Okanogan and the tributary valleys of the lower and mid-Columbia fleeing the Yakima Reservation. Besides traveling up and down the river to receive the refugees, he supervised the camps, issuing orders from his tipi like a "Boston" general at a command post. In the spring, he ordered the women to plant pumpkins, squash, potatoes, and corn in one of his gardens like the one in Moses Coulee, a well-watered spot protected from cold spring winds by a natural fence of towering basalt. In late spring he dispatched segments of his villages to the root grounds and fisheries, and in late summer, others to the berry grounds and again to the fisheries. Since trips to the Plains were becoming infrequent because of more danger and fewer buffalo, he sent his men more often into the Cascades to hunt deer and bear. He ordered the women in the coulees to dig large holes and line

[8] Splawn, *Ka-Mi-akin*, 213.
[9] Richard F. Steele, *An Illustrated History of Stevens, Ferry, Okanogan, and Chelan Counties, State of Washington*, 670–71; *and Walla Walla Union*, July 21, and August 18, 1877.

47

them with rocks, poles, and matting for storing winter food, and had them hack down with crude scythes ryegrass for the livestock. He ordered wranglers to round up their horses and drive them to winter pasture on the sheltered lower Crab Creek ranges and rounded up the people himself to follow the horses to the river camps at the Big Juniper Flat (Kahskahtqua) by the Columbia near present-day Vantage.[10]

During winter confinement, tempers erupted, keeping the Chief busy untangling domestic problems stemming oftimes from polygamy, which Alexander Ross termed "the greatest source of evil existing among this otherwise happy people."[11] Sometimes when a woman would come to him with the complaint that her husband rested his head on his other wife while resting his feet on her although theoretically the two held equal status in the lodge, Moses would order the man to abandon either his partiality or his scorned wife. The thought of losing a good worker would make the reprimanded husband regard the less favored wife more highly for a while.

He felt responsible for his people's religion and morals. During their ceremonials he went about camp intoning sober "hallelujahs" and "amens," undisturbed that he did so in the milieu of pagan worship. He disciplined small boys sneaking off to the sand dunes or coulee rocks to smoke their fathers' pipes, and prevented those fathers from sneaking off to Portland to prostitute their women or to carry liquor from white traders to other Indians.[12]

In disciplining his people, Moses had a valuable ally in his mother, the aging Karneetsa, who rose early every day for years and preached right conduct to her people. One day she left with some of her children for another camp where she was taken ill and died. Her chieftain son never saw her again.[13]

Although Moses often went about camp and urged his people

10 Peone Interviews.
11 Ross, *Adventures of the First Settlers*, 295.
12 Secretary of the Interior, *Annual Report*, 1867 (40 Cong., 2 sess., *House Exec. Doc. No. 1*), II, 73.
13 Peone Interviews.

to sobriety, he did not always practice what he preached—an inconsistency best explained by one of his followers: "Moses he drank too but he was a big man and it didn't hurt him." The Indians' addiction to drink was recent, but nonetheless demoralizing. Early in the century Ross Cox, the fur trader, had written that "all the Indians on the Columbia entertain a strong aversion to ardent spirits, which they regard as poison."[14] Not any more. "Whisky hells" were springing up all over. On taking over command at Fort Colville, Major Lugenbeel had pleaded in vain with the civil authorities to close those along the upper Columbia.[15] Two ruffians were even selling whisky at a trading post at Moses' birthplace on the Wenatchee Flat until they were hustled off to the penitentiary, but many others remained in the interior to peddle their wares.[16] Stories of Moses' fondness for liquor are legion. The incident best known to white men occurred in June, 1869. He was camped at that time on the west side of Crab Creek at Rocky Ford, where with Wanapums, Yakimas, and Umatillas his people often entertained Palouses, Spokanes, Nez Percés, Kalispells, and other tribes from as far away as eastern Montana who camped on the other side of the creek.

On this occasion, Jack Splawn, on a cattle hunt, entered the camp. Moses left the festivities and invited him to his lodge, which held as an aid to the fun-making a ten-gallon keg of whisky with the head knocked out and a tin cup hanging at the side. Before the thirsty Chief could take a draught from it, a large body of Indians rode down from Wilson Creek in a warlike mood. He asked them to explain, and they said they were seeking a medicine man (very likely one who had failed to cure a patient). He told them the shaman had sought asylum in his lodge and would be protected, and that if they did not leave, he would order his men to fire on them. At this, they quickly departed. After the interruption he returned to his lodge, where he filled and drained the

14 Cox, *Adventures on the Columbia River,* I, 321.

15 Major Pinkney Lugenbeel to County Commissioners of Spokane County, July [no date], 1861. Winans Collection, No. 38.

16 For an account of their eventual incarceration after some questionable maneuvers in frontier justice, see Splawn, *Ka-Mi-akin,* 269–71.

contents of the tin cup. Splawn, frightened by the liquid freedom of the camp, stole down to Moses Lake and hid in the tules. The big Chief had a keen sense of hospitality toward his guests whether they were medicine men or cattle drovers. When he discovered that young Splawn had left, he hurried to a large rock near his camp, unhitched his horse always tethered there, and rode off to find him. Overtaking the escapee, he asked why he had left in such a hurry. Splawn, still shaking in his boots, frankly told him, but promised to say nothing about the whisky to the soldiers.[17]

One of the Chief's greatest concerns was the relationship of his people with those of other bands. In these matters he was aided by intelligence agents circulating freely among neighboring bands gathering information. While camped with his people on the Yakima River one time, he heard that a young girl, one of his relatives, had been bought as a wife by a younger brother of a Yakima chief, Shuluskin. He rode to Shuluskin's camp and angrily announced that the girl had the regal blood of the Half-Sun and had married beneath her station. Shuluskin outlined his own lineage stemming from the great Weowikt family, to show that the marriage had been between equals. This satisfied Moses; so did the gift of ten horses Shuluskin offered to seal the union. The two chiefs shook hands, and Moses rode away.[18]

One of the greatest threats to his people came from just across the Columbia in the form of a hunchbacked prophet, Smohalla, the *Yantcha* or spiritual leader of the Wanapum people. In the backwash of the wars, disillusioned natives had flocked like flies in salmon time to Smohalla's wedge-shaped lodge at P'na Village (a Fish Weir) at Priest Rapids. Many of them had intended to cast their lot with Moses, only to change their minds on hearing the *Yantcha* tell them to avoid white influence and continue in the native ways so that they could be present in a bright resurrection day when the Greedy Ones, spawners of the recent war, would be overthrown.[19] With his *Washani* (symbols) of the sacred

17 Splawn, *Ka-Mi-akin*, 335.   18 Splawn, *Ka-Mi-akin*, 342.
19 The Wanapums remained unreconcilable. The only "treaty" they ever signed

trinity, Sun, Moon, and Star, cleverly worked into his trappings and dances called the *Washat*, Smohalla had medicine his Columbia rival could not match.[20] The closeness of the two camps encouraged association, and many times Moses' followers crossed over to the Wanapum village to join in the pagan *Washat* dance. Moses himself went there frequently, and he once brought a Wanapum woman back to his camp; however, she made herself unpopular with her husband's people by indiscriminate eating of the "Sunday Food," the *Welkaloops*, special food set aside to be eaten only on that day. Two baby daughters later, he sent her back to her own people.[21]

Moses did not go as far as his rival in opposing white influence, but he remained aloof as far as he dared. He continued to refuse the gifts of calicos and blankets that the Simcoe and Colville agents were passing out in growing numbers.[22] Returning north from his winter camp in the spring of 1870, he and the other non-treaty Indians received a note from George W. Harvey, the farmer in charge of the Colville District, to come to a council.[23] Quickly the Chief called a strategy meeting of his subchiefs, Sheeway, Schoothumekun (the Bull's Head), Chooeeal, Kemas, and his other principal men. Then they departed for the council at the Rock Creek root grounds on the Walla Walla Trail some thirty miles below the Spokane, where Kamiakin and about fifty of his band were living in heart-breaking exile. There, on May 7, they

with the white man was an agreement made by a remnant of the tribe with the Grant County (Washington) Public Utility District on January 15, 1957, in which that agency agreed to pay them twenty-thousand dollars for rights to the site on which Priest Rapids Dam was built.

20 For a description of Wanapum forms of worship, see Click Relander, *Drummers and Dreamers*, 61–86.

21 Peone Interviews.

22 G. A. Paige, special agent at Fort Colville, sent letters and notices to the Okanogans, Spokanes, and Pend Oreilles, inviting them to come in for gifts, and he later had to send special messengers assuring them the gifts were not in exchange for their lands. Even so, the Columbias were adamant in their refusal to accept them. Paige to T. J. McKenny, April 18, 1868, and W. P. Winans to Superintendent of Indian Affairs, December 31, 1870. Washington Superintendency Records, 1853–80.

23 George Harvey to Colonel Samuel Ross, May 26, 1870. Washington Superintendency Records, 1853–80.

met with over one thousand other Indians—Kalispells, Spokanes, Coeur d'Alenes, Lakes and Colvilles, Okanogans, San Poils, and Methows. Harvey addressed the council through his interpreter, George Herring, a half-blood son of a Colville woman and a Hudson's Bay Company factor.

Moses, who impressed Harvey as "the most intelligent of the lot," complained of the murder of one of his men by a young chief of an adjoining tribe. This chief, being ill, had sent a messenger to Moses requesting the services of one of his medicine men. Moses had complied, sending an elderly shaman. The shaman treated the young chief until he recovered, whereupon the ungrateful patient not only refused to pay the shaman for his services but poisoned him, in all likelihood thinking he had robbed him of his power. Since the old shaman did not die as soon as the young chief had wished, the ingrate took a rope and hanged him. Moses asked Harvey to settle the matter and to charge the young chief with first-degree murder.[24] This was obviously an embarrassing request to Harvey, who was unsure of the legal technicalities of the case and fearful lest his interference touch off an intertribal war. Consequently, he let the matter ride.

Harvey used the council to air his own grievances, specifically his opposition to the recent appointment of W. P. (Park) Winans as Colville agent. Moses was perhaps too much concerned with his own problems to detect Harvey's clever admixture of his own welfare and that of the natives. The following March, Winans reported Harvey's words to the Superintendent of Indian Affairs of Washington Territory, General T. J. McKenny: "The whites have been abusing you. They will drive you to the mountain tops. They will make slaves of you, use you like horses and cattle, make you pull your own plows. This land is your land and you are being robbed of it. You will be told that to hold the land you must fence and cultivate it, the same as white men. They who tell you so lie. It is your land. No one shall deprive you of it. I will protect you with my last drop of blood. Park Winans will come among you representing himself as an Agent. He is not an

24 *Ibid.*

agent. Don't have anything to do with him . . . if you listen to Park Winans you will be driven like sheep to the mountain tops." The speech had its desired effect; the following month, chieftains of the various bands along with several white citizens of Stevens County, Washington Territory, petitioned Colonel Samuel Ross, superintendent of Indian affairs of the territory, to have Harvey appointed their agent.[25] Every major chief at the Rock Creek council signed the petition save one—Moses, who, in spite of a personal respect for Harvey, apparently wished to show no interest in agency matters, possibly fearful that the government might use it as a wedge to extend its control over him. The petition proved to be in vain, national politics being what they were, and Winans took the job.

Moses returned with his men to the Coulee to enjoy its privacy, but their isolation was short lived. About June 27, a runner, Pukakheen, came from the San Poil with a message from Winans asking Moses and his followers to meet him in four days at the mouth of the Okanogan. There the agent planned to take a census of Moses' and other tribes in the area. "White men have noses like a hunting dog smelling out my country," Moses would often exclaim in situations like this.

As Winans' train of eight horses, with interpreter, guide, packer, and census taker, picked its way west to the Okanogan River over a hoof-cutting route, Moses rode north, probably rehearsing the tone and content of his speech. He must not appear too hostile, because that might encourage the government to confine him on a reservation; yet he must speak with enough firmness to impress the government with his isolation. On June 28, Winans reached the council site, the ruins of the Hudson's Bay Company fort, about a mile above the river near the graves of Indian victims of one of the smallpox epidemics. Here he nervously awaited the natives. He had carefully timed his visit to fall between the root-digging and berrying seasons, when they

25 Harvey's speech is found in Winans to McKenny, March 6, 1871. Winans Collection, No. 34. The petition to Ross, June 16, 1870, may be found in Washington Superintendency Records, 1853–80.

would probably be in their river villages, but he had no assurance they would come to the council. The evening of the next day his spirits rose with the arrival of Innomoseecha Bill of the Chelans and Enkawhakekum (Wappato John) from near Lake Chelan. He was impressed with Innomoseecha's powerful build and shrewdness; he was even more interested in Wappato John when he learned that he had a farm, a mining claim, and a house with a clock in it. He may not have learned that John had seen clocks in Portland, where he once worked as a cook and went by the name of "Jack."

As if to give dramatic and psychological impact to his arrival, Moses waited until the last of his four days to appear. This maneuver caused a much relieved and grateful Winans to declare that the "noble chieftain" wielded more influence than any other east of the Cascades in the territory, and that he was a man who always kept his word. In opening the council, Winans stated that he had come to gather the names of the chiefs and headmen of each tribe, the number of their men, women, and children, to learn whether or not they had religious instruction, and if not, whether they would prefer Protestant or Catholic teachers. After assuring them of governmental protection and help in acquiring titles to farmlands and in adopting other ways of white men, Winans recognized Innomoseecha, the first to speak. "Bill" assured the agent of his friendliness and of his wish for Protestant preachers and teachers for his people. This got the council off on the right foot, where it remained all through a speech by the Methow chief, Swahmous or "Cultus (Bad) Jim," who prayed in a manner hardly *cultus* for the Great Spirit to give him and Winans a good heart.

Then they stepped aside to hear the words of Moses. The council stilled. "*Nika Moses*," he began. "I am ignorant, you are educated, therefore, you are older in knowledge than I, but I wish to speak my heart as a child speaks to its father." Then, speaking quite unlike a child to his father, he condemned the government's too many "fathers' " handling of Indian affairs: "You agents all say that you are sent by the superintendent and

54

each one speaks differently so that my heart is divided towards you." Then with mounting anger, blasting white men who called themselves Christians: "The Indians don't receive any better treatment from the whites on account of their religion. . . . The Indians think they do right to pray but when the whites see them assembled for worship they mock them; and treat them the same as they would a band of fast horses; they drive them off. The white man is the cause of our sorrow. . . . I fear the ruin of my people is coming." With increasing anger: "Now you tell me to fence and cultivate my land [and that] after a time the government will give me a deed for it and then it will be mine. My parents gave birth to me here, and I fancy that this is my Country. . . . I don't expect always to live; but when you white and we red men die we shall have to give an account of ourselves before our Maker." And, finally, these words, which he would repeat many times in the years to come: "Let me remain in my own Country and I shall die contented. I have spoken."

Before the council broke up, Winans offered specific gifts to the bands. Reporting later, he wrote that the "haughty, arrogant and insolent" Isle de Pierres (Rock Islands), as he called Moses' people, had refused to accept the gifts, one of which he thought would have been very beneficial to them—a seine for use at a wide and dangerous place on the Spokane. Moreover, they had refused to supply him information about their tribe, claiming that with a government of their own, they did not recognize that of the United States—that the only authority they recognized was God, who already knew their numbers. This left him to depend on information that he described as "most reliable" to ascertain their population which he reported as 255 men, 245 women, 270 boys, and 230 girls. Moses' independence was not absolute, however, for he swallowed his pride just enough to show up at Fort Colville a month later to receive from the government fifty pounds of flour and one pound of tobacco.[26]

26 For Moses' acceptance of the government gifts, see statement A, "Statement of Articles Issued as Presents to the Chiefs and Head Men at Fort Colville, W. T. During the Quarter commencing July 1st and ending September 30, 1872." John A.

Shortly after returning to Fort Colville by way of the Okano-gan, Winans warned his superiors that several northern bands in stormy councils had talked of war against the whites to stop their settlement along the proposed route of the Northern Pacific Railroad.[27] Less than a fortnight from his meeting with Winans, Moses stopped at the trading post at the Wenatchee Flat where he met D. C. Linsley, who was the locating engineer of that railroad then making a reconnaissance of the country near the forty-eighth parallel between Idaho and the Pacific Ocean to carry the main line from Clark Fork to Puget Sound.[28] The railroad finally with-drew its right of way along the northern route and thus freed the land for government use. The Colville Reservation was subse-quently established by executive order, July 2, 1872. It lay west and north of the Columbia, east of the Okanogan, and north to the British Columbia line.[29] Thus the dreaded reservation system was brought to the borders of Moses' ancestral homeland.

With its northern route abandoned, the railroad now shifted its surveys south through the Plateau. One day in that same year (1872) Moses gathered some of his people, and perhaps with more sorrow than curiosity, rode down to Crab Creek to watch the survey crew preparing the way for the "chick-chick wagon." First the head flagman came with his red and white rod, and red pennon fluttering its location to the transit crew. Next, came the chaining party, moving up rapidly and driving stakes into the earth of Moses' fathers like hunters stabbing wounded prey. To the rear, moving into view, came the leveling party with a mule or two, while off to the south a pack train passed westward to camp. These operations were repeated until the party disap-

---

Simms Papers, 3A (Holland Library, Washington State University, Pullman, Wash-ington). The itinerary of Winans' trip and the census are found in his annual re-port. Winans Collection, No. 34.

27 *Ibid.*

28 D. C. Linsley, "Pioneering in the Cascade Country," *Civil Engineering*, Vol. II, No. 6 (June, 1932), 339–44.

29 Kappler, *Indian Affairs: Laws and Treaties*, I, 916. The preceding year, 1871, Congress had legislated that Indian tribes should no longer be considered foreign nations with whom the United States might contract by treaty; hence the new policy of executive orders.

peared beyond the bunchgrass stretching away to the Columbia.[30]

The big Chief must have been shaken by these rapidly chang-ing events. His old rival, Smohalla, taunted him for his helpless-ness, because only he, the *Yantcha*, had medicine powerful enough to stem the white advance. In the summer of 1872, just a short distance away on the Yakima Reservation, the missionary Henry Spalding was holding meetings at the big camps after having been encouraged to carry the flames of revival there be-cause of recent successes among the Nez Percés, to whom he had returned after an absence of many years.[31] Why did the worried Chief not hurry to Simcoe to hear words of comfort from the one who had taught him how to face the white man? In the first place, he avoided Spalding because, like other natives along the Colum-bia, he had indulged in the very practices which the missionary had warned him against. He also had avoided Simcoe because its Methodist agent, the Reverend "Father" James Wilbur, believed it his sacred mission to gather Moses and other scattered Colum-bias to his civilizing fold as he was said to have once herded New York toughs to Bowery missions as a policeman.[32]

Now the taunting Smohalla said the only way to escape the trap of white civilization was to pray to the Creator, Nami Piap, for its destruction. Smohalla announced that the Great Spirit would soon show his displeasure by shaking the earth. It had been the Prophet's practice to impress his following by foretelling eclipses, cleverly basing his predictions on information from white men's almanacs. But an earthquake? That was something else. Coinci-dence, the white man called it, when midway in the second Month of Snow (Sustikwu) by native reckoning, or December 14, 1872, in the Christian measure of time, the Spirit met his children in the power of Yimumtompt (the Earthquake). As shock waves

[30] Thomas Nelson Strong, "The Indians of the Northwest," *Pacific Monthly Magazine*, Vol. XVI, No. 2 (August, 1906), 169–77.

[31] Spalding, *Diaries and Letters*, 403.

[32] Wilbur was one of the church-related agents appointed to carry out Grant's "Peace Policy." For an account of the policy at work on the Yakima Reservation, see Robert L. Whitner, "Grant's Indian Peace Policy on the Yakima Reservation," *Pacific Northwest Quarterly*, Vol. L, No. 4 (October, 1959), 135–42.

rolled through the Columbia Valley, a large cliff a few miles up-stream from the Wenatchee Flat collapsed and its massive hulk fell into the river, partially damming it. Frightened natives rushed into the trading post on the Flat begging its new owner, Sam Miller, to read to them from the big black magic book (the Bible). In the epicentral Chelan country as sulphurous matter oozed from the earth, natives scurried about for old prayer books, fell to their knees, and asked the Great Spirit to forgive them for beating their too numerous wives. Farther upriver along the San Poil and Nespelem, water filled the Indians' underground houses and drove the inhabitants into the hills, where they re-peated Roman Catholic prayers or ran around tearing off their clothes. Others in the north country streamed into Colville beg-ging the priests to baptize them.[33]

Smohalla worked the earthquake for all it was worth. Even Moses, shaken as the earth, hurried to P'na Village to dance the *Washat*. Nami Piap was not content to give the Valley just one jarring. White settlers coming into Walla Walla in the spring of 1873 said that since the middle of February the country between the Wenatchee and Lake Chelan had not seen one day free from tremors. As the earth shook on through the better part of the year another prophet also made the most of the disturbances—the shadowy Wenatchee-River seer, Patoi, who drew many of Moses' people to his camp to pledge themselves to sobriety and right living.[34]

Moses seems to have felt the need of a medicine more powerful than that of his rivals. Apparently for the only time in his life, he came within a hair's breadth of becoming a Christian. In the late spring when the Indians collected for the root harvest at

[33] Agent John A. Simms to R. H. Milroy, December 31, 1872. Washington Superintendency Records, 1853–80. See also Rev. Urban Grassi, S. J., to Rev. P. Giorda, S. J., November 10, 1874, manuscript; Edward S. Holden, "A Catalogue of Earthquakes on the Pacific Coast, 1769 to 1897," *Smithsonian Miscellaneous Collections*, No. 1087 (Washington, 1898); Edson Dow, *Passes to the North*, 44–49: Verne F. Ray, *The San Poil and Nespelem: Salishan Peoples of Northeastern Washington*, 108; *Spirit of the West* (Walla Walla, Washington, Territory), December 4, 1874, p. 2.

[34] *Oregonian*, May 15, 1873, p. 1; *Walla Walla Union*, December 27, 1873, p. 3.

Pine Grove in the Spokane country, his old teacher, Spalding, joined them for a harvest of souls in response to an urgent request from the Spokanes for him to "preach Jesus to the people," baptize them, and marry them "according to the laws."[35] It was reported that he baptized as many as 160 natives in one day.[36]

Whether for the root harvest or for the express purpose of seeing Spalding, Moses was present at this gathering. When the two met, the thirty-four years of separation fell away in a great surge of the old affection. As the missionary reported it, Moses "came out boldly for Jesus . . . showed great memory of Scripture taught him long years ago, threw his arms around me & proclaimed me his father, proclaimed his strong desire that this father & no other should come to his country (beyond the Col. River over 340 miles from Kamiah) & receive himself & he thinks most of his large tribe into the church of Christ. I hear good reports of his wonderful labors as an exhorter."[37]

During the meeting Moses spoke to the assembled Indians, but instead of "exhorting" in the spirit of the religious revival, he used the occasion to air a bitter grievance against the white man. The famous Modoc War was raging at the time with the Modocs under Captain Jack making their desperate stand in the Lava Beds of southern Oregon. It had touched off a general Indian scare, and settlers in the thinly populated areas of southeastern Washington had fled for refuge to Walla Walla. Irresponsible rumors linking Moses with the hostilities had been circulated, and he feared that if these stories persisted, the government would put him on a reservation. Thus he launched into a passionate defense of his conduct and a condemnation of the white men who spread the slanders.[38]

After the meeting Spalding returned to Kamiah. He and Moses had agreed that he would return in five weeks to meet the Chief and his tribe at "a great fishery beyond Pine Grove." (A year

35 Spalding, *Diaries and Letters*, 409.
36 *Oregonian*, July 22, 1873, p. 1.
37 Presbyterian Historical Society, *Spalding-Lowrie Correspondence*, 47–48, 53, 55–56, and 95.
38 *Oregonian*, July 22, 1873, p. 1.

later Spalding referred to Priest Rapids as the designated rendezvous.) But this meeting did not take place. Spalding made three
more trips to the Spokanes, all the while apparently conducting a
fruitless search for his former pupil, but with the seasonal migra-
tions the Chief had left the area. His quest, as he related it, often
involved traveling sixty miles a day, riding beyond his strength,
plunging through gorges and defiles, and sleeping with aching
bones among the vermin. In mid-September he wrote from the
Spokane country that he hoped Jesus would "open the way &
furnish means should I make an other tour to Spokan, to go on
to the interesting people under the chieftain ship of Moses."[39]
About that same time, Moses and some of his "interesting people"
were camped in Moses Coulee and were about to receive a white
visitor, but not a missionary. As they were breaking camp, they
spotted R. H. Milroy, superintendent of Indian affairs for Washington Terriory, and his young son riding down a rocky trail in
company with Colville agent John Simms and an interpreter,
George Herring. Milroy was returning from a reconnaissance of
the Colville Reservation. His appearance must have reminded
Moses that the government would soon be moving natives to that
confine. That evening Moses went to Milroy's camp for a parley
which got off to a friendly start, as such meetings often did when
there was a white child present. As the boy gazed up at the lordly
Chief, who was bigger than his father, the elder Milroy eyed the
Indian's beautifully tanned deerskin outfit with collar and cuffs
of fluffy fur. To make the garment, the skilled Shantlahow had
scraped a deerskin, soaked it in a deer-brain solution, stretched it
on a drying frame, and crowned her creation by scraping and
hand rubbing it with an application of white clay. Moses was
known to make several changes of outfits on a single occasion. His
people had nicknamed him Sispilh Kalch, "Seven Shirts," after
the magic shirts had helped him escape the soldiers at Hangman
Creek. With his increasing fondness for varied apparel, the name
appeared to have taken on new meaning.

"Where did the Indians come from?" asked Milroy.

[39] Presbyterian Historical Society, *Spalding-Lowrie Correspondence*, 48, 53,
94–95.

"From the North in a great multitude according to the legends," replied the Chief.

Having heard that he had five wives, Milroy then queried, "How many children do you have, Moses?"

The Chief began to count many times over on his fingers, then confessed, "I don't know."

The next morning Milroy's party rode out of the Coulee with the Indians. Milroy asked them to explain a bright red spot far up the mountain. A deposit of material they put on their faces before going to war, they told him, almost implying that the material could still be used if necessary. Leaving the band, Milroy and party were transported across the Columbia to Sam Miller's post by native canoemen talking excitedly about the mountain which had tumbled into the river the year before. Milroy asked Miller about a store he had seen on a flat just east of the Columbia near Badger Mountain. He assumed it was a whisky shop since he had seen its proprietor pouring whisky down the throat of a snakebite victim. Miller assured the Superintendent that he had guessed rightly and told him that the liquor was brought down from Canada to the store, where it sold for less than in Seattle.[40] In the late spring of the previous year, Moses, at the head of a party, had stopped one of these vendors at Grand Coulee, demanding to know what liquor he had in his wagon. The shrewd trader, aware of Moses' fear of the Yakima agency, said that if the Chief touched so much as one keg of his cargo, he would report it to the Simcoe agent.[41] It is unlikely that the staid Father Wilbur would have given the freighter much sympathy, but the ruse apparently worked and the vendor moved north.

Moses knew that Father Wilbur wanted to trap him like a salmon in the Simcoe weir. Spalding also persisted in the hope of

[40] Elias Nelson, "Reminiscences of R. B. Milroy," *Yakima Morning Herald*, January 7, 24, 31, 1937; February 14, 1937.

[41] Charles Schneider to R. H. Milroy, December 19, 1872. (Washington Superintendency Records, 1853–80); on May 11, 1873, a government surveying party on the plateau below the Columbia River was stopped by three Indians of the Moses and San Poil bands who claimed their chiefs had given them authority to prevent the surveys (Milroy to Simms, May 23, 1873—Simms Papers). Moses later denied that he had given the three any authority to block the surveys (*Walla Walla Union*, July 5, 1873, p. 3).

bringing the Chief into *his* fold, although approaching winter and illness prevented him from further travel. The following June, 1874, when he was on his death bed, he again wrote of the affecting reunion with his former pupil and the Indian's words, "My father come & receive me & hundreds of people into church."[42] When the old man died on August 3, he was confident that his helper, the Reverend Henry T. Cowley, would succeed in bringing the work to this glorious consummation.

Cowley searched the Spokane country in vain, then pressed his search westward to the Coulee, arriving there in mid-May, 1875. Moses, with his usual outward show of hospitality, treated the missionary cordially and assured him that he was looking forward with much interest to the time when he and his people might receive baptism. It did not take Cowley long to see that he had come at a poor time, for the Chief was entertaining tribes from as far away as the buffalo country with games and dances, and medicine men were much in evidence. Moses, somewhat embarrassed, suggested that the shamans and pagan ceremonies were such as to interfere with Christian worship and that it would be better for the missionary to come back some other time. After staying in camp for a day and a half to rest his horses, Cowley returned to the Spokane.[43] Fortunately, Spalding would never know of his colleague's failure.

Had Moses wished, he could have escorted Cowley, as he had once planned to escort Spalding, to Priest Rapids to frustrate Smohalla with superior medicine. Deciding otherwise, he forfeited his last opportunity of employing spiritual weapons to defeat his adversary. Of course, he could have gone down and physically attacked the Prophet as he had often threatened to do. Legend has it that he stormed down to P'na Village, where he created the biggest aftershock of the quake by beating the *Yantcha* to within an inch of his life. The half-dead Smohalla, so the story goes, dragged himself to a canoe and floated down to the Umatilla,

---

42 Presbyterian Historical Society, *Spalding-Lowrie Correspondence*, 95.

43 "The Reminiscences of H. T. Cowley," *The Early History of Spokane Washington Told by Contemporaries* (ed. by J. Orin Oliphant), 42.

where some white men picked him up. Then he began a period of wandering, but where no one knows for sure, although by his own admission, according to the tale, he traveled to the Mormon country ostensibly to observe religious forms there, in order to set himself up on his return a bigger *Yantcha* than ever. Although the Prophet likely did not travel as widely as this legend would have it, his teachings did—through devious channels, where they set in motion a shock wave of events forcing Moses to make an agonizing decision, perhaps the greatest of his life.[44]

[44] A correspondent of the *San Francisco Chronicle* may have been the first to publish the story of the "fight" between Moses and Smohalla. See *Weekly Pacific Tribune* (Seattle, Washington Territory), August 7, 1878, p. 4. It was so widely circulated in newspapers that James Mooney describes it in his "The Ghost Dance Religion, "(*B. A. E. Fourteenth Annual Report*, Pt. 2, 718–19). Some of Moses' people claim the "fight" occurred; however, Mrs. Peone says that Moses' wife, Mary, never mentioned it. Click Relander, the leading authority on the Wanapums, writes that none of the old people of that tribe ever mentioned it to him (*Drummers and Dreamers*, 180).

IV. War Drums or Peace Pipes?

"Now, this day I have a hard knot given to me to untie."—
Moses' letter, February 19, 1879, from Fort Simcoe to General O. O. Howard.

THE STORY OF SMOHALLA's "miraculous return from the dead" helped spread his teachings like a Plateau bunchgrass fire. One of its sparks fell on Toohulhulsote, a nontreaty Nez Percé, who became a Smohalla disciple because of resentment over the white man's "forked tongue" diplomacy. The Nez Percé chiefs had been at the Walla Walla council in 1855, and had signed away much of their land. Even the land in the Wallowa country in northeastern Oregon which they had retained was soon also taken away, and they were ordered to concentrate on the Lapwai Reservation in central Idaho. This twisted series of events, capped by some highhanded actions of General Oliver Otis Howard, commander of the Department of the Columbia, gave weight to Toohulhulsote's influence in the Nez Percé councils.[1]

From his Coulee, Moses viewed the Nez Percé crisis as no mere observer. He, too, faced white settlers poised to occupy his lands. Moreover, his people and the Nez Percés were bound together by ancient ties proven by mutual aid in buffalo hunts and wars against their common enemies on the Plains; and Joseph, soon to become known in history as the Nez Percé leader, was his friend. General Howard from his headquarters at Fort Vancouver watched the crisis unfold with equal anxiety. In late May, 1877, accompanied by Lieutenant M. C. Wilkinson, his aide, and Colonel E. C. Watkins, inspector of Indian affairs for the Department of the Interior, he traveled by steamer and portage railroad up the Columbia in the direction of the trouble. At The Dalles

---

[1] George Fuller, *A History of the Pacific Northwest*, 265, 273–74. For the complete story of the Nez Percé war, see Francis Haines, *The Nez Percés*.

he interrupted his journey to turn north to Simcoe, the head-quarters of the Indian agency on the Yakima Reservation. He had received a letter from Andrew D. Pambrun, son of an old Hudson's Bay Company trader, warning him that Moses was receiving arms and ammunition from a freighter known as "Wild Goose Bill" Condon, and was organizing a general Indian out-break to help the Nez Percés.[2] Were even he and his party safe as they bumped along the lonely road to the Simcoe agency?

Early in June they reached the rectangular cluster of buildings that still bore the military stamp of its former days as a fort. Here the agent, Father Wilbur, ruled the natives by a combination of immense physical prowess, religious fervor, and paternalism—ranging from a whipping post to plowing their fields in order to bribe them to attend church.[3]

Colonel Watkins and Father Wilbur immediately sent couriers to the principal chiefs of the area: Moses, representing his own band, the Methows, Okanogans, and other bands of the upper Columbia; Smohalla, the Wanapums; and Young Chief, One-Eyed John, Thomas, Calwash, and Jatoiah, the scattered bands of the lower Columbia. It took the messengers three days to reach Moses in the country above Priest Rapids. The Chief greeted them courteously, and, in his eagerness to present his story to Howard, traveled the distance to Simcoe in a day and a half, arriving there June 9.

Since the Yakima War, Moses had avoided the beautiful oak grove of Simcoe as though it were a patch of poison oak. His wariness of Wilbur was well known, and Simcoe held unpleasant memories for him antedating the advent of the "Father." How could he forget the treachery of Kiyuya (David), who had stolen his horses and had set him afoot in the Yakima War, and Kiyuya's white masters, who had left their Simcoe den like rattlesnakes to strike the natives? But Colonel Wright, the vengeful terminator of the war, had drowned off the California coast; and Governor Stevens and Major Garnett, the builder of the fort, had been

2 Andrew D. Pambrun, "The Story of His Life as He Tells It," MS 181.
3 Lyman, *History of the Yakima Valley*, I, 541.

killed in the Civil War. Now he heard that Howard was a friend of the red man, and he must hurry to Simcoe to see for himself. (Howard indeed had headed Grant's peace commission during the Apache wars in Arizona.) Perhaps the most important force driving him to a rapprochement with the military was his growing belief that only through it could he find protection from the ever encroaching white civilization.

When Moses and Howard met that hot June day under the Simcoe oaks, they cast measuring glances at each other, as might be expected of military men meeting for the first time; and the strange alchemy of respect began its work at once. The proud bearing of each was marred somewhat by a physical handicap. For the General it was a missing right arm, a casualty of the Civil War; for Moses, inflamed eyes, a casualty of campfire smoke, plateau dust, and Columbia sand. Howard, conscious of military apparel, noticed that Moses was wearing a broad light-felt hat with thin veil, a striking buckskin coat and trousers interrupted by a leather belt containing a long knife and holster with an ivory-knobbed pistol, and handsome beaded moccasins.[4]

The white general was impressed by the military bearing and formality of the chieftains as they readied themselves for council in the big tent in the grove.[5] They sat on benches and chairs, while Howard, Agent Wilbur, and Colonel Watkins sat at a table facing them. The chiefs, recognizing Moses as their ranking leader, stepped aside to give him first position. Next to him on the front row sat Smohalla, and then in order of importance One-Eyed John, Calwash, and so on. Behind them, shading off into the background, crouched reservation men, women, and children resplendent with clean clothes and clean hands and faces—living testimonials that godliness among Wilbur's children had not been gained at the expense of cleanliness.

After an opening prayer, first Watkins and then Wilbur spoke

4 Oliver Otis Howard, *Famous Indian Chiefs I Have Known*, 200.

5 The council is described in the writings of General Howard: "Report on the Nez Percé Campaign," (Fort Dalles Papers 869, Box 15, Huntington Library); *Nez Percé Joseph*, 78–84; *My Life and Experiences Among Our Hostile Indians*, 346; *Famous Indian Chiefs I Have Known*, 363–64.

through the interpreter, Pambrun, stating that the United States required the Indians to come to the reservations, and that should they think otherwise, the military commander would enforce the requirement. Howard, directing attention to the Nez Percé trouble, impressed on his audience the idea that since these Indians had no chance against the military, any thought of waging war in their behalf would be futile.

Howard's firmness, dignity, and impartiality kept the opening of the council from being difficult. Since the Indians were tired from their long journeys, the council was soon adjourned with an invitation from Wilbur to attend religious services at the same spot the next day, Sunday. An "amen" to this suggestion came from the religious Howard. In the meantime, the visiting natives observed the Simcoe farms, schools, houses, and wagons, as Wilbur had hoped they would, as an inducement to move to the reservation.

The Sunday service was an old-fashioned Methodist camp-meeting "love feast" with everyone participating. Father Wilbur was in charge, with Watkins, calmly, and Wilkinson, nervously, exhorting the natives. They were followed by several reservation Indians who in their own tongue began "pleading for the cause of Christ." Well-dressed and happy Indian school children cemented the unforgettable service with song. Smohalla and several other "wild" chiefs responded with "much apparent sincerity and feeling." Smohalla's other responses were not so definite.

Early Monday morning, June 11, Wilbur came to Pambrun stating that Howard, Watkins, and he had discussed Smohalla's vague answers about coming on the reservation and had decided to give the interpreter considerable latitude in communicating with the evasive prophet. As soon as the council convened at eight o'clock in the morning, Pambrun asked Smohalla to give a definite answer. He answered that he would come in about two months—as soon as the white salmon fishing was over. "Your law is my law," he said. "Yes, I will be on the reservation by September." Moses, when asked to state his intentions, replied, "My

Indians are scattered over a large country. I cannot say what they will do. I am ready to tread on *any* reservation. If it is better for me to go on some reservation other than this, all right. The Indians above the Spokane, several tribes, have invited me to become their chief; and if they shall have a reservation, I would like to go to them." After the other chieftains had given similar assurances, the council adjourned. It is evident that Moses had cleverly stressed the Spokanes' desire to have him as their chief to divert attention from Simcoe as a possible reservation for his people, a strategy by which he wished to obtain a compromise reservation in his ancestral home between Spokane and Simcoe. Howard answered that a council would be held shortly near Spokane Falls where the tribes and bands to which Moses had referred would be brought together; should they then express their desire to go with Moses, the latter's wish would be considered. Moses assented to this agreement, marking his approval upon a formal paper with an "X."

After the council, Pambrun, still not convinced of Moses' peaceful intent, warned Howard to hasten to Lapwai to protect the white settlements from a possible Moses–Nez Percé alliance. Howard quickly gathered his party and in company with a lively cavalcade of Indians bounced along the Yakima River in a spring wagon and then drifted in a dugout canoe down the Columbia to an unhappy place in American history.[6] He held high hopes of meeting Moses soon in the Spokane country. At the same time, Moses rode up the Columbia, apprehensive of the forthcoming meeting. Strangely, circumstances would interpose so that neither Howard nor Moses would attend that council.

Moses moved up to the Spokane Fisheries to meet the tribes gathered there for the late spring salmon runs. About the latter part of June, reports reached Walla Walla that he was on the Spokane with three or four hundred warriors of several northern tribes and was preparing to lead them to a juncture with the Nez Percés in an all-out war against the whites.[7] Gatherings at fishing

6 Pambrun, "The Story of His Life as He Tells It," MS 181.
7 *Oregonian*, July 7, 1877, p. 1.

grounds were commonplace among natives, but to white settlers they appeared to be spawning grounds of war and plunder. Coincident with the Spokane gathering came word that the Nez Percé crisis had finally exploded into war, with some initial Nez Percé successes. This threw the white settlers into a frenzy.[8] Volunteer militia companies, like the Palouse Rangers, living along the path Moses would take to join the embattled Nez Percés, hurriedly organized and frantically bombarded the Washington territorial governor, E. P. Ferry, for arms and ammunition to supplement their own hodgepodge of weaponry. Panicky citizens fled over the rolling Palouse Hills to Colfax or Walla Walla. Farther north, the panic spread to the Crab Creek settlements. Yakima Valley citizens, being only a short distance from Moses' home base, were unnerved by all sorts of rumors that his band was on the warpath. In the Kittitas, settlers hastily threw up breastworks or scurried to Yakima City to join its people in building makeshift fortifications.[9]

When Moses was on the Spokane, the Nez Percés kept in almost daily contact with him, attempting to entice him into the war.[10] His consideration of their requests was not taken lightly. He talked the subject over with other leaders and chiefs, even with Skolaskin, chief of the San Poils, with whom he was usually at odds. The San Poils were a peaceable people, sometimes accused of laziness; and their chief, a hunchback with body so twisted he could not stand or walk without support, maintained his control over them by prophetic trances and visions. Now he told Moses they would not join the Nez Percés. "God made the world for us to live on, not to fight or sell," he said.[11]

8 Miles C. Moore to Governor E. P. Ferry, July 6, 1877. E. P. Ferry, State Documents 1876–80, Indian Affairs.

9 For an account of the hysteria and preparations for war, see William Sidney Shiak, *An Illustrated History of Klickitat, Yakima, and Kittitas Counties, Washington*, 162–67.

10 Chief Moses revealed many times these Nez Percé pressures (*Spokane Falls Review*, October 31, 1890, p. 1); early in July, Calkin, a Moses subchief, with a chief of the San Poils, assured a citizens committee in Walla Walla that Moses was peaceably disposed (*Walla Walla Statesman*, July 14, 1877, p. 3).

11 Henry Covington Interview, Colville Reservation, Washington, January 18, 1958; Harry Nanamkin Interview, Nespelem, Washington, March 4, 1961.

Moses may have been touched by the appeals of the Nez Percés, but he was convinced that diplomacy, not war, was to be his defense against the white man. Strategically it would have been foolish to cast his lot with them, for by this time they were rapidly retreating across the Rockies away from all help. Moreover, many of his braves were trading and visiting across the Cascades at Nisqually on lower Puget Sound.[12] The presence of his men there alarmed white citizens east of the mountains, who feared that the warriors would join their coastal allies, as they had in previous wars, in a devastating sweep into the Yakima country. The interpreter, Andrew Pambrun, was sent by way of Simcoe to find and pacify Moses; but Agent Wilbur, miffed at Watkins' criticism of his management of the Yakima Reservation, refused to co-operate. Pambrun, warned that Smohalla and the Wanapums had threatened his life because of his part in the Simcoe council, decided it was unsafe to go farther in his search for Moses.[13]

Moses and his people broke camp near the Spokane in July, after assuring the missionary, Cowley, they had no hostile intent in the Nez Percé troubles.[14] They returned to the Moses Coulee country, where it appeared to Jack Splawn they had only shifted the base of their hostile operations.[15] Splawn was then a full-grown man in the cattle business with E. D. (Ed) Phelps and W. I. Wadleigh. With Phelps he rode to within six miles of the Wenatchee, where "As far as we could see on the north side of the river Indian lodges were strung along, while the plains were covered by grazing horses, kept from wandering off by an occasional rider." On a high range of hills to the north they saw dust rising and soon sixteen warriors with gun barrels flashing in the sun coming down to water their horses. The warriors spotted the cattlemen, manned two canoes, and paddled over to meet them. As they neared the shore, Splawn saw that the warrior in the

<hr/>

12 *Spokane Falls Review*, October 31, 1890, p. 1.
13 Pambrun, "The Story of His Life as He Tells It," MS 181.
14 *Puget Sound Weekly Courier* (Olympia, Washington Territory), August 3, 1877, p. 1.
15 Splawn, *Ka-Mi-akin*, 335–37.

bow of one craft was none other than Moses. The Chief stepped out of the canoe, walked straight to the men, and asked why they were there. They said they had come because the settlers feared the Indians were going to war. Moses advised them to ride to Sam Miller's store at the Wenatchee Flat and to stay there overnight, promising to meet them there the following morning. The two moved cautiously upstream, counting 190 lodges along the way. Later they were told that farther on, Innomoseecha Bill of the Chelans was camped with 100; and above him the Okanogans and San Poils were encamped with 150. Moses' main camp was on the Plateau just east of the Columbia. They approached the post gingerly, half expecting to find Sam Miller dead, but Moses would have never permitted his braves to touch the scalp of his friend, the man with the big, black, magic book.

The next morning Moses was on hand at the store with Smohalla and Innomoseecha Bill. On the Flat in front of the store, so the two cattlemen were told, were five Nez Percé chiefs of Joseph's band. The two did not like what they saw and asked the Chief to explain the presence of so many warriors. He replied that he had no intention of entering the Nez Percé War, and, as for the warriors—he had asked them to come so that he could keep an eye on them. On the way, however, some of them, thinking he had called them together to make war, had burned cabins of settlers and had driven off horses and killed cattle. He assured the two that he had the warriors under constant surveillance so that they would not slip out to resume their depredations.

As one of Moses' people later put it, "Not many a chief could do that!"

While the Chief kept the restless warriors in line, the Colville agent, John Simms, kept in touch with him through messengers riding back and forth between the agency and the camps.[16] Moses informed Simms that he wished word could be sent to the Crab Creek settlers and others who had fled their homes to return, that he would be personally responsible for their safety. During the crisis with all its strain, Moses protected Alexander ("Slick" or

16 *Oregonian,* July 23, 1877, p. 3.

"Alex") McCauley, a rancher from the Okanogan who occasionally took extended trips through Indian country, and also welcomed to his lodge another white man named King.

Soon, hoping to reassure the settlers returning to their homes, he ordered the men who had stolen horses to restore them to the ranges. He then dismissed the Indians to return to their own homes. In containing the excited braves about him during the tense period, he had helped contain a northwestern Indian war![17]

There was still the problem of his future. Colonel Watkins had called for a council on June 27, at Fort Colville, with Moses and the other chiefs to discuss that problem, but it had been delayed because of the Nez Percé War. Finally, with Joseph in full retreat, the meeting was held at Spokane Falls on August 13. Colonel Watkins was there. Colonel Frank Wheaton, with five hundred of Howard's troops, no longer needed in the pursuit of Joseph, was there. Several Coeur d'Alene chiefs were there with Father Joseph Joset, who was in charge of a mission among their people and who had brought them at the request of Watkins.[18] The Spokanes, Colvilles, Kalispells, Palouses, Okanogans, Lakes, and San Poils were there—but where was Moses? They waited two days, but still no Moses. Later, his excuse was that the invitation from Simms had through a mixup been delivered by a woman and not by the white messenger he expected.[19] Also, he said, Chief Garry did not want him there. True enough, Garry resented Moses' presumptions to a Spokane chieftaincy, but he was sorry Moses was not present to be assigned to a reservation, preferably a long way from the Spokanes. Watkins assured Garry that Moses had promised in writing to go on a reservation, and that if he did not, General Howard and the army would see that he did. The uncertainty of the location of this reservation did not satisfy the

17 Elwood Evans was perhaps the first to realize and evaluate Moses' role in the crisis and stated that he not only held the key to a general Indian uprising in 1877 but also the key to Joseph's fate. Evans, *History of the Pacific Northwest: Oregon and Washington*, II, 83.

18 John Joseph Augustine Joset was born in Switzerland during the reign of Napoleon Bonaparte.

19 Howard, *My Life*, 349.

Spokane, and he sat glumly through the rest of the council. Had Moses attended the council, he might have been pressured by the officials to accept a reservation more certain in its location and less to his liking. Apparently he had absented himself from the gathering in hopes of securing a better reservation.

When the smoke from the last council fire cleared, all tribes except the Upper Spokanes and other holdout Spokanes under Garry had signed agreements to go on reservations. Moses' other neighbors—the Lower and Middle Spokanes—agreed to go to a reservation just north of the lower reaches of their river. The Okanogans, San Poils, Lakes, and Colvilles agreed to accept the Colville Reservation with some minor changes. Moses and his people were still uncommitted.

Now he was surer than ever of one thing—he would not go to the Yakima Reservation, a sentiment he expressed to S. F. Sherwood, a prominent Colville citizen, who passed the information on, as Moses hoped he would, to Colonel Watkins. "There is not room enough for my people on the Yakima Reservation," he complained. He professed disappointment at the failure of the council to attach a reservation to the Colville one for him; but this was his means of presenting one of his own choosing. As he described it to Sherwood, it would commence at the lower end of Rock Island on the Columbia, thence east to Rock Creek where the Colville and Walla Walla wagon road crossed it, along that road to the bridge on the lower Spokane, and down that river and the Columbia to the place of beginning.[20]

On September 24, at Cowlitz north of Fort Vancouver, Lieutenant Wilkinson met General of the Army W. T. Sherman, then visiting the Northwest, and showed him the area on the map. Sherman took one look at it and blurted, "No; no more reservations. Tell Moses and Smohallie that we have lots of young men who are anxious to fight Indians. They must go on reservations as laid down, or take the consequences."[21]

---

20 For an account of the council and of Moses' reservation proposal, see Secretary of War, *Annual Report*, 1877 (45 Cong., 2 sess., *House Exec. Doc. No. 9*), II, 649–50.
21 *Ibid.*

Hearty approval of these words came from settlers in the Yakima country, who were becoming fearful of an unconfined Moses and were casting covetous eyes on his homeland. Aware of their mood, he traveled as near Yakima as he dared on his way to the Kittitas in October to assure the "pale face Bostons" that he had only the kindest regards for them. In the Kittitas, he called on Francis ("Frank") Streamer, former editor, friend of the red man, eccentric, and frontiersman of many parts.[22]

Streamer sized Moses up as "the only practical Christian I have met on the coast, for the simple reason he always does what he says he will do." His conversations with Streamer increased the Chief's anxieties about what the government was planning to do with him and his people. He wrote to Howard expressing his fears that the soldiers were planning to force him to some reservation. On February 9, 1878, Howard wrote the commanding officer at Fort Walla Walla that arrangements were being made for Moses and the other Indians to secure titles to homesteads just like the whites and that he, Howard, would like to have a talk with the red leader. A few days later, the cattleman, Ed Phelps, rode into Moses' camp with a letter from Howard, which he read and translated to the chief:

Chief "Moses"
SIR: Mr. E. D. Phelps will carry this letter to you. I hear that you want peace with the whites and with the soldiers. I remember what you said to me at Fort Simcoe and am very sorry not to have met you at the Council at Spokane Falls but I could not be there on account of my war with the Nez Percés.

As soon as I return from Washington I would like to see you and talk over the whole subject of your country and of your being chief of the tribes you named to me at "Simcoe."

There are no orders to send soldiers against you or your Indians and I am, as you know, your friend. I thank you for helping us to keep the peace among discontented Indians and white men last summer.

When I see you again I will explain how every Indian who wishes to do so can get some good land for his own.

22 Streamer, Miscellaneous Notebooks, Folder No. 2., entry for July 15, 1877.

Be sure and not believe any timid or lying people who keep the country in trouble.

Mr. Phelps will tell you how friendly I am. If the Indians make war, then I fight, of course, but I do not love war. As I told [The Nez Percé chiefs] White Bird and Looking Glass and Joseph, so it came to pass. They lost their country and their houses forever.

Yours Truly

(sgd.) O. O. HOWARD

Brigadier General

Comd. Dept.[23]

Moses must have felt considerably relieved. Also, during this time he had found an amanuensis in Streamer to tell his story to the public. The *Weekly Herald* of Omaha, Nebraska, on March 29, 1878, carried from Streamer's pen the plaintive words of Moses, "the great high chief of all the Cascade Indians . . . as delivered in the Grand Medicine Council of Chiefs." No evidence has been found as to the council; and it is even possible that Streamer invented the council and wrote the Chief's speech, but in any case it presented his problems, and is in harmony with known statements he made on other occasions:

CHIEFS: we have heard from the great White Father and the great White Chief at Washington. We have asked to give us peace, and let our old men and old women rest on these lands that belong to the great chief of our fathers. We have asked them to let our young men and young women go free, to fish where they will, to hunt where they can. We have asked them to take away their soldiers, their agent and their traders, and let us all, old and young buy where we want to sell where it suits us. We have asked them to set us free, and not tie us down like wild ponies are tied down—to a stake on the sage sands. We have asked them to let us have our own religion, our own preachers and our places to meet the Great Spirit, and talk with him in our own way—in our own belief. We have asked them to make a good straight road, that all the white men and the black men and the red men could travel on it in peace, and not push

23 Howard to Moses, February 11, 1878. Washington Superintendency Records, 1853–80.

each other off in anger. . . . We have asked them to punish our bad people under the same laws they punish their bad whites. We have asked them not to kill our old men and our old women, because some of our bad young men had done wrong, when the bad whites stole their lands their ponies, and made them drunk on bad firewater (Revenue Whisky). We have asked them to make strong words with us now, and keep them strong as long as these waters run (Columbia river) or that mountain Cascade) stands. We have asked them to let us go to where the sun rises, when we want to see the Great Father and talk with him, and to come where the sun sets when we want to rest from our long trail—just the same as his white children come and go and go and come. We have asked them to hear [what] all our people have to say, to come and see us—to see how poor we are, to see how sick our old men are, and to see our naked bodies and bleeding feet. You see how the grass has died away from these lands they have tied us to [referring to the tribes on reservation]; how the deer and fish have gone, and how our children cry for something to eat. We have asked them to take pity on us, and not get angry with us and drive us like dogs onto the sharp briars and rough stones, away yonder to where no water runs, no grass grows, no fish swim, or deer trail.

The Great White father and the Great White chief have ears but they do not hear the poor Indians cry for help. . . . They hear the cry of the black. . . . They hear the cry of the yellow man. . . .

Chiefs, what can we do? The white men are as many as the leaves on yonder trees—as many as sands on yonder shores. The Indians are as few as the leaves on one tree, or the sands [on] one shore. If we go to war we will all be shot down like dogs; if we stay on the reservations we will all starve and die, like salmon out of water. Let us go to the white man's chiefs, and tell them to go to their Great White Council (Congress) and get their great council to set us free, as it set the black man free, and as it set the yellow men (Chinese) free. They have many ears and many hearts. . . . Some of them will feel our pain and take pity on us. Then the great papers will tell all the good whites how poor we are, and we will be set free to go and hunt where the game is, to fish where the salmon runs, and to raise our ponies and corn where the grass grows and the rains

Courtesy of Eastern Washington State Historical Society

Chief Moses, mounted on a war pony in the streets of Yakima City, 1897.

Chief Joseph of the Nez Percés, wearing war bonnet, 1900.
Joseph was an ally and lifelong friend of Chief Moses.
Photograph by DeLancey Gill

fall and the water runs. Then, if the Great White Council will not hear us, or is cold and stony, let their soldiers then come, and we will fight and die on our own grounds, and die brave and good, and cry no more. Chiefs: I am done, my words are spoke.[24]

The local press was understandably less sensitive to Indian grievances than the papers farther east, but Streamer made it possible for Moses to inform them also of his plight. In a letter to the *Weekly Standard* of Portland, he condemned (with Streamer's hearty concurrence) the various agencies handling Indian affairs: "Indians don't want so many tyees [chiefs] no more than the whites do." As for General Howard: "General Howard wants to do what is right, but the great chief at Washington keeps him back and makes him do bad." As to prospects for peace: "Indians are for peace now and all time to come but they will fight hard before they will be driven away like dogs from their salmon and buffalo illihies [camps or lands] this grass [summer] time."[25]

In Ellensburg, Moses talked with John Shoudy, trader and founder of that Kittitas Valley settlement. Although he appeared outwardly peaceful, he made it clear it would be unwise to put him on the Yakima Reservation. He said he had recently passed the same warning on to Chief Lot (Whistlepoosum, the son of Big Star) of the Lower Spokanes with a proviso that, if forced to a reservation, he would settle on the Colville. Shoudy reported Moses' words to Howard in a letter. At the same time he translated a letter to Moses from the General. This prompted the Chief to say that as long as the one-armed man was his friend, he feared no trouble, but, if the Indian Office insisted on sending him to Yakima, he and his bands would resist and then head for the Canadian border. Looking to this contingency, he sought to strengthen his ties with the Okanogan bands near the boundary.[26]

His efforts might have been more successful had Tonasket (an Okanogan chief living east of that river) come to his aid. Remembering that Lieutenant Wilkinson had warned him at Spokane

---

[24] Moses' letter was dated from Kittitas, W.T., March 11, 1978.

[25] *Weekly Standard*, March 22, 1878.

[26] Memorandum from General O. O. Howard, May 14, 1878. Washington Superintendency Records, 1853–80.

the previous year to report any signs of trouble, Tonasket hurried to Fort Colville on May 6 to report to its commandant, Captain W. C. Cook, that Moses had made overtures to him and that several hundred warriors, including those of Smohalla and Thomas, were concentrated in Moses Coulee for an attack on General Howard. Hiram F. "Okanogan" Smith, a white settler from Lake Osoyoos on the border, apparently accompanied Tonasket to Colville. In a sworn statement before S. F. Sherwood, clerk of the District Court, he said that for some time the Okanogans had been communicating with Moses' band and that unless some show of military strength were made, a general uprising would occur. Captain Cook immediately informed Howard of the situation.[27]

After receiving this word, Howard notified Father Wilbur of the danger and suggested that he send one of his "excellent delegations" to inform Moses that he could not come up the river for a conference until after the Fourth of July. Howard then telegraphed a request to the Adjutant General of the Military Division of the Pacific in San Francisco that no troops be sent to the trouble spot because it would be better for the Okanogans to join Moses than for a war to break out. Furthermore, he said, all of Moses' messages expressed friendship. The following is typical of the letters Moses was sending the General at that time:

GENERAL HOWARD:

I, Moses, chief, want you to know what my *tum-tum* [heart] is in regard to my tribe and the whites. Almost every day reports come to me that the soldiers from Walla Walla are coming to take me away from this part of the country. My people are excited and I want to know from you the truth, so that I can tell them, and keep everything quiet once more among us. Since the last war [the Nez Percé] we have had up here rumors that I am going to fight if the soldiers come. This makes my heart sick. I have said I will not fight and I say it to you again, and when you hear white men say Moses will fight them [tell them] 'No.' I have always lived here upon the Columbia River. I am getting old and I do not want to see my blood shed on my part of the country. Chief Joseph wanted me and my people to help him. His orders were

27 For the exchange of letters pertaining to the crisis, *see ibid.*

many. I told him, 'No, never!' I watched my people, faithfully during the war and kept them at home. I told them all, when the war broke out, that they must not steal. If they did, I would report them to Father Wilbur [the Indian agent at Simcoe].

It is time for us to begin spring work. We all raise lots of vegetables, and wheat and corn, and trade with Chinamen to get money. I wish you would write me and tell me the truth, so that I can tell my people that they may be contented once more and go to work in their gardens. I do not want to go on the Yakima Reservation. I wish to stay where I have always lived and where my parents died. I wish you would write to me and send your letter by the bearer of this, and be sure I am a friend and that I tell you the truth.

his

"(Signed)　Moses　X　Chief."

mark[28]

An important theme in Moses' correspondence with Howard was his people's peaceful adjustment to crop agriculture in the land of their fathers, another way of saying they were as happy there as they would be on a reservation somewhere. At the same time, circumstances, unknown to Moses and to the land-hungry settlers wishing to unseat him, were coming to light that caused government officials to believe Moses should remain with his crops and lands. Howard, in a letter to the Adjutant General in San Francisco on May 11, gave an estimate of what it would cost to send troops against Moses. He said they would have to be pulled from eight northwestern posts and sent to Wallula, the jumping-off place on the Columbia for the Moses country; and, adding the estimates for transportation, ammunition, and rations for a three months' campaign, he came up with a total of $100,000 if there was to be any kind of war at all. An immediate answer from San Francisco asked why he supposed hostilities were probable. He wired back that Moses was mustering well-armed forces, and he hinted—although he recognized the danger of stepping

28 Howard, *My Life*, 350–51. The *Walla Walla Statesman*, May 18, 1878, p. 3, reported that Moses had persuaded a white man by the name of White to write a letter to Colonel Cuvier Grover, commandant at Fort Walla Walla, assuring him that he was for peace during the crisis.

on toes in the Indian Office—that the source of the trouble lay in an order which he claimed Watkins had issued at the Spokane Falls council for Moses to go to the Yakima Reservation. (Officially, it appears that the Inspector had not designated a specific reserve for Moses.) He went on to say that he had just been informed by cattleman Phelps that Agent Wilbur was at that very moment delivering an order to Moses to go immediately to the Yakima Reservation, and this, according to Phelps, meant war.

San Francisco then relayed to Howard a message from Sherman that there were no War Department orders to use force to drive Moses to any distinct reservation; that Howard should do everything possible to allay the Chief's excitement, because "The appropriation for army transportation is so nearly exhausted that we are in no condition to inaugurate warlike measures." Thus economic concerns canceled out the arrogant boast Sherman had made a few months before. On May 13, Lieutenant Wilkinson carried the olive branch to the Chief near Priest Rapids and two weeks later followed him to the Kittitas to assure him that no soldiers were being sent to force him to a reservation.[29] At the same time, John Shoudy wrote to Howard from Yakima assuring him of the wisdom of the army's peaceful policy. The lives of about three hundred citizens, he said, would be endangered if Moses were to fight, and, if the government were wise, it would leave him just where he was.

In late May, Joseph Petty, a young stockman fresh from a six weeks' stay in Moses' camp, traveled to Portland to report that Moses had about five hundred fine-looking warriors, well supplied with horses, arms, and ammunition but lacking in ready money and means of subsistence. Moses always told him, said Petty, that he intended to stay with his people on the *illihee* of his fathers and would resist any move of the government to unseat him. Petty added that Moses was elated over a letter he had received from Howard a short time before with the news that the General planned to visit him, and that he was trying to purchase a wagon to receive his guest in style.[30]

29 *Weekly Standard*, May 31, 1878, p. 4.   30 *Ibid.*

On May 30, Streamer walked across the Wenatchee Mountains in mud, rain, and snow, carrying a precious notebook to Sam Miller's store. Moses rushed to see him and the notebook, for it contained his very own speech as recorded in the *Omaha Herald*. This set the mood for a friendly powwow that night. The next morning, after assuring Streamer that he was his friend, Moses left for the Wenatchee Fisheries.

Ten days later the Chief came back to Miller's to hear Streamer read to him one of Howard's many communications just in from the Ellensburg post office.[31] Under the date line of June 4, Howard sent Moses still another letter saying he was sorry they had not met in Spokane Falls as planned and that because of a threatening outbreak of Bannock Indians (in southern Idaho Territory), he could not meet him, but would arrange a conference when the troubles were over. Howard ended the communication with an expression of his dependence on the Chief to keep the peace, for he had just been informed by the commandant at Fort Lapwai that, although against Moses' wishes, his people wanted to join the hostiles—in fact, seven villages (whether or not some of them were under Moses' control the commandant did not say) along the Columbia had already done so.[32] The previous winter several Indians (if Moses' people, he again did not say) had crossed the Bitter Root Mountains to communicate with tribes of the Upper Missouri. With the outbreak of hostilities, Howard hurried to what became known as the Bannock-Paiute War to prevent the hostiles from forming an alliance with the Columbia River tribes.

One day a delegation of Bannocks arrived and made camp just below Wenatchee Flat. Moses' people had never been on good terms with these Snakes, as they called their visitors; but the latter knew that their success along the river depended on aid from its most powerful chief. Moses was camped with his forces across the river and a little above them. Just after dark Sam

31 Streamer, Miscellaneous Notebooks, Folder No. 1, p. 18.

32 Howard, *My Life*, 350; Secretary of War, *Annual Report*, 1878 (45 Cong., 3 sess., *House Exec. Doc. No. 1*), I, 212.

Miller saw the outline of a flotilla crossing the river in the direction of the Bannock camp. The unusual maneuver drew him to the scene. On spotting him, Moses flew into a rage, ordered him back upriver, and threatened to kill him if he did not obey. Miller, stunned by the command, retreated homeward.[33] Did Moses wish to protect him from hostile Bannocks? Or was he afraid his friend would observe his rendezvous with them and report it to the authorities? Was he considering a union with the Bannocks?

Settlers in the Yakima country thought so. They believed he was going to place himself between the Wenatchee and Kittitas valleys while Smohalla would take a station on the upper Naches and wait for the Bannocks and Paiutes to cross the Columbia so that they could join them in a slaughter of the whites. Moses would wipe out the Kittitas, cross the Umtanum Ridge, and sweep the Wenas. Smohalla would give the same treatment to the Naches and Cowiche valleys while the Paiutes raided the lower Yakima. They would then converge for a massive slaughter at Yakima City and the Ahtanum. The panic sweeping that country and the preparations for its defense were greater than those of the previous year at the time of the Nez Percé uprising.

A territorial militia company of fifty men, the "Klickitat Rangers," under the command of Colonel Enoch Pike, a Civil War veteran, thought they could handle the Moses problem by themselves. With needle guns and ammunition secured from the Territorial Armory in Olympia and an interpreter guide, they struck out across the Horse Heaven Hills to the Columbia and headed north to Moses Coulee and its chief. As they rode into the Coulee, they saw several hundred Indians riding out from behind a hill about a mile ahead, all naked, daubed with war paint, and decked out in feathered bonnets. About half of them carried guns, and the rest carried clubs, spears, and bows and arrows. Descending to the Coulee floor, the warriors closed ranks in a

---

[33] "History of Chelan County," *Wenatchee Daily World*, May 31, 1910, p. 3; "The Real Life of Sam Miller," *Republic* (Wenatchee, Washington), December 13, 1906.

large semicircle and rode toward the Rangers. Moses, on a spotted horse with his aide, the fierce-looking Innomoseecha Bill, beside him, rode out ahead of the main force in silence save for the creaking of saddles and the soft crush of bunchgrass beneath their horses' hoofs. When about one hundred yards from the company, Moses turned and signaled his warriors to halt. Then he and Innomoseecha rode on with right hands raised, palms facing the Rangers. Colonel Pike halted his command and with his interpreter rode to within ten paces of the two chiefs.

Innomoseecha broke the stillness: "Me interpreter, Chief Moses wants to talk with you. Chief Moses say you go back over the river and mind your own business! That's all."

Colonel Pike hurriedly consulted his interpreter. "You are in command, Colonel," said the interpreter, "but if you want my opinion I think you had better take his advice!" Pike ordered the Rangers to about face, and they rode out of the Coulee.[34]

Personnel at the War Department in the national capital and in San Francisco anxiously pored over their maps and reports from the northwestern trouble spot. On July 8, they telegraphed Colonel Wheaton, commandant at Fort Walla Walla, for information regarding what had been or what could be done to prevent Moses and his men from joining the hostiles. Wheaton wired back that he had done all in his power to prevent Moses' and Smohalla's people from leaving their hunting and fishing grounds. Just a few days before, General Howard had sent a Mr. Charles McKay with a message to Moses.

McKay found the Chief and some three hundred of his braves in the Kittitas, where they were encamped to escape the heat of the Columbia's sands and to avoid, possibly, the Bannocks moving north along that watercourse. He found the warriors armed and excited in the belief that soldiers were coming upstream to put them on a reservation. The peace pipe was passed around, and McKay delivered his message from Howard. Then Moses calmed his men with a three-hour speech and sent three of them to inform the other bands of the true state of affairs. When

34 Robert Ballou, *Early Klickitat Valley Days*, 341–42.

finished, he gave McKay an earful to take back to the military: "I will be happy to meet the one-armed general in council at any time." Then referring to the Puritanical restrictions imposed by Wilbur on the Yakima Reservation, he continued, "All I want is the same liberty enjoyed by white men. If I want to play cards I ought to be allowed to play; it is nobody's business but my own. I will sell the land I am on, but I will never be driven from it. Smohalla and I are planning no hostile moves together. Someday I am going to take a rope down there and hang him."[35]

Moses had no intention of carrying out his threat against Smohalla, but his speech indicated that, despite a common fear of white encroachment, the bad blood between the two continued to boil. An incident about that time contributed to this mutual animosity. Moses and his wives went down to Smohalla's camp to a root feast, where it appears Smohalla drank his rival's whisky and became so drunk he couldn't hold his spirit dance. The Prophet's wives were deeply incensed at what had happened and asked Moses' wives why they had allowed "the old fool Moses" to make Smohalla drunk. One of them grabbed a tipi pole and brandished it about, barely missing one of Moses' wives, who was carrying a baby on her back, and hitting Shantlahow (Mary) on the ankle. The usually calm Mary jerked the pole from her attacker and joined her people in packing their goods for a huffy withdrawal to their own camp.[36]

Moses' people were now agitated over something far more ominous than Smohalla. Colonel Wheaton reported on July 8 that Moses had sent him a friendly letter warning that he might not be able to restrain a thousand restive men under him; whereupon the Colonel had stationed at his post nearest Moses an entire company of his regiment, a contingent of thirty-four enlisted men and three commissioned officers. He also reported that gun-boats were patrolling the Columbia to prevent hostiles of the Bannock-Paiute uprising from joining Moses. These hostiles were

35 *Weekly Standard*, July 12, 1878, p. 1; *Walla Walla Statesman* (Walla Walla, Washington Territory), July 13, 1878, p. 1.
36 Peone Interviews.

actually natives living between Wallula and The Dalles (conveniently designated as Umatillas by the military) who had joined the Bannock-Paiute cause, but were now deserting those tribes for asylum with Moses. At the very time Wheaton was reporting, one of the patrol boats below Umatilla attacked and dispersed three bands of Columbia River Indians at different points and captured and destroyed native boats and camping outfits. Farther upstream Lieutenant Wilkinson, commanding the gunboat *Spokane*, gave the same treatment to other natives attempting to cross the river to the north bank. In returning the fire, the fleeing Indians riddled the *Spokane*'s pilot house. In retaliation, the patrol fired into a peaceful camp along the river, scattering corpses in all directions. Later, many finely worked buckskin dresses and shirts showed up in the saloons of Portland and Vancouver as trophies of the massacre.[37]

The Columbia River gunboats had the last word. The reverberating salvos from their decks were responsible for a stark tragedy in the lonely hills between the Columbia and Yakima sending jolts of fear through the country. No one was to feel the impact from that event more than Moses, the Columbia chief.

37 Secretary of War, *Annual Report*, 1878 (45 Cong., 3 sess., *House Exec. Doc. No. 1*), I, 168–69; Pambrun, "The Story of His Life as He Tells It," MS 193.

V. Paddle Wheels and Deals

"If the President complies with my request it will make me so much the stronger."—Moses to General Howard at Priest Rapids, September 8, 1878.

IN THE EARLY HOURS of July 10, 1878, Lorenzo Perkins and his wife, owners of a cattle ranch southwest of White Bluffs, prepared breakfast on the nearby Columbia. Then Mrs. Perkins packed a lunch as her husband readied their mounts for a trip to Yakima City, where she was to be delivered of her baby. The Perkinses engaged a neighboring rancher to row them to the west bank of the river. Safely across, they gathered their horses, which had swum behind the craft, and rode on.

At the same time, and on the same side of the river, seven Umatillas—Tewonne, Tomehoptowne, Winecat, Moostonic, Saluskin, Chuckchuck, and Kype—rode north. They were among those who, chased by the military, had fled north across the river after some of their relatives had been killed by the indiscriminate firing from the gunboats. Now the renegades, seeking protection and an opportunity to avenge their losses, were riding to the camp of the great Chief Moses. The first opportunity for revenge arose when they met the rancher and his wife, the "pregnant one," as the Indians still call her.

The couple invited the Indians to share lunch. They accepted the hospitality and then murdered their hosts. They had gotten their revenge. The cry, "Perkins Murder!" pierced the frontier as whites fearfully prepared to seek their own revenge.[1]

[1] For additional information on the Perkins murder, see *Weekly Pacific Tribune*, July 31, 1878; *Oregonian*, June 20, 1879 (the confession of one of the murderers); Shiak, *An Illustrated History of Klickitat, Yakima, and Kittitas Counties, Washington*, 165–67; James Wilbur to General O. O. Howard, July 26, 1878 (Yakima Agency Letter Record Books, 1878–79). In addition, we note in a letter from Click Relander, November 7, 1961, the following citation from a manuscript in his library: "Much of this story was related by Orlando [Bob] Beck, who was in the

Townspeople in Yakima City and on the Ahtanum, believing the deed a signal for an all-out Indian war, frantically began building fortifications. On July 12, it was reported that Moses, joined by contingents of coastal Indians from as far north as the Skagit River, had carried out his planned attack on the Kittitas and was moving down to meet the Yakima Indians to massacre settlers on the Ahtanum. Nearly all the families rushed to a meadow in the valley where they formed in true western fashion a large wagon circle around an inner circle of men prepared to protect their loved ones from the scalping knife. The report of Moses' movement was false, but nerve-shattered residents of Yakima County again had Agent Wilbur request of Governor Ferry two hundred stands of arms and ammunition. Settlers in the Spokane, Crab Creek, and Palouse areas were equally excited. Rumors in Lewiston had it that Moses had warned the few whites at Spokane Falls to safeguard themselves in case of an outbreak as he would be unable to restrain his braves.[2]

Renegades along the Columbia kept everyone on edge, including Moses, for their continued depredations threatened his chances of a favorable settlement with the government. When the Perkins couple were killed, he met one of these bands near his camp on the Wenatchee with an ultimatum not to cross that stream. The renegades turned away to raid the surrounding countryside. Knowing settlers in the Yakima country were boiling mad over the murder and pointing accusing fingers at him, Moses, the diplomat, kept the trails warm between his camp and that region with reassuring messages. In reply to a message from Agent Wilbur, the leading spokesman of that area, he proclaimed to all renegades in the country, "Your hands may be stained with blood, and if you come among my people you will get me into trouble." He was so touchy about the affair that he refused to go near Yakima City to meet two parties who came there in the latter part of July to hear what he had to say about it. Instead, he

posse, attended the trial, and also acted as guard at the several hangings [of the murderers]."

2 Shiak, *An Illustrated History of Klickitat, Yakima, and Kittitas Counties, Washington*, 162–67.

dictated to Sam Miller a letter to that town stating that he had under surveillance the Indians who had killed the Perkins couple and that he would turn them over to General Howard if he would come and get them with troops, but with no other armed men—meaning, perhaps, volunteer outfits like the Klickitat Rangers. He added that if a Mr. Burbank would send three unarmed men to him, he would deliver to them Burbank's horses, which the renegades had stolen. In response to this invitation, Burbank and his men traveled with Moses to a camp of over 150 renegades between the Wenatchee and Priest Rapids, where they stumbled onto some 1,500 horses hidden near the camp, but retrieved only a few of their own.[3]

From Fort Vancouver on August 20, Howard reported the explosive situation on the Columbia to Division headquarters, stating that he would soon visit Moses "to secure a permanent settlement of difficulties that keep that region in hot water." He found himself in hot water when the division commander informed him that as a military officer, he, Howard, had not been authorized to settle any question with Moses and had taken upon himself the responsibility of the Office of Indian Affairs. "Military commanders," he was warned, "should not attempt to adjust difficulties with Indian tribes which by law, an established Bureau and regularly appointed officers are required to adjust." He was further reminded that "out of respect for another department of the Government and [under] . . . instructions of the General of the Army of March 13, 1877 . . . the management of the Indians is to be 'conducted by the agents of the Indian Bureau; the military authorities merely protecting and aiding them in the execution of their instructions.'" Howard's forwardness in dealing with Moses may have been due to the fact that he had missed an army circular of May 27 stating that Moses was not to be forcibly placed on any reservation without previous orders from the War Department.[4] That department obviously was beginning to move

3 *Oregonian*, August 5, 1878, p. 1. See also Ben Snipes to Howard, August 19, 1878 (Washington Superintendency Records, 1853–80).

4 Washington Superintendency Records, 1853–80, contain telegraphic communications between Howard and division headquarters.

cautiously in its Indian dealings because of censure it was receiving for encroaching on Indian Office prerogatives in promises Howard had made to Chief Joseph at the time of his surrender.

Thus duly instructed, Howard traveled up the Columbia from Fort Vancouver to his oft-postponed meeting with Moses, at Priest Rapids, the site chosen for the conference. On August 29, he was at Wallula nervously pacing the bank, waiting for the steamer, *Spokane*. He had been at the same spot the previous year, preparing for his journey up the Snake River to the Nez Percés. The memory of his trouble with those people and anxieties over his proposed mission to Moses, which could suffer the same fate, must have filled him with tensions. His subordinates were crushing the Bannock-Paiute uprising, and the chances of Moses' participation in it were lessened. Yet, since there was still the possibility that in his bitterness at the failure of the government to settle him, he would exchange the Priest Rapids invitation for the warpath. Howard knew that the Indians were being supplied arms and ammunition by unscrupulous white men on the coast in spite of his efforts to stop the traffic. He may have known, too, that Moses' braves were ranging across the Canadian border to the Kootenay country to obtain arms from traders there.[5] Hearing that Moses was at Priest Rapids, he sent a mounted infantry column northward toward the mouth of the Okanogan to "interpose an obstacle" between the Indians of that region and the white settlers of Crab Creek Valley.[6]

About sunset of the thirtieth, the *Spokane* churned into Wallula with Major Henry Mizner's command aboard. Early the next morning the boat was off on a paddle-wheeling journey up the river, carrying, in addition to Mizner's command, Howard and his aides, Lieutenants Joseph A. Sladen and C. E. S. Wood,[7]

[5] *Walla Walla Statesman* (Walla Walla, Washington Territory), December 21, 1878.

[6] Preparations for the council, and a brief narration of it may be found in Secretary of War, *Annual Report*, 1878 (45 Cong., 3 sess., *House Exec. Doc. No. 1*), I, 234–35.

[7] Lieutenant Charles Erskine Scott Wood, Howard's closest aide in the Department of the Columbia, had attended West Point where he appears to have excelled primarily in military drawing. At the conference he sketched Moses; throughout

as well as Colonel Wheaton, commandant of the District of Clear-water, in whose district the conference was being held. Also aboard were the interpreter, Pambrun, and Judge A. J. Cain of Waitsburg, a former Indian agent and friend of the red man.

Several miles upstream from Wallula, the *Spokane*, on September 1, tied up to take aboard a Columbia chief, Homily, of the Walla Wallas and two other Indians. Early the next morning the craft was off again, inching its way through strong currents to the foot of Priest Rapids. From the deck Howard anxiously scanned the sterile landscape for an Indian encampment. He saw none. After docking at ten o'clock in the morning on the east bank, he set up camp and sent one messenger upriver with an invitation to Moses and another down-river to Wallula with a telegram to Division headquarters suggesting that the Interior Department invite a Walla Walla citizen to the council to insure much needed co-operation between that department and the army.[8]

The soldiers with Howard tried to overcome the tension of the camp by improvising little songs:

> *For Howard proposes*
> *To visit Chief Moses*
> *To see if his tune is hostile or no.*[9]

The next day, the anxious Howard dispatched another message to Moses. Then, on September 3, a messenger in company with an Indian was seen riding across the flat to the river. The Indian was "the Beaver," in all likelihood Chillileetsah or "Jim," the son of Moses' sister, Sinsinqt. There was considerable significance in the young man's coming; his uncle had chosen him as his heir and successor to the chieftaincy and had entrusted to him this diplomatic mission. Chillileetsah assured Howard that Moses

---

his life he made many other sketches and did some writing, which was in a somewhat radical vein. He died on January 20, 1944, at the age of ninety-one. Edwin R. Bingham, "Oregon's Romantic Rebels, John Reed and Charles Erskine Scott Wood," *Pacific Northwest Quarterly*, Vol. L, No. 3 (July, 1959), 77–90.

[8] Howard, "Diary—Bannock Indian Campaign" (Manuscript in Huntington Library).

[9] *Daily Bee* (Portland, Oregon), September 12, 1878, p. 3.

had sent word of the council to the various bands and that he was waiting on the Wenatchee Flat for his own men to return from hunting in the Cascades, when he would come down to the Rapids.

The interpreter, Pambrun, having lost none of his suspicion of Moses from the Simcoe conference, taunted Howard that the Chief was holding out and would never come in. Possibly under this goading, Howard, unaware of the pre-eminence Moses had given Chillileetsah and piqued that he had sent the young man as a substitute, hustled him under escort back to his uncle on the Wenatchee. In the meantime the General moved camp across to the west bank, where on the sixth he wrote a single entry in his diary, "Waiting." About noon of the seventh, a lone rider came down the trail from the Moses country carrying a white flag. Immediately, Howard ordered the *Spokane* to recross the river to the east bank. About three o'clock Moses rode in, flanked by Sam Miller, subchiefs Wappato John and Kachhachtaskin, and about seventy braves. They did not see the camp hidden on a flat behind a rise until within a quarter of a mile of it. When the Chief spied it, he had his men stack their arms as a friendly gesture, then rode with them to within a few feet of Howard and his aides, dismounted, and walked over to shake their hands. Howard breathed more easily.

The principals of the council went to a low bluff a short distance below the river bank to board the 150-foot *Spokane*. The natives, remembering the reputation of the strange canoe for making bad medicine on the lower river, must have done so cautiously. They made their way to the lower deck and stationed themselves amidships with Howard and his aides, Chief Homily, the crew of the *Spokane*, Judge Cain, and several Yakima citizens previously informed of the meeting by Howard through "a very judicious officer," a Captain Whipple. The Yakima citizens, far from convinced of Moses' innocence in the Perkins murder, were apprehensive that the government would give to a "criminal" lands they felt were rightfully theirs.

At three-thirty in the afternoon, Howard brought the council

to order. In the absence of a chaplain, he invited those wishing
to do so to unite with him in the Lord's Prayer. After the "amen"
he reviewed first of all the conditions which prevented him from
meeting Moses at an earlier time. Pambrun repeated Howard's
words in the Shahaptian tongue, a language Moses spoke very
well, but one which he quickly pointed out was not understood
by some of his Salish-speaking Indians aboard. Consequently,
Pambrun translated from English to the Shahaptian, and Homily
translated from that tongue to the Salish. With this technicality
worked out, Howard proceeded to condemn white men who had
spread rumors that he was coming to fight Moses, but praised
Miller, Shoudy, and Phelps, who had kept him informed of
Moses' peaceful intentions. Miller at that point interrupted to
say that many troublemaking white men had rumored that
Howard's and Moses' letters had not reached each other.

In answer to Howard's query about the Perkinses' murderers,
Moses admitted that they had been in his camp one day, but said
that when he went to find them they were gone. This opened the
matter of Indian depredations along the Columbia, particularly
horse-stealing, which drew from Moses a promise to search out
all horse herds and to take special note of strange brands. The
Chief told of difficulties in keeping the peace while members of
outside tribes ran from camp to camp carrying stories. He said he
had screened numerous "renegades" (Indians displaced by the
wars) in his camps, permitting only the peaceful ones to remain.
"You have followed the Snakes all summer, General Howard," he
said. "They have worn you out. The Indians around me have
tried me as much as the Snakes have you." "But," observed
Howard in an aside to one of his aides, "his hair has not become
quite as white as mine."

> Changing the subject abruptly, Howard asked, "Where are
> the San Poils?
> Moses: West of the Spokane.
> General Howard: Some of the Spokanes, San Poils, Okanogans,
> and other Indians have been quite restless and have signified
> a desire to come together and have him [Moses] for their

leader. I want to ask him[10] if they signified such a desire lately and mean for him to become their chief.

Moses: They are my people already. My relatives are among them. I sent my messengers all among them to say that you had got here and were waiting.

General Howard: If the Indians have any plan in their minds that they have agreed upon for themselves [and] not for these alone that are living but for their children's children that succeed them, any plan that will give permanent peace, let them submit it to me. I will be happy to hear it. The rumor came to me several weeks ago that . . . a British Columbia tribe . . . came to Moses and proposed to him to raid. I would like to know if it was true. I would like to know if they did indeed come down from British Columbia.

Moses: I do not know anything about these people. They have not sent me any delegations.

General Howard: These had sort of an idea that Moses was to be a great leader against the whites.

Moses: NO.

General Howard: Now, with reference to the plan, have the Indians thought it over. Something they would like to ask. Something that would make a permanent settlement.

Moses: They have made up their minds that they do not wish to have trouble. That they wish to be left in quiet and in peace in their own country. Other Indians may go to war, but they do not want to. All they want is to be left alone in their own country . . . .

Moses knew these last words of the first day of the council would be the first of the next, and so he asked Miller, Cain, and Pambrun to tell Howard that he wished to make a request regarding the boundaries of the proposed reservation. On that day, September 8, after convening the council and again leading in the Lord's Prayer, Howard asked the Indians to make their wishes known. Moses asked that a map be brought and spread out on the deck. As he began to trace the boundaries he wanted, the Yakima citizens must have nudged in to see how this would affect their

---

[10] Because he was speaking directly to the interpreter, Howard referred to Moses in the third person.

interests. As Moses pointed out the locations, he interrupted himself from time to time to explain how he was doing the right thing for the Indians. Howard broke in to make certain the Indians understood the lines he was tracing. At one point, the Chief, fearing a break in communications between himself and Howard, confessed, "God is really the dictator. I fear to dictate for myself."

After considerable parley and interpretation, the line the Chief wanted drawn began fifteen miles up the Spokane to include its fisheries, then it swung north and back west eight miles parallel to the Columbia's right bank. From there it continued southward to include the root grounds like those at Chelohan in the Kittitas and then appeared to run down the Wenatchee, Umtanum, and Yakima Ridges to the crest of the Rattlesnake Range. From the crest it dropped to the Falls of the Yakima to include more fisheries. From the mouth of the Yakima it ran north to White Bluffs and thence northeasterly to the point of beginning. The area requested was considerably larger and more threatening to the ambitions of the Yakima citizens than that of the previous year, which had extended no farther west than the Columbia River. Why was the request greater than before? Did Moses believe that he now had greater bargaining power with the government in its rapidly softening policies regarding the red man?

"I am sorry, very sorry," said Howard, "to have to say this, but while he can speak for all his people today I must lay it before the authorities at Washington. I will faithfully carry the request to the President and I will let Moses know the reply just as quickly as I can get it." Sensing another potential problem, Howard asked if there were any white men within the limits Moses defined. With sharp humor the big Indian replied, "Mr. Miller—my friend is the only one and we like him. He does everything he can for me to help me along. Writes for me. If he changes his heart and does not behave I will report him to you (laughter)." A citizen on board informed Howard that on the lower reaches of the general area Moses wished were some half-dozen stock

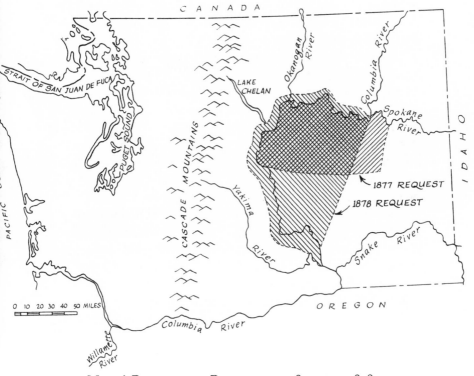

MOSES' RESERVATION REQUESTS OF 1877 AND 1878

ranches, including that of the large firm of Lockwood and Brey-man. Had Moses forgotten that these ranches existed, or did they lie in an area so peripheral to his own activities that he knew nothing of them?

In a long address Howard thanked the Chief for keeping the peace during the Nez Percé and Bannock wars, but warned that white people had been killed and that Moses and all the Indians at the council should find the murderers. He stated that he had no objection to the Columbia River Indians' staying with Moses if they would turn back to him or Sam Miller the property they had stolen. Then softening, he said he thought Moses had made a fair request. "Meanwhile," he added, "we will all keep the peace and as soon as word comes from the President, I will send it

95

to Moses. He can call his people together, and whatever the President decides we will keep the peace at any event. If Moses says *that* we will shake hands."

Moses arose quickly and shook Howard's hand, saying, "If the President complies with my request it will make me so much the stronger." He continued on a firm note: "I wish you to tell all the white people to quit this carrying arms and pointing at my people. It makes them all wrong. The Snakes are all gone, there is no trouble and we want to be as we were before. Not pointing guns at each other." Aware of Moses' habit of presenting his case to the public through the press, Howard said his request would be put in the papers. At this, Moses declaimed, "I wish the white people to tell no more lies of me. They try to make a liar of *me*. I want that *stopped* and I will stop the Indians from carrying stories. My people will all be pleased when they learn that all things have been reported." Again, Moses spoke the last word: "If you and I understand each other, there will be no trouble." At ten-thirty in the morning, the council adjourned.[11]

Believing he had exchanged the bugaboo of the Yakima Reservation for one to his own liking, Moses rode away in good spirits. At last he would find the peace he was seeking, in his ancestral home in the Plateau, safely behind his Columbia moat and a buffer of eight to twelve miles to keep greedy settlers away. One of their spokesmen, the editor of the *West Shore* magazine, said he should have been happy because his "superior cunning" had completely "bamboozled" the white man at Priest Rapids.[12]

As Moses surveyed his promised land, General Howard was issuing the following notice:

To all whom it may concern:

All persons are hereby notified not to take up lands within the following limits, till the pleasure of the President shall be made known, as to whether or not he shall grant the request of the Columbia Indians, that it shall be set apart as an Indian Reser-

11 Washington Superintendency Records, 1853–80.
12 "The Indian," *West Shore*, (Portland, Oregon), Vol. IV, No. 1 (September, 1878), 1.

vation. This notice to take effect with this date viz, the 9th day of Sept. 1878.

Boundaries as follows:

From the extreme eastern point on Columbia River at White Bluffs running northeasterly in direct line to the mouth of the Spokane river, thence crossing the Columbia river northerly along right bank of said river eight miles, from this point along the ridge westerly parallel with the Columbia river and distant twelve miles to the crest of Rattlesnake range. Thence in direct line to the Yakima falls, (about fifteen miles from mouth of said river) thence following the Yakima river to its mouth, thence following Columbia northward to place of beginning.

O. O. HOWARD
Brigadier General
Commanding Department[13]

The happy Chief would shortly find that before learning the pleasure of the Great Father in Washington regarding a reservation home, he would have to reckon with the displeasure of the Father's white children near that home. With them he would soon become involved in the most agonizing experience of his life.

[13] Washington Superintendency Records, 1853–80.

VI. Reds, Whites, and the Blues

"These chains are working a lie against me."
—Moses' statement in the Yakima City jail, December 25, 1878

ANGRY SETTLERS in the Yakima and Kittitas valleys shouted vituperations against General Howard for the notice released after the Priest Rapids council. In their bitterness they mistook it for an order. Howard must have been alarmed to learn of their reaction, for he had regarded it only as a statement to restrain land-hungry settlers until Moses' request could receive a hearing from the President. With the Bannock-Paiute and Nez Percé wars fresh in his memory, he was the last person wanting trouble.

The settlers, unlike the Great Father, had no intention of giving the red man a hearing and were alarmed that the government would even consider a Moses reservation—a stumbling block of land to their expansion. The Washington Territorial Democratic and Republican conventions that year had gone on record as favoring the abolition of reservations, and there were those who wished to make the abolition of reservations in the territory an example for the government to follow elsewhere.

On September 15, nearly every able-bodied man in the Kittitas assembled in a mass meeting to protest. Two days later, Yakima citizens held a similar meeting. No Indians, they vowed, must be permitted to remain in the bunchgrass Canaan along the Columbia or on the Plateau. The reservation, they complained, would cheat them not only of valuable grazing and timber lands, but of access to the Columbia River and hence to the outside world. They sent copies of their objections to the War Department[1] and to the newspapers in hopes of bringing public opinion to their side. This strategy backfired somewhat when the influential *Oregonian* of Portland editorialized in Moses' favor, less from

1 Washington Superintendency Records, 1853–80.

98

sympathy for him than from fear that he would plunge the region into war over the "worthless reservation wasteland."[2]

The land-grabbers had more government support than they realized. At the very time that Moses was meeting with General Howard at Priest Rapids to discuss the possibility of a reservation of his own, Agent Wilbur was in Washington, D. C., conferring with the Commissioner of Indian Affairs, E. A. Hayt, and hoping for a decision to move Moses to the Yakima Reservation. Returning West, the agent stopped off in Vancouver, met briefly with Howard, and then returned to the Yakima. He had no sooner arrived home than Howard, hearing that the agent had publicly refuted the plan for a separate Moses reservation, on October 18 asked him to come to Vancouver for a conference. Wilbur refused to go, stating that he had received a telegram from the Commissioner requesting him to find and confer with Moses.[3] It is obvious that Wilbur and Howard, like the governmental departments they represented, had conflicting plans for the Indian.

With the fear of jeopardizing a peaceful transfer of Columbias to the Yakima, Wilbur would not pass on to the General a citizens' request to send troops to the Kittitas and Yakima valleys. He told citizens wanting Moses confined on a reservation that Howard's actions (presumably at Priest Rapids) had forestalled the plans of the Interior Department to locate him on the Yakima. Yet, one news article reporting Wilbur's sentiments apparently intimated that Howard would now help with department plans. This statement angered Howard, who complained to the agent that his public utterances in Yakima City and the news article (a clipping of which from the *Oregonian* embellished one letter) had put the General in a trying position.

Wilbur answered that he had told the Secretary of the Interior in Washington that a few thousand dollars paid to Moses might induce him to come on the Yakima, thus eliminating the possibility of a separate reservation for him, a prospect which "greatly

2 September 19, 1878, p. 2.

3 Wilbur to Howard, October 31, 1878. Yakima Agency Letter Record Books, 1878–79.

99

excited" the citizens. Their request for troops had apparently reached the General in spite of the agent's refusal to relay it, because Wilbur wrote that he would not oppose a troop placement in the area since the General had the right to put soldiers where he wished. And, continued Wilbur, as for the interpretation of the public statement with which he was credited, it is not accurate—the policy of the Secretary of the Interior is to consolidate the existing reservations rather than to oppose the creation of new ones. Furthermore, Wilbur went on to say, he returned from Washington without department instructions in relation to Moses.[4]

The department's request that Wilbur find and talk to Moses to learn his attitude was sent on October 11.[5] He accordingly sent three runners, with Eneas, head policeman of the recently organized Indian police force, in charge.[6] Eneas and Moses had been enemies since the Yakima War.[7] The three emissaries rode across forty miles of barren hills east of Simcoe and crossed the Columbia to Moses' camp, then situated on Crab Creek. Finding the Chief, Eneas read him Wilbur's letter:

> I send Eneas, Big Jim and Hoptowit to take this letter to you to give you the talk I gave them which I brought from the President at Washington. I was at Washington and talked with the President about the Indians on the Reservation and he asked me about Moses and his people. I told him that Moses had kept a good heart towards the white people and he had kept his men from joining the hostile bands. That Moses was a good man and would do what the President wanted him to do. He was not like

4 The agent acknowledged receipt of Howard's letters bearing the dates of October 30 and November 9, 1878, and the clipping from the *Oregonian*, which is not dated. Wilbur to Howard, November 20, 1878. Yakima Agency Letter Record Books, 1878–79.

5 In reply to Howard the agent gave the date of the telegram from the Commissioner of Indian Affairs directing him to contact Moses. Wilbur to Howard, October 31, 1878. Yakima Agency Letter Record Books, 1878–79.

6 An act of Congress May 27, 1878, authorized agents to hire Indians as police to preserve order on reservations and prevent illegal traffic. The Simcoe force was organized July 12, 1878. For a further explanation of the Indian police, see G. O. Shields, *The Blanket Indian of the Northwest*, 240.

7 Splawn, *Ka-Mi-akin*, 315.

Joseph and his people and the Snakes and Bannocks. The President wanted me to send up some men to ask Moses to come down here to Fort Simcoe that I might talk with him and send the talk of Moses to him that the President might know his heart. I want you to come down Moses and make us a visit and then you can return to your people and I can return an answer to the President. I have a good heart toward you and your people and the President thinks well of Moses.[8]

Moses had been hopefully awaiting a message from General Howard about his reservation, and in his anxiety had recently sent a runner, Weattatatum, to Judge Cain in Waitsburg to learn if the expected answer had come from Washington. It had not.[9] Did Eneas now bring the news Moses waited for?

Apparently Eneas assured him that such was the case. Later in the month Moses asked Frank G. Middleton, a correspondent for the *Oregonian*, to contact General Howard for him. Middleton wrote the General:

After a careful investigation, I find that Eneas, one of the police force at the agency, is the party who told Moses that you wished to see him at Fort Simcoe, or that a message from you was waiting him there.... Moses is emphatic in the assertion that Eneas stated that what I have written.[10]

The lure worked. With five of his men the Chief hurried toward Simcoe, arriving there on Saturday, December 7. Wilbur noted that he was in excellent spirits as his men were put up at the agency and as he sat down to confer with the agent. But if he asked for the message from Howard, Wilbur made no mention of it in a letter he wrote to Commissioner Hayt six days later. In this communication the agent reported on what he called "three important matters that I presented to him [Moses] and those of his people who were with him."

8 Wilbur to Moses, December 2, 1878. Yakima Agency Letter Record Books, 1878–79.

9 A. J. Cain to General Howard, December 24, 1878. U.S. Department of the Interior—Moses Reservation—Special Case # 65, 1879–1907 (hereafter referred to as Moses Reservation).

10 Frank G. Middleton to General Howard, December 31, 1878. Moses Reservation.

1st What is your mind and the mind of your people about coming to the Yakima agency to live?

In the 2d place I wanted to know of him and his people if they knew anything about the men who killed Mr. and Mrs. Perkins?

In the 3d place I wanted him to tell me especially what his heart was toward the whites so I could send it back to Washington.

Here, according to Wilbur, were Moses' answers to the "three important matters":

To the first—coming to the Yakima agency:

"I met General Howard last summer at Priest Rapids on the Columbia and we had a talk. General Howard took his map and marked around and asked me if I would be pleased or satisfied with a reservation like the one he had marked out? I told him I would. He General Howard promised to send to Washington to know what they would do about this new reservation and when he got word he would let me know. Moses said he did not want to say anything about coming on the reservation until he heard from General Howard when he got the word from him if they said Moses could have the reservation that would be all right. If they did not give it to him he was not going to have a sick heart if he did not get it he would talk with me about coming and residing on the agency."

To the second—the Perkins murderers:

"Moses replied all he knew about them was what other Indians had told him, they were not his people but belonged to the Umatilla agency in Oregon. His people had given him the names of seven who were engaged in the murder. His people gave us information where these Indians (as they thought) can be found."

To the third—his feeling towards the whites:

Moses answered that, "I should think the white people by this time would know what my heart is towards them. When Joseph and his people were fighting the whites, I, Moses, kept all my men from going to the war; and kept them where I could hold them in perfect subjection; not one of them joined Joseph's fighting band.

"Last summer when the Snakes and the Indians were fighting the whites my Indians I kept right about me, not one of them joined the Snakes against the whites. The whites many of them said Moses was going to fight. He, Moses, had always said No, my friends, Moses is not going to fight. He had worked hard having one hand on his people and the other on the whites for two years trying to keep the whites and the Indians good friends. When strange Indians had come about him he had driven them off and would not allow them to come about his people, knowing if bad Indians were kept by him or his people the whites would say Moses was stealing or Moses Indians were doing everything bad —he was the friend of the whites and all good Indians."

Wilbur promised Moses that if he would move with his people to the Yakima, he as agent would give him good farm land, a house, and cattle, so that "he would be with us a bigger man than he could be off the agency." It seemed to Wilbur that Moses regarded the proposal with favor. This might have caused him to construe the Chief's response as an acceptance of the offer. It will be remembered that when he was in Washington, D. C., he had, unknown to Moses, proposed to department officials that they bribe Moses to come on the Yakima. But in spite of Wilbur's efforts to persuade him, the wary Chief was not taken in by the proposals; he indicated that he had to wait for an answer from General Howard.

In his report the agent summed up his own conclusions for the Commissioner:

> The Reservation asked for by General Howard, if given to Moses and his people without an agent (or with one) in my judgement would bring on a speedy trouble between the whites and Indians. The country asked for is sparsely settled by stockmen but to request them to leave would occasion the uprising of the whole country against such an arrangement.
>
> Two things are necessary in the case of Moses and his people. Either let them remain where they are without a reservation or induce them to come to this agency. Either of these two, in my judgment is better than to make a new reservation.[11]

It is not known whether Wilbur or Moses suggested a joint effort to find the Perkinses' murderers and bring them before the

[11] Wilbur to Hayt, December 13, 1878. Yakima Agency Letter Record Books, 1878–79.

authorities, but regardless of who suggested it, Moses "signified his willingness" to participate. He agreed to send some of his men with a party of agency Indian police to hunt and arrest them. Would he go with Wilbur to Yakima City to lay the plan before the citizens? Yes. It might allay white fears and put his intentions on record.[12]

On Monday morning, December 9, they left Fort Simcoe for Yakima City some twenty miles to the east. The settlers, learning of their coming, deserted their fields and crops, rode to town to meet their red opponent, and left only enough men to defend the sod fortifications on the Ahtanum and the Wenas. These were very meager defenses, they believed, as were the 102 rifles sent them from Fort Vancouver in August and the 40 sent to nearby Klickitat County to the south. How could these weapons withstand hordes of savages who, well armed with weapons purchased from merchants in Portland, Seattle, and other towns on the lower river and Puget Sound, according to rumor were about to swoop out of the hills in a general uprising?[13] On the streets of Yakima City they shouted cries of defiance. In little groups they whispered rumors of white women raped by Indians.

Accompanied by Dr. George Benson Kuykendall, the agency physician, Wilbur escorted Moses and his men to Centennial Hall. The building was packed with spectators. Father Wilbur sought to get the meeting under way on as friendly a note as possible by reminding his hearers that they were all children of the Great Father, of one family, and that it was wrong to take another's life. Then he approached the subject of the Perkins crime.

The audience must have been less interested in the agent's words than in the big Indian before them whose savagery was masked in a long Prince Albert coat, black trousers under buckskin leggings, white handkerchief about his neck, and a wide-brimmed Spanish hat on his head.

"The greatest chief in our territory is present and can, if he

12 For additional information on the Moses–Wilbur conference, see Thelma Kimmel, *The Fort Simcoe Story*, 18–20.
13 *Weekly Pacific Tribune* (Seattle, Washington Territory), December 22, 1878.

will, be of great help in capturing this band of outlaws," said Wilbur introducing him.[14]

Moses stepped forward and stood "perfectly quiet for some time" before what must have seemed to him a sea of defiant faces. Then he blew "a mighty bugle blast" from his nose and wiped his hand on his leggings.[15] He straightened, then began, *"Nika Moses."* As he launched his remarks, the citizens sized him up as one "dwelling upon his own greatness." They were unimpressed when he told them that he was a friend of the whites and that he and his people had "no bad hearts toward them."[16] He talked two or three hours, his speech slowed by the difficulty of interpretation, denying complicity in the murders and agreeing to assist in apprehending the criminals.[17]

He promised to send some of his men to join a posse to capture the murderers, who were believed to be in three camps in the lava beds up on Crab Creek approximately forty miles from his lodges. Some of the crowd objected—they not only wanted the murderers apprehended, they also wanted to recover the horses stolen by the Indians. Moses said he knew the brands of the horses, and, as he came across them, he would capture and return them.

Then a proposition was made. Wilbur offered fifteen Indian police for the search. But Moses said, "No you better send at least twenty Indians and twenty whites."[18] Although the number of men to make up the posse was discussed, the eventual decision is in doubt because of the subsequent misunderstanding. The chance for error in interpretation and its slowness for anxious people may have been a factor in producing this uncertainty. To

[14] Splawn, *Ka-Mi-akin*, 311.

[15] *Yakima Morning Herald*, February 17, 1898; Lyman, *History of the Yakima Valley*, I, 258.

[16] Wilbur to Hayt, December 13, 1878. Yakima Agency Letter Record Books, 1878–79.

[17] Shiak, *An Illustrated History of Klickitat, Yakima, and Kittitas Counties, Washington*, 167.

[18] Wilbur to Howard, December 19, 1878. Yakima Agency Letter Record Books, 1878–79.

complete the details of the hunt, a second meeting with the citizens was held. At this time Moses agreed to meet the Indian police from Simcoe and citizens from Yakima City on the Columbia across from his Crab Creek camp, to which his men would ferry them in dugouts.

On Wednesday, December 11, Moses set out for home with his men, cautioning them to spread no word of their plans to assist in capturing the murderers. Later, Wilbur's Indians would report that they had learned from Moses' people "that one of Moses Men, who was with him at Fort Simcoe returned before Moses, and gave information to Camps where Some of the Murderers were, that the Police and Volunteers were on their way to arrest them."[19] In spite of Moses' injunctions to secrecy, the news of his promise preceded him to his camp.

Before leaving Yakima City, Moses and his men had learned that whites planned to waylay the Chief. Undaunted, they continued homeward. One of their horses gave out before they left the Yakima River so they borrowed another from an Indian family. Traveling with speed, they narrowed the hours required to cross the sagebrush stretch between Yakima City and the Columbia. At the river they dismounted, paddled across in dugouts, pulling their horses after them, and headed to camp several miles upstream from the mouth of Crab Creek.[20]

In camp, Moses sent Billy Curlew (Kulalikiyu), a potential warrior seventeen years old, to Badger Mountain to bring the cattle down to winter pasture. In the rapid sequence of events and in his concern over the possible invasion of his lands by the white man's cattle, the Chief had forgotten to bring his own down to the Crab Creek ranges. His beloved horses were already down, feeding there on the nutritious bunchgrass. Billy rode off obediently to the north to round up all twenty-six of the *molops* (this figure is at variance with the hundred-odd that the whites accused Moses of having—as though it were an offense for an Indian to

19 Wilbur to Hayt, December 25, 1878, addendum to letter dated December 25, 1878. Moses Reservation.
20 Billy Curlew Interview, Ephrata, Washington, October 7, 1956.

own so many). A few days later, the boy returned with the herd, fat and sleek as the fall had been mild.[21]

Moses found it much easier to ride herd on his cattle and horses than on his own men. The news of his promise to help capture the murderers had preceded him to his camps. It was disturbing to many of his warriors, who would rather fight the "Bostons" than co-operate with them. Now they tried to goad him into hostility. Even his own half brother, Paul (Watasass),[22] leader of the hostiles of Moses' and allied tribes, went around stirring up the hotbloods. The renegades in Moses' camps continued to tell him that he was as weak as a mare and to call him an old woman, the worst possible insult. He dared not alienate these malcontents since he was beginning to see them, along with his available pool of eager braves, as levers for bargaining with the government. His camp held sixty of his own Columbias, renegade Snakes, Wanapums, Walla Wallas, and Yakimas. His allies among the neighboring tribes numbered fifty Wenatchees, twenty Entiats, nearly fifty Chelans, seventy Methows, forty of Sarsopkin's Okanogans, perhaps one hundred Spokanes and allied tribes, and a number of Canadian Okanogans, who were willing to disregard the international border and the tattletale Tonasket.[23]

Twenty-four hours after Moses left the Yakima Valley, the posse rode out to join him. The first night out it camped across from White Bluffs. The next morning it moved up the west bank of the Columbia preparing to cross over to Crab Creek. An excited runner burst into camp to tell Moses of the posse of citizens and Indian police. There were many more than the number agreed upon, and Eneas was in the lead! Were they coming to arrest him? At this news the young warriors rode their horses back and forth shouting, brandishing guns in the air, and throwing the camp into turmoil.

One can conjecture Moses' feelings. The posse was coming after him. It was very clear now—Wilbur and the government

21 *Ibid.*
22 *Oregonian*, March 24, 1879.
23 *Oregonian*, March 24 and March 27, 1879.

with Eneas' assistance were going to confine him on the reservation so that the citizens could take his lands. Perhaps his discontented warriors had been right all along. Eneas had deceived him once; why would he not do it again?

Arriving at the rendezvous point, the posse searched vainly for the boats Moses had promised to carry them over to Crab Creek. They became convinced that he had never intended to cooperate, but was planning to attack them instead. After a hurried council they retreated down-river to a point some eight miles below Saddle Mountain Gap, where they held another council and elected William Splawn as captain.

The posse then crossed the Columbia. Wilbur later wrote that, as soon as the men and horses were crossed, a man was sent to Moses to ascertain why he had not carried out his agreement to ferry them over; and that Moses told this man, whom the agent does not name, that the talk he (Moses) had had with Wilbur in Yakima City was foolish talk, that he had changed his mind, and that he believed Eneas and the other police had come to take him prisoner.[24] This varies from the statement Moses would give a few days later, on December 25. He said then that he told his men to watch for the "Bostons" and the agency Indians on their arrival at the river preparatory to taking the boats to the designated place: "I directed my people, when the party reached there, to send a man to my house, eight miles distant, and let me know. I then went home and slept there. A young man came to my house as directed and said the Bostons had come on the west side of the river, but they did not come to the place he was watching, where the boats were waiting. They had gone below."[25] Moses did not explain why he had not ordered his men to move the boats to the place on the river to which the posse came, nor is it clear why the posse had not moved up to where the boats were, if indeed boats were waiting on shore. As the country is open in that area, it seems that, if the Indians had been along the river with their craft, the posse could have seen them and moved to the location. A more plausible reason for Moses' failure to carry out his

24 Wilbur to Hayt, December 23, 1878. Moses Reservation.
25 Howard, *My Life*, 356.

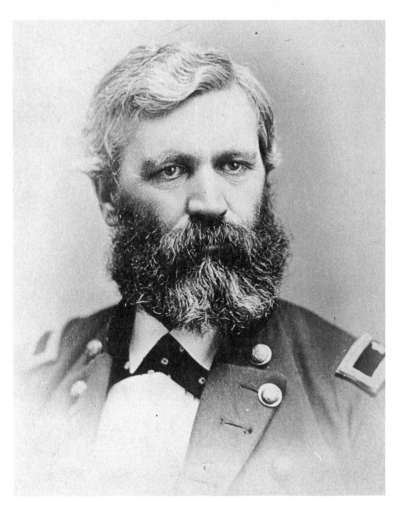

General Oliver Otis Howard, victorious over Chief Joseph and his Nez Percé followers, friend of Chief Moses, to whom he mailed this photograph after he left the Northwest as commander of the Department of the Columbia.

Francis Streamer, while editor of the Omaha *Herald*, 1873. Streamer believed himself commanded by a heavenly spirit to record items about Chief Moses.

promise to ferry the posse was his fear of capture—especially since the number of men arriving at the river was greater than he seems to have expected and since Eneas was with them.[26]

In a letter to Commissioner Hayt, Wilbur quoted Moses' justification, but in an addendum written two days later he stated that his Indians sent to Moses' camp reported that ". . . it appears, that Eneas did go to the Columbia River where Moses agreed to furnish the Boats for Crossing the men, and No Boats were there. And that no arrangement had been made by Moses to furnish Said Boats."[27]

After the failure to make connections at the rendezvous, runners kept Moses informed of the posse's every move—that it had ferried the river in dugouts above Priest Rapids and was heading toward his camp. On hearing this, the warriors crowded around their chief for a short parley. Then they all rode south to meet the posse.

26 The accounts vary considerably on the number of men who joined the force to hunt for the murderers. Lyman in his *History of the Yakima Valley*, I, 258, quotes Mrs. Louise Heiler Cary, a pioneer, as stating that sixteen men (citizens) and seventeen (Indian) police were to make up the force. Lieutenant E. B. Rheem in a letter to Howard, December 24, 1878 (Moses Reservation), wrote that after talking to "Agent Wilbur, who in my opinion is the most trustworthy person in this section of the country," there were to be thirty volunteers and fifteen of Wilbur's Indian police in the party. Yet, in a letter to Commissioner Hayt of December 23, 1878, Wilbur stated that the "Indian police force went out from here with Six additional Indians from the Reservation in Company with 25 men [White] volunteers to Capture the murderers of Mr. and Mrs. Perkins." Wilbur to Hayt, December 23, 1878. Moses Reservation. Previous to this, Wilbur wrote that he was to have sent fifteen Indians and twenty whites (Wilbur to Howard, December 19, 1878. Yakima Agency Letter Record Books, 1878–79). The *Oregonian*, December 20, 1878, p. 1, contains an article stating that Wilbur promised to send fifteen Indians to be joined by twenty whites to join five of Moses' warriors. The same article states that the whites raised thirty-five men. In his own words Moses related: "The proposition was to send fifteen men of the agency police. I said: 'No; these murderers are strong; fifteen men are not enough.' I promised to send five of my best men, making twenty in all" (Howard, *My Life*, 356). Pleas Rader, one of the posse, later wrote, "The people, fearing Moses was laying a plan to get 10 men [from Yakima City] out there and do them as they [the Indians] had done Perkins decided to take more men. Thirty men volunteered to go and 15 Indians were taken with us from the Yakima Reserve." *Wenatchee Daily World* (Wenatchee, Washington), November 20–22, 1922.

27 Wilbur to Hayt, December 23, 1878. Yakima Agency Letter Record Books, 1878–79. See also the *Okanogan Independent*, April 1, 1930, p. 3; Shiak, *An Illustrated History of Klickitat, Yakima, and Kittitas Counties, Washington*, 167–69.

A lone rider galloped toward them. It was Eneas! The police-man asked Moses why he had not kept his promise. As Moses subsequently related this meeting, "I met Eneas and told him to go back to his party and I would come on."[28] Eneas wheeled his horse about and galloped back to tell Splawn that Moses had refused to answer and that he was planning a hostile move. Splawn ordered his men to ride to meet the Chief, by that time a short distance away. With Moses and Innomoseecha in the lead, the nearly one hundred warriors pressed forward to their con-frontation with the posse. They were armed and stripped except for breechclouts, some feathered, with their bodies and faces and their horses daubed with blue paint.[29] The air was crisp and frosty. As the two parties neared each other, Moses ordered no shooting, except at his command. Then he ordered his men forward at full gallop down the slope toward the posse.

Another Custer's stand?

The posse stopped. The warriors raced to within fifty feet of it and then stopped. Splawn and Eneas rode out ahead a few paces from the ranks. Moses and Innomoseecha faced them. Splawn, his revolver drawn, demanded of Moses why he came in a hostile manner.

This was the way he had met General Howard, was his re-sponse.[30]

28 Howard, *My Life*, 356.

29 The sources extant vary in the number of warriors who rode down with Moses to meet the posse. In his own version of the incident Moses said, "Forty or fifty of my people went with me" (Howard, *My Life*, 356). Lieutenant Rheem in a communication to General Howard gives the number of warriors reported to have been with Moses as sixty (Rheem to Howard, December 24, 1878. Moses Reser-vation). After his inquiry into the matter, Wilbur wrote: "Moses came with [as estimated] about 100 men," (Wilbur to Hayt December 23, 1878. Moses Reserva-tion). In his annual report Wilbur wrote: "He came down . . . with about 60 men" (Wilbur to Commissioner August 25, 1879. Yakima Agency Letter Record Books, 1878–79). Pleas Rader of the Yakima Posse later wrote: "There were 100 of them in number and ready for battle" (*Okanogan Independent*, April 1, 1930). Another account gives the number of warriors as 100 (Shiak, *An Illustrated History of Klickitat, Yakima, and Kittitas Counties,* 168).

30 Moses' statement varied from the other sources. He said that he shook hands with Splawn—which seems unlikely in view of the chilly encounter. He also stated that he had told Splawn that the reason his men came as they did was because they wished to see (presumably) the posse, and that not all were going to hunt the

The tables were now turned. Moses was on his home ground protected by his men—not in Centennial Hall facing hostile citizens.

Splawn snapped another verbal volley asking Moses if he thought his presentation with so many warriors prepared for battle at a moment's notice was in keeping with the spirit of the agreement made in Yakima City. "We have come for the murderers," said Splawn, "and do not desire war with the Columbia River tribes, but if you wish to fight, all you have to do is to open the attack."

Moses turned and spoke to his men. The posse, motionless, waited for the next move. The warriors executed a well-ordered movement which placed them two columns deep in a line facing the posse. Many shouldered their rifles—needle guns (Franco-Prussian War discards sold to immigrants) and a few muzzle-loaders.[31] The posse countered, shouldering weapons, shifting in haphazard formation to match the natives' maneuver. One false move, the sound of a cocking trigger from the forest of rifles, would have unleashed a volley that could have left few to tell about it.

Splawn stood his ground, restraining his fire. Then another verbal blast, "Moses, if you want to fight, cut loose. For you and me there can be but one result—death. We'll die. If you don't want to fight, pull your men off." After an awkward moment, Moses turned without formal leave-taking, commanded his men to withdraw, and then sped with Innomoseecha to the head of the column, waving his men toward camp.[32] The posse moved south into Smohalla's camps, many of which were empty of warriors gone to join Moses. There it arrested Moostonic, one of the Umatilla murderers, and continued down to White Bluffs, where it encamped.

murderers, but only those he picked to do so. He said, moreover, that he spoke to Eneas at the meeting with the posse, but other accounts do not substantiate this. Howard, *My Life,* 357.

31 Frank Graham Interview, Spokane, Washington, February 7, 1958.

32 Wilbur to Hayt, December 23, 1878. Yakima Agency Letter Record Books, 1878–79. See also *Okanogan Independent*, April 1, 1930; Shiak, *An Illustrated History of Klickitat, Yakima, and Kittitas Counties, Washington*, 167–69.

At the creek Moses withdrew from his men and rode several miles upriver to his lodge. He charged his agent, Tatahala, to alert his intelligence network and sent runners to Canada to cover his escape there should the government's attempt to force him to Simcoe precipitate a war.[33] To implement this plan, his friend Chief Sarsopkin, of the Okanogan, promised to evacuate him and his immediate family to British Columbia should the whites press war or should renegades in his camps escape his grasp.[34] Signal fires, flashing brightly and frequently, flickered messages from tribe to tribe along the Columbia.[35] Moses' spirits may have been lifted with the knowledge that other northwestern chiefs were following his cat-and-mouse game with the settlers. When native intelligence was incomplete, the Spokane and Coeur d'Alene chiefs inquired about his situation from their federal agents.[36] All the tribes were especially concerned with the fate of the Umatillas whom the gunboats had dispersed in July, of the seven who had taken vengeance on the Perkins couple, and of the ten times that number of Umatillas who subsequently escaped north and now camped at the mouth of the Grand Coulee from whose fastness they could strike to avenge their losses and possibly involve all the tribes in war.[37]

One of the Indian policemen was dispatched from White Bluffs with a letter from Splawn to Wilbur at Simcoe. He stopped over in Yakima City, where some of the citizens read the dispatch and D. P. Ballard, an attorney there, reported it to the *Oregonian*.[38] The policeman continued then to Simcoe, arriving on December 15, two days after the confrontation of Moses and the posse. Wilbur wrote to Splawn the same day, probably in answer to the message the policeman carried. (It cannot be determined whether or not Wilbur had received the message before writing; his letter

[33] Peone Interviews.

[34] *Oregonian*, March 24, 1879, p. 1.

[35] Grace Wine Interview, Ephrata, Washington, July 28, 1961. Mrs. Wine's father was posseman Reed.

[36] H. C. Merriam to Assistant Adjutant General, Department of Columbia, March 19, 1879. Moses Reservation.

[37] *Oregonian*, March 24, 1879.

[38] *Oregonian*, December 20, 1878, p. 1.

cannot be found in the agency files, but it was mentioned in a reply written by Splawn.[39]) It is possible that Wilbur had already learned of the hostile meeting. If a courier was sent out ahead of the policeman, possibly on the day of the confrontation, he should have arrived in Yakima City and Simcoe on Saturday the fourteenth. One account written years later states that George Goodwin, a member of the posse, was sent to Yakima City for reinforcements on the day after the confrontation (the same day the policeman was dispatched). This account says that Goodwin was back at White Bluffs in three days.[40] It is possible that the two traveled together and that Ballard mentioned only the policeman.

Someone must have left the scene of the confrontation very soon after its occurrence with information for parties other than Wilbur and Yakima City citizens, for General Howard seems to have learned of the touchy situation very early. He wired Wilbur on Saturday, November 14, asking if his police force were in any trouble.[41] Wilbur had certainly chosen not to inform the General of trouble if he knew of any.

The news from White Bluffs carried to Yakima City must have evoked many "I told you so's" from its citizens, who were now assured of Moses' intention to start a war. They met for repeated sessions to discuss the immediate crisis, formed a committee, and dispatched Ballard to The Dalles on December 16, with authority to telegraph General Howard in Vancouver to rush troops upriver, as the posse was surrounded by the hostile savages under Moses.[42] Reports reaching Yakima City magnified stories of Indian treachery. The citizens appealed to Governor Ferry for arms and ammunition. While waiting for help, Yakimans anathematized Secretary of the Interior Carl Schurz and Agent Wilbur, whom they accused of pampering the Indians and thus bringing

39 Splawn to Wilbur, December 17, 1878. Yakima Agency Letter Record Books, 1878–79.

40 Shiak, *An Illustrated History of Klickitat, Yakima, and Kittitas Counties, Washington*, 168.

41 Howard's telegram to Wilbur is not available to the authors; however, a telegram from Wilbur to Howard, December 19, 1878 (Yakima Agency Letter Record Books, 1878–79), acknowledges Howard's inquiry of the fourteenth.

42 *Oregonian*, December 20, 1878, p. 1.

about the trouble. In a later communication Ballard wrote that the crisis stemmed from "an exhibition of the Quaker-Schurz-Wilbur peace policy" which was to come upon us "in all its civilizing beauties."[43]

Some shocking report or rumor from the Columbia or from some other quarter reached Yakima City on December 19. The *Oregonian* for the following day stated: "From sunset last night until daybreak this morning you could have heard the clatter of hoofs on the frozen streets." Settlers scurried to get volunteers, forty of whom came forward to join the posse at White Bluffs. In every quarter of Yakima County, settlers pulled guns from their racks, and messengers spread the alarm to Walla Walla, the Klickitat, and the Kittitas and asked for volunteers to join the posse.[44]

How Wilbur occupied his time in connection with the Moses trouble during the three days preceding December 19 is not known, but this day the agent's fingers must have felt the effects of gripping his pen. He prepared a long report to be telegraphed to Hayt detailing the situation with the posse and Moses.[45] He wrote a message to the Kittitas on the same matter in which he stated that this was "the time to settle this vexed question," and asked for fifty men and oats for horse feed, to reinforce the posse.[46] He penned a lengthy letter to Splawn, Goodwin, and others at White Bluffs expressing disappointment in the conduct of Moses. He suggested that Splawn invite Moses to the posse's camp ostensibly to assist in taking the murderers, and then, when sure he and his men were in the posse's power, to bring Moses in a captive, if he would not come voluntarily.[47] Finally, he wrote a detailed letter to be telegraphed to Howard answering the General's

43 *Oregonian*, February 27, 1879, p. 1.

44 *Oregonian*, December 20, 1878.

45 Wilbur to Hayt, December 19, 1878. Yakima Agency Letter Record Books, 1878–79.

46 Wilbur to Gentlemen of the Kittitas Valley, Washington Territory, December 19, 1878. Moses Reservation.

47 Wilbur to Splawn *et al.*, December 19, 1878. Yakima Agency Letter Record Books, 1878–79.

previous inquiry and requesting that troops and provisions be sent as early as possible by steamer to White Bluffs.[48]

In the meantime, on December 17, five white men came from the Kittitas to the Columbia opposite the mouth of Crab Creek. They crossed the river and rode to Moses' lodge, which they found surrounded by about forty warriors.[49] Their spokesman, F. D. Schnebly, told Moses, whom they knew, that, after hearing about the Yakima meeting with him, they had come to help the posse find the murderers. Moses told them the Yakima posse had been frightened off and had probably returned home; and he warned them against going any further up Crab Creek without an Indian escort, as the natives were quite enraged with the whites. Schnebly thought it best to retreat across the Columbia. Safely on the west side, he and his group rode down to White Bluffs, where they joined the posse.[50]

The posse at White Bluffs, continuing its search for the murderers, whom they felt Moses was shielding, sent a detachment to a point on Crab Creek fifteen miles north the day before Wilbur sent his dispatch explaining his new strategy of taking Moses into custody.

It appears Moses had likewise changed *his* strategy. Well informed of the movements of the posse, he must have decided to co-operate in the search for the murderers because he took nine of his men up Crab Creek, riding hard through falling snow in order to move ahead on the creek, apparently for the express purpose of being intercepted by the posse. One explanation for Moses' apparent change of attitude is offered by Charles B. Reed, who had ridden with Schnebly from the Kittitas. Reed was acquainted with Pee-el, a friendly Kittitas Indian, who later told him he had been in Moses' camp when Schnebly and his party arrived. Knowing the white men and their serious determination

48 Wilbur to Howard, December 19, 1878. Yakima Agency Letter Record Books, 1878–79.

49 Washington Questionnaires, Charles B. Reed, PB 82:15. Typescript copy in Bancroft Library.

50 Shiak, *An Illustrated History of Klickitat, Yakima, and Kittitas Counties, Washington,* 168–69.

to search out the murderers, Pee-el had warned Moses that if any of them were killed in his (Moses') country, Howard might have something to say when he returned from Washington, where he was making an effort to get a reservation for Moses.[51] (Pee-el, of course, was mistaken about Howard's being in Washington.)

Well after dark, after a fifteen- or twenty-mile ride, the Indians stopped to make camp back from the stream and built a large fire, apparently to attract the attention of the posse. They hobbled their horses and settled for the night. Shortly before daylight, they heard the pounding of horses' hooves bearing down on them. They lay motionless around the fire. The posse rushed up and surrounded them.

Moses ordered his men to lie still and not get up as the posse rode up. "*Nica* [sic] *Moses, Nica Moses, pe halo poo, pe halo poo.*" ("I'm Moses, I'm Moses, don't shoot, don't shoot.")[52]

Moses heard a voice cry out: "It is Moses! Moses! Moses!"

Preparing to die, he stood and wrapped himself in his blanket. The posse dismounted. Moses called out, "Do not do so. We have come to help you![53] Several of the posse wanted to shoot him on the spot. Splawn gave orders to his men not to attack. He ordered some to dismount and take the captives' six-shooters, knives, and rifles.[54]

Again, Eneas was in the posse!

The men had what they wanted—a chance to bring Moses in. Moses had what *he* wanted—a chance to calm the troubled waters by helping bring in the murderers. When daylight came, the posse forced Moses' men to round up their hobbled horses and then proceeded to herd the Indians to the creek. Some of Splawn's

---

[51] Washington Questionnaires. In Moses' statement of these events he said that an old man told him of the whereabouts of the volunteers. He then, according to the statement, decided to go with nine of his men (four more than he had promised) to help arrest the murderers. Howard, *My Life,* 358.

[52] Shiak, *An Illustrated History of Klickitat, Yakima, and Kittitas Counties, Washington,* 168–69; Wilbur to Hayt, December 23, 1878 (Yakima Agency Letter Record Books, 1878–79); *Okanogan Independent,* April 1, 1930, p. 3.

[53] Howard, *My Life,* 358.

[54] Shiak, *An Illustrated History of Klickitat, Yakima, and Kittitas Counties, Washington,* 168–69.

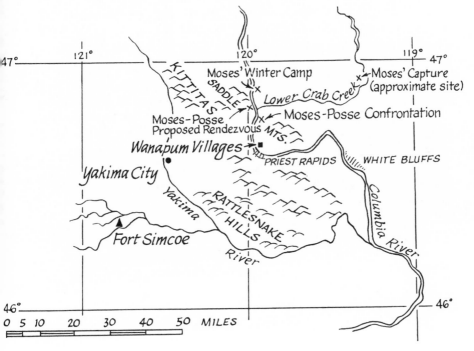

MOSES POSSE SITES

men made camp and some tended the horses, while others guarded the Indians. All day, Thursday the nineteenth, they conferred in camp with Moses, who made a number of pledges to help in the search.

Moses explained that he and his men were so far away from their lodges because they were looking for the hiding place of the murderers. He said some were camped in the rocks not far away. He would guide the posse there. Had Moses really gone to find them or had he purposely joined Splawn to render his services? Some of the posse searched for the fugitives, but it is not clear whether or not Moses was permitted to join them. One account states that Moses and his brother Jim were permitted to search for them and espied horse tracks in the snow coming from the rocks about three miles down the canyon. Their investigation

117

revealed where the Indians had camped, and the tracks showed the direction in which the culprits had fled.[55]

Another account says a search may have been made, but "Some of those who were present fail to remember this reconnoissance [sic] of Moses and Splawn."[56]

In all likelihood the stumbling block to satisfying negotiations between Moses and Splawn was Eneas, who is said to have told the posse captain that the tracks in the snow were made by decoys of Moses' people trying to lead the whites into a trap. Moses' actions had not been above suspicion, and since Splawn realized that one Indian knew how another thought, he tried to decide on a proper way of handling the situation.[57]

The party spent the night in camp along the creek. In the darkness the night watch heard the horses snort and prance on the ridge above camp. Erroneously believing an Indian was stampeding them, he fired his gun to awaken the camp. It is evident that the whites were jumpy.

During negotiations the next morning, Moses said, "Give back the guns, the nine men [Moses' men] shall go with you to capture the murderers; I will go home." The answer was "No." Moses then advised the posse not to go back to White Bluffs as the criminals were in the opposite direction. He proposed that three of his men should go with three of the Indian police and two whites to hunt the murderers. Again the answer was "No." Next he proposed that six of his men make the search and that they be given their rifles. This proposal was accepted, but Splawn would not permit them to have their rifles, only their pistols. He decided to allow six of Moses' men to accompany some of the Indian police, but chose to hold Moses as a hostage, an action undoubtedly calculated to prevent entrapment of the police detachment.[58]

Well after daylight, Splawn and some of his men returned with Moses and three of his Indians to White Bluffs, where Splawn

[55] Splawn, Ka-Mi-akin, 312–13.
[56] Shiak, An Illustrated History of Klickitat, Yakima, and Kittitas Counties, Washington, 169.
[57] Ibid.
[58] Howard, My Life, 359–60.

received Wilbur's letter, written the day before, asking that Moses be brought in as a captive. These members of the posse with their hostages left the next day for Yakima City, spending the night along the way. Wilbur meanwhile had become unnerved over the fear of an Indian uprising and of the resulting slaughter of settlers' families. Perhaps the excitement of the Yakimans contributed to his alarm. He followed up his recommendation of December 19 to Splawn with another letter—probably written the following day, the date is not entirely legible—in which he cautioned Splawn that capturing Moses would expose the inhabitants of the country to a raid by Moses' men, and advised him to avoid any collision with the Chief except in self-defense.[59] It is not known whether this suggestion that the posse go easy on Moses arrived at White Bluffs before the party started back to Yakima City or whether it reached them along the way. At the same time Howard had ordered two hundred troops from Walla Walla to proceed to White Bluffs, but they had not arrived when the posse departed. The General must have taken the action reluctantly because he trusted his Indian friend to keep the peace.

When the posse arrived in town, it rode to the jail with its captives. Chains were clamped to the Chief's ankles, and all four Indians were locked up. Moses' spirits fell. The "Bostons" had wanted to arrest him after all! He sat out the night of Sunday, December 22, and the long early-morning hours of the next day listening to the posse and townspeople on the street celebrating his capture. It must have been the darkest night of his life.[60]

[59] Wilbur to Splawn *et al.*, December 20[?], 1878. Yakima Agency Letter Record Books, 1878–79.

[60] Wilbur to Hayt, December 23, 1878. Yakima Agency Letter Record Books, 1878–79.

VII. Forked Tongues and Twisted Trails

"The Indians want the great council in Washington [Congress] to make a good, straight road."—Moses to Francis Streamer, Spring, 1877

CHRISTMAS CAME. On that day, the Chief broke down, venting his feelings over the events of the preceding fortnight in a flood of words, insisting the recent happenings were due to a misunderstanding. After relating details leading to his capture he continued:

I have watched my people, not only those about me, but all around the country, and if they had done badly I would have caught them and put chains on them as you have put them on me. If my people had caused the trouble for which I am held I would not feel so hurt about it, but it is in consequence of the acts of renegade Umatillas that I have these irons on and am made to suffer. The Bostons in the Kititas [sic] Valley have a good heart toward me and treat me all right, but here everything is dark. I have a thick bundle of papers from General Howard and other *tyhees*. I shall not throw these away and go to fighting.

When the sun comes up one day I do not talk one way and the next day another. I have only one straight way. When the Bostons, one, two, or three, no matter how many, pass through my country my people do not disturb them. My mind is not to die by violence in war, but to die when I get sick or old like other people. I do not know who brought these irons upon me, whether Eneas or some other, but it is the lying that has done it. These chains are working a lie against me.

When General Howard and I had the talk at Priest's Rapids last summer about a reservation I did not expect an answer right off. After the talk my mind was at rest until he should give me an answer. I believed all the time that he and I were friends.

While he was fighting last year and the year before I was holding my people back so that they would do nothing bad. General Howard did exactly right, and I am trying to do the same. We have been a good way apart,—General Howard and I,—but our minds have been together—our hearts are one.

While the Bostons and friendly Siwashes (police) have lied about me and brought the chains on me, if I am liberated I do not mean to have a bad heart toward them. My mind is to go along the road with good men—those that tell the truth and do not lie. In staying here I am getting very tired and I would like to hear from General Howard very soon, so that I can go to my own house.[1]

On Christmas Day the rest of the volunteers and Indian police returned to Yakima City from White Bluffs. Shortly after they left White Bluffs, the troops sent by Howard to rescue them arrived there. At the same time Lieutenant E. B. Rheem was in Yakima City, having been sent there from Vancouver by General Howard on verbal instructions, probably to observe the situation and report to the General. Wilbur, now regretting that he had asked for troops, joined the Lieutenant in sending a message to Howard in which they stated that the troops would no longer be needed since the disturbance had subsided.[2] In the meantime, two more Perkins murderers had been captured and jailed in Yakima City. Another, about to be captured by Moses' men, committed suicide —leaving three still at large.

The capture of Moses and most of the murderers did not stop the zealots from stirring up discontent. In Yakima City, under Ballard's guiding hand, an anti-Moses committee was formed; it consisted of E. R. Welch, chairman; E. P. Boyle, secretary; and D. W. Stair, J. W. Goodwin, P. J. Flint, and Ballard. Ballard handled the publicity. He directed a flow of letters, demanding the removal of their adversary from the country, preferably to the Indian Territory (the present Oklahoma), to nearby communities, to the press in The Dalles and Portland, and to General

[1] A complete text of Moses' statement of his capture appears in Howard, *My Life*, 356–61.
[2] Rheem to Howard, December 24, 1878 (Moses Reservation); McDowell to Sherman, December 24, 1878 (Washington Superintendency Records, 1853–80).

Howard in Vancouver.[3] The rest of the Indians, they maintained, should be forced to abandon their tribal ways, acquire homesteads, and become United States citizens, responsible for their acts under the white man's laws.

Some of these agitators wanted to bring on war—having as its purpose the removal of all the Indians and the opening of the Yakima Reservation to the whites. Lieutenant Rheem called them a "wild, bad reckless element who will not scruple to do anything to accomplish their object."[4]

These anti-Moses factions were emboldened by sympathy from Governor Ferry—particularly by a letter he had sent the previous October to Secretary of the Interior Schurz containing a lengthy newspaper editorial expressing anxiety over the possible outbreak of Indian wars in Idaho Territory and Oregon, whose citizens wished all reservations abolished. The editorial had proposed that all the Indians be removed from their "Botany Bay" reservations to two more remote—Neah Bay in the far northwest corner of the Territory and the Colville—where the military could "watch" the "savages" to keep them from purchasing ammunition from unscrupulous merchants and from committing crimes against innocent victims.[5]

In jail, Moses probably thought less about himself than about his people. He feared that without his leadership they might be suffering or planning war. Sarsopkin, Innomoseecha, and other subchiefs had decided to withhold action until they should hear from him, although they found this difficult in the face of rumors circulating through the camps—of whites capturing Indian babies, piercing their bodies with sticks, roasting them over fires, and inviting Indians to the feast.[6] The hotbloods would never be penned up in the face of such rumors as these. However, the less inflamed of Moses' families began moving onto the Yakima Reservation once he was in Yakima City. Wilbur had lost no time

3 *Oregonian,* December 20, 1878, p. 1.
4 Rheem to Howard, December 24, 1878. Moses Reservation.
5 Ferry, *Report of the Governor of Washington Territory Made to the Secretary of the Interior* 1878, pp. 7–9.
6 *Weekly Standard,* March 4, 1879, p. 4.

sending out his Indians to invite them in, and by Christmas about two hundred had made the change.[7]

Many citizens wanted to storm the jail to take Moses' life. Aware of this, Wilbur negotiated for his release with a promise to confine him at Simcoe—for protection rather than punishment.[8] General Howard's aide-de-camp, Lieutenant Wood, probably reflected the General's feelings when he wrote: "[Wilbur] succeeded in getting Moses placed in his own custody in the guard-house at the reservation, it being the desire and policy of Father Wilbur to use this imprisonment of Moses as a means of forcing him and his tribe to come upon the reservation and under civilizing influences, a pet project which Mr. Wilbur had for a long time unsuccessfully endeavored to accomplish."[9]

At the same time Wilbur mildly censured the General when he wrote to Commissioner Hayt: "My judgment is, they [Moses and his people] Should be upon the Yakima Reservation—that all the lingering hope that Moses has about this New Reserve, Reported by General Howard, Should be wiped away at once— that he should understand this through General Howard who Encouraged him to believe he was likely to have it Set off to him and his people."[10]

Wilbur went ahead with his "pet project" by asking Colonel Pike and members of his militia company to escort the Chief to the agency, not daring to leave the task to Yakima citizens. The agent must have looked like an angel to Moses when he entered the jail and removed the fetters from his ankles. He took the Chief and the three other prisoners, surrounded them with a cordon of Pike's militia, and rode off with them toward Simcoe. Pike's command had unsuccessfully faced Moses a few months earlier in Moses Coulee, and many of his men were stinging over their retreat from that encounter. One Joe Lancaster reckoned he would even the score. With a bead on the Chief, he cocked his

---

[7] Wilbur to Hayt, December 23, 1878. Moses Reservation.

[8] Rheem to Howard, December 24, 1878. Moses Reservation.

[9] C. E. S. Wood, "Famous Indians; Portraits of Some Indian Chiefs," *The Century Magazine*, Vol. XLVI, New Series Vol. XXIV (1893), 443–44.

[10] Wilbur to Hayt, December 23, 1878. Moses Reservation.

rifle and was within an eyelash of pulling the trigger when Pike rushed up and disarmed him with a sharp reprimand.

"He'll get it sometime," snarled Lancaster; "I thought I had just as well give it to him." To prevent anyone else from similar action, Pike grouped his men in a square convoy so that they could watch each other and their prisoner in the center.[11]

At Simcoe they put Moses in the guardhouse. Wilbur, hoping to overcome his determination for a new reservation, talked with him and tried to convince him that he was not being held as a criminal but only for appearance' sake until the Interior Department should decide what to do with him and his people.[12] The agent felt the necessity of protecting Moses from whites who would murder him and mutilate his body the minute he was freed.[13]

With Moses in custody and with large blocs of his and Smohalla's people fleeing to Simcoe,[14] Wilbur believed he at last held the upper hand in his controversy with General Howard. He stepped up his communications to Commissioner Hayt in an effort to convince him that he was in an advantageous position to settle the Indians at Simcoe on fine farms with fine stock, thus rescuing them from inevitable collision with whites along the Columbia and banishment to the Indian Territory. (Chief Joseph and his people had been sent there as unhappy exiles after their defeat in the Nez Percé War).

The agent allowed Moses certain visitors. One of them was Middleton, the *Oregonian* correspondent, whom the Chief recognized as an old acquaintance. Convinced that the journalist was there to report the situation with fairness, Moses poured out his feelings to him, blaming his present predicament on Eneas' trickery. He asked Middleton to tell Howard that his heart trusted him as it had at Priest Rapids in September. While bitter toward those who had misrepresented him, he wept when telling

11 Ballou, *Early Klickitat Valley Days*, 343.
12 Wilbur to Hayt, December 31, 1878. Moses Reservation.
13 Wilbur to Hayt, January 30, 1879. Moses Reservation.
14 Wilbur to Hayt, January 2, 1879. Moses Reservation.

the correspondent of his unshakable friendship for the whites; no matter what lay ahead for him—confinement or freedom—he would have a good heart for the whites and would forget the irons that had been strapped to his legs. Fearing that the idea of a reservation for him might be forgotten, he asked Middleton to let the General know he still wanted very much to hear from him. At The Dalles, en route to Pendleton, Oregon, the correspondent put Moses' wishes in a letter which he sent to General Howard at Vancouver.[15]

Wilbur, for his part, wanted Howard to forget Moses. On December 30, he telegraphed Commissioner Hayt: "By all means let no reservation be set apart for Moses. The sooner he knows he is to have no reservation, the better I shall hold him at the agency. Now is the time to move his people to the reservation. Smohalla and his people are nearly all on the reservation now and some of Moses' people. No attempt has been made, nor will any be made to force Indians upon the reservation. All volunteers and Indian police have returned, not a gun fired. I await for instruction."[16] He followed the message with a lengthy explanatory letter to the effect that now was the time to settle the Moses matter and wipe away the last hope of the Chief and his people for a separate reservation. If the department would sustain him in that position, he would order Moses to come to his agency.[17]

The new year, 1879, came in unhappily for Moses. To add to his worry, there was much bickering between the reservation Indians at Simcoe and his people who had come there. Things were different in Yakima City. On New Year's Eve the jubilant citizens honored Moses' captors, the posse, with a big free "soldiers' supper," toasting the brave volunteers who had brought to justice the "bloody chief and lousy digger." They sang "Marching Through Georgia" and other spirited songs and got the new year off to a good start with two resolutions: one, thanking those who had helped in the capture; and the other, thanking Agent

15 Middleton to Howard, December 31, 1878. Moses Reservation.
16 Wilbur to Hayt, December 30, 1878. Moses Reservation.
17 Wilbur to Hayt, December 31, 1878. Moses Reservation.

Wilbur—"Resolved: that we regard the action of Father Wilbur throughout the late campaign as highly commendable and that any thrust at him for alleged neglect is unsupported by the facts and deserving of our just condemnation."[18]

Many voted approval of the resolution that night only as a holiday gesture: actually they were opposed to Wilbur's policies every inch of the way. Some maintained that Roman Catholics should administer the agency. Others feared that Wilbur's Methodist control would be too soft on Moses, should he remain at Simcoe. Still others feared that his braves would use the agency as a base from which to launch forays against nearby cattlemen. Wilbur's idea of the "plow and the Bible" might be all right, they believed, provided the "Father" saw to it that his flock followed the Bible by beating their weapons into plowshares and confined their plowing to Simcoe.[19]

Meanwhile Moses awaited some break in the deadlock. Early in January he received a letter from Howard at Vancouver:

> Mr. Middleton, a newspaper correspondent, has written me a letter and says that you are very anxious to hear from me.
>
> I promised to send your request to Washington. I did so by the hand of Lieutenant Wood, the officer who made a picture of you at Priest Rapids. He went to Washington and placed your request before the Indian Department and the President's Secretary. The Secretary said it will be much better for Moses and his people to go on the Yakima Reservation, than to have a new one. The Secretary thought Mr. Wilbur would be able to get Moses and his people upon the Yakima without trouble. Still, the President has not yet refused the request you made, and he has not granted it.
>
> Lieutenant Wood will be back here about the middle of this month, and I hope by that time that I may have a definite answer for you. I promised to send the answer before. I promise it again.

18 *Oregonian*, January 17, 1879, p. 1.
19 Wilbur's critics thought him unchristian as well. A letter sent after Moses' capture evoked the following poem:
In Clouds of the above matters defamitory
We gaze and wonder
While Wilbur in all his selfish glory
Strives to rule for plunder.

The Columbia River is now frozen over, so that the boats cannot run.

Bear your suffering with patience. I hope there are brighter days in store for you and your people.[20]

Moses must have found little cheer in this letter as he turned from it to gaze out at the Simcoe landscape as barren and dead-locked as his own future. Living in the guardhouse on the east end of the parade ground, 420 feet across from Wilbur's residence, he was as comfortable as he would have been in his winter lodge. He had the free run of the grounds—that is, until one late January day when the deputy sheriff and two men from Yakima City, succumbing to pressure from the Ballard group to get Moses back in chains, came with a warrant for his arrest. Wilbur refused to turn him over and, while the law officers were there, kept him locked up in the guardhouse. The next day the sheriff and his men returned. When Wilbur again refused to surrender Moses, they demanded the guardhouse key. This Wilbur refused because he feared the officers much less than "the rabble," who would have killed Moses had he been taken away.[21] As soon as the sheriff rode off, Wilbur may well have hoped the incident had frightened the Chief into settling at Simcoe. As soon as he deemed it safe, he again gave Moses the run of the grounds.

Certain citizens were outraged at the Chief's relative freedom. Said the *Weekly Pacific Tribune*: "The people east of the mountains are justly indignant at the action of the government in the case of Moses, the old reprobate Chief, recently arrested by a sheriff's posse and placed in limbo to answer for the part he has played in shielding the Perkins' murderers. He has been set at liberty, it seems, by an order from Washington." The *Tribune* then quoted an editorial from the *Dayton News* of Dayton, Washington Territory, which said among other things that not only had "this old red-handed reprobate" been liberated but was now free to join his tribe and "concoct deviltry" for his warriors to

20 Howard to Moses, January 7, 1879. Moses Reservation.
21 Wilbur to Hayt, January 30, 1879. Moses Reservation.

perpetrate when the bunch grass was in good condition and the weather "warm and genial."[22]

One can only guess what promises and acceptances passed between Wilbur and Moses during this time. Possibly the Chief came close to yielding to the agent's persuasive pressures. One thing which might have weakened his resistance to Simcoe was word that his friend Chief Homily, of the Walla Wallas, was talking of leading his people there from the Umatilla Reservation, whose agent, N. A. Cornoyer, he blamed for the department's failure to recognize him as chief because he had two wives.[23]

Lieutenant Rheem returned to Vancouver urgently recommending that the military make a speedy decision regarding Moses, before the uncertainty of his disposition could ebullate into war.[24] To the east, a Mr. P. Gilbert wrote Congressman Richard Williams of Oregon that Indians could easily raid Hangman Creek in the Spokane Falls area before the military could arrive there. The settlers, he said, had not forgotten how the Coeur d'Alenes living near them had joined the Nez Percés when they began their war against the whites, and how they had afterwards returned with loot taken from the soldiers in that fight. These settlers wanted guns and ammunition, he said, and he asked Thomas H. Brents, delegate to Congress from Washington Territory, to find a means of arming them.[25]

The Indians of the Interior sought news of Moses' progress. Subchief Pierre of the Spokanes had openly expressed to Colonel Henry C. Merriam, commanding Camp Coeur d'Alene, Idaho Territory, his sympathy for Moses, who, he asserted, would do no wrong to the whites.[26] Spokane Garry was likewise agitated by

22 *Weekly Pacific Tribune*, February 9, 1879.

23 *Weekly Pacific Tribune*, March 30, 1879.

24 McDowell to General Sherman, January 14, 1879; Secretary of War to Secretary of the Interior, January 16, 1879. Moses Reservation.

25 Gilbert to Congressman Richard Williams, January 8, 1879. Moses Reservation.

26 Merriam to Assistant Adjutant General, March 19, 1879 (Moses Reservation); Moses' troubles were also a matter of conversation and deep concern to Indians as far distant as the Great Plains (*Pacific Christian Advocate*, December 11, 1879, p. 2).

news accounts of Moses' difficulty; the Spokane leader was hoping also for a reservation of his own.

Jumpy settlers between Spokane Falls and Walla Walla sought to intimidate the natives by suggesting that Moses be brought to trial for attacks he was alleged to have made on white miners a quarter of a century before. Typical of the stories about him was one in the *Waitsburg Times* narrating his "sneaking attack" on a lone white miner in the Spokane country during the summer of 1858. Fearing prosecution, said the paper, he had hypocritically presented himself as a man of peace.[27]

Aware of these developments, Wilbur kept the telegraph keys clicking optimistic messages to Commissioner Hayt urging immediate settlement of Moses at Simcoe. He indicated his belief that Moses would move there once he was told that he could not have a reservation of his own. He said that his police had done a good job of finding and bringing in the murderers, that Moses wanted the Commissioner to know he was not in chains and did not have to be locked up at the agency, and that he had no idea of escaping.[28]

Wilbur's beneficent pressures did not divert Moses' attention from General Howard, his main source of succor. When Lieutenant Wood had not returned from Washington by January 25, Howard telegraphed Schurz for word on any decision so that he might inform Moses, quiet his anxiety, and perhaps prevent conflict. The next day Schurz wired back that Wilbur already had instructions to settle Moses at Simcoe. It must, therefore, have been perplexing to Howard to receive a wire from Wilbur asking him if he had as yet any answer regarding the proposed reservation for his Indian charge. The General apparently reasoned that the agent had not been instructed or that someone was passing the buck, and he referred Wilbur's inquiry to Schurz.[29]

While governmental authority was being passed around in a

27 January 17, 1879, p. 4.
28 Wilbur to Hayt, January 16 and 20, 1879. Yakima Agency Letter Record Books, 1878–79.
29 Howard to Schurz, January 25 and 26, 1879; and February 3, 1879. Washington Superintendency Records, 1853–80.

flurry of exchanges like a game of *jeu de main* or "Who's got the button?" Yakima citizens knew exactly what they wanted—the reincarceration of Moses in their city because of increasing fear he might escape from Simcoe. Again, the sheriff and two of his deputies came to the agency for him, only to be turned away again by Wilbur, who once more locked up his "prisoner" in the guardhouse.[30] Shortly, the sheriff and his men returned with a demand for the guardhouse key. When Wilbur refused, the officer threatened him with arrest.[31]

To add to Wilbur's problems, Captain W. H. Winters arrived on February 2, with some new residents for Simcoe—friendly and hostile Paiutes and a few Snake prisoners from Camp Harney in eastern Oregon.[32] Moses had a long-standing hatred of the Snakes, but there were fears that their Paiute allies in the recent Bannock war would join him against the whites. Wilbur must have rejoiced when Commissioner Hayt—apparently in response to Howard's inquiry—sent him a telegram dated February 5 stating: "No reservation will be set apart for Moses. Make his people comfortable on the Yakima Reservation. Make peace with them in the Indian sense."[33] At last there had been a meeting of the minds in Washington, D. C. Immediately, Wilbur began planning how he might make Moses and his people comfortable at Simcoe.

The matter was not as completely closed as Wilbur believed; he did not know that circumstances were altering his well-laid plans. General Irvin McDowell, of the Department of the Pacific at San Francisco, sent to the War Department Howard's messages that, if an attempt were made to force Moses and his Indians to the Yakima Reservation, they would go on the warpath. These communications were passed on to Hayt, who informed Secretary

---

[30] Wilbur to Hayt, January 30, 1879. Moses Reservation.

[31] Wilbur to Hayt, March 18, 1879 (Moses Reservation); *Oregonian*, March 4, 1879, p. 1.

[32] Wilbur to Hayt, February 28, 1879. Moses Reservation.

[33] Hayt to Wilbur, February 5, 1879. Moses Reservation.

Schurz of the explosive situation in the Northwest and suggested that the situation be given further study by the departments concerned.[34]

Like Wilbur, Moses was unaware that recent deliberations in the national capital were changing his fate, as he looked out February 6 on a bleak countryside covered by a three-foot blanket of snow isolating the agency from the outside world. His people's horses, suffering from lack of hay, would have starved to death if Wilbur had not allowed them to be fed straw he had been laying up for three years. On February 8, Lieutenant Wood, after returning from Washington and conferring with Howard at Vancouver, set out for Simcoe to tell Moses that the Secretary, with the concurrence of the President and his cabinet, had decided against a separate reservation.[35] Two days later Wood was trapped by a severe storm that buried the countryside in snow and obliterated the trails. He had no way of knowing that on the twelfth the Interior Department would send word to the War Department that Moses should be settled at Simcoe, and would later that same day decide that he should come to Washington with a delegation headed by Agent Cornoyer and Chief Homily, who were going east to settle problems left over from the Bannock War.

Early on the morning of the eighteenth, a telegram from Schurz informed Wilbur of this new plan for Moses. The agent must have been taken aback by the decision, but he was still hopeful that if Moses went to Washington, officials there would be able to persuade him that Simcoe was a good place to live. By that time Wood had reached the agency with Howard's letter to Moses conveying the disappointing news of no separate reservation. At seven forty-five that morning the Chief was called into council with Wilbur, Lieutenant Wood, Dr. Kuykendall, Captain Winters, Abe Lincoln the interpreter, the agency blacksmith, agency mechanic, and two Indians, George, a friend of Moses', and

---

34 Hayt to Schurz, February 12, 1879. Moses Reservation.
35 McDowell to Adjutant General, U.S.A., February 26, 1879. Moses Reservation.

Hiachenie, a Cayuse of the Umatilla Reservation. Wood read Howard's letter, attempting to soften the blow by assuring Moses that the government had a friendly feeling for him and his people. He explained that Howard and the military could not interfere with the management of peaceful Indians; that was Agent Wilbur's responsibility.

The Lieutenant was certain that Moses understood Howard's message, for the Chief repeated it in his own words.[36] Wilbur assured Wood that he could induce Moses to live on the Yakima Reservation; and, as Wood stood watching him exert his powers of persuasion, he paid a silent tribute to the agent as "one of the shrewdest in the management of Indians I ever knew." Yet the Chief held his ground. In the verbal crossfire, his compliments were as exaggerated as Wilbur's.[37]

Studying the big Indian's actions, gestures, and expressions, Wood reached the conclusion that "in order to secure his freedom," the Chief had previously made promises that he did not intend to keep and that he and his people would not come to live on the Yakima. Moses seemed to him like a politician wanting the support of the whites so that he could be head chief of all the surrounding tribes on his own reservation; and, although he was not reckless for war, his followers were bitter, and that bitterness could well burst into open hostility unless affairs were settled.[38]

During the conference Wilbur told Moses about the telegram inviting him and one of his principal chiefs, along with an interpreter, to come to Washington, D. C., with Agent Cornoyer. Moses looked on the invitation with suspicion. Was this to be a trip to Washington or a trick to exile him like Joseph to the Indian Territory?[39]

[36] Wood to Adjutant General, Department of the Columbia, March 4, 1879. Moses Reservation.

[37] Wood, "Famous Indians: Portraits of Some Indian Chiefs," *The Century Magazine*, n.s., Vol. XXIV (1893), 443–44.

[38] Wood to Adjutant General, Department of the Columbia, March 4, 1879. Moses Reservation.

[39] *Oregonian*, March 4, 1879, p. 1.

Again Wilbur took advantage of the Chief's depression to offer him money and a house and cattle for his people. Moses replied that the gifts were very desirable and that he would accept them without hesitation, but it would be no use for him to come and live upon the reservation alone. He would have to consult with his people, and unless they would come also, he did not care to do so.

"Give me my gun and my knife [taken from him when captured at Crab Creek] and I will go and see them, and unless they are very foolish, they will be glad to receive all these benefits, and come and live in peace and plenty with so good a man as you."

"If I give you your gun and knife," said Wilbur, "you will be sure to encounter some white man, and he will shoot you; and you, to defend yourself, will shoot at him, and whether he kills you or you kill him, then there will be a great war."

"That is true," said Moses; "you are very thoughtful. I will not take either the gun or the knife, but will go unarmed, which will show that I have peace in my heart; and I will keep to the secret trail of the mountains, that no white man travels, so that there will be no reason of this danger that you fear."

"But your tribes live in the wilderness, and it will be very difficult for you to go unarmed, and very unsafe. You might possibly be caught in the snow," responded Wilbur.

"Oh, these are very small matters to an Indian," said Moses. "I think nothing of them; I will reach my people safely."

"But it is better that you should stay here with me," Wilbur objected, "and I will furnish you with messengers to send word to your people to come in and see you and have the council here."

"Yes," said Moses, "that would do very well, perhaps, at another time, but not now. They have heard of my arrest; they are all excited; it was all I could do when I was up with them to keep some of them from going upon the war-path. Now, when they get your message, they will say: 'This is childish. Moses is a prisoner, and the whites are using his name only to lure us into captivity. If Moses were free, he would come to us himself, not send a messenger,' and so they might perhaps kill the messengers, but surely they would never come. No; Father Wilbur, that is not a good plan. I must go to them myself."[40]

Lieutenant Wood witnessed the scene, impressed. Surely, the white man had no monopoly on cunning! Wilbur consented to release Moses to visit his people. The conference lasted through the morning and into the afternoon.

In the evening Wood, without Wilbur, Winters, or Kuykendall (who was growing increasingly skeptical of the Indian's sincerity), visited Moses in the guardhouse for a private talk to bolster him with assurances of the interest of the government in his welfare. Moses asked the Lieutenant to write a letter to Howard for him. He dictated:

> First of all, I wish to say you have always been good to me. I understood you correctly at Priest's Rapids, and took you to my heart. The talk which you had with us there was taken to our hearts. After that interview all the eyes of the Indians in this upper country were upon General Howard; and they came to me saying, "When, when, when is that paper coming back?" Now this day this paper has come back and there is no land given. We have understood today that there is no land for us—for Moses, Hiachenie, Homily and all the others; therefore we must think the situation over. Now, this day I have a hard knot given me to untie. It is an awful undertaking for me to go back to all these people and tell them they have been refused. I have nothing for them. It is a hard task. We have so thought upon this reservation matter and talked of it so often that our hearts had become as one; the people were a unit; now, when I tell them I fear they may scatter in many directions according to their interests, and they will laugh at me. I am afraid, because I told them General Howard would surely get this for us. For my part, I am ashamed; for we are defeated men, and the Indians will laugh at us. We are both beaten, and those that have opposed us have won; we have been outwitted.
>
> I have been looking to you heretofore, and, though you have nothing to do with us now, I want to ask you to use your influence to let us work slowly, and do not drag us and jerk us onto any

40 Wood, "Famous Indians: Portraits of Some Indian Chiefs," *The Century Magazine*, n.s., Vol. XXIV (1893), 443–44.

reservation. I always, always, always had perfect confidence in you, and my heart loves you now. Happen what will, you and I will always be friends; I will never, never take arms against you.

It seems very strange that the bad men are always successful. I have kept my rifle behind me, have tried to be good but the bad are in the lead; they can go ahead of the chiefs and the generals.

With all the humiliation I have been subjected to, dragged away, disarmed, maltreated, thrown into irons, disgrace heaped upon me as dirt, my heart to its very bottom has been faithful to General Howard.

There are many, many, Indians; they won't all come to this reservation. If there were two reservations, properly arranged, they might divide and part go on one, part on the other; but I am not at all sure of their coming here.

You Americans have many means of communication, and the newspapers bring the news to all of you at once; but with us we have no such things. Soon, now, this news you have sent me will begin to spread. It will fly from camp to camp, it will in time travel far and near; some will hear it and will say, "I will go see Moses himself." They will come to my camp. To all such I will tell the truth. All the various people that speak my tongue will talk it over together. Some will curse; the good will try to pacify the bad. They will weight it long in their hearts. They will look at it on every side, to see what they would gain by going to war; they will decide as seems best to them and according to the persuasions of the chiefs. This cannot be done in a day; the whites must be patient and give us time. It is by hurrying such things that they bring on trouble.

As long as you remain a general, I think we can imagine these things very well. The Indians like you, and they like me, but you ought to have some power and control over the people.

I wonder if the whites know what I have done for them? I know they don't but you do. During your war with Joseph, I worked as hard as you did. My people were crazy; I held them back with both hands. Last year the same. They abused me; I had almost to fight them; they showed me what they could make, but I held them down. Now what have I for a reward? Not what I asked for— nothing but outrages that humiliate me.

I have but one mind—but one speech; I will not fight; my rifle must stay behind me all the time.

General Howard, that is all I have to say.

The next day, Wilbur, Winters, and Wood went to Yakima City to tell its jittery citizens of Moses' proposed Washington trip. Wood assured them the commander would use his forces to protect them, if it were necessary, and begged them to be calm. But the impressions he gathered caused him to report to Howard that war could be anticipated.[41]

While he was in Yakima City, Wilbur exacted from F. D. Schnebly, who had succeeded J. K. Mullican as sheriff of Yakima County, a promise not to capture Moses when he went to his people to attend to matters preparatory to his journey. Back again at Simcoe, he freed his captive with the injunction to return in a month unless instructions from Washington should require him to come earlier (praying all the while that he would indeed return). Would he leave the security of his native fastnesses for the uncertain chances of the agency? Although he trusted Wilbur, he was afraid that the white chiefs in Washington might use the troops stationed at Simcoe to transport him to the Indian Territory. There was also the threat of violence from the white settlers.

Many of these whites were furious upon learning of his release. They charged that he would become a "Sitting Bull Number Two," harassing settlers and stockmen; some hoped that, like the Sioux Chief, he would retreat across the Canadian border and drop out of sight. Even some of the army personnel doubted that he would return after his thirty days.[42]

One of the Perkins killers had surrendered. A retreat to the border proved futile for Saluskin, another of their number. Word of his capture in British Columbia and confinement at Fort Colville came to Yakima City just two days after Moses left Simcoe for his camps. In prison, Saluskin "confessed" that Chief Moses had promised asylum to the murderers of the "pregnant one" and

[41] Wood to Adjutant General, Department of the Columbia, March 4, 1879. Moses Reservation.

[42] *Oregonian*, March 4, 1879, p. 1.

her husband.[43] To substantiate the story, another Perkins murderer in the Yakima City jail, seeking to make Moses his scapegoat, staunchly maintained that, with the Chief's full knowledge, he had been present at the Priest Rapids council and Moses had not lifted one finger to apprehend him. Wood interviewed the Indian and thought the story credible.[44] Winecat, the last to be captured, was not apprehended until after Moses had left for Washington.[45]

Safely east of the Columbia on his thirty-day leave, Moses called a council to organize his people for his absence in Washington. It was a gloomy affair. His people, having traveled back and forth between Crab Creek and Simcoe during his confinement, were disorganized and were unable to settle on a permanent winter camp. In discouragement one of his nephews, Charlie, had moved over to the Skagit River to live with relatives, whose ancestors had married into the Columbias many years before. Some of the firebrands urged Moses to escape the Washington trip. Placing his brother Paul in charge, he warned these hotheads not to start any trouble and that, if they did, he would be held as a hostage in Washington City. He also worked out plans for his escape from the Indian Territory, if the trip should come to that, and announced that he would take his favorite, Chillileetsah, with him. He knew that if the young warrior were to take over as chief, he would certainly profit by observing negotiations with the white men.

As the time for their departure neared, it looked as though war might break out before the delegation could get under way. It was reported to General McDowell—erroneously, it seems—that to the east near Payette Lake, in Idaho Territory, settlers had killed thirty-six Indians and that the Cayuses were preparing to move northward to retaliate. To help stave off the spread of hostilities, McDowell asked for War Department permission to

43 *Ibid.*

44 Wood to Adjutant General, Department of Columbia, March 4, 1879. Moses Reservation.

45 *Oregonian,* April 23, 1879.

establish a camp in the Yakima and Kittitas valleys.[46] While runners to Moses' camp brought information of these rumors, word came from Wilbur asking him to return to the agency early.[47] Moses promised to be at the ferry on the Yakima River just below the "Gap" where it cuts through the foothills of the Cascades, on March 11.

On the day of their departure to Simcoe, Chillileetsah ordered six cattle butchered so that the women could prepare a barbecue. Observing that many of the people were fearful of ever seeing their leaders again, Chillileetsah made a speech urging them to keep stout hearts because their Chief would return and everything would be all right.[48] Extended farewell ceremonies caused the two to be a day late at the ferry.

Wilbur nervously awaited their arrival at that place—aware that Moses would have been arrested if he had arrived at the ferry on March 11, the designated day. This is borne out in a letter he penned to Commissioner Hayt: "At the time he was Expected to Cross the Yakama [sic] River at a Certain Ferry I took Captain Winters My Interpreter and one of the Reservation Indians and went 27 miles with Said party to Meet Chief Moses and his party at Said Ferry, to prevent if possible his arrest, and to hasten his departure to Washington—Moses and his party did not arrive at the Ferry on the 11th as I Expected and I found the River patrolled by the Sheriff's posse . . . ."[49]

Disregarding his promise to the agent, Sheriff Schnebly had placed all the major Columbia and Yakima river crossings under

46 McDowell to Adjutant General, U.S. Army, February 26, 1879. Moses Reservation. The following appeared in the *Weekly Standard*, March 25, 1879: "The only Indians now anywhere in this department known to be hostile are the forty or so in the vicinity of Salmon City, erroneously said to have been killed by settlers on the Weiser."

47 Presumably, two Indians, one of whom was Abe Lincoln, went to Moses' lodge. Wilbur wrote, February 28, 1879: "I shall send out my interpreter and one of my reliable men in two days to have him return and then I shall know whether he keeps good faith or whether there is trouble in having him and his people settle according to promise," Wilbur to Hayt, February 28, 1879. Yakima Agency Letter Books, 1878–79.

48 *Morning Call* (San Francisco), March 31, 1879, p. 3; Wilbur to Hayt, March 15 and 18, 1879 (Moses Reservation).

49 Wilbur to Hayt, March 15, 1879. Moses Reservation.

surveillance; and when the unarmed Moses and his nephew approached, he arrested them three miles short of the ferry.

The "wide awake sheriff," as Ballard described him in a dispatch to the *Oregonian*,[50] justified his action by Moses' tardiness in returning from his people,[51] but it really stemmed from the fears of the Ballard group that the Chief's trip might result in his freedom. As soon as the posse reached town, they promptly arraigned their prize before the court, charging him with complicity in the Perkins murders. Ballard and Stair, serving as prosecutors, secured a court adjournment for twenty-four hours, a delaying tactic to keep Moses from going east and to give time for Saluskin to be brought down from Fort Colville to testify against him.

On March 13, the prosecution, claiming that it was still not ready, asked for an adjournment of eight days. It was becoming evident that it wished to confine Moses until the October court. To prevent this, Wilbur paid one hundred dollars for counsel, waived examination, and with citizen P. G. Gearvis posted bond under which Moses was released.[52]

Secretary Schurz (probably on the basis of Wood's reports) was aware of Moses' reluctance to go to Washington and of the pressures to keep him at home, and he telegraphed Governor Ferry to urge Moses and his men to make the trip.[53] Ferry, knowing Moses' faith in Howard, invited the General to accompany him (Ferry) up the Columbia to Walla Walla, near which place the others in the Washington, D. C.–bound party would be gathered. The officials arrived on March 13. In the bustling southeastern Washington Territory town, they were entertained that evening at a social by nearly two thousand citizens, wishing them well on their way to gather the chiefs for the important Washington conference.[54]

---

50 March 13, 1879.

51 Wilbur to Hayt, March 15 and 18, 1879. Moses Reservation.

52 *Oregonian*, March 19, 1879.

53 *Oregonian*, March 24, 1879, p. 3; Ferry to Schurz, March 9, 1879. Moses Reservation.

54 *Walla Walla Statesman* (Walla Walla, Washington Territory), March 15, 1879, p. 3.

Although Wilbur had snatched him from the hands of the prosecutors, Moses could not shake off his fear of the trip. A runner told him that the Governor and the General expected him to go to Washington and asked him to meet them at The Dalles. On the fourteenth, Wilbur sent a message to Hayt[55] and one to Ferry assuring each that Moses was safe at Simcoe and would start for The Dalles on Monday. He asked the Governor to relay the information to Agent Cornoyer. Wilbur then briefed Commissioner Hayt on the forthcoming conference, asserting that when the Indian leader learned there would be no new reservation for him, he would go to Simcoe as he had agreed, although his people had not. Wilbur also advised the department to promise Moses the head chieftaincy, a yearly salary of five hundred dollars, a house, and lands.[56]

Wilbur planned the trip for Moses and Chillileetsah right down to their wardrobes, so that they could meet the white man in style—for each, a suit, four shirts (two being cassimere), two suits of underclothing, a tie and a button to hold it down, a pair of socks, a box of collars, a pair of boots, a valise, and a satchel.[57] The boots, they would never wear, thwarting Wilbur's desire to make his red charges over in the white man's image from head to toe. Wilbur also wrote a letter of introduction for Moses to Commissioner Hayt: "Sir, I have the honor herewith to introduce to your favorable notice Chief Moses and his traveling companion Jim. Gentlemen will find Moses a man of good sense and deserving your kind attention. Hoping his visit may do him and his people a general and lasting good, I am, sir, your obedient servant. James H. Wilbur, U. S. Indian Agent."[58]

With credentials in hand, Moses prepared for the fateful journey. He hoped the trip would result in an honest plan to settle him and his people on their own land; he feared it would be a sinister plot to exile him to Indian Territory. Soon he would know.

55 Wilbur to Hayt, March 14, 1879. Moses Reservation.
56 Wilbur to Hayt, March 15, 1879. Moses Reservation.
57 Wilbur to Hayt, April 11, 1879. Moses Reservation.
58 Wilbur to Hayt, March 15, 1879. Moses Reservation.

VIII. *Down from Camp to Father*

"I wish to speak my heart as a child speaks to its father."
—Moses to Indian agent, Okanogan River, June 30, 1870

EARLY IN THE MORNING, Monday, March 17, 1879, Moses, Chilli-leetsah, and the interpreter, Abe Lincoln, set out for The Dalles in company with Captain Winters. Deep snows on the Satus forced the party to drop to the Columbia at Umatilla.[1] There they met and joined, aboard the stern-wheeler *Annie Faxon*, Howard, Ferry, and Washington, D. C.–bound chiefs, Homily of the Walla Wallas, and Hiachenie, a Cayuse from the Umatilla Reservation.[2]

When the stern-wheeler reached The Dalles, Moses sent a message back to Paul, instructing him to stay out of trouble, not to worry over the stolen horses the whites were complaining about, to plant seed soon, and above all to keep the peace because their leader was with friends and was all right.[3] The last was no small order for Paul, as dissident elements of his people believed that Howard was deceiving Moses. Moreover, white men, hoping to cause trouble by making the most of Paul's tenuous hold over the Columbias, claimed he was trying to make a name for himself as war chief in order to usurp leadership of the renegades.[4]

Soon, Ballard, in reply to a "long and interesting" letter from Ferry, asked the Governor to ship Moses to Canada and to send Wilbur with him. He said:

So-happy [a Yakima Indian] and other leading subchiefs and men including Eneas, the chief of Wilbur's police have been to consult me and they tell me as do all Indians that they have lost all confidence in Wilbur and have full faith in Howard. In fact

1 *Oregonian*, March 19, 1879.
2 *Oregonian*, March 16, 1879.
3 *Weekly Pacific Tribune*, March 30, 1879.
4 *Oregonian*, April 2, 1879, p. 3.

they fear and respect General Howard and look to him as the
person to look after the cultus [bad] siawash.

The whites have less confidence in Wilbur than they have in
the Indians.

The only foe we dread is the present Indian policy.

Ballard's afterthought is interesting: "P.S. And Private. Use
the above if desired. If you can get Wilbur removed as the man
who does will sweep Eastern W. T. in 1880."[5]

Ballard was aided in his crusade by J. B. Huntington of The
Dalles, who collected anti-Moses communications from Yakima
people, such as those describing the posse's unfriendly experiences with the Indians.[6]

Moses, however, had a few backers among the whites. His
friend Streamer, now a helper at Shoudy's trading post in Ellensburg, continued to write pro-Moses articles for the *Oregonian*
and other papers, doing so not entirely from a sense of righteous
compulsion; Shoudy's store did considerable business with Indians. Indian trading was truly good business. To keep it that
way, frontier merchants like Shoudy and Sam Miller kept on good
terms with their red customers. No wonder one of their fraternity,
Joseph Oppenheimer, then living in Portland, should be one of
the first persons to visit Moses shortly after his arrival in Vancouver, the first major stop on his way east. Oppenheimer, who
for fifteen years with his brother Marcus had traded in the Colville Valley, had some suggestions for bringing prosperity to that
part of the world. Enlarge the Colville Reservation, he said, by
extending its southern bounds east along the Spokane River to
the boundary between Washington and Idaho territories. He
reminded Moses and Howard that the Washington territorial
legislature had recently memorialized Congress to set apart that
area as a reservation for the Columbia Plateau Indians. He

[5] Ballard to Ferry, April 2, 1879. Secretary of State, Indian War Canister. The
reference to Ferry's political ambitions is obscure. His service as territorial governor
ended in 1880, but so far as the authors have been able to determine, he was not a
candidate for any elective office that year. Perhaps he was counting prematurely on
statehood. He was elected as the first governor of Washington state in 1889.

[6] Wilbur to Hayt, April 4, 1879. Moses Reservation.

pointed out that the Colville Valley, in the heart of the extended reservation, would be an ideal sanctuary from the pressure of cattlemen. The country was timbered and a little hilly, but capable of supporting 25,000 Indians. (A goodly number of customers, he must have mused.)

Oppenheimer would like to have gone to Washington with the party to present these ideas in person. He had already expressed them in a detailed letter to Congressman Williams. Immediately after his conference with Moses, he urged Governor Ferry to submit the idea of a northern Moses reservation to the legislature.[7]

Moses must have been impressed with the proposal, for some time before leaving Vancouver he confided to Howard that he and his Indians would be willing to live on a *western* extension of the Colville Reservation.[8] He knew he was not to have a reservation in his homeland, and the remoteness of a Colville extension may well have appealed to him. "He despises agents and would give up everything rather than live under one," reported the *Weekly Pacific Tribune* of Seattle;[9] and the *Weekly Standard* of Portland, Oregon, stated that although he kept his ideas in comparative secrecy, he probably reasoned that a reservation of his own, attached to, but separate from, an existing reservation would free him from agency and Indian Office domination.[10]

Moses became the center of attraction at Vancouver. An impressed correspondent of the *Weekly Pacific Tribune* described him thus: "His hair is like the Raven wing; his mien is proud and lordly; he is a wild impulsive, dashing Chief."[11] Another observer noticed that his hair was combed and straight, not braided, and that he wore his native moccasins instead of his issued shoes.

7 Oppenheimer's views were set forth well in his many letters, one of which was to Congressman Richard Williams, December (no date), 1878; another to Howard, March 24, 1879 (Moses Reservation); and another to Ferry, March 25, 1879 (Ferry, State Documents 1876–80, Indian Affairs).

8 Howard, *My Life*, 363.

9 March 30, 1879.

10 March 25, 1879.

11 *Weekly Pacific Tribune*, March 30, 1879.

Howard invited the press to meet the Chief in his new home, a show place, said to be the nicest in Vancouver. Around a large semicircle sat the General, Moses, Homily, Chillileetsah, Hiachenie, Abe Lincoln, who interpreted, and Tom Sutherland, a reporter for the *Standard*. (The Umatillas with Agent Cornoyer would arrive from upriver later that night.) After some general conversation, Moses asked Abe Lincoln to tell the General he wished to make a speech. Howard assented.

He spoke, as Sutherland described it, with great animation of voice, eyes, and gestures:

> I have a good heart; when General Howard was fighting the Bannocks I stretched out my arm and kept back my restless young men; the whites are scattered all over my country, and far up the Wenatchie [*sic*], and yet never has one been missed; my voice is loud for peace, and friendship for the whites, why then was I brought to Simcoe in chains and put in jail? This was terrible to me. General Howard and Moses are working hard together; General Howard and I are friends and I trust him. Both are working for the good of the Indians. I have no fears; my mind is resolved and strong. My people, even the old men and women are opposed to going on the Simcoe Reservation; this is the strongest thing in my mind. That is all.

Next Howard explained the Chief's troubles and his good behavior during the Paiute troubles the previous summer. Mindful of his own critics, the General said there were persons who wished to remove him as commander of the Department of the Columbia because of his friendship for Moses.

Homily then took the floor. After some discussion about a debt the government owed him for a horse killed in the last war, he said he wished to write a letter to one "Peabody," to have him send runners to all his people—the Palouses, Tom's band, to Munday, to Unechine, and to those beyond to keep together and not go wild; that they could hunt and fish but must stay out of mischief. He wanted none of them to worry about him. Howard promised to see to it that he had help with the letter.

At this point Moses broke in: "When I was asked if I would go to Washington, I was in prison, without money, not knowing where to get any, yet I said yes, I will go. There are other things of which I will think to speak to you before I go."[12]

Howard invited the Washington-bound party to dinner Tuesday evening, March 25. Moses came, as did Homily, Captain W. H. Boyle, who had been assigned to accompany them to Washington, D.C., as military representative, Agent Cornoyer, and Andrew Pambrun, who was serving as interpreter with the Walla Walla delegation. Ladies at the gala affair cast timid, curious glances at Moses. When it came time to eat, he removed his tie, coat, and vest, threw them into the corner of the room, piled on a chair, and consumed his dinner ravenously.[13]

The next morning, the party left by steamer for a day's outing across the river in Portland. Moses, Chillileetsah, Abe Lincoln, and Homily, accompanied by Captain Boyle, made a beeline for Fishel and Roberts' clothing store. Curious citizens rushed into the store to see the "savage" who had sent shudders of fear throughout the region only a short time before. Moses moved through the throng with difficulty, to purchase a large broad-brimmed, cream-colored hat, a pair of dark trousers, a sack coat, a white shirt with stand-up collar, and a black tie. Radiant in his new clothing, he faced his six-foot frame before a mirror and made no attempt to hide his pleasure at what he saw in it. *"Nika hias close!"* he exclaimed. *"Heap Mamook look!"* ("This is satisfactory! I look fine!") Then he blew his big nose into his hand and looked about for a pocket handkerchief, which an embarrassed clerk quickly procured. The others also made purchases, Chillileetsah patterning his after those of his chieftain uncle.[14]

With their military escort and a reporter dogging their heels, the Indians then left for dinner at a restaurant on First Street, where they made quite a bill of fare for the other diners. *"Kah Napkin?"* ("Where is the napkin?"), asked Moses, as was his custom when he sat down to the white man's table.[15] That after-

12 *Walla Walla Statesman*, March 29, 1879; *Weekly Standard*, March 25, 1879.
13 Pambrun, "The Story of His Life as He Tells It," MS 201.
14 *Daily Bee*, March 21, 1879.   15 *Daily Bee*, March 22, 1879, p. 3.

noon, he was taken to the dome of the post office building to view the waterfront, which he had visited thirty years before when Portland was little more than forest and trails.

One reporter asked: "Moses, if you and your family should go to the Yakima Reservation to live, would those Indians who have agreed to make common cause with you and recognize you as their leader go with you?"

Moses reply was: "I do not want to talk too much about that."

The reporter persisted: "I only asked the question for your own good in order that you may be correctly represented to the people who you are going to see."

Moses: "You may be asking me the question to get me in a trap, [to] make me say something that I will have to stick to. You white men are a great deal smarter than the Indians and its pretty hard for me to keep up with them."

"Well Moses," continued the reporter, "I only want your opinion on the subject."

"I do not think it best to go ahead too fast," replied Moses. "My people and I have made common cause and where Moses is there will his people also be found."

Carrying their purchases in red carpetbags, the party returned to Fort Vancouver late in the evening. There Moses went shopping once more—to Nicholas Schofield's store for a blanket, a pound box of crackers, and two cans of sardines, of which he was extra fond. He charged his purchases.[16]

The delegation boarded the *Elder* on March 27 for the first leg of their journey from Portland to San Francisco, or perhaps, as they feared, to oblivion. As the ship floated down the broad Columbia, the illustrious passenger was probably ill at ease. He had made dangerous crossings of the river many times before in dugouts and on horses, but now he must have had a sickening fear that he was crossing the stream for the last time. The real danger of crossing its treacherous bar was not what would have worried him. (The *Great Republic* would capsize there within the

16 *Weekly Pacific Tribune,* March 30, 1879; *Oregonian,* March 27, 1879, p. 3.

week with the loss of a dozen of her crew.[17]) No doubt he attempted to mask his depression as he paced the decks of the *Elder*, his jet-black hair breeze-whipped around his broad face, ashened somewhat perhaps by the rhythmic swells of the Pacific. Chillileetsah, his proposed successor, must have felt the same way as he moved about the ship, his athletic frame covered with a long, red-trimmed blue overcoat. What a strange setting for these dry-land beings who found the decks of the *Elder* more rebellious than a wild cayuse's back.

The two must have found some security in the company of the white passengers aboard, but they undoubtedly felt more at ease with their red fellows—Young Chief of the Walla Wallas; Umapine and Wenamsnoot, the Umatilla chieftains; and Hiachenie, the Cayuse chief, who carried a sack of shiny twenty-dollar gold pieces, and who, according to rumors, footed the bill for the trip because Congress had failed to do so.[18]

The *Elder* slipped inside the Golden Gate to her berth at one o'clock Sunday morning, March 30. The sleepy delegation was taken to the newly refurnished Russ Hotel on Montgomery Street. The next day the reporters descended upon them. Northern Indian troubles had been good copy in San Francisco papers for years, and Moses was well known to San Franciscans by reputation. Abe Lincoln ushered into the Chief's room one reporter, who was amazed to find the "primitive" Indian using a chair and wearing white man's clothes. Moses answered the usual questions—the name of his father, his tribe, the number of his warriors, the description of the land he wanted, and so on. All the while, short, rotund Homily good-naturedly took in the show, with head drooped over the side of the bed and booted feet propped on a pillow, and managed to get a word in here and there about his great-uncle, "Pia Pia Moksmoth" (Peu Peu Mox Mox), who had taken scalps in the Yakima War of 1855.

Umapine sat on top of the washstand with legs adangle, so intent on the conversation that the dampness from a small trickle

17 *Oregonian,* April 21, 1879.
18 *Oregonian,* April 14, 1879, p. 3.

of water set off by one of his accidental movements failed to break his concentration. Abe Lincoln, conspicuous with crimson neck sash, shut off the water. The reporter was impressed as Umapine told how as Howard's scout he had penetrated the Paiute camp and pointed out their famous chief, Eagen, thus causing his capture. Wenamsnoot, who had drawn the middle bureau drawer out sufficiently to sit in it, told of his home on the Umatilla Reservation. The reporter then moved to another room, where Hiachenie (noted for his pinched expression) and Young Chief reclined as though beside a campfire. Young Chief explained that he was subchief of the Cayuses and the paid chief of the Walla Wallas, since the real chief, Homily, had been deposed by the chaste Interior Department for having two wives. The reporter was most impressed with Chillileetsah, observing that he was tall, young, handsome, though somewhat pallid from seasickness, and never forward in the presence of Moses, even imitating the actions of the Chief.[19]

On Sunday afternoon, the Indians toured a wonderland of streetcars, tall buildings, and Woodward's Gardens on Mission between Thirteenth and Fifteenth streets. At the Gardens, laid out in 1860 by R. B. Woodward, they saw the biggest white medicine of their lives—a "zoographicon," art gallery, marine aquarium, conservatory, music hall, menageries, statuary, and an amphitheater. They concluded the tour with thirsty glances at the saloon whose wares they had to pass up for water from a drinking post with attached cup.

Monday evening, Moses and his companions appeared between curtains at the Baldwin Theater, where the popular actress, Rose Eytinge, shared the limelight with the Indians.[20] Moses had a strong sense of the dramatic. The older Indians still say that he should have been an actor. This trait was evident throughout his life in his speeches to white audiences, at native councils, and in private conversations; but it is probable that this first appearance on the stage gave him little opportunity to exercise his histrionic

19 *San Francisco Chronicle,* March 31, 1879, p. 2.
20 *Ibid.*

instinct. By coincidence, that same night "Buffalo Bill" Cody was appearing in another San Francisco theater in his latest Wild West show, *Knight of the Plains.*[21]

The next day, the party boarded the train for the nation's capital. At last, Moses was on the iron horse described by Mc-Clellan to his people many years before. As mile after endless mile stretched by, the steam cayuse jolted his big frame as its clicking hooves sped over an iron trail. From his window he could watch the big land fly past—mountains, plains, prairies—much bigger now than Spalding had described it.

Arriving in the capital Wednesday morning, April 9, on the Pennsylvania Railroad, the delegation was taken to the Tremont House, where they took board and room for a stay of nearly two weeks. Moses must have been impressed with the size of the crowds as the Interior Department people had hoped he would be. Who could ever think of beating the white man's tribe? The impression must have continued the next morning when the delegation had an introductory meeting with Secretary Schurz and Commissioner Hayt. The Office of Indian Affairs was housed in the old Patent Office Building, a huge building with long halls and many rooms. The endlessness of it all! How could an Indian powwow in such a place as this?

Newsmen were as intrigued with Moses as he was with the sights of their city. One of them wrote: "Moses is a man of fine presence. He seems to have the powers of leadership, if not the meekness of his biblical namesake."[22] Two days later another reporter noted Moses' resemblance to Henry Ward Beecher (others had noted a similar resemblance) and compared him with the Nez Percé Chief Joseph, in being like the latter, "the most remarkable of living Indians."[23]

The delegation met again on Friday with Secretary Schurz and Commissioner Hayt, who soon learned that, in spite of Wilbur's letters to the contrary, Moses had no intention of going on the

---

21 *Daily Evening Bulletin* (San Francisco), March 21, 1879, p. 2.

22 *Evening Star* (Washington, D. C.), April 10, 1879, p. 1.

23 *Evening Star*, April 12, 1879.

Yakima Reservation and that he would not tolerate supervision by department agents. He gave an articulate presentation of recent events, which offset the propaganda of cattlemen who opposed setting aside grazing lands for reservations. On Sunday he was the attraction at the Calvary Baptist Sunday school, where he shook hands and talked to parishioners and teachers. He was happy, he told them, to see so many men, women, boys, and girls studying the good book and practicing the arts of peace and husbandry.[24] The next evening Drs. T. A. and M. C. Bland, editors of *Council Fire and Arbitrator*, a magazine devoted to championing Indian rights, invited Moses and his party and nearly fifty other guests, including several Congressmen, military leaders, and members of prominent Washington families, to their parlors on Thirteenth Street to hear the Indian side of the story. The one who introduced Moses observed: "Some one name always stands as representative of the Indian question. It was Captain Jack. It was Sitting Bull. Last winter it was Joseph. Just now it is Moses." Moses responded with a speech urging peace, and Hiachenie followed with a similar plea.[25]

The conferences with government officials continued throughout the week. Hayt suggested that Moses' people be given a permanent home immediately west of the Colville Reservation. Moses agreed. This was similar to Oppenheimer's suggestion except that the new reservation was to be west of the Colville rather than an extension of it to the east.

Between these sessions, Moses had ample time to see Washington. He could not have dreamed such a place existed. He was to describe it many times to the listening children in his old age. There were the big stone houses and the horse-drawn streetcars. There were the street lights—lighted at six-thirty in the evening and extinguished shortly after midnight. And the firewater served by Washington society in shiny glasses from fancy bottles—no barrels and dangling tin cups here.[26] There were so many people —thick as leaves on the trees as Spalding had said.

24 *Evening Star*, April 14, 1879, p. 4.
25 *Washington Post* (Washington, D. C.), April 17, 1879, p. 2.
26 Peone Interviews.

Down from Camp to Father

A letter from Moses to the editor was published in a paper back home. It read:

MR. EDITOR:

When I left my native land, I promised Mr. Duff, on Pine Grove to write to you because he takes your paper and wants to hear from me in print, but I am here. This is a great city. All my tribe put together would not fill the great Father's back yard. I cannot sleep and would die if forced to take the district [*sic*] of Columbia for my reservation and live on it. They have no game here, only what they raise, and the hills and plains, even the streams are covered with houses; cars with ponies and cars without, vessels with white wings and vessels that crawl on their hands and knees and run like the wild deer, but the people here are very good to us. They understand our hearts and know when we are hungry. Myself and the Umatillas are getting dyspeptic. Too much good eating kills the Indian. Maybe that's the reason they are so scarce around here. I shut my eyes when I lay me down to rest and dream but sleep not. I am bewildered and want to go home, be a good Indian and tell my people what I saw. By the time I tell all I know I'll be dead. We have lots of money; it comes and we know not why. Last Tuesday the boss of a theater offered me $95 and the Umatillas $40 each to go with him and show ourselves. We went and all we had to do was to sit on the stage, look wild, smoke the pipe of peace, and give an occasional yell. While we were doing this a white man made a speech to a thousand people, telling them that we were the original owners of the soil, the landlords and the true Americans, while all the rest were tenants, retaining possession by force; that the white men on the frontier were the savages, not the Indians. At this junction something came whistling through the air. It missed the speaker but hit one of the Umatillas between the eyes and bursted, but there wasn't much lost. It was only a spoiled cabbage head, and the speaker took a big drink of water and went on to say, that the Indians had been abused, robbed out of house and home, etc. I tell you that man made a good Indian speech, but it would have been better had it been true. The great Father Hayes is a good man and has a good heart. He gave me all the country I wanted; more than I need. There are white men living in my country. Some can stay forever

151

and some must go the moment I come. People who raise hogs in my country must go with their hogs, because they kill out the young camas, and to kill that is to starve us. It's our bread and we cannot eat earth. We do not want to work and don't know how. Indians are too old to learn that when five years old. We must fish and hunt and our squaws must dig camas and other roots, and when you touch us on any of these points, then we carry our rifles on the right and left of us. Indians will always be Indians and Moses will be Chief. Peace is my aim and peace will last while I live, unless my Indians should kill me, and sometimes I think they will, but I will return. Send my next paper to Vancouver in care of Mrs. Schofield, the storekeeper. I owe her yet for a blanket, also a pound of crackers and two boxes of sardines, and if I never pay her she can keep the paper.

> Your large hearted
> X   MOSES[27]

Negotiations with the government officials were completed April 17. Hayt then prepared a memorandum of the agreement and the draft of an executive order establishing the reservation.[28] These were submitted to Secretary Schurz and transmitted to President Rutherford B. Hayes for his signature. The memorandum read:

Memorandum of an Agreement made and entered into at Washington, District of Columbia, this the Eighteenth day of April A. D. 1879, by Chief Moses, acting for and in behalf of himself and his people.

Witnesseth, that for and in consideration of the following described Reservation in Washington Territory, which is set apart for the permanent use and occupancy of said Chief Moses and his people and such other friendly Indians as may Elect to settle, with his consent, thereon. Viz: Commencing at the intersection of the forty mile limits of the Branch line of the Northern Pacific Railroad with the Okinakane [sic] River, thence up said river to the boundary line between the United States and British Columbia; thence west on said boundary line to the 44° of longitude, west

27 *Daily Intelligencer* (Seattle, Washington Territory), May 20, 1879.
28 Hayt to Secretary of the Interior, April 17, 1879. Moses Reservation.

MOSES (COLUMBIA) RESERVATION BY EXECUTIVE ORDERS
OF APRIL 19, 1879, AND MARCH 6, 1880

from Washington,[29] thence south on said degree of longitude to its intersection with the forty miles limit of the Branch line of the Northern Pacific Railroad; thence with the line of said forty mile limits to the place of beginning, does hereby relinquish to the United States all right title or interest, possessory or otherwise, in and to any and all lands now or heretofore claimed by himself or people in Washington Territory.

And the said Chief Moses does hereby agree that he and his people will immediately remove to the reservation above described, and settle upon the same that they will not leave said reservation without the consent of the Commissioner of Indian

[29] Washington D. C. is 77.01° west from Greenwich. By standard Greenwich reckoning the west line of Moses' reservation was at 121.01°.

Affairs, and they will never hereafter engage in hostilities against the United States or without the consent of the United States, against any Indian tribe, but will forever remain at peace with the United States and the various Indian tribes."[30]

The following year the reservation would be extended beyond the "forty mile limits" of the railroad grant. The railroad officials relinquished their claim, and a supplemental executive order of March 6, 1880, would extend it to the south bank of Lake Chelan.[31]

Many points raised in the talks between Moses and department officials were not detailed in the memorandum, thus opening the way for future misunderstandings. Moses, for example, later claimed that certain gratuities were offered him—mills, a school, and agricultural implements—which were not listed in the memorandum. He also interpreted in broader terms than the department seems to have intended the authority he should exercise over Indian tribes that might elect to settle with him.

An agreement with the Umatillas and Walla Wallas was completed after separate negotiations.

On April 19, the executive order setting aside the land for Moses reached the desk of President Hayes, who signed it and returned it to the Office of Indian Affairs. That same day, the Indians were taken to the White House. They filed quietly into the library to shake the President's hand—mechanically, all but Moses, who gave it a strong grip. Then they stood back in an irregular line, Abe Lincoln in the corner.[32]

Back home the *Oregonian* carried the story of the meeting. It

[30] Memorandum of Moses Agreement, April 18, 1879 (Moses Reservation); Kappler, *Indian Affairs: Laws and Treaties*, I, 904–905.

[31] For details relating to the Northern Pacific claim, see Sworn Statement, Captain W. H. Boyle to J. A. Sladen, 14th Infy., May 13, 1879 (Selected Documents Relating to Chief Moses; Photostatic Copies of Records of the National Archives, Department of War, Record Group No. 94, 1879–83; referred to hereafter as Selected Documents Relating to Chief Moses, NA, RG 94, 1879–83) and Secretary of the Interior, *Annual Report*, 1882 (47 Cong., 2 sess., *House Exec. Doc. 1, No. 5, Pt. 5*), II, 352.

[32] *Evening Star*, April 19, 1879, p. 1.

lasted about five minutes and consisted of the following conversation:

"I am glad to see you my friends," remarked the President. "I hope Secretary Schurz will make a settlement with you that will be satisfactory. We are friendly towards you and want to deal with you with exact justice. I hope you will always be our friends."[33]

Moses replied that when he got back he would be a bigger Indian than ever.[34]

Maybe he was not going to be a "bigger Indian," but at least he would be a happier one; he was to have a home in the Northwest and not a prison in the Indian Territory. Meanwhile preparations were being made for his return to his own home and "back yard."

[33] *Oregonian,* April 30, 1879, p. 2.
[34] Moses is reported to have made comments later of additional conversation that he had with the President. See John Esvelt, "Chief Moses of the Spokanes," *Pacific Northwesterner,* Vol. IX, No. 1 (1965), 10.

IX. Hail Columbia—Promised Land

"Indians want to be free and hold their lands and homes, same as the whites do."—Moses to Francis Streamer, Winter, 1877–78

SECRETARY SCHURZ telegraphed Governor Ferry to arrange with Howard for Moses' protection on his return home. Ferry answered that he would get in touch with Howard and meet Moses in Portland to accompany him to the new reservation, and that a council with other nonreservation Indians would be held to induce them to settle there.[1]

Howard was anxious to have Moses come home to help control the restive natives. Ferry was having his problems too, in controlling excited citizens. Shortly before his exchange of telegrams with Schurz, he had received a telegram from Sheriff Schnebly stating that Deputy Willis Thorp and a posse bringing back three Indian prisoners from the Okanogan and some recovered horses, packs, and rigging stolen from the whites had been attacked by other Indians, who wounded one posseman, forced the release of the prisoners, and captured the horses. Hoping to avoid conflict with the Indians, Ferry wired the sheriff to let the matter ride until Moses returned—which could not be too soon to suit him. The General instructed Captain Winters to proceed at once to Fort Simcoe and move his command toward the scene of the disturbance. Major John Green was to hold his two companies of cavalry in readiness for call.[2] Then Innomoseecha Bill, acting for his absent Chief, sent Indians to recover the stolen horses, packs, and rigging and to deliver all to Yakima City.[3]

When details of Moses' new reservation reached the West, the zealots saw red. Ballard fired reports to the *Oregonian* that the

1 Ferry to Schurz, April 26, 1879. Moses Reservation.
2 *Oregonian*, April 24, 1879.
3 *Oregonian*, May 1, 1879.

territory set aside for "King Moses" would provide a "barbarous kingdom" where there would be asylum for renegades to swoop down on the whites to steal horses, rob houses, and murder citizens.[4] Eight days later an account in the same paper read: "The new reservation given to Chief Moses is unpopular . . . because it is next to the British line which will always be a safe retreat for all the renegades in the country. They can always find a market there for stolen horses, and obtain ammunition and supplies."[5] The Yakima County commissioners ordered two hundred stands of arms for distribution, and Ballard continued his appeals for a good strong military post at Priest Rapids.[6] In view of the anger of the land-grabbers and the ferment of the hotheads in Moses' camp, a nearby military post seemed a necessity during the movement to the new reservation. Not at Priest Rapids, however. The army decided to remove the garrison from Fort Colville to a place that could guard the reservation all the way to the border. Howard first selected a site near the mouth of the Nespelem River, but later chose a location on Lake Chelan.

Meanwhile, the murderers of the Perkinses escaped from the Yakima City jail.[7] Although they were shortly recaptured, their escape provoked more hostility against the Indians. The day before the delegation left Washington, a reporter hurried to ask Secretary Schurz about the confession of Saluskin, charging Moses with shielding the criminals. Schurz replied that military intelligence contradicted the accusation of Saluskin, who was well known in Washington, D. C., as a despicable character. He added that he was favorably impressed with Moses—that there were too many white people trying to prevent peaceful settlements with Indian tribes, and particularly with Moses' tribe, in the hope of creating an Indian war for "the shower of greenbacks that it would bring to their country."[8]

Monday evening, April 21, Moses and his party went to Hamp-

4 *Ibid.*
5 *Oregonian*, May 8, 1879.
6 *Oregonian*, May 1 and May 23, 1879.
7 *Oregonian*, May 8, 1879.
8 *Evening Star*, April 24, 1879. p. 1.

ton, Virginia, to visit the famous Negro school, which at that time had some Indians enrolled.[9] They began the conclusion of their visit to Washington. A final conference with Indian department officials was held Thursday.

The Columbia Chief had reason to be proud of his achievement. He had secured for himself a reservation separate from the Yakima—and larger too. He had told Howard that the Colville Reservation might be acceptable if it could be extended west in the Okanogan. Now his new home was to be the Okanogan. Prophetic! At the farewell meeting, Schurz presented him and the others silver medals. They bore a likeness of former President Grant. (A surplus of these medals had been left over from that administration; that they didn't bear the likeness of Father Hayes probably failed to dampen the joy of the recipients.)[10]

The next evening, April 25, the party boarded the train for the trip home. At Omaha they lay over the entire morning of April 28. There, Moses and the others asked about taking a side journey to the Indian Territory to see Joseph.[11] They were not permitted the "inappropriate" trip, but returned West as they had come, arriving in San Francisco on May 2. Checking in again at the Russ Hotel, they found themselves once more a source of interest. Everyone was concerned about the Indian problem, perhaps because Sitting Bull was still loose in Canada and General Crook was running down the remaining Sioux as relentlessly as he had the Wenatchees twenty years earlier as a young lieutenant. Of course, there were those out to exterminate all Indians, but an increasing number of right-thinking citizens (away from the frontier) applauded Secretary Schurz's policy of placing them on reservations to protect them from white men who would provoke them to acts of violence.

Shortly after the side-wheeler *Ancon* safely docked in Portland from its run up the Pacific and across the treacherous Columbia

9 *Washington Post*, April 22, 1879.
10 *Evening Star*, April 24, 1879; *Oregonian*, May 10, 1879, p. 2.
11 *Oregonian*, April 29, 1879.

River bar, Ferry, as he had promised, met the delegation it carried. Moses went to Vancouver to be questioned by Howard about the trip and its results; there he told how "me and the President" (as he would later come to look upon his relationship with Hayes[12]) had set aside land for his people. He showed the General a map that included the Northern Pacific Railroad land, which had been excluded from the agreement.[13]

The Chief's name had become a household word throughout the Northwest. It appeared even in newspaper advertisements. The Walla Walla *Weekly Statesman*: "Moses is Raising a Row— So am I, because I am selling groceries cheaper than anybody else."[14] The *Waitsburg Weekly Times*: "Chief Moses captured in Egypt! D. W. Kaup leads the peaceful forces in the machinery and implement business."[15] The *Walla Walla Watchman*, in a hostile editorial, suggested that the next time the territory elected its delegate to Congress, it should choose "a 'buck Indian,' for they can do less and get more from the general government than all the territorial delegations put together."[16]

On May 14, the homeward-bound Indians, with Governor Ferry, General Howard, Lieutenant Wood, and other army personnel, boarded the *Northwest* for the journey up the Columbia to Wallula. Here they were joined by Colville Agent Simms, and on May 15 an informal conference was held on board. Plans were made for a big council to be held at Lake Chelan, with Moses sending runners to all nonreservation tribes to invite them to attend it. Moses was now the officially recognized chief of the Wenatchees, Entiats, Chelans, Methows, Okanogans, and others who might wish to come and live with him on his reservation; and, so far as he was concerned, he was chief over the San Poils, Nespelems, and Colvilles on the Colville Reservation. Had not

12 *Yakima Morning Herald*, February 17, 1898.

13 Secretary of War, *Annual Report*, 1879 (46 Cong., 2 sess., *House Exec. Doc. No. 1*), II, 151.

14 March 15, 1878.

15 July 4, 1879.

16 May 6, 1879. This same issue announced the death of Moses' friend, Judge Cain, who first came to the Northwest as the private secretary to Governor Stevens.

he been made chief of all the tribes of the upper Columbia! The meeting aboard the *Northwest* revealed that the Washington conference might have developed more problems than it settled. It was pointed out to Moses that the Indians who came under him must go on the new reservation. He agreed that free Indians should go there, but since he was chief of all the tribes, he would make his lodge on the Colville at a more centralized spot, not far from the place Howard had first considered for his military post. Ferry and Howard insisted that since he had his own reservation, he had to live on it. Ferry, however, wired Secretary Schurz for clarification. A telegram came back from Schurz: "The addition to the old Colville Reservation west of it was made for the benefit of Moses and his people, but he may live on the old Colville Reservation together with the Colville Indians. There is no objection to his locating his home where your dispatch states."[17]

Simms agreed that Moses could make his camp on the Colville, but explained that while he, as agent, had no authority over Moses' reservation, he was in charge of the Colville and Moses was no chief there. Moses would soon learn that he was not to be absolute monarch on his reservation either, for the military planned to keep a watchful eye on him from its proposed base at Camp Chelan.

Moses had insisted that since he had now been recognized by the Great Father as head man of the nonreservation Indians, the symbols of his authority—his knife and gun, last in the possession of Father Wilbur—should be returned to him. Ferry sent a communication to Wilbur requesting the weapons; but Wilbur refused to send them across country unless some reliable party, perhaps Captain Winters, would receive and receipt for them and carry them to Moses. Returning the weapons would be a symbolic gesture for Wilbur—a token of his failure to civilize Moses at Simcoe.[18]

After the Wallula conference Moses received his weapons at

[17] Ferry to Schurz, May 16, 1879; Schurz to Ferry, May 17, 1879. Moses Reservation.

[18] Wilbur to Ferry, May 27, 1879. Yakima Agency Letter Record Books, 1878–79.

Priest Rapids, to which place Howard and a military guard safely escorted him.

Here he detected more activity than the year before when he had met the General in council. The *Northwest* had been making trips upriver to a landing at the base of the Rapids, from which four hundred troops and supplies had been unloaded and moved over a new wagon road through Honsan Canyon to a temporary encampment in the Kittitas Valley.[19] At that place the troops, commanded by Colonel James W. Forsyth, rested quietly, preparing to see that Moses and his people were placed at their new home without incident.

Before Moses left the escort at the Rapids, plans were made to change the meeting place of the big council from Lake Chelan to the mouth of the Wenatchee, and the date was set at May 29. The Chief took leave of Howard and the Governor, and they disappeared through the canyon on their way to Colonel Forsyth's camp.[20] Grateful for the fine saddle Howard had given him, he went on to a happy reunion with his tribe on Crab Creek and Moses Lake; then he left with them for their summer camp on Badger Mountain. Many of the nontreaty tribes were along the river or in the root grounds, so he sent runners up and down the Columbia and Okanogan valleys and their tributaries, and across the Plateau to the east to invite them to the big powwow.

The troops arrived at the mouth of the Wenatchee, Wednesday evening, May 28, and set up camp. Most of the Indians came in the next day—armed and painted braves in fur mantles, loose buckskin shirts, breechclouts, and fringed leggings—shy buckskin-clad women riding astride, saddles hung with bags, utensils, and sometimes papooses swinging in cradles at the pommel—bronze children atop bales of camp goods—half-naked boys riding bareback—finally, the pack horses loaded under a "thousand barbaric things," as Lieutenant Wood described the arriving bands. "Then the camp with its wild groupings, its color, its gorgeous setting in the evergreen and snow-clad hills; the eternal

19 *Oregonian*, June 3, 1879.
20 Secretary of War, *Annual Report*, 1879, II, 152.

snow-peaks high in air against the blue sky; the irregular streets of dusky tepees; the lounging men, the playing children, the sneaking dogs, and the working women! It is the thrilling life of the wilderness. What a pity it should all be passing away and no great artist think it worthy of his brush!"[21]

A small sprinkling of curious cowmen and miners came and mingled with the Indians in their camps. Squawman John Galler, already famous along the Columbia for his fine grape wine, was there. Probably he found customers, eager to sample his product.

The council grounds were next to Sam Miller's store on the Flat, a memorable spot of earth for Moses—his birthplace, if his claim is correct, and for ages the scene of important councils of his people. After invoking divine aid, Howard spoke through Interpreter John McBean. He told of the delegation's trip. "They brought back a writing and map showing the new reservation, called Moses' reservation . . . where Moses and his people are permitted to live. And all Indians who desire to make that their permanent home are permitted to do so, provided Moses and the secretary of the interior are willing." Moses must have smiled to hear the words "Moses' reservation," a much better name for his new home than "Columbia Reservation," its official designation.

He rose, dignified—clearly the man of the hour. He urged the Indians to be peaceful and friendly with the whites and the United States, against whom resistance would be useless and disastrous. He expressed satisfaction with the new reservation and stated that all who wanted to follow him to the new country were welcome.

Then, according to a contemporary newspaper, he held out the inducements of reservation life in contrast to the land tenure and citizenship of the white man. The Indians are too poor and shiftless and will not make good farmers, he was reported as saying. They will find it difficult to work hard and pay taxes like the white men. The Indian is not used to working for his daily

[21] C. E. S. Wood, "An Indian Horse-Race," *Century Magazine*, n.s., Vol. XI (1887), 447–50.

bread. The berries and camas and game are everywhere and have only to be gathered. Game comes within reach of bullets. Moreover, schools and other advantages will be provided on the reservation.[22]

True to his reputation for brevity, he concluded amidst cheers.

One chief after another indicated willingness to go with him, rather than take land as citizens or remain wanderers. Subchiefs followed with similar expressions. Everyone was happy. "You can't make me believe all white men are rascals," proclaimed Harmelt of the Wenatchees, so infected was he with good will.

Then Governor Ferry spoke, warning the Indians that peace must be maintained in the territory. Any bad Indian must be arrested and punished. Any Indian who would not occupy a reservation or who had not built upon or improved land would have to go with Moses to the new reservation. Otherwise, the Indians would have to work like white people, pay taxes, build their own schools, and educate their children. Those who did not go on the Moses reservation or settle down and become good citizens would be regarded as bad Indians.

Many Indians followed the Governor with short speeches in response. Most said they would go with Moses, but a few expressed the wish to stay at their present homes.

Now Howard again: "Two years ago I had difficulty with the Nez Percé and last year with the Paiutes and Bannocks. During these wars Moses kept his people peaceable." These words must have given Moses a certain feeling of smugness. "Notwithstanding these wars," continued the General, "I am your friend, so long as you do right. But if you kill the whites I shall punish you. Don't steal horses or other property—find those who do. . . . We are going to establish a post between you and the settlements and then we expect permanent peace."

Moses understood Howard's words. It must have cheered him to hear the one-armed General say, "If Moses finds any difficulty he will report to my nearest officer who will send word to

22 *Daily Intelligencer,* July 1, 1879, p. 3.

163

me and the Governor, when such steps will be taken as to correct all evils."[23]

Because of the peaceful and orderly nature of the council, four troops of the cavalry returned to the Kittitas, leaving Howard, Wood, Ferry, and two troops under Forsyth to continue to Lake Chelan. Before they set out, they witnessed one of the most thrilling horse races they had ever seen among the Indians. On the Flat, the fully mile-long track was cleared. The natives drew a line on the ground to mark the starting point and held a horsehair lariat taut to mark the end of the course. They separated into two groups, determined by the betting on two horses, one a white, and the other, the challenger, a gray. They wagered heavily—pelts, blankets, saddles, and other possessions, which they threw on the ground in two large piles. Women on the fringe of the track held back what household articles they could from their eager men, who kept piling treasures on the growing mounds—knives, traps, tobacco, beads, canoes, everything but their precious guns. When all bets were made, the riders vaulted to their places. Only a single horsehair lariat swung from each horse's mouth. At a signal, the animals were off. Noise and choking dust filled the Flat. The horses sped neck and neck down the course until the white pulled away from the challenger to win by half a length. The winners moved in to gather their prizes.[24] It was a great victory; the stakes had been high. Watching the excitement with his white friends, Moses knew that in the councils he had won a greater victory—and much higher stakes.

Howard honored Moses by traveling with him the twelve miles up Badger Mountain to his camp near the pines and cottonwoods. There in the pleasant well-watered, tipi-studded camp, the two had a cordial conversation and then returned to the Wenatchee encampment to see it break up—to Sam Miller's regret; business at his post had never been so good, with a brisk trade in shawls, knives, blankets, shirts, traps, gloves, and white men's pipes.

[23] Secretary of War, *Annual Report*, 1879, II, 152.

[24] Wood, "An Indian Horse-Race," *Century Magazine*, n.s., Vol. XI (1887), 447-50.

Moses and Innomoseecha moved north with Howard's command along the east side of the Columbia, since the huge rock mass dislodged by the earthquake seven years before blocked the trail along the west side of the river. They made several stops—across the river at the future location of the proposed Lake Chelan post, at Foster Creek, at a spot farther up the Columbia near the San Poil where Skolaskin the lame dreamer welcomed Howard but snubbed Moses, and finally at their destination, Spokane Falls.[25]

Howard made a quick inspection trip to Fort Coeur d'Alene and then returned to the Falls to meet the Spokanes, whom he hoped to induce to come with Moses to the new reservation. Moses appeared resplendent in his Washington go-to-council clothes. But Spokane Garry, the literate chief of the Middle Spokanes, had apparently read or heard about Moses' success and made up his mind before the council met that he would not submit to his domination. He wanted a reservation home for his own people and stubbornly resisted the proffered mills, schools, and agricultural implements which would be theirs if they would follow Moses.

The Lower Spokanes under Chief Lot, many of whom were related to Moses' people, were more kindly disposed to the new reservation. Thus the Spokanes were a house divided. Howard, anxious to stop the bickering, suggested that they adjourn until the next day, Sunday. Moses objected, on the grounds that Sunday was not a proper day to do business.[26] He had out-Howarded the religious Howard.

One would like to know whether Moses succeeded in saving the Sabbath from desecration. The record does not say. On that day, or perhaps on the Monday following, Governor Ferry opened the council, augmenting and emphasizing Howard's views. He was followed by Lieutenant Wilkinson who asked why they were not good Indians like Moses? See what the Great Father has done for him. Wilkinson's psychology backfired somewhat, for several drunken Moses Indians rode across the prairie to the

25 Secretary of War, *Annual Report*, 1879, II, 151–55.
26 *Weekly Standard*, June 27, 1879, p. 3.

council impertinently proclaiming the Spokanes to be their future slaves.[27]

Garry rose to answer Wilkinson: Years before when there was gold excitement on the Fraser River and a large company of miners passed through this country on their way to the mines, they spent one night in the Grand Coulee in the Big Bend, and the following morning one of the party was left sleeping in one of his blankets and the party went on. An Indian who had been hiding in the brush, stole upon the sleeping miner, cut his throat, and took his belongings.

"That Indian was Moses, your good chief. If he is a good Indian, then is Garry a bad one, for Garry never killed a white man. Oh, no! There is no blood by these hands. I was born by these waters. The earth here is my mother. If the great father will not give me land at this place, I will not go to another reservation, but will stay here until the whites push me out, and out, and out, until there is no more out."[28]

Some of the Indians under Lot chose to go with Moses; most of them, however, held out with the hope that by doing so they might still get a reservation in their own country, such as had been discussed with them by Colonel Watkins in 1877.[29] Howard, accompanied by Forsyth, continued to Lapwai.[30] Moses turned from the council disappointed that he had lost the skirmish at the Falls, but encouraged that he had won a reservation. But he did not see dark, formidable obstacles on his trail ahead, which would make the continuing celebration of his return home an empty gesture.

[27] Myron Eells, *History of Indian Missions on the Pacific Coast*, 83.

[28] *Wilbur Register*, August 24, 1894, p. 6.

[29] Secretary of the Interior, *Annual Report*, 1877, I, 582. War and Interior Department officials visited the Spokanes in July the next year in another attempt to persuade them to remove to a reservation. Moses, apparently an unofficial guest this time, was brought to the council by Lot. The Chief's presence aggravated factional disunity among the Spokanes. See *Northwest Tribune*, July 7, 1880, p. 4.

[30] Secretary of War, *Annual Report*, 1879, II, 151–55.

X. Ill-Fated Illihee

"You white men have a nose like a good hunting dog smelling out my country."—Moses to Indian agent, Okanogan River, June 30, 1870

DESPITE THE ENTHUSIASM marking his return from Washington, Moses soon found that his own people, like the Spokanes and other nonreservation Indians, made no great rush to leave their old habitats for the new land. There were also dwelling in that land, unknown to the Great Father who had promised it to him, cattlemen and miners who were determined to keep it for themselves. Moses did not turn to the Interior Department for help in removing them. He went to the military at Fort Colville rather than to Agent John Simms of the Colville Agency, a Roman Catholic and as unpopular with the pagan Columbias as he was with the Protestant Lower Spokanes. He also asked the military to have the government pay him for the fence and other improvements on the tract he had ceded at Moses Lake.

He was happy about the proposed military post on Lake Chelan. Until it materialized, he enjoyed the company of the soldiers bivouacked in the Kittitas near his peoples' ancient camp, Chososcan, by the mouth of the Nanum. Things had quieted down in the Kittitas. The dirt-filled wheat sacks that had fortified settlers' houses the previous year had been removed and families were living just a short distance from Moses' camp. Nearby, Ellensburg had now become so civilized with its school and several businesses that an incident at Sam Olmstead's store was almost bizarre. Olmstead, an old-timer, was away for a brief time, leaving his wife, a newcomer, in charge. Moses came seeking gunpowder. He gestured and "jargoned," but could not make the frightened woman, who expected to be "massacred" on the spot, understand. Finally, he picked up a loaf of bread and a cup of brown sugar, bolted outside, held the bread to his chest, and whacked off big chunks of it for his ravenous fellows.[1] There were no such misunderstandings between him and Francis Streamer, with whom he passed many hours in religious and philosophical discussions.

His people were concerned with matters closer to earth, like the poor salmon catches that year, the result of the *suiapees'* (whites') canneries near the mouth of the Columbia. He rode with Mary, his favorite wife and confidant in tribal matters, over to the ancient Wenatchee Fisheries. Between lodges where racks of salmon dried in the smoke of willow fires, he may well have heard the grumbling that there were not so many fish as in the old days.

Although Moses' people had not moved to his new reservation, he sought to obtain its riches by leasing to cattleman E. D. Phelps of the Yakima City firm of Phelps and Wadleigh a lush strip of land running south between the Similkameen and Salmon rivers. He informed other cattlemen operating on that part of the reservation that he would lease the lands to them as he had to Phelps. The proposal angered them, because Moses had been given lands they had occupied freely for years.

Then there were the miners, whose claims—some twenty-six recorded locations and relocations—were situated in the copper-, silver-, and gold-rich draw streaking the Similkameen River from the Canadian border to the Okanogan River. The first claim had been located there some twenty years before in the backwash of the initial discoveries of the late 1850's. The miners had first formed a mining district in 1860; then in 1873 and finally in 1874 they had reorganized under the recently enacted United States mining laws as the Mount Chopaca and Similkameen Mining District with boundaries corresponding roughly to those later granted to Moses. When they learned of this grant, they met in a hurried session, also attended by cattlemen of the area, at Toats Coulee on July 9, 1879. Hiram Smith, the oldest white settler of the region, presided over the meeting. A resolution was adopted

[1] Clareta Olmstead Smith, *The Trail Leads West,* 18.

demanding that the Moses Reservation be abolished or, if it should become permanent, that the government reimburse them for their interests there.[2] The miners had a strong legal position.[3] The cattlemen, on the other hand, had no legal claim to the land they were using. It had been a part of the public domain, and no individual could obtain title to it until it should be opened to homestead entry.

Smith appealed to Governor Ferry for help and forwarded the resolution to Secretary Schurz. The Secretary was embarrassed; his department had known nothing of the miners or of their district when negotiations for the reservation were being worked out with Moses. He referred the communication to Commissioner Hayt with the wish that the miners suffer no wrong. At the same time, Smith wrote privately to Schurz protesting the Moses-Phelps lease. The Secretary expressed to Hayt his conclusion that Moses had "gone far beyond his competency" in leasing the reservation.[4]

At the very time Smith was corresponding with Ferry and Schurz to limit Moses, the Chief's friend, Captain Winters, was corresponding with the Governor on his behalf. He was still charged with complicity in the Perkins murders, and wanted to know whether a *nolle prosequi* could be entered in the case. The Governor referred the question to the judge who held court in Yakima City, and learned the judge would be unwilling to consider the *nolle prosequi* without instructions from Washington, D. C. However, the judge entered into an agreement with Ferry that Moses would not be "molested" if he were indicted. At the national capital the Secretary of War, the Attorney General, the

2 Hiram Smith to Schurz, August 5, 1879 (contained an enclosure of the resolutions of the July 9, 1879, meeting). Moses Reservation.

3 U.S. General Land Office, *United States Mining Laws and Regulations Thereunder*, October 31, 1881, Sec. 2319, states that all valuable mineral deposits in lands belonging to the United States both surveyed and unsurveyed were free and open to exploration and purchase. Sec. 2322, states that locators of mining properties prior to May 10, 1872, had exclusive right to possession and enjoyment of the same.

4 A. R. Thorp *et al.* to Ferry, July 14, 1879; Schurz to Hayt, August 23, 1879; Hal Price to Secretary of Interior, August 1, 1882. Moses Reservation.

Secretary of the Interior, and the acting Commissioner of Indian Affairs all became concerned, but decided the case came under the jurisdiction of the territorial courts.[5]

General Howard had hoped the hearing could be held at Walla Walla—away from the anti-Moses atmosphere of the Yakima country, where a conspiracy was being formed to assassinate the Chief.[6] Nevertheless, it was scheduled for Yakima City, where the grand jury would convene October 6. Two weeks before this date, four of the Perkins murderers escaped for a second time to the Simcoe hills. Five days later, the deputy sheriff's party shot and killed Winecat. Two others were captured and taken back to Yakima City, but Tomehoptowne eluded the searching party. The episode created a tense setting for the opening of court. On top of Moses' other troubles, one of his brothers died on September 27.[7]

Nine months after being shackled in Yakima City, Moses rode back there as the grand jury hearing commenced, apprehensive of the treatment he might receive this time. The proceedings were conducted with decorum and without demonstrations. More than sixty hostile witnesses testified. Wilbur was present in Yakima City—a friendly gesture that must have been encouraging to the Chief. Moses must have realized that his friends of the army could not help him if he were indicted. A jury would hold his fate. The results at last! No bill found. He was free to return home on October 17.[8]

The same attorneys appointed for Moses, J. W. Hamilton and Edward Whitson, defended the Umatillas who were indicted for the Perkins murders. Moostonic turned state's evidence and was not prosecuted. He gratefully paid his lawyers with thirty horses. Kype, Saluskin, and Tewonne were sentenced to hang.

5 Winters to Ferry, August 8, 1879; Ferry to Winters, August 13, 1879; Brooks to Ferry, September 22, 1879; Schurz to Ferry, September 24, 1879. E. P. Ferry, State Documents 1876–80, Indian Affairs.

6 Howard to Ferry, August 8, 1879. E. P. Ferry, State Documents 1876–80, Indian Affairs.

7 *Daily Intelligencer*, October 23, 1879, p. 2.

8 Wilbur to Hayt, October 18 and 31, 1879. Yakima Agency Letter Record Books, 1878–79.

They attempted a jail break on November 1, but all were wounded by gunfire and quickly apprehended. Tewonne joined Chuchchuck (who had committed suicide) and Winecat (killed following the previous jail break) in escaping the rope; he died of his wounds the day before the hanging. Tomehoptowne remained at large. About eleven twenty-five in the morning, November 23, Kype and Saluskin climbed the steps of the scaffold. Saluskin calmly scanned the crowd that had gathered from around the country to witness the execution. He surveyed the rope and then glanced above to the yardarm—or perhaps to heaven—and smiled. Kype spoke as Abe Lincoln interpreted: "You see me here today. This day I lay my body in the ground. You can hang my body but you can't hang my spirit. That is all."

Saluskin spoke, proclaiming his goodness—that the good Father took care of all his children in this world and the next. Father Wilbur offered a prayer. The black caps and nooses were adjusted. At eleven-fifty-five Sheriff Schnebly chopped the rope holding the trap door. Saluskin struggled briefly.[9]

Tomehoptowne, still at large, would not be captured until about two years later,[10] when he was tried, convicted, and hanged.[11] While frightened settlers awaited his capture, they appealed for federal troops. Did they really feel the need of so much protection from one lone renegade? To find the reason for their request, one must go back to September, when Sheriff Schnebly had gone over Howard's head to visit General McDowell in San Francisco ostensibly to ask for troops for Yakima City during Moses' trial. Actually his visit was to investigate the possibility of having a post established in the Kittitas rather than at Lake Chelan.[12] McDowell shrewdly divined that the reason every man up there wanted a military post at his door was to have a ready market for his farm produce. One newsman wrote that

9 Wilbur to Howard, November 24, 1879 (Yakima Agency Letter Record Books, 1878–79); *Olympia Transcript* (Olympia, Washington Territory), November 29, 1879.

10 *Puget Sound Weekly Courier* (Olympia, Washington Territory), August 5, 1881.

11 *Dalles Times-Mountaineer* (The Dalles, Oregon), January 25, 1882.

12 *Olympia Transcript*, September 27, 1879.

in revenge for the sheriff's poor reception in San Francisco, the Yakima people would "lick the stuffings out of Chief Moses at the first time they can get a good whack at him."[13]

Moses had a better reason to feel comforted with the military post at *his* door. That fall the troops from Fort Colville arrived and were bivouacked at a temporary "Camp Chelan" on the Columbia near the mouth of Foster Creek. One day Moses rode down there, greatly agitated, and in the absence of interpreter McBean poured out his problems in Chinook to Colonel H. C. Merriam, the new commandant. He said that two Indians had come to him with news that Indian-haters in Yakima City were threatening to hang him even though he had been freed by the court. He confided that he had not been able to sleep the night before. Merriam, aware of the two pistols strapped to the Chief's waist, assured him that the military would protect him. He felt much safer now walking about the camp, which in spite of its temporary buildings had an air of permanence, with troops bustling about, pack horses bringing in vegetables from the Indians' small farms on the Colville Reservation, and contractors hauling in wagonloads of wood from the Columbia.[14]

Moses established his winter camp near Omak Lake in the Kartar, an isolated valley nestled in the hills between the Nespelem and Okanogan rivers, in the southwestern part of the Colville Reservation; but to his concern, his people showed a tendency to scatter. One of his bands under Netsaspooshus (Hair Is All Gone from His Head) dug in for the winter in their lodges by the gardens in Moses Coulee. A few dug in on Crab Creek. Two lodges were put up at the Whitestone, where their San Poil relatives wintered with the prophet, Skolaskin. Others "lodged in" for the winter with Quequetas, the tribal leader of the Nespelems. Skolaskin and Quequetas, both bitter enemies of Moses, resented this intrusion of his people. To fill the void in his own camp Moses invited other bands like the Wenatchees to winter

13 *Herald* (Tacoma, Washington Territory), November 6, 1879.

14 Merriam to Assistant Adjutant General, November 11, 1879. U.S. Army Commands, Camp Chelan and Camp Spokane, Washington Territory, NA, RG 98.

The 1879 Washington, D. C., delegation. Seated left is Chief Moses; seated right is Chief Homily of the Walla Wallas; standing left is Moses' nephew Chillileetsah; standing right is Chief Hiachenie of the Cayuses.

Courtesy of the Smithsonian Institution

Chief Sarsopkin of the Okanogans, a member of the 1883
Washington, D. C., delegation.

with him, but their chief, Harmelt, chose to lead his people to
their usual cold-weather haunts along their river.[15]

With spring, 1880, the troops moved from their temporary
quarters to the south end of Lake Chelan on Moses' reservation
to build a permanent post where timber could be rafted down-
lake to a proposed sawmill. The same spring found Moses and his
people en route to their old haunts. The whites expected them to
abandon their roving ways now that they had a reservation of
their own, but it was not as easy as that. It is doubtful that they
could have survived in the new land, where most of the protected
campsites were already occupied by Sarsopkin's Indians or white
cattlemen. Some cynical whites claimed the Chief was on the
move because he could not get the other chiefs to submit to
his authority.

Seeing his people safely to their old hunting and fishing
grounds, Moses turned northward to collect his own harvest—
the lease money from the cattlemen. Phelps paid; others refused.
He found several white miners and cattlemen who had married
Indian women and thereby claimed the right to use the reservation freely. Then there were native bands, like Sarsopkin's on the
mid-Okanogan, who sold produce to the whites from their small
farms and resented Moses' intrusion as reservation landlord. The
unpopular Chief turned eastward across the Okanogan to an
equally cool reception from the people of Tonasket, a cattleman
himself, who considered his visitor a renegade. Moses spent
several warming spring days knocking about from camp to camp
in his attempt to collect his rents. To liven things up, he "hired"
Charlie Brown, a teen-age half blood to get him whisky from
some miners.[16]

With some rent money "in his belt" and whisky under it, he
hurried south the first part of May to check the progress of the
new camp at Lake Chelan. At midmonth with about thirty of his
families, he left for the root grounds north of Moses Lake. On
May 21, Colonel Merriam and a party rode into his camp while

15 Peter Dan Moses Interview, Nespelem, Washington, November 24, 1961.
16 Cull White Interview, Nespelem, Washington, March 10, 1957.

173

searching for a better wagon road than the one they were using to freight supplies from White Bluffs to the new post. Moses appeared glad to see the Colonel to unburden to him the difficulties he had had feeding his people, mostly at his own personal expense. Merriam surmised that the Indians were hungrily roving their old haunt, because they had gone to their new home so late the previous fall with few supplies and "without help of any kind from the government." Moses guided the military party along a route that cut across the middle of the Grand Coulee and out to the northwest. In the evening, the party camped not far from Badger Mountain. Moses explained to Colonel Merriam more than once that the old Colville Reservation should be included in the one given him by the government, otherwise "he had no reservation."[17] Moses then rode back to join his people. Finding them the next day busily digging roots, he returned to Camp Chelan to spend the last few days of May and the first week of June with the soldiers. The military were his friends—they looked after him.

All the past winter the miners had not relaxed their efforts to oust Moses from their Similkameen El Dorado. One of the largest investors, Marshall Blinn, a retired lumber merchant from Olympia turned investment broker, spelled out their attitude in a letter to Hiram Smith, "Perhaps the D——d Indians will raise hell next year, and then what? From my standpoint it appears that an enterprise in that region will be attended with more or less uncertainty and risk until the blamed Indians are all dead and buried, but you have been there so long that I presume you look upon it in an entirely different light, but this as it may be, I regard my investment."[18] Cattlemen thought ahead as well. They made efforts to stay on Moses' reservation. General Howard at Vancouver was apprised of their activities. Merriam transmitted

[17] Merriam to Assistant Adjutant General, Department of Columbia, June 5, 1880. U.S. Army Commands, Camp Chelan and Camp Spokane, Washington Territory, NA RG 98. This was apparently his way of insisting that he should be head chief of all the Indians, including those on the Colville. Unless he got all he wanted, he got nothing.

[18] Blinn to Smith, November 21, 1879. Streamer, Miscellaneous Notebooks, Folder No. 3, p. 217.

reservation information to the General, as well as Moses' wishes to have the Colville Reservation recognized as a part of his domain, in which case other tribes would then belong to him—a consequence which he believed would follow were the Great Father to proclaim him head chief. Without going through channels, Howard relayed these complaints to Secretary Schurz. The Secretary wired back that Moses had been told he would be recognized as chief of the Indians willing to go with him; and, as for his Moses Lake improvements, there was no record of them in Washington, D. C. "Moses should remember," said Schurz, "that we saved him from being hanged, and ought to be grateful."[19]

Nevertheless, Howard immediately began to unkink the chain of command on Moses' behalf and directed Lieutenant Wood to see that steps were taken to drive the cattlemen off the reservation. Wood relayed the order to Merriam, and, on August 19, Merriam detailed Captain Cook to carry it out.

Accompanied by Special Indian Agent George W. Harvey, Cook traveled through the area, serving each of the cattlemen a written notice to move from the reservation without delay. One George W. ("Tenas George") Runnels and his son-in-law, Alexander McCauley, were especially defiant. Runnels was living with a Nespelem woman, the daughter of Chief Quequetas, and knew all the Indians, including Moses, whom he considered a bluff and a phoney, as did his wife's people and their San Poil neighbors.[20] Cook learned that the cattlemen, particularly Phelps, had lost many cattle during the cold winter. He took detailed notes of each settler's improvements, the number of acres each claimed, and how long each had been on the reservation. On September 16, he made a report evaluating their total claims at $3,575—considerably less than their valuation of $11,000.[21]

That same fall the military decided to move Camp Chelan because of the difficulties of transportation. Moses was deeply

19 Schurz to Howard, July 6, 1880. Moses Reservation. In ment'oning the improvements, Schurz apparently referred to a previous communication.

20 Cull White Interview, Nespelem, Washington, March 10, 1957.

21 Cook to Adjutant, Camp Chelan, September 16, 1880. Moses Reservation.

concerned. With the post gone, could the intruders ever be removed from his reservation? Colonel Merriam helped pick the site of the new post, a bench high above the south side of the Spokane River near its mouth. It became known as Camp Spokane. While the troops were moving, Lieutenant Thomas W. Symons talked with Moses at squawman John C. ("Virginia Bill") Covington's dirt-floor store at the mouth of nearby Hawk Creek. The Chief told Symons he was "in favor" of having a military post on his reservation, as he had understood it would be, in the agreement made in Washington, D. C. The Lieutenant explained why Camp Chelan was being abandoned and pointed out the advantages of a Spokane River post.[22] If one advantage considered was that its nearness to the Spokanes might have a quieting effect on them, this probably was not told to Moses. They had agitated a long time for a reservation of their own, and now they were being stirred up by vengeful Umatillas and Nez Percés. But this tension would soon be eased, for on January 18, 1881, an executive order established a reservation for the Lower Spokanes on the north side of the Spokane River.[23]

In the late summer of 1880, President Hayes had visited Washington Territory with General W. T. Sherman. He was apologetic to the miners, assuring them he had not been informed of their claims at the time of the Moses Agreement and suggesting that Territorial Delegate Brents assemble the facts and present them to Congress. The miners told the President that they planned to file a petition to have the mineral lands restored to the public domain. Hayes believed this a good suggestion—one which could result in an executive order to that effect.[24]

Although Moses had no way of knowing what the miners were planning, the activities of the cattlemen were more visible. The circulating Francis Streamer kept him informed and sympathized with him, all the while sending glowing reports of the area to the

22 Exhibit C of Gardner's Report, "Affidavit of Lieut. Thomas W. Symons," November 14, 1882. Moses Reservation.

23 Secretary of the Interior *Annual Report,* 1881 (47 Cong., 1 sess., *House Exec. Doc. No. 5*), II, 318.

24 Petition of Citizens to Schurz, December (no date), 1880. Moses Reservation.

newspapers. Moses' brother, Louie (Paneksteesah),[25] as a buck-aroo hired by Phelps and Wadleigh to help in the annual thousand-head drives from Moses' reservation to the Seattle market, gave fairly accurate intelligence of what the cattlemen were doing. This year's six-hundred-head drive, reduced considerably by the cold winter, began on September 20.[26] Like previous drives, it involved, among other hazards, the dangerous Columbia crossing near the mouth of the Okanogan.

A different kind of activity occurred at that place as Moses and the other chiefs gathered there to meet with a government official, coming to ask them to place their children in the newly established Indian Training and Normal School at Forest Grove, Oregon. (Later this school would be known briefly as Harrison Institute, and still later as Chemawa Indian School.)[27] The Blackrobe Urban Grassi, of St. Regis Mission in the upper Colville Valley, was in the area visiting various tribes at that time; and he attended the gathering to put its Roman Catholic chiefs on guard against sending their children to the government school. While they were waiting for the official, he told Moses and the others that he intended to build himself a small house in that vicinity and teach reading and writing to their children. Moses replied that the government had given the Indians the land, and for that reason the cleric could not use it for either a school or a church.[28]

The official did not arrive as anticipated, but instead went to Camp Spokane to await the chiefs. Of all the big chiefs, only Moses appeared; the Blackrobe had warned his children well. Moses probably would not have attended the meeting either had it not been held at his favorite haunt. The agent unfolded his

25 It will be remembered that Moses' brother Quiltenenock was called Louis. The reason for the identity of names is not known. Indians were often given Christian names by whites, and it may have been purely a coincidence. However, Indians have been known to take the names of dead relatives when they acquired that person's power spirit, appearance, or special gifts of prowess, and this brother may have been named after the other for one of these reasons.

26 Streamer, Miscellaneous Notebooks, Folder No. 1, p. 162.

27 Marion County Historical Society, *Marion County History*, Vol. V, 37; Olof Larsell, *The Doctor in Oregon: A Medical History*, 32.

28 Grassi to Cataldo, April 19, 1881. Manuscript, Crosby Library, Gonzaga University.

plan of gathering children for the school. Moses objected. He may have thought that with the children gone to the faraway school, his people would not be able to go as family groups to the camas fields, the salmon fisheries, and the gaming grounds. What he said, however, was that the Blackrobe was going to build a school in his own country. In revealing this fact to the agent, Moses was employing his native shrewdness; he had no intention of sending his children to that school either. The government representative turned away, angered at the response to his invitation. In July of the following year, Captain Wilkinson, then in charge of the Oregon school, would come to nearby Cheney for another try. Again Moses would refuse to send his children; the Spokanes' Chief Lot would send seven girls and four boys.[29]

Meanwhile, Father Grassi had gone up to the Omak Lake country to visit Chief Suiepkine to discuss the establishment of a mission there. Suiepkine, probably influenced by Moses' anti-priest sentiment, refused permission to erect the building, with the excuse that doing so would invite other white men to the area to take up Indian lands.[30]

Moses knew what it was to have whites on Indian land. After Captain Cook's expedition and investigation, the miners employed Seattle attorneys to present their case to government officials. The attorneys reported that there were fifty-nine mines in a mineral-rich ten-mile-wide strip along the Canadian border. When Congress convened in December, Delegate Brents presented to that body affidavits of settlers, transcripts of the Mining District's records, and proofs of filings. Petitions were being circulated, too: one that the miners be given title to their claims and another that the ten-mile strip be cut off Moses' reservation. Attempts were also made to enlist General Sherman, with the reminder that he had discussed the matter with the President during their visit to the territory.[31]

29 *Daily Intelligencer*, July 17, 1881, p. 3.

30 Grassi to Cataldo, April 19, 1881. Manuscript, Crosby Library, Gonzaga University.

31 Struve, Haines, and Leary to Schurz, October 8, 1880; Thomas T. Minor to Schurz, December 11, 1880; Young to Sherman, December 19, 1880. Moses Reservation.

Moses' problem with the miners and the cattlemen could wait; winter could not. He was unwilling to take his people to his turbulent reservation. On a trip to Camp Spokane with one of his brothers and Chillileetsah, he visited at the big San Poil Fisheries, above the mouth of the San Poil River, to inform Skolaskin that they would soon be digging in with winter lodges at Komellakaka, on the north side of the Columbia, across that river from Quequetas' camps.[32] The San Poil seer opposed this self-issued invitation, but Komotelakia, a San Poil subchief, pulled Moses aside, saying, "Yes, go there." The Columbia Chief accepted Komotelakia's hospitality and rode off. Skolaskin shook his head, "He is just like his people before him. They came to our camps when the men were off on hunts and hanged our old people, burned our babies, and stole our salmon. They will do us no good."[33]

Moses' Indians drove their horses and their few cattle north across the Columbia into the Nespelem Valley and then returned to set up their lodges at Komellakaka. Their lodges were stocked with goods purchased by their chief on a shopping trip to Ellensburg in late September and early October. (Not all the money from the leases had gone into his own pocket.) On that trip one of his braves had been shot in a squabble with a white man. Shortly before that, a Crab Creek cattleman had even taken a pot shot at his favorite, Chillileetsah![34] Apparently the settlers could not understand why the Indians did not stay on their own reservation.

Moses' people crossed the Columbia to its north landing, called by its natives "Sixteens," but soon to be called "Moses Crossing." They turned east about a mile, and here on the Colville Reservation, which Moses claimed as a gift from the Great Father but which was also claimed by the Nespelems and San Poils by right of ancestral possession, they set up winter quarters. They selected a bench some hundred feet above the river, built a long house,

32 Peter Dan Moses Interview, Nespelem, Washington, November 24, 1961.
33 Clara Hughes Moore Interview, Belvedere, Washington, March 4, 1961.
34 *Northwest Tribune* (Cheney, Washington Territory), September 8, 1880.

and dug out floors for their lodges of poles and woven reeds, banked with earth. Before snow came, Moses sent for Nesaspooshus and his people in Moses Coulee to join him at Komellakaka.[35]

This place was one of the warmest in the area. Huge piles of driftwood hung up along the river bank to be used to warm the lodges. Snow was not as deep here as it was out on the Plateau or in the mountains or even along other parts of the river. Campfires flickered yellow. Sounds, now sharp from winter stillness, could be heard—ever rushing Columbia water—animate noises—chants of the winter dance in the medicine meeting—laughter from the games—the yelp of dogs—the hushed chatter of women near the bend of the river.

Once moving with the force of a moisture trickle from a snow-bank, by spring, 1881, the idea of cutting the ten-mile strip from Moses' reservation showed signs of moving like a Chinook-born flood. The Interior Department under the new national administration was considering the white men's resolutions without so much as conferring with the military or the Indians. Then, Thomas M. Nichols, acting commissioner of Indian affairs, directed Agent Simms to have a showdown on the matter with the Chief. Simms wisely invited Moses to Camp Spokane rather than to the agency at Chewelah, to the north. Moses had no love for agents—Simms in particular. But the snows had melted; he would go. On April 21, the agent unfolded to him the plan to take for the miners a ten-mile strip of his land from along the Canadian border. At first Moses hesitated to confer with him, claiming that he had been promised that all communications for him would come through the military. When Simms asked what reply he could give the Commissioner, he answered that since the matter had come upon him suddenly, he did not care to express his opinion at the time but would give him an answer in two days. He returned in two days to advise the agent that he was unwilling to commit himself to the withdrawal of the mineral land. He would not say yes or no, he said, for the Secretary had

[35] Peter Dan Moses Interview, Nespelem, Washington, November 24, 1961.

180

given him the reservation and should have known what he was doing. He hinted that if the Commissioner was going to take back his land, he would communicate with the official through a channel other than the Colville Agency.

When reporting the results of the conference, the agent informed the Indian Office that he thought "interested white men" would urge Moses to protest the loss of his land so that he could be compensated for its withdrawal, and he advised the Commissioner that the Chief by living off his reservation had failed to comply with the terms of his agreement.[36]

The air was already filled with the spring fuzz of cottonwoods when Moses visited the grazing lands of his reservation to exact his lease money, with what success it is difficult to determine. The cattlemen had ignored the orders of the military to remove their stock. While Moses was away on this errand, his people went back to make the rounds of their old camps. Everywhere they saw increasing numbers of white men, come to occupy lands they had ceded.

The Fourth of July that summer found Moses with Chillileetsah and some of his other young men celebrating at Camp Spokane. There, Nettie, the daughter of Squawman "Virginia Bill" (who had moved up from Hawk Creek to set up a dance hall and saloon), waited on tables and entertained the troops. Her pixy ways and dark, flashing eyes, like those of her San Poil mother,[37] had first captured Chillileetsah when he flirted with her in her father's store on Hawk Creek. In camp the young men with Moses celebrated themselves into a stupor from whisky sneaked out from "Virginia Bill's" and obtained from other squawmen out to make a fast buck.

Moses enjoyed his sojourn at the post—an escape from the headaches of his reservation. Years later, soon after the Chief's death, S. F. Sherwood in a magazine article recalled some of his

36 John A. Simms to Commissioner of Indian Affairs, April 25, 1881. Moses Reservation.

37 William Thornburg Interview, Lincoln, Washington, November 21, 1959. Mr. Thornburg used to play for dances at the fort after Chillileetsah lived there. Henry Covington Interview, Keller, Washington, November 22, 1959.

reactions to the land-grabbing on his reservation. When offered this tract, he was fearful it would be taken from him in pieces, as other tribes had lost land, despite Schurz's assurances that it would be his as long as the Cascade Mountains stood. Then he allegorized a tale of two white men who came one day to look at its rocky surface. The Chief told them it was a present from the whites. Suddenly a rock fell from one of the visitor's hands. It broke and exposed gold and silver on the inside. The two men started fighting for the precious metals; and they told Moses that what was on the outside was his, but what was on the inside belonged to them.[38]

That summer General Nelson A. Miles, the new commander of the Department of the Columbia announced that he would come up from Fort Vancouver to look over the situation in the upper country. His suggestion, that the government follow the precedent-setting opinion of the United States district attorney for California in 1864 prohibiting mining claims on a military establishment, was support for Moses. One day a runner came from Camp Spokane to tell Moses to come in to confer with the General. Arthur J. Chapman, a military interpreter, learned later that someone told Moses not to be "like a common Indian" but to "put on style"—to "go off into the mountains" and have Miles send for him.[39] According to Chapman's informants, Moses soon became sorry that he had succumbed to this suggestion and hurried to the post with two wives and a confidant to talk with the General. He reached the place at sundown the first day of September—too late; the General had left that morning.[40] Miles, though he did not meet Moses, had learned enough to make him highly concerned over the situation. On September 6 he sent a communication from Fort Vancouver to General McDowell to find

[38] S. F. Sherwood, "The Cunning of Chief Moses," *The Washington Historian,* Vol. I, No. 4 (July, 1900), 172–73.

[39] Chapman to Howard, December 21, 1881. Selected Documents Relating to Chief Moses, NA, RG 94, 1879–83.

[40] Board of Foreign Missions, "Mr. Deffenbaugh's Visit to the Indian Chief Moses," *Presbyterian Monthly Record,* Vol. XXXII, No. 11 (November, 1881), 380–82.

out what steps could be taken to protect either the Indians or the whites in the eventuality of open conflict.[41]

At the post Moses learned that a missionary to the Nez Percés was looking for him and was encamped up the Spokane River. Perhaps regretting his blundering avoidance of Miles, he went to meet the man of God. His party dismounted not far from the missionary's camp. As his wives prepared the evening meal, the Chief sought solace in his jug. He sent his confidant to the missionary, Dr. George L. Deffenbaugh (a Presbyterian missionary to the Nez Percés and helper of Reverend Cowley in the Spokane field), who returned with him to Moses' camp, accompanied by Robert Williams, a trusted Nez Percé helper, and Jacob, their Spokane guide. Moses still persisted at the jug.

The missionary greeted the Chief. Moses told him he had come this far in search of him, to which Deffenbaugh replied that he too had come a long distance to see *him*.

Moses listened "attentively" while the minister explained the purpose of his visit—the establishment of a mission among his people. Moses responded by giving an account of his visit to Washington D. C., of what was said and done, and ended with a "tirade against the whites in general." "You put on long faces and worship God, then turn around and steal, tell lies, drink whisky, play cards, etc. What good is your religion?"

"In the main you speak true words," the minister replied, "but you must make a distinction between worshippers and those who steal, etc. If you find a true worshipper, you will find a man who does not do such things." (Deffenbaugh thought that Moses' ill humor might have stemmed from the jug.) "It is late," the minister continued, "we have not long to talk, let us come to business. And to make our talk short and as satisfactory as possible I will ask you a few questions."

Moses assented.

To the question whether he and his people wanted a minister and a school, he replied, "Yes." Then he told of refusing to send

41 Miles to Adjutant General, Division of Pacific, September 6, 1881. Selected Documents Relating to Chief Moses, NA, RG 94, 1879–83.

any children to the government school at Forest Grove. "The school must come to our children," he said. He was "emphatic" in asserting that he would allow no Roman Catholic to come among his people.

Would he help start a mission? "Yes, but will not command my people to worship."

Would he insure the safety of a missionary among them? "Yes, certainly."

As Deffenbaugh prepared to leave, the Chief told him that he would start in the morning to overtake General Miles. The minister did not expect to see him again, but in the morning Moses was waiting at the river across from the former camp. He crossed over and remained there until after breakfast. He said he had been thinking during the night and was ashamed of things he had said against the whites, and wanted to be regarded as their friend —that he had opened his heart and was for a mission, heart and hand, and that he would even go with someone to look over three likely places that might be appropriate for its location. The kind of man he wanted for his people, he concluded, was one with one heart and no children, so that he could take the Indian children into his heart and love them as his own.

Deffenbaugh told him that it was too late in the season to begin work, but someone would be sent the following spring. By now the missionary had mentally measured the Chief and surmised that he was no fool, was impatient at dillydallying, and, since he was not a religious man, was more interested in a school than a church. "He feels his importance," wrote Deffenbaugh in reporting the interview.[42]

Moses' failure to meet Miles and his bitter words to the missionary were typical of his unco-operative attitude that fall. He refused to give any information to Joseph E. Labrie, who was sent by the Colville Agency to take a census of the Indians. His responsibility was to the military only. He told Labrie that the

[42] Board of Foreign Missions, "Mr. Deffenbaugh's Visit to the Indian Chief Moses," *Presbyterian Monthly Record*, Vol. XXXII, No. 11 (November, 1881), 380–82.

military had advised him to answer no questions and give no information to civilians. Labrie encountered the same attitude when he visited other tribes. It was his opinion that Moses had reached them first and had persuaded them not to co-operate.[43] White men have never been able to understand the Indian's fear of a census.

At the same time General W. McMicken, the surveyor general of Washington Territory, came to look over the ten-mile strip. He had come at the urging of the mining interests, but he was reluctant to make surveys without first seeing Moses. Agent Simms sent for Moses to meet with him and McMicken; but Moses replied that he would not meet them since he did not wish to sell his land.[44]

Moses raced horses at Walla Walla that fall, then trekked to the Kittitas for winter supplies and to the reservation to collect his annual *chickamin*. He probably did not do too badly, either. Total collections must have been almost one thousand dollars.[45] But most white men in the area would rather have spat on their creditor's face than to have handed him their fees. They had plenty of company from Indian chiefs, bitter that they could not reap a similar harvest.

A certain tribal disintegration was apparent in Moses' camps that winter. Some of his people went to Priest Rapids to join Smohalla, who charmed them with his dreams. Others went to the San Poil to be with Skolaskin, who told them that the evil Moses was stealing his lands. Remaining with Moses' families

43 Labrie to Simms, September 30, 1881. Colville Agency Records, Letterbox 19, United States Bureau of Indian Affairs, Federal Records Center, Seattle, Washington (hereafter referred to as Colville Agency Records, Letterbox 3).

44 Smith to Secretary of Interior, Samuel Kirkwood, September 18, 1881 (Moses Reservation); Blinn to Smith, January 12, 1882 (Streamer, Miscellaneous Note books, Folder No. 3, pp. 218–19).

45 Walla Walla Statesman, October 29, 1881. When Arthur J. Chapman, military interpreter, came to the area in December, 1881, on an inspection trip for Miles, he made a report of the amounts of money certain white men, located on Moses' reservation, paid the chief. Chapman to Miles, January 17, 1882. Moses also "leased" an area to one cattleman from British Columbia for the right to cut hay from it and pasture stock on it. Sidney Waters, agent of Colville Reservation to Commissioner H. Price, February 9, 1885. Colville Agency Records, Letterbox 3.

were seven lodges of Umatillas housing such braves as Itukes, Iesha (Charlie Scott), Tatshama, Chuweah, Hoote (Billy Simpson), Watastomakolich (Charlie Simpson), and others who had fled from below the Columbia in the late summer of 1878 to accept asylum with him rather than on Oregon reservations.[46] Even in this main camp, the winter mat houses were more scattered than usual—like sparks crackling off a campfire. Nearly twenty lodges were pitched down-river from Moses Crossing and as many were up the Nespelem above the cataracts. Others were upriver from Komellakaka, and still others a short distance up the draw on Peter Dan Creek. The lodges, some containing five families, were grouped in twos and threes, mud-banked with walkways between. Inside, low fires curled smoke up to roots and berries hanging from poles to dry, alongside the Winchester and Sharps rifles and revolvers that now replaced needle guns and muzzle-loaders. Of Moses' warriors, 120 were able to bear arms.[47]

Nearly one thousand horses ran loose that winter in the Nespelem Valley. A few *molops* were there too, some of which Moses had given to Chililleetsah. He hoped his "son" would care for them as proper training for the chieftaincy, rather than hang around the soldiers at Camp Spokane, drink whisky, and live with Nettie. Growing up were Moses' own daughters: Tomquinwit, the daughter of the Wanapum wife, who had died shortly after returning to her own tribe; and Sinsinqt, Quemollah's daughter, who had been named for her aunt.

During that whole winter the miners and cattlemen worked actively to save their holdings. They held meetings, sent communications to the Interior Department, and enlisted the support of territorial officials. On September 15, Hiram Smith came up with a proposal that a *fifteen*-mile strip be shaved from the Moses Reservation and that the Chief be compensated by a tract on the south end of the Colville—ignoring with typical obtuseness the fact that this land belonged to other Indians. Resolutions

46 George Friedlander Interview, Nespelem, Washington, July 16, 1961; Exhibit B of Gardner's Report, "Affidavit of S. F. Sherwood," November 6, 1882 (Moses Reservation).

47 Chapman to Miles, January 17, 1882. Moses Reservation.

were passed protesting against the "arbitrary acts" of the military in ordering the trespassing cattlemen to leave.[48]

Even some of the Indians backed the white men. Tonasket favored selling the mineral strip, the proceeds, of course, to be distributed among all the Indians, not just Moses' people. (Tonasket's band, some thirty-eight lodges, were not living on the Moses Reservation, but near the east side of the Okanogan and farther east on the Kettle River, where they raised their cattle.) Some of the families of Sarsopkin's nineteen lodges and of the Methow lodges quite expectedly came out in favor of the cession. These people were more inclined to farming than were Moses' people and, now that there were fewer Chinese in that area, were in a favorable position to sell produce to the miners.[49]

On October 5, William A. Newell, now governor of the territory, advised the legislature:

> The Chief Moses, Colville, Yakima and other Reservations in Eastern Washington, alone, contain five millions of acres of the best agricultural, grazing and mineral lands of the Territory, with not more than four thousand tribal occupants. The Indians are decreasing in numbers, are very peaceable, some of them advancing in civilization and cultivating the acts of peace.
>
> The Indian question, which so vexes the public mind and strains the public purse, is easy of solution in this Territory. Abolish Reservations, conceding liberal homesteads, which shall be inalienable for a period of years; dissolve tribal relations and subject Indians to the same authorities and laws by which other people are governed, then predatory and hostile excursions will cease.[50]

These recurring suggestions that the tribal relations be dissolved, that the reservations be abolished, and that the Indians

---

[48] Smith to Secretary of Interior, September 19, 1881; Petition of Mount Chopaca and Similkameen Mining District, December 1, 1881 (Moses Reservation); Secretary of Interior, *Annual Report*, 1879 (46 Cong., 2 sess., *House Exec. Doc. No. 1, Pt. 5*), I, 69.

[49] Chapman to Miles, January 1,, 1882. Moses Reservation.

[50] Charles M. Gates (ed.), *Messages of the Governors of the Territory of Washington to the Legislative Assembly*, 1854–1889, University of Washington *Publications in the Social Sciences*, XII, 227.

be "allotted" individual farms ("lands in severalty") under fee simple titles were in accord with the current theory of Indian administration. It was to become the established policy of the government after the passage of the General Allotment Act in 1887. Although it was supported by sincere friends of the Indians, its most vociferous advocates were the land-hungry frontiersmen. Obviously, if each Indian family received a "homestead," much of the reservation would become surplus and available for white settlement. Further, it had been shown that an Indian standing alone could not protect his deeded farm against widespread frauds and biased courts.[51] It was asserted that these practices could be prevented by making the allotment inalienable for a term of years, but the sequel was to show that this scheme would not work either.[52]

Moses, of course, was not aware of these forces that were working to destroy all reservations. He was pleasantly surprised the day before Christmas by a visit from Chapman, who came from Vancouver by way of Simcoe and Camp Spokane as an emissary of General Miles. The Chief told his story to his military protector and confessed the reason for his failure to meet Miles the previous summer. He said that he was very anxious to have the General visit his country "to settle many complicated questions," and that three years had passed since the Secretary of the Interior had given him a reservation along with the Colville, over which he was to be head chief and from which all whites were to be removed. The whites were still there, he lamented. And besides, the Secretary had promised wagons, plows, other farm implements, a gristmill, and a sawmill, none of which had come. And that was not all—he had to go long distances for flour and had to pay cash for it. He wished Miles to know he still wanted these improvements and, furthermore, wanted them in the Nespelem

51 For examples see the works of Grant Foreman: *Indian Removal*, 129–34, for the experience of the Creeks in Alabama in 1834; *The Last Trek of the Indians*, 196, for similar frauds practiced upon the Wyandots in Kansas during the 1850's.

52 For the wholesale exploitation that followed the dissolution of the Indian Territory reservations at the turn of the century, see Angie Debo, *And Still the Waters Run*.

Valley, the place he had selected as his home; but they should be under the jurisdiction of the military, as he had "no confidence" in agents. Simms, he said, was "an old woman," who "never looked out for the Indians"; he had "lied" about his (Moses') reservation and told the Indians that he (Moses) was no chief; and that he wanted to buy ten miles of mineral land from his reservation. Simms could not have it; but if General Miles advised him to sell it, he would. He unburdened another complaint —the Smohalla Indians, yet free, should be made to go on a reservation.[53]

Chapman hired horses from Moses to finish his trip, which took his party over to Lake Osoyoos, thence across the mountains eastward, down Rock Creek to Old Fort Colville, and back around to Camp Spokane. Along the way he visited other chiefs to gather their impressions of Moses and the settlers. He found many Okanogans dissatisfied with Simms and angry with the encroaching whites, some of them almost to the point of taking up arms. He visited the Lakes and Colvilles living in the Colville Valley to inform them, to their unhappy surprise, that the land east of the Columbia would be surveyed for white homesteading, at which time they would have to move on to the Colville Reservation.[54]

Back in Vancouver, Chapman reported to Miles. The General asked him to make an estimate of the cost of buying the entire Moses Reservation if doing so would cause less opposition than the purchase of the fifteen-mile strip. Chapman estimated that of the 2,992,240 acres scarcely one-fifth, or 640,000 acres, could be sold for agriculture, grazing, or mining for a total $800,000. The remainder, though apparently worthless, might—should it prove rich in minerals—bring an additional $800,000. He recommended that Moses and his Indians be paid one-fifth of the value of the usable land, or $160,000; that they be settled on the Colville; and that except for reasonable annual cash payments to the chiefs, the money they would receive from the sale should be used

---

[53] Chapman to Miles, December 24, 1881, and January 17, 1882. Moses Reservation.

[54] Chapman to Miles, January 17, 1882. Moses Reservation.

for schoolhouses, mills, farm implements, and cattle. Finally, he suggested that the government buy both the reservations and give the Indians lands in severalty. Only in this way, he concluded, could they adjust to a better way of life.[55]

After digesting Chapman's proposal, Miles drafted and sent through channels to the War Department his own proposals: that all Indians who so desired might relinquish their claims in the Moses Reservation, move to the Colville Reservation, and there be granted a patent for 640 acres of land, tax free for twenty-five years; that $30,000 be included in the current year's appropriation for expenses of the Indians making the move; and that $10,000 be appropriated annually for a period of twelve years for their benefit. He tried to evaluate these suggestions objectively: Moses' grievances would be redressed by giving him a home of his own, as would those of the citizens with their mineral lands. The situation Miles characterized as "rivalling [that of] the Black Hills," where the theft of land from the Sioux for its minerals precipitated war and the defeat of Custer; and the Nez Percé Reservation, where the theft of land for the same reason drove Joseph to his war of resistance. The conflict over the Moses Reservation would climax in similar hostilities unless immediate steps were taken to satisfy both sides.[56]

[55] Chapman to Miles, February 4, 1882. Selected Documents Relating to Chief Moses, NA, RG 94, 1879–83.

[56] Miles to Adjutant General, February 13, 1882. Selected Documents Relating to Chief Moses, NA, RG 94, 1879–83.

X. White Giver

"Now you go back and tell the Secretary that if he will raise
me $400.00 I will stop talking from now on and forever."
—Moses to S. F. Sherwood, July 6, 1883

GENERAL MILES was so apprehensive of war that on February 13,
1882, he sent his aide, Lieutenant Frederick Schwatka, the famed
Arctic explorer, to the assistant adjutant general of the Department of the Pacific in San Francisco with a letter stating: "The
difficulty between the white settlers and the Moses Indians appears to be increasing. . . . If the matter is delayed it may result in
an outbreak, or the Indians may get an exaggerated idea of the
value of their Reservation." Feeling the urgency of the situation,
Miles requested permission of the assistant adjutant general for
Schwatka to travel to Washington, D. C., with his recommendations for settling the controversy.[1] The request was denied, but
the papers were forwarded to Washington.[2]

Winter quiet betrayed the bitterness smoldering in the lodges
from the Okanogan to the Colville. No doubt angry braves spent
the time talking, as they had a few years before, of taking up arms
against the white man. In one lodge, a chief must have thought of
his position among the tribes and feared that their bitterness,
jealousies, and dislocations would splinter his authority. After
the snows melted, he escaped his winter confinement with enough
lease money left over to propel himself to the libations and gaming of the trading posts and the "happy grounds." There he saw
his old cattlemen friends again. Some not so friendly white cattlemen challenged the free passage of his Indians across the Plateau.

Besides cows, there was also the threat of the iron horse. A

[1] Miles to Assistant Adjutant General, Military Division of the Pacific, February
13, 1882. Moses Reservation.
[2] Richard Coulter Drum, Adjutant General, to Major General Irwin McDowell,
February 21, 1882. Moses Reservation.

decade earlier, Moses had watched surveyors of the Northern Pacific Railroad hurrying across the Plateau; now that railroad was grading and laying track from Ainsworth, at the mouth of the Snake River, across the lower reaches of that sweeping land to meet tracks being laid down from the east. The "chick chick wagon" would bring more white men. Settlers were already skirting the shores of Moses Lake, interfering with the harvest of duck eggs and forcing the natives to gather the delicacy to the north in the Kartar Lakes yet hidden from the whites. There, the women rolled up their gingham skirts and aprons, threw off their moccasins, and waded through the shallow water as the mallards quacked a raucous warning at the intrusion. Parting the brush with one hand, they gathered the eggs from the well-hidden nests with the other, sacking their harvest in the rolled edges of their clothing. On shore, they dug pits and lined them with rocks, which they heated and covered with a blanket of soil and then a cushion of wet green grass. On top of this, they laid the eggs to steam beneath another layer of grass and soil. Then—a feast of tender unhatched ducklings![3] How long would they enjoy such feasting?

From the Kartar, Moses crossed the Okanogan River to collect his lease money from the stockmen, who squawked at his intrusion like the mallards at the lakes. His threats to report them to the military if they did not pay angered them all the more. They took their spite out on all the reservation Indians, like Sarsopkin's "miserable little wretches," whose fences and gardens they let their stock overrun. No wonder Sarsopkin's people blamed their ills on Moses. "Moses talks and talks," they said, "but gets nothing done for the Indian. He collects lots of money but keeps it all to drink and gamble and all he does is quarrel with his own people."

Moses hurried from the hostile atmosphere of the Okanogan back to the friendlier, unpenetrated areas of the Colville. These places would not be unpenetrated for long. In early August, Lieutenant Henry Pierce under orders of General Miles, traveled from old Fort Colville to Puget Sound by way of Lake Chelan

3 Dan Condon Interview, Nespelem, Washington, November 25, 1961.

and the Skagit River to look over the area.[4] Miles was a friend, but expeditions of this kind spelled trouble. That same August, Hal Price, commissioner of Indian affairs, sent Inspector Robert S. Gardner to investigate the feasibility of the suggestion that the Indians relinquish the Moses Reservation so that its mineral lands could be returned to the whites.[5]

There were still more intrusions. Also in August, Lieutenant W. R. Abercrombie, stationed at Fort Coeur d'Alene began a tour with old time Colville resident, S. F. Sherwood as interpreter-guide, to enumerate the northern Indians. The party had not traveled far when it ran into the stubborn San Poils under Skolaskin. After a cool reception they moved on, spending August 9 and 10 in the Nespelem Valley. Not finding Moses or other Indians there, Abercrombie looked for improvements to gain some idea of the number who had lived there the previous winter. The only improvement he could find was a grain field near where Sunacka Creek enters the Valley, but he observed that the region held great prospects for development. The party missed the fine gardens of Moses' shaman, Tompasque, on the flat above the Columbia at the Crossing; and those of Chillileetsah, which produced a good yield of potatoes, beans, squash, and melons. Continuing west, Abercrombie enumerated the Indians on Lake Chelan and talked with Innomoseecha Jim, now a chief in that area since his father's death. He then swung north to the land of the Methows, where he discovered that they had gone to the Kittitas for winter flour. He then crossed the Okanogan to visit Suiepkine's tribe on Omak Lake, before recrossing that river to take the count of Sarsopkin's people.[6]

Meanwhile, Moses took stock of his own affairs. On September 15, he met a trans-Columbia resident, William Granger, who wished to lease the pasture of old "Buckskin" John Utz's ranch on his reservation. He accepted Granger's offer of one hundred

---

[4] Nelson A. Miles, *Personal Recollections and Observations of General Nelson A. Miles,* 400.

[5] Memorandum, R. V. Belt, August 2, 1882. Moses Reservation.

[6] Exhibit B of Gardner's Report, "Affidavit of S. F. Sherwood," November 6, 1882. Moses Reservation.

dollars annually, with half the amount to be paid every six months, and the first payment shortly.[7] With this business taken care of, he put together a pack outfit and, on September 17, started for Sprague to purchase flour and other winter supplies for his people.[8]

When he returned with the supplies, he received word that Abercrombie wished him to bring his people to the mouth of the Okanogan. He agreed to go. The next day he headed down-river with only thirty of his followers. Speaking through Sherwood, he explained to Abercrombie why he had brought so few: some were sick with smallpox; others were mourning for one Sillilsa, who had been killed recently; and others had been attacked by whites in the Kittitas and were unable to come. He reaffirmed his good relations with the military by stating that he co-operated with them and that they would settle his problems; however, he refused to give a census of his people that day, but promised he would do so in the future. He complained that the Secretary of the Interior had told him personally that he would supply his people with farming tools and implements, but had not fulfilled his agreement. Why had Moses not lived on the Columbia Reservation, Abercrombie wanted to know. He answered that no improvements had been made there because his people had not been given the promised implements. Moreover, certain white occupants had not been removed from his land, and Tonasket questioned his right to reside on the Colville and be recognized as head chief.[9]

(The trespassers to whom he referred were Hiram Smith, the settlers on Toats Coulee, and six families southwest of Osoyoos. He did not include rent-paying cattlemen.)

That fall the "*hi-yu* fire" (smallpox) raged through the tribes, felling one of Moses' wives, his little daughter, and his brother, who was living in the household. He had been hurrying them to the Nespelem Valley for winter and was but one day from his

[7] Granger to Abercrombie, December 7, 1882. Moses Reservation.

[8] Streamer, Miscellaneous Notebooks, Folder No. 1, pp. 220–21.

[9] Exhibit B of Gardner's Report, "Affidavit of S. F. Sherwood," November 6, 1882. Moses Reservation.

destination when it struck, forcing him to set up his lodges quickly on the first bench, three-quarters of a mile upriver from the Crossing. As the stricken ones became more feverish, he sent for his shaman, Tompasque, to hurry to the temporary lodge to make medicine. On such occasions a shaman often stood over the ill person chanting measured cadence to match the movements of his body as he sprinkled his patient with power water obtained from near the place where he had received his spirit power. If his ministration seemed to fail, he called in another medicine man.

A second medicine man was in attendance in Moses' lodge on November 8, when Patrick McKenzie, an old squawman and agency interpreter, approached the camp, carrying a dispatch for the Chief from Indian Inspector R. S. Gardner, who was on a mission from the Indian Office to get detailed information on his situation. The Chief received McKenzie, and heard him read and interpret the message asking him to meet with Gardner in Spokane Falls November 14 or 15, or such other time as suited him, to discuss his reservation affairs. Moses told McKenzie he was sorry, but he could not come because of the illness in his family. McKenzie saw the sick, so ill that he thought they would die.[10]

Moses' failure to meet Gardner forced that official to seek information from other sources, including McKenzie, Simms, Lieutenant Symons, and Sherwood. He also received a communication from a member-elect of the legislature from the county in which the mines were located, insisting that the region be opened to citizens.[11] In his report the inspector recommended that Moses be given an area on the Colville Reservation bounded on the

[10] Gardner to Secretary of the Interior, November 29, 1882 (Moses Reservation); Exhibit A of Gardner's Report, "Affidavit of Patrick Mackenzie," November 15, 1882 (Moses Reservation).

[11] Joseph Stitzel to Gardner, November 9, 1882; Gardner's Report, Exhibit A, "Affidavit of Patrick MacKenzie," November 15, 1882; Exhibit B, "Affidavit of S. F. Sherwood," November 6, 1882; Exhibit C, "Affidavit of Statement of Lieut. Thomas W. Symons," November 14, 1882; Exhibit D, "Proposed Location for Moses and his People"; Exhibit E, "Map of the Colville and Columbia Reservations"; Exhibit E, "Map of the Department of the Columbia." Moses Reservation.

south by the Columbia, on the east by the San Poil River, on the north by a line extending west from the source of the San Poil to Bonaparte Creek and along that creek to the Okanogan, and on the west by that stream. He also recommended allotments to adult males, a cash payment and an eight-year annuity to the tribe, and wagons, horses, and tools to assist them in farming.[12]

Moses' wife and brother died. The daughter survived on tea made from sage-hen droppings and, when she was able to take a little nourishment, on salmon skin chewed for its oils. When her sensitive stomach was able to tolerate solid food, her father moved all the lodges to the Nespelem Valley for the winter.[13]

Meanwhile trouble was developing between some of his lessees. Granger moved his family to the Utz ranch and departed in late October for Sprague. On November 10 while he was still away, two whisky peddlers and part-time cattlemen, who claimed Granger had taken a hay meadow they had rented from Moses, approached his cabin and ordered his wife to leave. She refused, whereupon the ruffians forced their way in and built a fire on the floor. The plucky woman grabbed a shotgun from the wall and chased them from the premises. On returning home, the angered Granger fired complaints to Lieutenant Abercrombie at Fort Coeur d'Alene and demanded military protection. Not to be outdone, one of the intruders, in January, addressed his complaints to Colonel Merriam at Fort Spokane.[14] (The post had received the new name the previous February.) The Coeur d'Alene commandant also referred Granger's letter to Merriam. Merriam did not take kindly to refereeing fights between Moses' lessees. He characterized the incident as a quarrel between frontier rogues, who, if allowed enough rope, would hang each other and save someone else the trouble. The military, however, saw no reason to prohibit Moses from leasing, although General J. M. Schofield in San Francisco expressed the hope that the Indian

---

12 Gardner to Secretary of the Interior, November 29, 1882. Moses Reservation.

13 George Nanamkin Interview, Nespelem, Washington, November 25, 1962.

14 Granger to Abercrombie, December 7, 1882; Gillett to Merriam, January 14, 1883. Moses Reservation.

would be taught to utilize the pasture for cattle rather than to expend the income for whisky.[15]

It appeared the Indians would shortly have no land to lease. The miners and their attorneys were actively lobbying at the national capital that winter, and their interests were strongly backed by Delegate Brents. The recommendations of General Miles and Inspector Gardner had reached official desks. They could expect a sympathetic hearing from Henry M. Teller, the new secretary of the interior, who hailed from Colorado and had the miners' point of view.[16]

On February 14, Teller directed Commissioner Price to draft an executive order to restore to the public domain a ribbon of land not less than fifteen miles wide across the northern end of Moses' reservation to include all the mineral lands. The order was issued February 23, 1883.[17]

No one in official circles notified the Indians of this action. White settlers told Moses the news. Other whites told Sarsopkin's people that the reservation was to be carved up into pieces. This caused them to react like a rattlesnake poked with a stick. Miles feared that the rattlesnake would coil for a strike.

The newspapers generally rejoiced at the news with glowing reports of the withdrawn strip and urged people to visit it to see for themselves. Greedy, taunting miners began running over the Indians' property and damaging their belongings.[18] Moses hurried off to Fort Spokane with a letter from Streamer asking the military for an explanation. Merriam advised him that he had no official information. It must have saddened the Chief to learn that there was yet no word from his friends, the military, of the

15 Fourth endorsement of Enclosure, Merriam to Major General J. M. Schofield, Military Division of the Pacific, January 13, 1883; Schofield to Secretary of War, February 21, 1883. Moses Reservation.

16 E. T. Young to Henry M. Teller, December 8, 1882; Vance to Secretary of the Interior, January 8 and February 8, 1883. Moses Reservation.

17 Teller to the Commissioner, February 14, 1883 (Moses Reservation); Secretary of the Interior, *Annual Report*, 1883 (48 Cong., 1 sess., *House Exec. Doc. No. 1, Pt. 5*), II, 224–25; Kappler, *Indian Affairs: Laws and Treaties*, I, 904–5.

18 *Oregonian*, April 9, 1883, p. 2.

land-grabbing by the overbearing whites. The post commander asked Moses if he would like him to ask General Miles.

The Chief's reply came in a torrent of words:

> A few years ago I had trouble in my heart. I carried a gun everywhere and expected sometime to die in battle. I saw General Howard. He asked me to be friendly and sent me to Washington to see the great Chief, President Hayes. He was kind to me and marked out a reservation for me and my people. He promised that it should be permanent. It made me very happy. I trusted the government. I put away my gun. I made up my heart to live in peace, and to die a natural death. I have been told by Indians and white men that the government was only trifling with me and would take away my land again. I would not listen to such talk, and I have been laughed at. The common Indian and the common white man amount to very little and their talk has disturbed me. The soldiers and the commanders amount to more; but the great chief at Washington is a mighty chief, and he speaks. His word is law. I will wait now until I know what he says.

Merriam reported to Miles, and Miles wired for Moses to come down to Vancouver for an interview. The *Northwest Tribune* of Cheney sarcastically observed that the stately and dignified "murderer," Chief Moses, accompanied by Colonel Merriam, traveled to Vancouver in a military ambulance.[19] Captain William Miles, left in charge at Fort Spokane, replied to Streamer that Moses had gone to Vancouver and asked him to tell Indians and whites in the Okanogan that no official information had come relative to opening the land to the whites.[20]

When Moses met Miles at Vancouver Barracks, his uneasiness and anxiety were apparent. Vancouver's mayor, Dr. Randolph Smith, interpreted until John McBean could come down from Simcoe to serve. Moses was particularly interested in one topic of their conversations—how much compensation the government would give him for the strip from his land. Miles said he thought ten thousand dollars would be sufficient should the Great

[19] April 13, 1883.
[20] Miles to Streamer, March 31, 1883. Streamer, Miscellaneous Notebooks, Folder No. 3.

Father pay him so much. Moses had no idea of the value of this amount of money until Miles told him it would buy a thousand ponies. This satisfied him.[21]

Miles must have wondered how long it would be before the whites wanted the next parcel of Moses' land. He was certain his previous suggestion was sound—that all of the Moses Reservation be purchased from its chief to keep the white man from chewing it to pieces. Moses could live on the Colville, where he spent much of his time anyway. Miles knew how injudicious and arbitrary it was to take away a part of the reservation, an action which, as he put it, "might result in war." To prevent such an eventuality, he ordered two infantry companies under Captain Boyle toward the trouble spot.[22] Preparing for a trip to Washington, D. C., he promised Moses to do what he could for him and his people to renew their faith in the government and the people who made the laws. He undoubtedly had some conversation with Moses about whether the Chief would travel east to confer with the Great White Father if authority were granted, for the next day, Thursday, April 4, he telegraphed the War Department, requesting the trip.[23] The department sent the request, with a favorable recommendation, to the Secretary of the Interior on April 7.

Moses must have been especially concerned over the abuses his people were suffering from the crowding whites. The *Oregonian* was sympathetic, editorializing that the action taken by the government was shaking Moses' authority with his people and that it was his faith which prevented an outbreak.[24] The Walla Walla *Union* stated that the miners wanted the mineral land taken from Moses' Reservation because they feared the Chief, who had murdered some miners in 1858 and 1859.[25]

21 *Oregonian*, April 9, 1883, p. 3.

22 Schofield to Adjutant General, April 2, 1883; Robert Lincoln, Secretary of War, to Secretary of the Interior, April 4, 1883. Moses Reservation.

23 An endorsement by Schofield recommended that Miles' request to send Moses to Washington be favorably considered. Schofield to Adjutant General, April 5, 1883. Selected Documents Relating to Chief Moses, NA, RG 94, 1879–83.

24 *Oregonian*, April 6, 1883, p. 2, and April 9, 1883, p. 2.

25 *Walla Walla Union* (Walla Walla, Washington Territory), May 12, 1883, p. 4.

In his stateroom aboard an outbound steamer ready to embark for the capital, Miles was interviewed by reporters. They asked if his trip east had anything to do with Moses.

"What are the feelings of Moses and followers to President Arthur throwing open part of the reservation?" they inquired.

Miles answered, "His followers are sorry. Moses has enemies who will use this to break down his authority."

"Will this cause war?"

"No," said Miles. He explained that Moses would be satisfied with payment for the land.

"Have you made provision to check an outbreak should one occur?" he was asked.

"Yes, two companies have been sent toward the reservation, and will move if needed."

"What action should the government take?"

"I shouldn't express my views."

"What will Moses do?"

"He will probably start home Tuesday morning."

"What if Moses can't restrain his people?"

"They number only three hundred in all," answered Miles.

"How long will you be gone?"

"About six weeks, I think," Miles told them.[26]

Back in the Indian country Sarsopkin's people, having taken all the abuse they could, called a big meeting at Toats Coulee. Still angry with Moses, they sent him no invitation. They called on the British Columbia Indians to join them, and some were present. At the meeting they bitterly condemned Lieutenant Abercrombie (recently in that area if not still there),[27] whom they believed responsible for their plight since it was he who had counted their families. Streamer was present and incited the Indians in his usual way to stand up for their rights and keep their lands.

When Streamer learned that Moses had returned from Van-

<hr>

26 *Oregonian*, April 9, 1883, p. 3.

27 Captain William Miles in his letter to Streamer, March 31, 1883, enclosed a letter for Lieutenant Abercrombie. Streamer wrote in his diary that the letter for Abercrombie was delivered to him (Streamer). Streamer, Miscellaneous Notebooks, Folder No. 3, p. 203.

couver, he moved the assembled Indians across the Okanogan River to a big medicine council with the returned Chief.[28] Word of this meeting reached the settlers a short distance south in the Big Bend, Moses' old home, now dotted with white farms. (By summer, sixty-seven whites, including children, would occupy the area near Moses' old summer camp on Badger Mountain.) The news sent them streaking eastward to the nearest white community, Sprague, in fear of immediate attack. Jumpy whites thought two Indian "squaws" going to Fort Spokane were an advance guard of Moses' people preparing to scalp them.[29]

Meanwhile, the Indian Office, fed up with the Moses situation, refused the War Department's request that he be brought to Washington because he had been given a chance to tell his story, but had not even shown up to confer with Inspector Gardner.[30] No allowance was ever made for the fact that three members of Moses' family were lying at the point of death when he "refused" to meet Gardner. The War Department replied that unless something was done to relieve the strained situation, hostilities would break out; but Secretary Teller thought only of suggesting that the War Department take necessary measures to protect settlers and their property, and—if necessary to preserve the peace—arrest Moses and hold him in captivity until he should submit.[31]

General Miles impressed the War Department with the importance of placating the Indians, and through his insistence the Moses problem was carried as far as the President's cabinet for discussion. Finally, on May 1, Teller consented to see Moses if the War Department would pay the expense of the trip and if—besides an interpreter—two other chiefs were brought along, thus dividing Moses' authority.[32]

The Walla Walla *Statesman*, hoping for peace in the north for

28 *Yakima Weekly Record* (Yakima City, Washington Territory), May 12, 1883, p. 3.
29 *Northwest Tribune*, May 19, 1883.
30 Price to Secretary of the Interior, April 14, 1883; Teller to Secretary of War, April 16, 1883. Selected Documents Relating to Chief Moses, NA, RG 94, 1879–83.
31 Teller to Secretary of War, April 19, 1883. Moses Reservation.
32 Teller to Secretary of War, May 1, 1883. Moses Reservation.

the many settlers poised to go there, approved the decision: "Moses seems to have the best of the controversy thus far," it editorialized. Several weeks earlier that paper had blistered Delegate Brents for saying that part of Moses' Reservation should be opened because with only four hundred individuals in his band there was "so much wealth here and so few Indians to utilize it." In fairness to Brents, it should be said that he had expressed surprise that the action was taken without Moses' knowledge.[33]

Some of Sarsopkin's people came to Fort Spokane to complain that their farms in the mining district were being overrun by aggressive whites. Colonel Merriam assured them that they would be protected. The two infantry companies Miles had promised Moses were sent from Vancouver Barracks under Captain Boyle and placed under Merriam's command. With two hundred rounds of ammunition per man and rations for twenty days, they were ordered to make camp near the mouth of Foster Creek, across from the reservation near the lower Okanogan Valley. With this security from the military, Sarsopkin's Indians were again ready to accept the white influx as so many new customers for their produce. If Moses' people would only go to work, they reasoned, they too could have more peace.

To investigate the situation, Captain Frank D. Baldwin, acting judge advocate for the Department of the Columbia, was sent to the Okanogan. Both Tonasket and Sarsopkin asked him, "Why does the government place over us, who make our living by farming, a man who never works, but gambles, drinks and races horses with the money he collected from the white men who graze cattle on our reservation? We want a chief who works, and sets a good example for our young men."[34] Baldwin reported that excitement on the Moses' Reservation was abating and that the whites and Indians in the vicinity were in accord. "All the Indians laugh at Moses' pretentions," he wrote.[35]

The Okanogans were all the more disturbed when they learned

33 *Walla Walla Statesman*, May 12, 1883, p. 2, and April 14, 1883, p. 3.
34 Miles, *Personal Recollections*, 406.
35 Baldwin to Assistant Adjutant General, Vancouver Barracks, May 11, 1883. Moses Reservation.

that Moses was going to Washington. Skolaskin was jealous too; no one had invited *him* to Washington to ask if the intruder Moses and his people could live in the San Poil country.

After his trip north, Baldwin recommended that the military pick Sarsopkin and Tonasket to go east with Moses; in the light of their differences with him, he believed they should also be represented. Wheaton, left in charge of the Department of the Columbia, wired Washington, D. C., for permission to send the two chiefs.[36] The next day a wire from the War Department advised that Moses be permitted to select the Indians to accompany him, but, the following day, the department wired authorization for Tonasket and Sarsopkin to be in the delegation.[37] To even the score, Moses chose Lot of the Spokanes to go with him. At a prejourney powwow Moses met other chiefs on the Kettle River for a strictly Indian council to talk over the trip to the Great Father. Possible evidence of Moses' waning influence over other tribes was the fact that the location of the meeting was not on his home ground, but on Tonasket and Oropaughn's. Both these northern chiefs attended. Sarsopkin also attended. Skolaskin, resenting any real estate transaction involving San Poil land, avoided the council. Tonasket opened the conference, although Moses shortly assumed leadership. The real grievance, probably aired more in the stuffiness of close private sessions and brought out cautiously in open council, was the proposal that they permit Moses to live on the Colville Reservation. Any prior agreement and understanding on this matter might help them in Washington. Tonasket was ready to consent, provided Moses would use the proceeds from the "sale" of the fifteen-mile strip for the benefit of all Indians, to build a school, a gristmill, and a sawmill on the Colville. Sarsopkin said he preferred living where he was, with the Okanogan River between him and Moses.

Comments made aside from the meeting were that Moses

36 Wheaton to Adjutant General, May 16, 1883. Selected Documents Relating to Chief Moses, NA, RG 94, 1879–83.

37 Chauncy McKeever to Commanding Officer, Department of the Columbia, May 17, 1883; Drum to Commanding Officer, Department of the Columbia, May 18, 1883. Selected Documents Relating to Chief Moses, NA, RG 94, 1879–83.

wanted the money from the sale of the land for gambling and whisky-drinking, that he made himself conspicuous with the whites whom he bluffed and deceived, that he was an actor.[38] They would have agreed with one Indian—a known Cheney street loafer—when he said, Moses gets broke, makes a fuss, gets taken to Washington, is supplied with the best in land and money, and returns home and repeats the same all over.[39]

Although Moses' popularity sagged among his own race, his stock among sympathetic whites had never been higher. The Blands referred to him in the *Council Fire and Arbitrator* as one of the "most talented and influential Indians on the Continent," and challenged Teller to disclose what persons were behind the land-grabbing on his reservation. Commissioner Price replied with a lengthy justification, which appeared in the June issue, but it probably did not convince friends of the Indians.[40] Members of the clergy attempted to influence the government officials in behalf of Moses and his Indians, who were "draining the cup of disappointment to the dregs."[41]

Meanwhile, on June 12, the Washington-bound party assembled at Fort Spokane for the journey. Besides the chiefs and Baldwin, who was in charge,[42] the party included two interpreters, S. F. Sherwood, employed by the government, and George Herring, of Curlew Lake, the Indians' choice. General Miles, now back at Vancouver, wired his department of their departure and urged that the Indians be paid $150,000 for relinquishing their reservation and be induced to take lands in severalty on the Colville. The impressed War Department passed the message on to Secretary Teller.[43]

---

38 Helen Toulou Interview, Kewa, Washington, August 9, 1961.

39 *Northwest Tribune,* June 15, 1883.

40 T. A. Bland and M. C. Bland (eds.), *Council Fire and Arbitrator,* May, 1883, p. 66, and June, 1883, pp. 87–88.

41 Rev. A. L. Lindsley to Rev. John C. Lowrie, May 18, 1883; Lowrie to Price, June 1, 1883. Moses Reservation.

42 Special Order 76, June 6, 1883. Selected Documents Relating to Chief Moses, NA, RG 94, 1879–83.

43 Miles to Adjutant General, Washington, D. C., June 15, 1883. Selected Documents Relating to Chief Moses, NA, RG 94, 1879–83.

Courtesy of Sadie Moses Williams

Chief Lot of the Spokanes, a member of the 1883
Washington, D. C., delegation. ·

Courtesy of William Compton Brown

Skolaskin, self-appointed leader of the San Poil Indians, refused to sign treaties with the government or accept its gifts.

This time there was no roundabout travel by way of San Francisco. Except for one short gap, the Northern Pacific now spanned the continent. The party boarded the train at Spokane Falls, once the camping grounds for Chief Garry and his people, but now swarming with railroad construction crews and prospective city-builders eager to develop the location as an important railroad center. They rode to the end of the line near Missoula, Montana. (Track crews building east would reach Missoula on June 23.) Then they traveled by stage to Helena, which the westbound crews had reached on June 12. This part of the journey must have evoked many memories in Moses as, with an Indian's capacity for total recall of physical features, he recognized the landmarks of his youthful journeys—the pass with the travois winding through, the sheltered camp in the deep valley, and the sites of hunts and battles. He was especially impressed by the stage ride; in his later years he would tell his family many stories about it, even of a robbery that took place on this or the return trip.[44]

The party reached Helena on June 17 and boarded the train for St. Paul, where they arrived two days later. There they changed to the Chicago, Milwaukee, and St. Paul Railroad.[45] They arrived at Washington on Friday, June 22.

In the big city Moses must have displayed an air of confidence before his wonderstruck fellows. He had been there before. He was also familiar with the Tremont House, where the delegation was accommodated. Most Indian delegations to Washington stayed there, for the proprietor, E. W. Denison, catered to their peculiar tastes in diet and special comforts and provided board and room for them at $2.50 a day.[46]

Captain Baldwin reported at once to the War Department, and then to the Interior. The latter furnished enough cash ($40.00 for each) to purchase suits of clothing for the travel-worn

[44] *See below,* p. 341.

[45] *Pioneer Press* (St. Paul and Minneapolis), June 20, 1883, p. 7.

[46] Denison to Secretary of War, June 18, 1883; McKeever to Baldwin, June 18, 1883; McKeever to Denison, June 19, 1883. Selected Documents Relating to Chief Moses, NA, RG 94, 1879-83.

and shabby Indians, but refused payment for other expenses, or even to see them.[47] This latter refusal continued through all of the following week. When the Commissioner was informed that Moses had succumbed to the bottled spirits of the capital city, he quickly pointed out that the delegation was the War Department's responsibility, not the Interior's.[48]

There were some persons who wished to see Moses before he left the city. To air the controversy for the readers of *Council Fire and Arbitrator*, the Blands arranged an interview with him to get his side of the fifteen-mile land grab. What should have been a pleasant visit turned into a disappointment when the Blands detected that the interpreter had been drinking.[49]

Fearing that the questions and answers were not being properly conveyed, they asked the interpreter if he knew Moses well.

"Oh, yes, I've known him for many years."

"What is your opinion of his character?" asked one of them.

"Well, he is a mighty smart Ingin."

"Is he truthful and honorable?"

"Oh, yes, he's as square as a brick. I'd take his word as quick as I would any white man's."

"Do you think he has been badly treated?!

"Yes, he's been treated scandalous, both by the settlers and the Government."

Spying an old army acquaintance wandering into the Tremont, the interpreter broke away to converse with him. The Blands pricked up their ears when he began discussing Moses. They could not help overhearing his representations of Moses as a "drunken, dissolute vagabond, a notorious liar, an inveterate gambler. . . . Moses has no following to speak of, and what ingins he has with him are a set of worthless renegades and thieves. It was ridiculous to let him hold all that land and keep settlers out of the country."

47 *Evening Star*, June 23, 1883, p. 5, and June 25, 1883, p. 1.
48 *Washington Post*, June 28, 1883, p. 2.
49 From the account of the meeting given by the Blands, it is not possible to determine whether they had reference to Herring or Sherwood. There is ample evidence that Herring was given to drink.

The Blands slipped away thinking Moses was in the hands of the Philistines.[50]

By the time the second Monday of the delegation's visit rolled around, the Interior Department still would not consent to listen to Moses.[51] Offices were closed Wednesday, July 4, when the capital exploded with a lavish Independence Day celebration, the likes of which the Indians had never seen. The following day, the Interior Department personnel relented and agreed to meet the Indians in conference. Perhaps they had been stirred to do so by the spirit of freedom generated by the Fourth.

In the give and take of that conference (Friday) with Commissioner Price, most of the delegation cowered at the strangeness about them, leaving Moses as the undisputed leader. He spoke with authority, yet impressed the officials as being co-operative. (He was shrewd enough to know that he might as well appear co-operative; the government would get what it wanted anyway.) Tonasket impressed the officials as a complainer, abrupt, and lacking in diplomacy, particularly when he said that Agent Simms was ignorant of Indian needs since the agency was too far from his (Tonasket's) people. The officials found Sarsopkin's manner unpleasant, a match for his oval, unhandsome face. It was Moses' sense of humor and drama which a number of times saved the conference.[52] The Interior officials proposed that the Indians cede the entire Columbia Reservation and that they live on the Colville. In return the department would furnish certain items to Moses and his people: to the band, a schoolhouse, a sawmill, and a gristmill; to each of the band, two cows; to each head of a family or adult male person, one wagon, one set of double harness, one grain cradle, one plow, one harrow, one scythe, one hoe, and such other agricultural implements as might be necessary; to Moses, one thousand dollars to be used in building himself a house, and an annual salary of six hundred dollars on condition that he and his people keep the agreement faithfully. Tonasket

50 T. A. Bland and M. C. Bland (eds.), *Council Fire and Arbitrator*, July, 1883, pp. 104–105.

51 *Washington Post*, July 3, 1883.

52 Helen Toulou Interview, Kewa, Washington, August 9, 1961.

and his people would be furnished a sawmill, a gristmill, a boarding school, and a physician. Sarsopkin and his people were given the choice of remaining on the Columbia Reservation, where they would be protected with the rights of settlers, or of removing to the Colville, in which case they would receive one hundred cattle for relinquishing all claims on the Columbia. Lot and his people on the Spokane Reservation would be provided with a church and a school.[53]

That afternoon as the session broke up, Sherwood handed the Indians their streetcar tickets. Moses waited in the corridor outside the conference room for Sherwood to appear; then he asked the government interpreter when he would get his first payment. Not until the agreement was ratified by Congress, Sherwood told him. Moses then confessed that for the first time he had been lost —embarrassed in the presence of the Secretary—and could not think of the many things that were required of him for his people. He asked the interpreter if he ever played poker. Only a little, was the answer.

"When you have a good hand you play it for what you think it is worth, do you not?" asked Moses.

"Yes," said Sherwood.

"Well," said Moses, "I had a good hand and I have not played it right. I have lost. Now you go back and tell the Secretary that if he will raise me $400.00 I will stop talking from now on and forever."[54]

The next morning, Secretary Teller met with the Indians for a final conference to settle details, after which the final draft of the agreement was to be drawn up, although it would not be signed until Monday, July 9.[55] Moses must have been elated to find he would be given an annuity of one thousand dollars— an amount approximating his yearly lease income, which he could no longer collect when his land was signed away. Perhaps

[53] First Report, "Result of Conference Held July 7, 1883, with Chief Moses and Other Indians of the Columbia and Colville Reservations." Moses Reservation.

[54] Sherwood, "The Cunning of Chief Moses," *The Washington Historian*, Vol. 1, No. 4, (July, 1900), 172–73.

[55] *Washington Post*, July 10, 1883, p. 2.

COLVILLE RESERVATION BY EXECUTIVE ORDER OF JULY 2, 1872

as a pacifier, Tonasket was to be "tipped" one hundred dollars
annually. No mention of Chief Lot or gifts for him was made,
possibly because his reservation was separate from the two involved. This final draft also provided that with Congressional
approval and appropriation, the government would secure to
Moses, his people, and all other Indians who went on the Colville
and engaged in farming, equal rights and protection with all
other Indians on that reservation, and necessary assistance to any
Indian to carry out the terms of the agreement. Until Moses and
his people should locate permanently on the Colville, his status
would remain as it was, with policing over his people vested in
the military. All money and other articles to be furnished them
would be sent to some point in their locality for distribution.

209

Because some of Sarsopkin's people cultivated land within the fifteen-mile strip, they would be allowed to keep it and to select enough unoccupied land in severalty to provide each head of a family or male adult with one square mile of land; and they would be furnished necessary farm implements. Sarsopkin himself was to get four square miles (2,560 acres) of unoccupied land in severalty on the Columbia Reservation.

All other Indians then living on the Columbia Reservation were to be entitled to one square mile (640 acres) for each head of a family or male adult, and the possession and ownership of this land would be guaranteed and protected; and each would be provided with necessary farming implements if they should move onto the Colville Reservation within two years and surrender all rights to the Columbia.

The council convened Monday to sign the final draft. Teller signed; then Price. Moses signed with his "X," followed by Tonasket and Sarsopkin with theirs. George Herring also made a mark. Sherwood and Captain Baldwin signed, and the conference ended.[56]

On the return trip the party changed at Cleveland, Ohio, from the train to a steamer bound for Duluth, Minnesota. The long journey on the Great Lakes confirmed for Moses what he had long suspected—that Washington, D. C., was on an island.[57] At Duluth they boarded the train again for the final lap of their trip, which included a ride through burning Idaho forests. From Spokane Falls Baldwin escorted them to Fort Spokane, where they stayed a day before starting for their homes.

After a reunion with his household, Moses proceeded to the military camp near the mouth of Foster Creek to report to the

[56] Secretary of the Interior, *Annual Report*, 1883 (48 Cong., 1 sess., *Sen. Exec. Doc. No. 1, Pt. 5*), II, pp. LXIX, LXX, and LXXI; Second Report, "Result of Conference Held July 7, 1883 with Chief Moses and Other Indians of the Columbia and Colville Reservations" (Moses Reservation); Kappler, *Indian Affairs: Laws and Treaties*, II, 1073–74.

[57] Henry Covington Interview, Colville Reservation, January 18, 1958. On July 27, General W. T. Sherman and his party boarded the train on which Moses was riding at Missoula, Montana Territory. Secretary of War, *Annual Report*, 1883–84, (48 Cong., 1 sess., *House Exec. Doc. No. 1*) I, 266.

Indians. If he had hoped to find an overflow crowd waiting for
him like the one at Wenatchee after his 1879 Washington trip, he
was disappointed. The presence of so few to hear him gave added
impact to the dramatic gesture related by Billy Curlew:

> Moses called his wise men and his chiefs and representatives
> from other tribes together. There were Umatillas and even those
> from Coast tribes, and told them the futility of resisting the
> white man. He made a pile of sand. [Curlew indicated by gesture,
> a foot-high mound.] He told one of his men to count the grains
> of sand in the mound. "There are too many," said the man.
> "That is the same way with the white man," said Moses. "There
> are too many!"[58]

While one of that race, Lieutenant George W. Goethals of the
Corps of Engineers, returned from a reconnaissance into the
Okanogan country and beyond, Moses went to his lodge.[59] Other
visitors were sure to come. He received a dispatch from Goethal's
topographical assistant, A. Downing, written September 18, requesting a council. Moses met Downing on the twentieth and was
pleasantly surprised to learn that the officer was examining the
falls of Bonaparte Creek and those of the Nespelem for likely
locations for mills.[60]

With so much excitement, Moses may have almost forgotten
that he would now be under the supervision of the Indian Office
and the local agent; but this blow was softened somewhat on
October 23 when Agent Simms was relieved of his duties and
replaced by Sidney Waters. Sarsopkin still feared that white encroachment would force his band from their homes, despite the
provision in the agreement that they could remain there. All too
quickly his fears proved to be true, as word of the cession stimu-
lated the aggressions of the intruders. These abuses drove the
unhappy Indians to greater vehemence than ever against Moses,
the "lying, thieving, drunken murderer" who had bartered away

[58] Steele, *Illustrated History of the Big Bend,* 528–29; and Billy Curlew Interview, Ephrata, Washington, October 7, 1956.
[59] *Army and Navy Journal,* Vol. XXI, August 18, 1883, p. 47.
[60] Miles, *Personal Recollections,* 406–10.

their rights, like so many ponies, while grabbing the Great Father's best gifts for himself.[61]

Meanwhile, Congress delayed action on ratifying the agreement. In December, General Miles, fearing that the Indians might be driven to violence, became so concerned that he would have sent Baldwin to the capital to jog the legislators, but he was overruled by his superiors. Baldwin was so disturbed that he wrote directly to Montana Territorial Delegate Martin Maginnis urging the need of ratification and stating that he would be "almost willing to go at my own expense" to work for it.[62] Moses went from time to time to the military to inquire about it, but the answer was always the same—"No action yet." On March 13, 1884, he had a talk at Fort Spokane with the new agent, Waters, who told him the Senate Committee on Indian Affairs had reported favorably. This pleased him and gave him faith that the government would at last give him and his people a permanent home so they could quit the wandering life and settle down to farming. He had kept telling them that in the end the government would keep its promises, but many did not believe him and repeatedly taunted him for giving up their land and homes. Moses felt these taunts and reproaches deeply.

The next day the agent, reporting to the Office of Indian Affairs, expressed great sympathy for Moses. "He today is a very poor man, while once he was rich and powerful," wrote Waters, who "earnestly" hoped that the agreement would be kept so that "at last this Chief and his people [can] find a resting place and a home. ... He has kept his people from committing acts of violence thus far, but will they listen to him if this agreement is not ratified? I fear not; From recent acts of his I know that he is very friendly to the whites." The agent closed his letter with a strong recommendation not to delay the ratification.[63]

One year after it was drawn up, the Moses Agreement was

[61] George W. France in his *The Struggles For Life and Home in the North-West,* 175–77, implied that the ouster of Moses from his reservation was a Masonic plot.
[62] Miles to Assistant Adjutant General, Division of the Pacific, December 3, 1883; Baldwin to the Honorable Martin Maginnis, December 10, 1883. Moses Reservation.
[63] Waters to Price, March 14, 1884. Moses Reservation.

finally approved, July 4, 1884.[64] Moses might have celebrated the occasion in glorious fashion—the way he had seen the white man celebrate the day in the capital the year before. To be sure, he knew how to "celebrate," but lacked the means—specifically, his thousand-dollar annuity. Tracking down this money and wrestling with other problems in his new home would soon involve him in fireworks more explosive than those of any Fourth.

[64] Secretary of the Interior, *Annual Report*, 1884 (48 Cong., 2 sess., *House Exec. Doc. No. 1, Pt. 5*), II, 42 and 262; Kappler, *Indian Affairs: Laws and Treaties*, I, 224.

XII. Farmers in the Dell

"We must follow the way of the white man or perish
like bunch grass before the plow."
—Moses to Governor John McGraw, Yakima City, Autumn, 1896

WITH THE INDEPENDENCE DAY RATIFICATION of the Moses Agreement, that chief officially yielded his independence to the Office of Indian Affairs. A paper change, however, did not alter his attitude; his faith was still in the military. Frequently he visited Colonel Merriam at Fort Spokane to air his grievances and to ask for his thousand-dollar annuity, only to be told that the Council of White Chiefs, the Congress, had not appropriated the funds. How strange these white men! They were in such a hurry to take his land; now they were in no hurry to pay him for it.

On one of his trips to the post, Moses learned that Special Indian Agent Major Charles H. Dickson, in the West to implement the Moses Agreement, would meet the chiefs at Spokane Falls. Moses hurried there in hopes Dickson would have news of the annuity. Agent Waters and Captain Baldwin were there, as were Tonasket and other chiefs. The Indians appeared independent; they spoke their minds well. Moses could see that his dream of chieftaincy over the tribes would be hard to achieve. Their independence also worried government officials, whose policy had generally been to lump tribes together under one head to manage them more easily.

Getting no satisfaction from Dickson about his annuity, Moses turned to needling Agent Waters for it. Under this pressure, the agent wired the Commissioner on October 17 to forward the money, but to hold back the thousand dollars intended for construction of the Chief's house for fear he would spend it on other things. Soon perceiving that Moses and his people were going to occupy the greatest share of his time, he wrote, on December 3, requesting the removal of agency headquarters from its peripheral location at Chewelah[1] to a spot nearer Moses' camps. He also requested a doctor and other services for Moses' people.[2]

Moses rode home believing his annuity a will-o'-the-wisp. Then he learned that it had been sent to the post—a pre-Christmas gift for him. Summoning his subchiefs, he rode there to receive his prize from Colonel Merriam. Waters happened to be absent in Washington, D. C., and this circumstance gave the Chief the impression that the military had gotten him the money. Clutching the coveted check, he and his subchief bodyguards rode below the post to have Ed O'Shea cash it at post trader James Monoghan's store. Posting his men outside to look for robbers, he burst into the building.

Moses ordered gold. No paper money. O'Shea handed over a stack of twenty-dollar gold pieces, but retained five of them for his services.[3] Moses grabbed up his gold, burst out the door, and jumped into his saddle with a command to his men to ride west. He felt safer with his bodyguard, the way the army paymaster felt escorted by the military guard as he carried the payroll to Fort Spokane. Between the post and Nespelem, he picked up two relays of horses he had thoughtfully placed there to speed him home.[4] His motives in safeguarding his gold were not altogether selfish; he needed it to purchase winter supplies for his people camped on the Nespelem at the lower end of the Valley meadows.

In the Valley the women had recently taken down the one canvas tipi (*spaqanot*) and the buffalo-hide tipis (*cepeesqt*), and the families were assembling in the long, many-hearthed, tule-mat winter houses (*skowwast*) to live out the cold months.

Moses' lodge bulged with his own family; he called them his

1 The Lower Spokanes on the Spokane Reservation, the Coeur d'Alenes on the Coeur d'Alene Reservation, the Pend Oreilles, and Kalispells were under the jurisdiction of the Colville Agency. The Upper, and certain bands of the Middle Spokanes were under no agency supervision.
2 Waters to Hal Price, December 3, 1884. Colville Agency Records, Letterbox 3.
3 Merriam to Charles H. Dickson, December 15, 1884 (Colville Agency Records, Letterbox 3a); Streamer to General Howard, January 15, 1894 (Streamer, Miscellaneous Notebooks, Folder No. 3, p. 37).
4 *Spokesman-Review* (Spokane, Washington), October 17, 1906

"children." There were his sister, Shimtil, and her sons, Sam and Yayoskin; another sister and her man, Skquichu; and Moses' brothers, Quintolah and Puckheim. Also sharing his lodge were two youngsters who had been orphaned in childhood—Killsmoolah and Kulalikiyu. Kulalikiyu's dead mother's cousin, Nahanoomed, preferred to live in Moses' house with her daughter, Kist, than with her Wanapum people. Also in the crowded winter lodge were Sokula and his son, who later married Kist; and a niece of Moses', Quanspeetsah, whose son, Weashuit (Peter Dan), lived in the creekside lodge of his Nespelem wife in the hills above Komellakaka. Moses' two brothers, Louie (Paneksteesah) and Kweecha (sometimes called Croissant or Crasam, the French fur traders' name for his father, Sulktalthscosum), lived on the meadows by the Little Nespelem. Louie lived with his wife, Quemat, and a one-year-old daughter, Kekimetsa (Madeline); his full-grown son, Joe, lived in a lodge nearby.[5]

Snow covered the Valley most of the winter. Between the lodges and particularly around Moses', it lay packed from use. Smoke lifting from the narrow slit at his lodge top signaled a welcome to come inside, where roots and meats hung from poles and the smell of smoke and grease lay heavy. Scattered about were piles of store-bought provisions, which might have been larger had not the master reserved a portion of the annuity for his own pleasure. The winter seemed shorter when he drank and gambled.

But the Great Father was not sleeping like a bear, forgetting his children. That fall Special Agent Dickson had wrestled with plans for buildings for Moses' and Tonasket's people. These included a boarding school for Tonasket to be located in the Okanogan and a day school for Moses. Then on February 14, 1885, Dickson contracted with Messers. Davis and Todd to build a flour mill and sawmill four miles south of Moses' camp and two miles north of the confluence of the Little Nespelem and the Nespelem. It would be run by water sluiced through a nine-

5 Nellie Moses Friedlander Interview, Palisades, Washington, June 2, 1957; George Nanamkin Interview, Nespelem, Washington, November 25, 1962, Madeline (Mrs. Robert) Covington Interview, Nespelem, Washington, November 25, 1961; Peter Dan Moses Interview, Soap Lake, Washington, July 30, 1961.

hundred-foot ditch leading from a dam on the Nespelem. A "shack" was also being planned to house the sawyer and miller.

The mill could not be built too soon to suit Moses. Skolaskin hoped it would never be built. He complained to the military at Fort Spokane and to his own people that Moses on the Nespelem and Moses' Umatilla friends (perhaps the forty who'd gone to Moses in 1880) at Twenty-One Mile Creek on the upper San Poil were thieves who had come to take his land. And the government had not even invited him to Washington to ask his consent! So he went around inciting his people to block the construction of the "soil contaminating" buildings for the intruder, Moses.[6]

Five days before Davis and Todd signed their contract, Skolaskin rode to the fort to talk with Merriam. He swung from his horse and with hands on knees waddled into headquarters. There he berated his Columbia rival with all the traditional bitterness of prophets and dreamers toward hereditary chieftains, and protested the building of the mills for Moses and Tonasket. Merriam thought him jealous. It was likely the stunted Indian wanted nothing built so permanent it would mean the intruding Indians were there to stay.[7] Merriam then wrote a note to Agent Waters in Chewelah suggesting that by spring-thaw time, or earlier if possible, the agent should meet with the various chiefs.

With the approach of spring, Moses turned his attention to the wagons, cattle, and other promised gifts that were to be delivered at the Columbia for his people. Finally he was notified of their arrival at Spokane Falls. The horses were easily rounded up to go after them, more easily in fact than were the dissident members of his camp. In stormy councils these irreconcilables talked of boycotting the contemptible gifts. Had they been infected with Skolaskin's teachings?

With as many as would follow him, Moses rode to the river and set up camp at Sixteens. There they waited. On the evening of April 15, Major Dickson, Captain Baldwin, and Acting Assistant

---

[6] A. Bupshaw to Benjamin Moore, February 18, 1886. Colville Agency Records, Letterbox 4; and *Walla Walla Statesman*, March 13, 1880.

[7] Merriam to Waters, February 9, 1885. Colville Agency Records, Letterbox 19.

Surgeon C. N. Merriam (not Colonel Merriam) came to the Columbia and made camp three miles from the mouth of the Nespelem River. (They had made a circuitous journey from Fort Spokane over the Silver Creek Trail to the Nespelem avoiding the Fort Trail past the camps—and possibly angry demonstrations—of the San Poils.) Moses rode the nearly six miles to visit the government party. The meeting was harmonious, with arrangements made for receiving the wagons and other items not yet arrived at the river.

The next day, the three government emissaries continued to the Okanogan through a four-inch blanket of sudden spring snow, which began falling at Omak Lake. At Bonaparte Creek they met Sarsopkin who had come in from Toats Coulee. Sarsopkin was heartsick at white men's threats of what would happen to him and his people if they remained to take up allotments on the old Moses Reservation instead of going over to the Colville. To lessen their anxieties, Major Dickson agreed to meet with those Indians wanting to stay where they were. The government party returned to Omak Lake with Sarsopkin to assure an assembled delegation of his people, the Chelans, and the Methows, camped at that place, that they could remain on their old homesites, which would soon be staked off and protected from unscrupulous whites. Dickson promised to return in five weeks with a surveyor to fulfill these promises. The plan of bringing a surveyor did not set well with one participant at the council—Innomoseecha Jim, who maintained that the lands of his Chelans should never be surveyed and allotted.

Moses went to see these officials when they returned to their camp near the mouth of the Nespelem. When Baldwin asked for an accounting of his people preparatory to the forthcoming issue, Moses replied that he had 109 women and children and 34 men in camp, exclusive of "nonconformists" and others preparing for a trip to the root grounds. Baldwin was skeptical of the count.[8] This bothered Moses but little; he was more concerned with the

[8] Baldwin to Adjutant General, Department of the Columbia, May 1, 1885. Moses Reservation.

dissension Skolaskin was causing among his people by urging them not to accept the agricultural implements, not to take up land, and not to build a mill and a schoolhouse. The San Poil chief threatened to destroy their improvements if they should build houses and cultivate the land. Baldwin had received the same information from others; thus, he concluded that the frequent appearance of troops in the neighborhood would be a good means of preventing trouble.

Skolaskin was not the only interference to Moses' people. Complaints were made of white men moving on the reservation. Bringing others' stock on to graze (undoubtedly for a tidy sum) was only one of the many means they used. Squawman Len Armstrong was one who made a slick entry in April with 150 horses belonging to another white man; his claim was based on the fact that his wife was a Nespelem woman, thereby giving him the right to live there.

The government party returned to Fort Spokane. Moses went to the Valley to wait for the wagons. When they did not arrive, he hurried over to the post. He had not been there long when Agent Waters rode in with reassurance extracted from the Dreamer that he would not obstruct the erection of mills and schools in the Nespelem and Okanogan Valleys. Under threat of punishment, the Lame Chief had agreed to desist from riding over the southern part of the reservation and stirring up the Indians. He had asked Waters to inform Washington that if he had been consulted before the Moses Indians had been located on San Poil land, it would have been all right with him. Moses had sold the Columbia Reservation without consulting the Indians living thereon, Skolaskin told the agent, and had used the money to buy whisky and gamble; and he would be as ready to sell San Poil land for more money when the time came. Before leaving the post for the agency, Waters had the "pleasure" of closing up "Virginia Bill's" saloon.

Before Moses left the post, he expressed his satisfaction that the government was carrying out the agreement made with him and said that he and his people would always be friends of the whites.[9] He had just left when Innomoseecha, still disturbed that the Chelan country was to be staked off and divided, rode in to talk with Merriam, who tried to convince him of the advantages of taking land in severalty. As soon as the Chelan had left, some white men who had signed leases with Moses on his old reservation rode in to state that they wished to continue lease arrangements with the government.

In the meantime, construction of the buildings in the Nespelem and the Okanogan was getting under way more slowly than anticipated. This forced Waters to set back the hoped-for completion date to some time in November and to forfeit money allotted for employees to operate them. J. M. Jones, the contractor for furnishing equipment for the gristmill and sawmill, came on the reservation to make estimates and then left to make his purchases and ready them for freighting to the Nespelem. When the machinery reached the Columbia, dissidents from Moses' camps threatened to prevent the teamsters from ferrying it across to the reservation. The teamsters called their bluff, crossed the river, and wheeled their cargo up the steep hill from the river and on up the Valley to the millsite.[10] One could surmise that Skolaskin had plotted the "insurrection"—not alone to prevent the white man's gifts from reaching the reservation but to build up a coalition against Moses.

But Moses had the prospect of new allies. Joseph and his Nez Percés had spent six unhappy years in the Indian Territory, where many had died from the change in altitude and climate and from plain homesickness for their mountain land. Apparently unknown to the government officials, Joseph had managed to send three of his men—Otskai, Joe Albert, and one other—with a message to Moses, asking permission to live on the Colville. They would recognize Moses as chief; and in case Moses should die first,

9 Waters to Commissioner Atkins, April 16, 1885 (Colville Agency Records, Letterbox 3); Secretary of the Interior, *Annual Report*, 1885 (49 Cong., 1 sess., *House Exec. Doc. No. 1, Pt. 5*), II, 183.

10 *Spokane Evening Review* (Spokane Falls, Washington Territory), May 6, 1885, p. 1.

Joseph would succeed him. Moses sent back word that the exiles would be welcome.[11] At the same time so much had been written about the Nez Percés heroic war, their defeat, and their miserable plight in an alien land, and so much public sentiment had been aroused in their behalf, that, in 1885, the government decided to send them back to the Northwest.

Not everyone felt as happy as Moses about the prospect. Needless to say, Skolaskin was furious. First Moses, and now Joseph; it was like measles following the smallpox. The white frontiersmen were equally aroused. The *Evening Review* of Spokane Falls—subscribing to the creed that "the very best Indians are those planted beneath the roses"—cried out in angry protest that the presence of Joseph and his pack of "thieves," "murderers," and "demons" in the country would deter miners and settlers from going into the rich Colville Valley, upon which the Falls relied for considerable business.[12] When the train carrying the Nez Percés reached southern Idaho, warrants for Joseph's arrest were in process of being served, and he would have been jailed had not the military protected him. At stations along the route, curious throngs gathered to catch a glimpse of the famous chief—deified in the East, but damned in the West.[13]

At Wallula Junction, at the mouth of the Walla Walla River, 118 of the Nez Percés were separated from the group and returned to Lapwai. The remaining 150, including Joseph, were brought to Spokane Falls.[14] On May 27, a large crowd gathered at the station there, as though waiting for a circus train to roll into town. But Joseph, "a large, fat-faced scheming cruel looking cuss," and his party, "a hard looking crowd as could well be collected," did not arrive that day—a great disappointment to the curiosity seekers. The next day the pitiable remnant of the once

11 Josiah Red Wolf Interview, Lapwai, Idaho, August 8, 1963. This story told by Red Wolf, a nephew of Otskai, is also corroborated by Mrs. Peone.

12 *Spokane Evening Review*, May 25, 1885, p. 2, and May 26, 1885, p. 3.

13 W. H. Faulkner to Commissioner, June 24, 1885. Selected Documents Relating to Skolaskin, National Archives, Record Group 75 (hereafter referred to as Selected Documents Relating to Skolaskin, NA, RG 75).

14 *Ibid.*

proud band arrived.[15] Forty-two soldiers from Fort Coeur d'Alene piled them bag and baggage into a fourteen-wagon caravan and escorted them to Fort Spokane. They arrived there on the twenty-ninth. Moses and other Colville chiefs were at the post to meet them.

Joseph greeted his old friend warmly, expressing his joy in a flow of Nez Percé words, which Moses understood. (Joseph could not speak in Moses' tongue). Flowery welcoming speeches were delivered by every chief present except Skolaskin, who stood closemouthed and uncordial.[16] The whites shared the Prophet's feeling. With Joseph's return, rumors of Indian uprisings were flying, like the June 1 report received at Walla Walla from Ritzville of an expected outbreak in the Okanogan, a story started by two horsemen who had seen some Indians in paint and feathers.[17]

Joseph's people were in no position to fight a war. They were poverty stricken and tattered in appearance. They possessed only their tipis and a few personal belongings; whatever horses and cattle they had accumulated in the Indian Territory had been left behind. The military was given the responsibility for purchasing rations for them until June 4. After that the expense fell to the Indian Office, but the military continued to issue the rations. The Nez Percés were placed across the Columbia from the post so that they could be protected—from the soldiers, who it was feared would ravish their women, and from Moses, whose drinking and gambling propensities would do them no good.[18]

Moses, leaving his favorite, Chillileetsah, to enjoy the company of the Nez Percés and the pleasures of the post, hurried his people home. The pleasures proved to be the young man's undoing. Late Monday night, June 8, he reeled in a firewater stupor to his horse and rode it to the Columbia. At the water's edge he limply dismounted, stumbled into a canoe, and with his horse in tow, started to paddle across the swollen river. He never reached

15 *Spokane Evening Review*, May 27, 1885, p. 1; and May 28, 1885, p. 2.
16 Agency Correspondence to Commissioner Atkins, June 3, 1885. Colville Agency Records, Letterbox 3.
17 *Spokane Evening Review*, June 4, 1885, p. 4.
18 Henry Covington Interview, Colville Reservation, May 18, 1958.

the other side. For a moment, his tall strong body bobbed like a piece of driftwood and then sank in the swirling waters.[19] Word of the tragedy flooded Moses with sorrow. The Columbia had swept away his hopes and plans for the leadership of the tribe.

On Thursday, Major Dickson, Dr. Merriam, Captain Henry Catley, and a detachment of troops left the post to issue the implements and cattle to Moses' people. When they arrived at Moses Crossing, the bereaved Chief asked them to delay the issue one week.[20] The officials agreed and decided to journey over to Lake Chelan to urge Innomoseecha Jim to have his lands surveyed.

Innomoseecha, backed by about twenty-five of his tribe, tried to explain the universal Indian abhorrence of cutting the earth into pieces, a concept the government officials were unable to grasp. He said "That the Great Spirit gave the land [which they were now living on] to his ancestors, who are buried where they always lived." His people had never asked anything of the government, but now they asked that they might "be allowed [in the future, as in the past] to dwell in peace upon the land which was their birthplace."[21]

In the meantime, Moses' followers waited for the Columbia to release its victim. They were still at the river watching when the government party returned on Saturday the twentieth and set up quarters on the south shore. The officials decided to wait there until Monday to issue the forty wagons, the eighty sets of harness, the plows, and the cattle, which had arrived there. On that day Captain Catley handed out the Great Father's gifts. An interpreter Charles Abraham, a young man of Lot's band and former pupil of the Indian School at Forest Grove, Oregon, instructed the Indians on how to ferry the wagons over the river in canoes.

After inspecting the bright new wagons the natives pondered

19 William Thornburg Interview, Lincoln, Washington, November 21, 1959. Thornburg lived his adult life in the Fort Spokane area and was well acquainted with happenings at that place and related the circumstances surrounding the accident.

20 Dickson to Commissioner Atkins, July 25, 1885. Moses Reservation.

21 *Ibid.*

the difficulty of transporting them across the river and getting them to the valley. They probably got little help from their Chief, still depressed over the loss of his nephew. The effort was abandoned after crossing about two wagons. Undoubtedly each turn of the wheels over the trail to Nespelem convinced them that the vehicles were symbols of work and that any Indian Office notion of their happily transporting grain on them was quite unrealistic.[22]

If the Indians were not eager for wagons, there were others who were. Certain settlers in the Big Bend exchanged money and whisky for them for a token of their real value. Agency officials were red faced with anger—and embarrassment—to learn that only two wagons of the issue had reached their destination. Their anger was not lessened by information from Washington that since the transaction had taken place off the reservation, no federal offense had been committed; as a result, there was nothing the government could legally do to recover the wagons.[23]

It would have been difficult for whites to purloin the large thresher destined for the reservation. Besides, the Indian Office gave the responsibility of supervising the transportation to Richard Hutchinson, sawyer and miller hired to operate the yet unfinished mills, so that he could start the Indians in the farming business. The only threshing for a while was threshing out plans for moving the giant machine to the Nespelem. It was finally decided to freight it across the Columbia on "Wild Goose Bill" Condon's ferry (located approximately halfway between the Moses Crossing and the crossing to the Okanogan Valley at Foster Creek, on a route from the southeast that crossed the Columbia and cut through the southwest corner of the Colville Reservation). The task was completed after some difficulty. Now the real

22 Waters informed Atkins by letter, July 10, 1885, that "about 2 wagons out of 40 issued" were crossed onto the reservation. He did not indicate how many sets of harness, plows, or head of cattle were crossed over. Colville Agency Records, Letterbox No. 3.

23 Secretary of the Interior, *Annual Report*, 1885 (49 Cong., 1 sess., *House Exec. Doc. No. 1, Pt. 5*), II, 183; Commissioner Atkins to Waters, July 22, 1885 (Colville Agency Records, Letterbox 3a).

problem lay ahead. In the absence of roads from the ferry to its destination, it was decided to move the machine cross-country on trails leading through the Kartar and thence easterly over the mountains to the Nespelem. For two days, twenty Indians and six cayuses shoved and pulled and pulled and shoved the monster. They lassoed it and tied the ropes to their saddle horns to keep it from rolling down the steep hillsides. At one place it tottered so precariously they had to hang on to it to keep it from turning over. Two days later, the exhausted wranglers dragged their mechanical maverick into the valley.[24]

Meanwhile, word that Chillileetsah's body had been found along the river bank two miles above the Moses Crossing sent Moses hurrying down to identify the bloated, discolored corpse and to bury it where it was found.[25] Who would succeed him now? He had no sons of his own to carry on the Half-Sun aristocracy. Mary had passed the age of childbearing. If a son were to be born of the Columbia woman sleeping in his bed, he would not be old enough to be a leader at Moses' death. Yayoskin, Shimtil's son, sharing a summer tipi next to his, would be the logical choice. Perhaps this young nephew could be trained in the ways of leadership in spite of his limited abilities and habits that were even more carefree than those of Chillileetsah.

But the firewater trade threatened to engulf Yayoskin as it had Chillileetsah. The contractor, Todd, as an adjunct to his building activity, carried on a thriving liquor business with the Indians.[26] Moses was stunned at the reasoning of the white authorities; they constantly harped at him to keep his people from drinking, but they did not stop one of their own people from supplying them with all the firewater they wanted. Finally, the United States prosecuting attorney caught up with Todd and shut off his supply. This left Jones, who had contracted to furnish machinery for the mill, to complete the building and the shack for the operator on the right bank of the Nespelem River.

24 *Spokesman-Review*, November 26, 1916.
25 Henry Covington Interview, Colville Reservation, January 18, 1958.
26 Commissioner Atkins to Agent Waters, August 25, 1885. Colville Agency Records, Letterbox 3a.

In his preoccupation over Chillileetsah's death and his other worries, Moses let his mount trample his instep, laying him up for two weeks during July. His friend Streamer, who happened to be ailing also, dropped by to keep him company; and the two lay around on Moses' buffalo robes commiserating over their ills. Joseph rode over from his camp near Fort Spokane to visit the convalescents and eat corn bread, potatoes, and fresh salmon, a long-missed delicacy for him.[27] He would drink nothing stronger than sugared coffee in spite of generous offers from his imbibing friends. Moses' spirits rose, his conversation more Christian with each dipper of whisky; and such generosity! "God loveth a cheerful giver." But his guests had long since learned that they had better not carry away the tokens of his liberality. When he sobered, he was not so magnanimous.[28]

He and his friend Streamer ranged over a wide choice of subjects before settling down to their favorite topics—religion and the mysteries of the universe—as was their custom during such visits. Dubious of the white man's thermal concept of hell, Moses in these conversations may have explained to Streamer his opinion of hell and the blackrobes. The devil was called something thrown away and was supposed to live under the earth where it is very hot. The priests wanted to baptize him and teach him to pray, and a government officer once told him that unless he were baptized, he would go to hell where the devil would burn him. Moses objected to this, for, if there were fire inside the earth, the water in the white man's well would boil. Consequently he would neither be baptized nor go to church because he did not believe in the devil.[29] Streamer's leaving the Valley the last of July forced Moses to return again to temporal matters— the building program, progressing at a fast rate.

During that same summer, things were happening on the old Moses Reservation. A survey was carried out under the supervision of Lieutenant John K. Waring and the protection of Cap-

27 Streamer, Miscellaneous Notebooks, Folder No. 3, July 31, 1885.
28 Peone Interviews.
29 Cline and Others, *Contributions*, 167.

tain Samuel Todd Hamilton and his cavalry troops camped at Camp Clark at the mouth of Foster Creek. Dickson followed the surveys and made thirty-seven allotments to Sarsopkin and his people in Toats Coulee. Instead of the better times Sarsopkin had hoped the allotments might bring, he became involved in numerous wrangles—with a white man who insisted on settling on the chief's (his) land and with another who flagrantly exhibited but refused to return a horse stolen from the Okanogan leader the year before.[30]

Meanwhile, Moses sought to strengthen his position further. During the fall he had received and welcomed Yakima, Kittitas, and Entiat families to his camps. Having mended his break with Kamiakin before the Yakima war leader's death, Moses also welcomed to the Colville the old warrior's sons. Tes Palouse, Tomeo, Sklumskin (Snake River), and Cleveland, and their sisters, Mary and Kiotanie.[31] During this time a tragedy struck the Chief's family. A few years before, his daughter, Sinsinqt, had married Locos, a son of Kamiakin. Moses was pleased with this union. Sinsinqt had waited until she was almost thirty years old before her family had found an acceptable suitor of royal blood whom she might marry.[32] Now the couple and their three-year-old daughter Nellie had made a trip to Spokane Falls and were crossing the reservation on their return home when Locos was murdered by a notorious Okanogan renegade and whisky peddler named Puckmiakin. As long as she lived, Nellie was to be haunted by her father's screams as the killer pursued him to lay his head open with an ax.[33] The child would soon lose

[30] Dickson to Commissioner, November 23, 1885; Hamilton to the Post Adjutant, Fort Spokane, September 19, 1885. Moses Reservation.

[31] Cleveland Kamiakin Interview, Ephrata, Washington, October 8, 1956; Hattie Red Star Interview, Nespelem, Washington, August 25, 1962.

[32] Lucy Friedlander Covington Interview, Nespelem, Washington, September 10, 1962.

[33] Secretary of the Interior, *Annual Report,* 1886 (49 Cong., 2 sess., *House Exec. Doc. No. 1, Pt. 5*), I, 449–50; George Friedlander Interview, Nespelem, Washington, August 25, 1962. Moses was summoned to Spokane Falls the preceding year when one of his tribe was murdered in the Brents area, off the reservation, by an intoxicated Indian who was captured and jailed. The murdered Indian was called Moses' son-in-law in a report appearing in the *Northwest Tribune,* October 22, 1885.

her mother, too. Sinsinqt died two years after the murder of her husband, and the little girl was adopted by Moses.[34]

Puckmiakin fled, boasting that no one would catch him.[35] It turned out that he was right, although he could not have understood the legal ramifications involved. The United States Attorney General had opined the previous spring that Indians charged with murder were subject to the criminal jurisdiction of the state;[36] and the Commissioner of Indian Affairs had interpreted the opinion as applying to the territory also. This meant that such murders usually went unpunished, for local officials were not concerned about crimes committed by Indians against other Indians when the white taxpayers were unwilling to bear the expense of prosecution.

As winter approached, Moses found that life for him and his people was no longer as it had been in the old times when the tribe freely provided for its needs in its own way. The stationary lodges were stocked with foods, some raised, some gathered, and some purchased with money earned by working for the whites. Taste for the whites' food also brought the hardship of obtaining it, so the men found it easier to hurry off to the mountains in the old way for the annual deer hunt, leaving the women to finish harvesting the gardens and repairing the mats to be used in the winter long houses. Moses also had a "harvest" to gather; he rode off to Fort Spokane the first of October, to keep an appointment with the new agent, Benjamin Moore, to "harvest" his annuity. Not finding the agent there, he went on to Spokane Falls. The next day Moore arrived, but, not finding Moses at the post, he too left for Spokane Falls, and on his way met Moses returning.

Indian relationships are often confused by non-Indians in trying to reduce them to our understanding. It would not appear from details learned from Indian interviews and from annual reports of the Secretary of the Interior that the above is the murder of Locos.

34 Peone Interviews.

35 Secretary of the Interior, *Annual Report*, 1886 (49 Cong., 2 sess., *House Exec. Doc. No. 1, Pt. 5*), I, 449–50; George Friedlander Interview, Nespelem, Washington, August 25, 1962.

36 Commissioner Atkins to Waters, March (date illegible), 1885. Colville Agency Records, Letterbox 3a.

At this meeting Moore advised the Chief to meet him at the post in ten days. Moses was there at the appointed time, October 14, but Moore did not arrive to pay him until November 16. During the month he waited impatiently around the post for his money, he visited with Joseph. The two must have talked much of the understanding they had reached while Joseph was still in the Indian Territory, that Joseph would join Moses on the Colville. This alliance would replace the worn-out alliances Moses once had with the Methows, Chelans, Okanogans, Wenatchees, and Wanapums. It would help offset Skolaskin's opposition.

Joseph's people were hungry. They were receiving only one-fourth of the standard weekly ration, and even so, the supply on hand was insufficient for that fiscal year. But emotions flared when Colonel J. S. Fletcher, new commandant of Fort Spokane, telegraphed his War Department superiors that the rations had to be increased. Moore shortly received permission from *his* superiors in the Interior Department to issue half-rations, but two months would elapse before he would be authorized to contract for the purchase of enough supplies for full rations. Meanwhile, the matter produced an exchange of messages between the personnel of the two departments, with Moore objecting to "orders" from Fletcher and Fletcher defending his telegram as containing "suggestions" only.[37]

Moses and Joseph together visited Moore before he left for the agency, at Chewelah, and the Nez Percé chief asked to be allowed to move his people to the Nespelem and take up farms.[38] Moses then went to Monoghan's store to cash his check and again demanded his pay in twenty-dollar gold pieces. Again, probably because of his preoccupation with getting his treasure and with getting the Nez Percés to Nespelem, he did not object too greatly

37 Secretary of the Interior, *Annual Report*, 1886 (49 Cong., 2 sess., *House Exec. Doc. No. 1, Pt. 5*), I, 449–53; Interior Department to War Department, endorsements and enclosure of a letter from Commissioner of Indian Affairs to Interior Department relative to the matter between Fletcher and Moore, December 9, 1885 (Colville Agency Records, Letterbox 3a).

38 Moore to Commissioner of Indian Affairs, November 27, 1885. Colville Agency Records, Letterbox 3.

when O'Shea held back one hundred dollars for the favor of cashing it. With a bodyguard he again made his "annuity dash" to the valley, where he found that the women had finished putting up the winter lodges.

Moore wired the Office of Indian Affairs for permission to move Joseph and his people to the Nespelem; and since this place was fifty miles from the post, he requested authority to issue their rations monthly instead of weekly. The Indian Office gave its approval.[39] Moses was delighted with the decision and prepared his people to receive the Nez Percés royally. Yellow Bull and sixteen of his people chose to remain at the camp opposite the post;[40] but the first week of December, Joseph and 132 Nez Percés rode into the Nespelem Valley to the cheers of Moses' people and the jeers of the Nespelems. Moses presented Joseph with several fine horses,[41] and others of his band gave the Nez Percés presents of one kind or another. Moses pointed out to Joseph a flat of good potential farm land about four miles north of the mill, on the west side of the Nespelem River. (Moses lived about five miles north of the mill, on the east side.) The suggestion set poorly with the Nespelems, who rushed in (quite possibly at Skolaskin's urging) to occupy the area, forcing Joseph and his people to huddle for the winter next to the river, two miles north of the mill. Still the Nez Percés were in the Nespelem. Moses' diplomacy had won him another victory!

Winter returned to the Valley. Moses' "children" beat a snow path to the Joseph camps, some to gamble with the Nez Percés, who bet their issued blankets for horses in an attempt to build up their herds. Moses' nephew Yayoskin, spent much time there, not to gamble but to court the lovely Iyutotum, whom he soon married. Cold weather brought much sickness. The Chinook dancers did their utmost, and their efforts seemed to bring results when towards the last of January a gentle Chinook blew. But it was only a teaser; there was no letup of bad weather or ill-

---

39 *Ibid.*

40 Henry Covington Interview, Keller, Washington, July 1, 1960.

41 Alice Moiese Andrews Interview, Nespelem, Washington, March 4, 1961.

ness. Moses spent long fretful nights around his lodge fires sharing his heartaches and future plans with his beloved Mary. The government had not built him the promised house. He would have to wait until spring to find the answer from personnel at the post. Mary did not share his confidence in the soldiers—they had killed her father and brother—but she kept her feelings from her husband, who increasingly depended on her domestic talents and perceptive powers to divine the deepening intertribal intrigues. He seems, however, to have perceived on his own that funds for his house were being held by the post trader, Monoghan, who had been authorized to let the contract for the structure. Hired carpenters were scheduled to build houses for the people in the spring with lumber from logs the natives were to haul to the mill. But the people did not respond. Despite Hutchinson's proddings, spring found the completed mill idle for want of logs to saw.

As spring approached, Moses and Joseph became concerned about the farming that the government was urging upon the Indians. An agency farmer, H. E. Hardy, had been sent to the valley and was sharing the miller's shack with the Hutchinson family until a house could be built for him. The chiefs came to him with their complaints. Moses' people had prepared four hundred acres; now they wanted to know about the grain which had been promised them for seed. Joseph was disgusted that farm implements purchased for his people had not been issued.[42] Moore always answered that the supply had not come. Joseph complained also that his people had no place to farm, for the Nespelems were occupying the good land. It seemed to the two chiefs that Hardy scarcely glanced up from his newspaper to listen to their troubles.

With his faith in the military, it seemed natural for Moses to appeal to the trusted General Howard to complain of neglect by the agency. Joseph had no reason to love Howard, who had commanded the forces against the Nez Percés during the war, but possibly he knew that Howard had opposed their exile to the

42 Atkins to Moore, June 14, 1886. Colville Agency Records, Letterbox 4.

Indian Territory. At all events, he joined Moses in writing to Howard, who was then commanding the Division of the East, far removed from Indian matters. The chiefs' letter followed the red-tape route up through the War Department, thence down through the Interior Department until late in June it landed squarely on Agent Moore's desk, not far from where it started.[43]

Moore was infuriated by a letter from Commissioner of Indian Affairs J. D. C. Atkins on the matter.[44] He replied to the Commissioner in justification of his inaction: that since the Nespelems had shoved Joseph's people from the tillable land, they had no need for farm implements; that there had been too much snow to journey over to the valley to correct the situation; that Moses' Indians had not raised enough wheat the previous year for him to buy back to give them for seed; and that it was too late this year to buy seed on the outside and take it over a stretch of trails to the farms, there being no roads into the Nespelem. As for the complaint that the agent could never find time to talk to Joseph and Moses, he had long distances to travel from the agency at Chewelah to the Coeur d'Alene Reservation and to the Colville, and that when he was traveling between April and June on reservation matters, he made one quick trip to the Nespelem to accept the mill. He was there without an interpreter, and for that reason did not visit with the chiefs. He wondered who was informing on him. It could not have been Indian Inspector Bannister, in the area earlier in the year, for the Inspector had neither met him when he was in the Nespelem nor talked to Hardy when he was at the post. Who but the military would inform General Howard? It must have been Fletcher. "Where he [the Inspector] obtained this false report (for such it is) unless from the military at the Fort, where more than one of the same kind of reports have originated," he did not know.[45]

He sped to the valley hoping to pacify the two noisy chiefs by

[43] Atkins to Moore, June 18, 1886. Colville Agency Records, Letterbox 4.

[44] Moore to Atkins, June 30, 1886. Colville Agency Records, Letterbook 31.

[45] Secretary of Interior, *Annual Report*, 1886 (49 Cong., 2 sess., *House Exec. Doc. No. 1, Pt. 5*), I, 449–53.

locating Joseph's people. He located most of them west and north of the mill, but permitted Two Moons, Joseph's medicine man, to locate on the east side of the creek at the ford half a mile below the mill. He located Kamiakin's sons, Tes Palouse and Sklumskin, west near the first falls of the river, and his other son, Tomeo, and a sister, west of the mill. It required two days for him to accomplish his task. His work had been completed too late in the season for the Nez Percés to farm their new lands. The government would have to subsist them for another year. He found over four hundred acres of Moses' land fenced, and half of this cultivated. (His report does not specify to what crop it was planted.)[46] In late summer, twenty wagons and as many plows and sets of harness were issued to the Moses band with specific instructions to Moore from Acting Commissioner A. Bupshaw to take receipt for them and to warn the natives well not to grieve the Great Father by selling them to white men.[47]

The Great Father was less grieved over the land they had sold to the white man. The Moses Reservation had been officially opened on May 1 of that year. Prospectors, land-seekers, merchandisers, adventurers, and speculators poured into the area. The town of Ruby, laid out within the first week on Salmon River, would become the first county seat, February 2, 1888, when Okanogan County was established. But apparently Moses almost overlooked what was happening on his old reservation. He was preoccupied with problems on his present one.

As the winter of 1886–87 approached, Moses visited Hutchinson frequently but avoided the do-nothing Hardy. Again Hutchinson encouraged the natives to cut and haul logs to the mill, and Moses listened as the program was hopefully explained. Knowing the miller was preparing to leave for Spokane Falls for his winter supplies, Moses told him the coming winter would be a bad one and asked if he would get sugar, tea, and flour for him and his people. Hutchinson replied that he could not do that, as he had

46 *Ibid.*
47 Bupshaw to Moore, August 12, 1886. Colville Agency Records, Letterbox 4. In this communication Bupshaw cites Sec. 363 of Regulations, 1884, as the authority.

no funds available, whereupon the Chief produced his annuity money, which had been safely in hand since October. He suggested that Hutchinson buy the food with this money, have the Indians buy it from him with otter, mink, and bear skins, which he should bale and ship to New York, and reimburse Moses from the proceeds of the sale. Hutchinson agreed to this arrangement. The method worked, and Moses would be reimbursed by the following May.[48] To his people, Moses was still provider; to the Nez Percés, the government was Provider.

Joseph lived that winter with his old fat wife, Iyattooweane-tenmy, and his young thin wife, Wiwintipyalatalecotsot, in their lodge below the mill, west across the ford from Two Moon's lodge and close by the other Nez Percés clustering within easy reach of their rations. A few Nespelem families under the influence of Meschelle, George, and Frank clung fast to the west side of the river above the mill hoping to keep the lands Moore had attempted to give the Nez Percés.

Winter illnesses raced from family to family through Moses' camp striking bodies susceptible to virus diseases. The medicine men and women—Tompasque assisted by Sokula, Snawtonic and his wife Sintque, Homas, Tolemiat, and Johawahliwicks—faced the spring gaunt and haggard from long hours ministering to the sick.[49] Although sickness did not strike Joseph's camps with such fury, the cries of his medicine men, Two Moons and Lapeethe-shentooks, pierced the air, pulsing back and forth through the Valley, a macabre echo to those of Moses' doctors nearby. Moses' camp lost nineteen children that winter while Joseph's lost only four. By spring, 1887, Moses' band had lost not only vitality but blankets and horses as well. Joseph's braves had bettered Moses' in the gambling sprees as they had in the disease toll.

Dr. C. F. Webb, stationed in the Okanogan with Tonasket's people, had been sent over the previous summer to care for the sick. Now in March the agent sent him over again to treat high fevers, sore eyes, diarrhea, rheumatism, skin diseases, dyspepsia,

[48] *Spokesman-Review*, November 26, 1916.
[49] Madeline Covington Interview, Nespelem, Washington, November 25, 1961.

scrofula, and lung disorders. He went first to Moses' camps, then to Joseph's, but Joseph's people, because of strong faith in their medicine men, refused treatment from the white doctor.[50]

With milder weather, Moses started again to ride almost daily down the valley, around the pond, and over the brush-, dirt-, and gravel-filled dam to Hutchinson's shack, arriving there usually about ten in the morning. Sometimes Joseph joined them. Seldom did the two chiefs visit Hardy; they would have interrupted his newspaper reading. Hutchinson was soon able to guess the agenda of their day's meeting by observing the manner in which Moses rode up and entered his shack. Sometimes the Chief brought fresh beef, venison, fish, or berries to repay the miller for the luncheons he ate with him. He would rather do this than have Hutchinson and Hardy help themselves to flour from the mill, as they often did. After lunch, they would have more discussion. Hutchinson briefed him on agency matters. Perhaps he told him of plans under way to move the headquarters from Chewelah closer to his camps. In turn, the miller learned of grievances, the whereabouts of the Indians, and the progress on Moses' house under construction. If Moses knew that Father Stephen DeRouge, a Catholic priest, had settled in the Okanogan Valley, it can easily be imagined he complained of this to Hutchinson. Usually around three o'clock in the afternoon, the chief rode home.[51]

As the days passed, Moses became more and more disappointed with his house. Although the carpenters were busy at work, no one in authority had ever gone up to see it. He began to suspect that in spite of Hutchinson's assurances to the contrary, no thousand dollars was being put into it; and he wondered why Hutchinson could not force Monoghan to give up the commission he was taking out of the house money. Hutchinson asked Moses what he thought of the White House where the Great Father lived. Moses was impressed; maybe, if his house could be painted white, he could live in a house like the President's. From

50 Webb to Agent Moore, March 9, 1887. Colville Agency Records, Letterbox 20.
51 *Spokesman-Review,* November 26, 1916.

that time on, Hutchinson referred to Moses' house as the "white house."

The miller was less jovial in discussing with Moses his excessive drinking. Maybe Moses rationalized as he was reported to have done in explaining it to Special Inspector F. C. Armstrong, who came to the Valley to check on a new site for the agency. According to an account that came to light a generation later, he said: "I have visited New York, Washington, Chicago, and San Francisco a number of times and your greatest men have invited me to drink and have drank with me. Liquor is a bad thing for the Indian, for it robs him of his property and his health, and through it came diseases never known by the Indian until the white man came, but the Indian is weak, and I want to tell you the only way to stop the Indian from drinking liquor is for the government to stop the white man from making it."[52]

It is unlikely that Joseph escaped Hutchinson's lecturing. Although the Nez Percé chief was a teetotaler, his people drank heavily and gambled too much.

Moses asked from time to time for a boarding school like Tonasket's. His day-school building was being used as a commissary for the storage of the Nez Percé rations, for no teacher had ever been supplied. But he and Joseph were not interested in a day school; they demanded a boarding school near their lodges. Moses had never forgotten his Lapwai days of fifty years before and of Spalding's plans for a boarding school at his mission. Both chiefs emphatically opposed sending their children to a Roman Catholic school. Moses, particularly, objected to Father DeRouge's teaching; it would cause, as he put it, "separation of the families," his way of describing what would result from the priest's antipolygamy sermons. One way to frustrate the Blackrobe's efforts, he felt, was to bring in a Protestant minister. The denomination was immaterial.

That spring during the bustle of seed planting, horse roundup, and preparations for food-gathering expeditions, word came that Agent Moore was leaving. This was good news. The new agent

52 *Ibid.*

could be no worse; Moore had been so wishy-washy, always promising to do things in a by-and-by that never came. The new agent, Rickard D. Gwydir, arrived May 3, 1887, as the Moses band was preparing to go to the root and fishing grounds. Joseph's people did not get under way to those grounds until after mid-May. Moses attributed the delay to their leader's lack of concern as to whether his people worked or not; and he was becoming critical of this attitude, lest it influence the Columbias. Actually, Joseph found it easier to wait for the food to come to his people than to urge them to farm or to go in search of it.

Louis Mayer, who had the contract to transport the rations, delivered the quarterly supplies: 313 pounds of bacon, 94 pounds of beans, 125 pounds of coffee, 66 pounds of salt, 16 pounds of baking powder, 219 pounds of sugar, and 1,568 pounds of flour. In addition, the Indians were furnished cattle, which were butchered and the meat handed out on the spot. Some of the animals were purchased from reservation Indians, and others more expensively on contract off the reservation. In early March, 1887, for example, Mayer drove the cattle over the Fort Trail to the Valley and floated the supplies down-river to that place to avoid the mud-clogged spring roads.[53]

The Agency's hope that Joseph's people would raise enough wheat this year to grind into flour for themselves and to feed their livestock was unrealized, for the Nespelems still occupied the best land. Meanwhile Hutchinson's milling for Moses' tribe came to a halt in early June when rising water from melting mountain snow washed out the dam.[54] During the summer, a Mr. T. Holmes repaired the damaged dam while a Mr. Sibin repaired the idled machines. Sibin did little, however, to repair relations between the Nez Percés and the Nespelems, advising the Nespelems to plow furrows around their properties to keep the Nez Percés from their lands. Goaded by Sibin's interference, the Nespelems

[53] Alex Shannon, agency farmer, to Moore, March 10, 1887; Louis Mayer to Moore, March 9, 1887; Mayer to Moore (no date clip to letter). Colville Agency Records, Letterbox 20.
[54] Hutchinson to Gwydir, July 26, 1887. Colville Agency Records, Letterbox 5.

carried tales to Skolaskin. This would soon lead to a real showdown.[55]

Hutchinson was still disappointed at the slowness of Moses' people to become agrarians and became irritated when he saw tools lying around the camps rusting from disuse. Because of their slow progress, the government switched some of their wagons and plows to the needy Spokanes, who had taken quite well to farming.[56] The Spokanes were ahead of the Valley Indians in other ways too, particularly in matters of law and order. They maintained a court of their own, an effective means of reducing crimes and whisky sales on their reservation. Gwydir also lay in wait for whisky peddlers, whose defiance of federal laws was producing not only a swath of drunks and gamblers, but thieves and prostitutes as well. His efforts were partially rewarded in the apprehension of one of the prize offenders, a squawman named Burke.

Skolaskin had a court, police, and jail as did the Spokanes, but his law-enforcement system was not sponsored or authorized by the government. There were stories drifting into the Valley that the crippled leader jailed his own men on false charges and then lived with their women while the men languished in prison unable to furnish the exhorbitant numbers of stock they would have to forfeit to get free.[57] Everyone knew that he kept a huge pile of logs near his home which he said would be used to build an ark to save his people from the flood that would one day come to drown the Evil Ones. He still exhorted his followers not to accept government gifts, or bribes, as he called them.

Joseph on the other hand was afraid his people might miss the government handouts. When several of them left to visit their relatives at Lapwai, he sent his nephew, Little Joseph, there to call them home to share a beef issue. These trips of the Nez

[55] Chapman to Assistant Adjutant General, Headquarters Department of the Columbia, February 11, 1888. Colville Agency Records, Letterbox 20.

[56] Gwydir to Atkins, June 13, 1887. Colville Agency Records, Letterbox 5.

[57] Clara Hughes Moore Interview, Belvedere, Washington, July 26, 1961; Madeline Covington Interview, Nespelem, Washington, May 29, 1961; Cull White Interview, Moses Lake, Washington, January 2, 1958; Herman Friedlander Interview, Coulee Dam, Washington, May 4, 1964; T. J. Morgan to Hal Cole, August 10, 1889 (Colville Agency Records, Letterbox 6).

Percés back and forth between the two reservations worried Gwydir and Lapwai agent George Morris. A new order had been issued the previous February by Atkins that all Indians leaving reservations must have permission—a formality that the Nez Percés overlooked. Back of this order lay the determination of Atkins to force all Indians to accept allotments and open their reservations to white settlement. Thus he tried to prevent tribes from visiting each other and forming a united resistance. Sitting Bull had strayed from his Standing Rock Reservation in Dakota to travel through Montana stirring up the Crows against the allotment of their land. Hence the Commissioner's general order, which—as it happened—antedated the passage of the General Allotment Act by six days.[58] The Nez Percés were unaware of all this; apparently only their respective agents worried about the matter.

Gwydir's real troubles were with the Indians who stayed on the reservation. When the Nespelems, stirred up by Sibin's meddling, came with their complaints to Skolaskin, the lame prophet became furious. In July, he carried his denunciation to Gwydir at the agency, just moved from Chewelah to a site across the Spokane River from Fort Spokane. Moses' and Joseph's people were murderers and horse thieves, he told the agent. He reminded Gwydir that his people had never stained their hands with white man's blood, as had the two intruding chieftains, and that on one occasion they had stood with firearms in their hands and defied Moses to take some white settlers who had fled to them to escape his fury. Before sending such people as Moses to San Poil and Nespelem land, Washington should have asked his permission.

Moore had been rather tolerant of Skolaskin. Although he was aware of the supernatural inspiration that was the source of the lame dreamer's power, he hoped that this might be modified by the mundane influence of the agency—that Skolaskin might become "one of the best converts we have."[59] But Gwydir knew

[58] Atkins to Agent, Colville Indian Agency, February 2, 1887 (Colville Agency Records, Letterbox 20); Angie Debo, *The Road to Disappearance*, 320–22.

[59] Secretary of the Interior, *Annual Report*, 1887 (50 Cong., 1 sess., *House Exec. Doc. No. 1, Pt. 5*), II, 288; Gwydir to Armstrong, July 19, 1887 (Colville Agency Records, Letterbox 20).

that something must be done to settle the explosive situation on the Nespelem. Anticipating trouble, he had asked the War Department for military assistance, and on Monday, July 18, Colonel J. Ford Kent, commandant of Fort Spokane, informed him that he had received authorization to comply. Assured of this backing, he told Skolaskin on Tuesday that he was setting out for the Nespelem to undertake the permanent location of the Nez Percés and invited the chief to accompany him.[60]

Skolaskin did not accept the invitation. He left the agency ahead of Gwydir, gathered his messengers, and sent them to Indians as far as the Okanogan with news that the agent was coming to take their land.[61] Meanwhile, Gwydir and Kent planned that the troops would be sent into the Nespelem in a roundabout way, under the pretense of going on summer practice. The detail set out across the Big Bend and crossed to the reservation on the "Wild Goose Bill" ferry to approach the valley from the west. Gwydir set out by a different route, with an interpreter and Alex Shannon, agency farmer. They ferried the Columbia in a canoe at a crossing just above the mouth of the Spokane and followed the Old Fort Trail until they came to the vicinity of a San Poil village. There, on Friday evening, July 22, Skolaskin called a meeting of his people and invited Gwydir to participate. In an enclosure that could hold two thousand people, the agent met with Skolaskin, two of his principal men, and fifty of his "picked warriors," in "all their barbaric bravery." They were a "formidable-looking band."

Skolaskin launched a violent verbal attack on the government for putting the Nez Percés on land belonging to San Poils. Then he said, "I would ask the Indian agent who is present if it is right for the Great Father to take the land of the San Poils . . . and give it to a people like Joseph's band of Nez Percés? If the agent would answer as his heart tells him he would say that the great father was doing wrong, but he will not speak his straight mind. He will

[60] Secretary of Interior, *Annual Report,* 1887, II, 288.

[61] C. B. Bash, *et al.,* County Commissioners, Stevens County, to Gwydir, September 9, 1887. Colville Agency Records, Letterbox 20.

say, 'My chief orders and I obey.' But I say the San Poils will not obey." Skolaskin sank into his seat exhausted.

Gwydir noticed the fierce expressions on the faces of Skolaskin's men. Seeing how deeply their leader's words had moved them, he forced himself to appear at ease as he rose to speak. He agreed with Skolaskin that once the land had belonged to the Indians, but wagons and roads had taken the place of the pack horse and trails. Railroads were built and the white men began pouring into the country changing its life; and so, too, would the San Poils have to change theirs. He explained that Lot, Tonasket, and Moses had taken the advice of the government. So, too, should the San Poils. He added that he could tell by the faces of his listeners that his remarks were not well received. He surmised that Skolaskin intended using force to oppose the locating of the Nez Percés, and that he had as yet no knowledge of the troop movement.

The next morning as Gwydir continued on his journey, Skolaskin with twenty of his warriors followed. As they passed other San Poil villages recruits joined Skolaskin, until he had nearly two hundred when the Nespelem was reached late in the evening. Here the agent found that the supporting troops had not arrived and that nobody knew their location. He sent a couple of runners to find them, inform the commanding officer of the precarious situation, and request that he hurry to the Valley. Before putting up for the night at the miller's house, he sent his interpreter among the Indians to learn their feelings.

There were two councils that night. Moses and Joseph and their people held one south of the mill; Skolaskin and his followers, the other. Campfires burned late. In the morning Moses sent an emissary to Gwydir, asking him to meet with the Indians. He refused, saying he was not yet ready. As noon rolled around, the agent still did not appear. Some of Moses' and Joseph's people waited at the miller's door. Word spread through the camps that Gwydir was afraid. This was true; he was waiting for the troops to appear. Then suddenly came his call for the Indians to meet unarmed at the mill. His interpreter had advised him that the

Indians were getting impatient and that, "If the two factions started a fight the finish would be like the fight of the Kilkenny cats, nothing left but head dresses."

With some fear, Gwydir made his way to the mill and stood in the doorway facing west. He directed Joseph and his people to gather to his right, Moses and his people to his left, and Skolaskin and his followers in the center. He must have seen tension in the faces before him. A few of the natives were in feathers, a sign that they meant business. Although he had ordered them to disarm, he suspected that they had weapons concealed beneath their harmless-looking blankets. Trying to disguise his nervousness, he began to speak. His purpose in coming at this time, he explained, was to notify the Indians that Joseph and his people were to be given land on which to locate on the reservation. This was an order from the Great White Father in Washington.

Immediately an uproar came from each camp—the *"Tah!"* (No) of the San Poils, drowned out by the *"Oriah!"* (Yes) from the groups on the left and right. When quiet was restored, Skolaskin was on his feet denouncing the agent and calling the Great Father a thief and Moses and Joseph murderers.

Gwydir sternly interrupted, admonishing him to cease talking in that manner or he would stop his talk entirely. The agent afterwards admitted that he did not know what he would have done had his bluff been called. But Skolaskin redirected his abuse from the Great Father to Moses, calling him a coward, a liar, and a murderer, and saying little about Joseph. When he finished, Moses rose. *"Nika Moses,"* he began. Cleverly recognizing Gwydir's sensitivity to abuse of the President, he said he had taken the advice of the Great Father. By doing so, he had helped his people, who now had land, a mill, a school, horses, and cattle. At one time, he continued, he was an enemy of the whites, but that was when he was ignorant as a child and did not understand the ways of the Great Chief and the good he was doing for his Indian children. He could see it now. His friend Joseph and the Nez Percés saw it as his people did. They would always obey and do as the Great Father wished them to do. He was glad his people were not ruled like the San Poils by a dreamer, who could not talk without frothing at the mouth like a dog and who was no better than a dog.

Gwydir stopped Moses from further talk. The San Poils became wild in audible anger. Skolaskin sat impassive "as a stone image." Gwydir must have thought this was it! And framed in the doorway, he made the best possible target. One word from Skolaskin would have ignited the fireworks. Gwydir thought the lame chief was debating whether or not to give that word. Should there be trouble, the Indian Office would hold him responsible for not having taken proper precautions: "I would be the goat, for the department would have to have one." Then, the blast of the bugle! The timing had never been better in a wild west show. Lieutenant Hoppin arrived with an advance guard, held a quick conference with the agent, ordered his men to dismount, picket their horses, form ranks in front of the entrance to the mill, and stand at ease. Gwydir knew all the Indians "could hear the military click as breech of the carbine was closed." The main body of troops rode up just as Lieutenant Hoppin disappeared with the agent inside the mill. Gwydir knew the crisis had passed. "Wily Skolaskin" perceived he had been "outgeneraled," and withdrew with his people from the Nespelem.[62]

However, Moses may have had the uncomfortable feeling that Skolaskin had not spoken his last word.

[62] Gwydir to Atkins, August 1, 1887 (Colville Agency Records, Letterbox 7); Secretary of the Interior, *Annual Report*, 1887, II, 288; Rickard D. Gwydir, "A Record of the San Poil Indians," *Washington Historical Quarterly*, VIII, No. 4 (October, 1917), 243-50. The foregoing article is an account written by Gwydir thirty years after the events occurred. He gave the date as 1888, but the contemporary records show that he was in error one year.

XIII. Prophets and Losses

"I am afraid the end of my people is not far off."
—Moses to reporter, Spokane Falls, October, 1890

AGENT GWYDIR spent Monday and Tuesday, July 25 and 26, 1887, locating Joseph's people along the valley flat where they had originally intended taking up farm land on their own.[1] Then he held a discussion with Moses before leaving to attend to some matters in the Okanogan.[2]

Although Moses had won the battle in his war with Skolaskin, Gwydir attempted to cut him down to size by warning him to stop his people's gambling and his own drinking. He even threatened him with imprisonment in the guardhouse if he failed to comply. Moses had another problem—the bearded Father DeRouge who was lecturing his people—tormenting his families, trying to make Catholics out of them, as he explained it to the agent. The priest wanted them to give up not only gambling and whisky, but also their wives. Years later Gwydir related a conversation he once had with Moses concerning this matter. As Gwydir tells it, he explained to the Chief that the government wished the Indians to adopt Christian ways, keeping only one wife as the priest suggested. Moses asked if the priest had a wife, whereupon Gwydir told him the priest was not allowed to have a wife.

After reflecting a moment Moses replied, "Tell the Blackrobe that I will give him one of my wives if he will keep his mouth shut!"[3]

---

[1] Gwydir to Atkins, August 1, 1887. Colville Agency Records, Letterbox 20.

[2] For additional information on Agent Gwydir's activities in the Okanogan, some of which were related to problems remaining from the agreements regarding the Moses Reservation, see Ann Briley, "Hiram F. Smith, First Settler of Okanogan County," *Pacific Northwest Quarterly*, Vol. XLIII, No. 3 (July, 1952), 226–33.

[3] Gwydir recalled years later that this conversation occurred in 1888, but, since other reports by him were off one year, it is assumed this was also. *Spokane Daily*

No one knew better than Moses that for doing work, two wives were better than one. The same could hardly be said of his braves who were trying to become farmers. At that, they outclassed the Nez Percés, who harvested no crops at all and let their timber lie in spite of the four yoke of oxen and two teams of horses that the agency provided them to haul it to the mill. A. J. Chapman, the interpreter, visiting the Valley in July (1887), urged the natives to cut and put up plenty of wild hay for winter use. When they went out to do so, they found that white herdsmen, some of them armed, had sneaked cattle and several thousand sheep on the reservation.[4] Moreover, prospectors were spilling over from Moses' old reservation.

The increase of population in the Big Bend aggravated the problem. However, advancing civilization brought some benefits, among them the new post office and store opened on August 31, at Barry on the south side of Moses Crossing. This facilitated communications between the agency and the reservation and supplied the latter with trade goods. Moses, however, still depended on stores in the Kittitas for most of his purchases. Some of his people joined him on his trips there. Leading his supply-laden pack strings homeward out of Ellensburg up the steep Nanum Trail, he often paused to eat with cattlemen in their camps and joke with them over their failure to supply napkins with their meals. Descending to the Columbia, his trains passed pantalooned Chinamen shuffling under burdens of live pigs and chickens purchased from a white rancher or driving pack strings of their own. At the river, his men unpacked their cargoes for a short camp. The next day, they loaded their supplies in canoes and ferried them across the Columbia under the watchful eye of their Chief sitting on the river bank and puffing on his bluish-

---

Chronicle (Spokane, Washington), March 12, 1917. In 1887, Gwydir reported on Moses' reaction to the priest's teachings on plurality of wives. Secretary of the Interior, *Annual Report*, 1887 (50 Cong., 1 sess., *House Exec. Doc. No. 1, Pt. 5*), II, 287–89.

4 J. Orin Oliphant, "Encroachments of Cattlemen on Indian Reservations in the Pacific Northwest," Reprinted from *Agricultural History*, XXIV (January, 1950), 1–4; Gwydir to Atkins, July 29, 1887 (Colville Agency Records, Letterbox 7).

green pipe. Across the river he repeated his pipe ritual, the men reloaded their packs, and they all struck off across Badger Mountain and through the Haystack Rocks to Barry and home.[5]

On his return from the Kittitas this year, Moses learned of the completion of Tonasket's boarding school despite the fact that its contractors, Davis and Todd, had been turned in for trading whisky to the Okanogan Indians for cattle. "Send your children to Tonasket's boarding school or to the Spokane Reservation boarding school," was all Moses heard from the government officials. But he still insisted that his children would attend a boarding school close to home or none at all.

Meanwhile, the Chief learned that his old friend Sarsopkin had died in August shortly after Special Agent Gordon had visited him hoping to protect his people in their lands from white indignities. It appears that after the Okanogan chief had celebrated in the rough mining town of Ruby, his son Peter had tied him to a horse and led it toward his ranch at Fish Lake. Crossing a dangerous stretch of trail, the chief and the horse fell over a bluff. Both were killed. There were those who believed Peter had given them a push. Moses struck off for the big Sarsopkin potlatch, pausing along the way to visit Suiepkine at Omak Lake. All of Suiepkine's talk was anti-DeRouge—the Blackrobe was taxing the Indians to build a church and thus preparing the area for an influx of whites. Now more distraught than ever, Moses continued toward the potlatch.

Natives at the potlatch were on edge. Skolaskin had traveled through the Okanogan the previous July, warning that the Colville would soon be opened to miners. Someone handed Moses a jug of firewater. Indians remember that he put it to his lips, gurgled its contents down his throat, and said, "*Lem! Lem!*" (good! good!).[6] The ensuing celebration was so noisy that C. E. Brooks, farmer for the Tonasket Indians, reported him and his friends to the agency.[7] On October 14, Streamer, attending the

[5] Peter Wheeler Interview, Wenatchee, Washington, October 9, 1961.

[6] Joe Someday Interview, Curlew, Washington, August 8, 1961.

[7] Brooks to Gwydir, October 10, 1887. Colville Agency Records, Letterbox 20.

potlatch, scribbled an agreement, which Moses and Tonasket signed, to permit Hiram Smith and his associates to construct a wagon road from above Grand Coulee across the reservation to Moses' mill road through the Nespelem, then "by the most feasible route" to Tonasket's mill, and on to Lake Osoyoos.[8] When word of the Okanogan revelries got back to Agent Gwydir, he asked permission of Acting Commissioner A. Bupshaw to throw the Chief in the guardhouse for his indulgences.[9] Bupshaw suggested that he be disciplined by withholding his annuity, a plan which could not have gone into effect until the following year since Moses had already received his yearly allowance.

In the meantime, Gwydir tackled the more pressing problem of discontent among the northern tribes. He rode north on October 28, to dispel rumors that the reservation was to be thrown open to the white men. In the Okanogan, he found good reason for the Indians' alarm; many white prospectors had illegally entered the Colville. He called a council and managed to calm the natives temporarily.[10] Tonasket was not present when the meeting opened, and in his absence those who were there complained that he drank all the time. Gwydir promised that he or any others arrested for drinking would be jailed until they revealed the source of their whisky. On November 6, Tonasket appeared at the council, and after a long powwow the agent prepared to appoint two policemen from the Okanogan to act as a court for handling drunks.

Apparently, Gwydir had arrived in the Okanogan before the potlatch was completed, when only Sarsopkin's personal effects, but not the substantial portion of his estate, had been distributed. The agent accordingly took steps to insure that this property should be given to "those legally entitled" to it. The Commissioner upheld his action and told him to turn it over to the civil courts of the territory, and should they fail to accept jurisdiction,

---

8 Statement signed by Tonasket and Moses, October 14, 1887. Colville Agency Records, Letterbox 20.

9 Bupshaw to Gwydir, November 18, 1887. Colville Agency Records, Letterbox 5.

10 C. B. Bash, Henry Wellington, and William Granger to Gwydir, November 15, 1887. Colville Agency Records, Letterbox 20.

to discharge any debts against it before awarding it to the legal heirs.[11]

Law and order were taking much of Gwydir's time—and Moses' too. The Chief was asked to watch for Poker Jim, an acquaintance of the two chiefs, wanted for murder at the Umatilla Agency. Poor Joseph was preoccupied with problems other than Poker Jim. The agency's eight oxen, kept primarily for the Nez Percés, had broken out twice, had knocked over the fence around the Nespelem Meschelle's haystack, and were eating the hay. In their wrath, the Nespelems demanded fifty dollars' damages of Joseph. Moses jumped into the squabble to protect his friend, an action angering Meschelle so much that he killed a Nez Percé yearling. Farmer Hardy listened to the arguments and requested two policemen from the Valley, one each from Moses' and Joseph's bands. The two chiefs bristled at this. None of their people would "take the billy stick"—even with pay. If the government wanted police, it would have to provide them itself.[12]

In December, measles hit the Moses tribe heavily. Joseph's people suffered less; they had acquired some immunity from repeated infections while exiled in the Indian Territory.[13] That same month Chapman again came to the Valley. Moses and Joseph visited him in Hutchinson's house to pour out their grievances against the Indian Office and the agency and asked him to write on their behalf to General John Gibbon, now commanding the Department of the Columbia, and to General Howard.

Moses had a long list. The thousand dollars to build his house had been left with Mr. Monoghan, who had kept the money two years before a house worth only three or four hundred dollars was built. No one came out to inspect it or to advise him, but left him to accept it or go without anything. The agents do not help Indians, he lamented. "They help other white men to rob the

11 Atkins to Gwydir, January 12, 1888. Colville Agency Records, Letterbox 20.

12 Sworn statement, Meschell [sic.] to Gwydir, December 1, 1887; and Hardy to Gwydir, December 13, 1887. Colville Agency Records, Letterbox 20.

13 Big Bend Empire (Waterville, Washington Territory), February 2 and March 29, 1888.

Indians." To get his annuity he had to go a long distance and wait weeks. Murders were committed, and stock was stolen, but his complaints were shunted aside. "I was put off with bye and bye, but bye and bye never came." He had been told an Inspector would come and investigate. He waited two years, but still no Inspector. The previous July Gwydir had come carrying Skolaskin, "that man that cannot walk," and "saying, 'here Moses, this is a good man, and I want you to follow him.' " They wanted him to send his children to a boarding school out of the Valley. He had kept his word to counsel in peace, to cease roaming, and to settle his Indians down to cultivate the soil.

Joseph complained of his people's idleness. They had cut some logs, which still lay in the woods. They had plowed some land the previous fall, but it was not fenced. If the white man [Hardy] "would get out and stir around, instead of lying in the house, reading newspapers all the time . . . we could do something." There was no feed provided for the oxen for winter, but these oxen would be needed in winter to haul logs to the mill on sleds. Land was plowed, but no seed was provided. Clothing needed during the cold weather lay over a month before being issued. (It was stored in the unoccupied schoolhouse.) The Nez Percés wanted a fine stallion to better the strain of their horses. (They had been famous throughout the West for their skill in horse breeding.) Joseph knew General Gibbon to be brave, and he thought he was kind also. His little girl and others appreciated the clothing he and Mrs. Gibbon had sent them. Government employees were responsible to some extent for the existing troubles between his people and the Nespelems. Two winters before, the government had failed to furnish supplies. As a result, white employees shipped in about $1,200 worth of goods, traded them to the Indians for their cattle, and then turned around and sold the cattle to the government, which gave them back to the Nez Percés as part of their issue—thus serving as contractor and government agent at the same time. The employees took wheat and bran from the mill for their own use. The Indians wanted an investigation.

Chapman catalogued the chiefs' complaints in a letter to the military.[14]

On January 27, 1888, a three-day rain began falling over an eighteen-inch snow cover. Hutchinson worked frantically to divert the water from the mill, but finally gave up to stay with his wife and daughter, who were down with the measles. The heavy precipitation turned the much-used walkways between the lodges of Moses' families and around his house into ribbons of mud. The mat houses were damp. The sick lay helplessly huddled on soggy skins and blankets, some too lethargic to take nourishment. Medicine men worked over the greasy, brown bodies. They helped matters none by pushing sweat-bath-weakened victims of the disease into the cold muddy waters of the Nespelem. Acting Agent W. Lewis sent Dr. R. M. McAdoo from the Okanogan to the Nespelem February 15 to help the ailing tribes.[15] Before McAdoo could get there, Hardy hurried off the reservation to bring in Dr. B. F. Youngt, a doctor in private practice. In the meantime, McAdoo treated some of Moses' Indians, but could do nothing with the Nez Percés, who quarantined themselves from all help. When Youngt arrived, he handed Hutchinson some bottles of medicine and left.[16]

Upper respiratory infections and lung congestions followed the measles and stalked the children into March. One of their victims was Joseph's only child, the daughter of Wiwintipyala-talecotsot. Wailing from the Chief's lodge announced her death, sending fear like the fever racing through the Valley. Skolaskin spread the rumor that it was the white man's medicine that was killing the Indians. Fortunately, the disease was on the wane.[17] Many of those who had accepted medicine from the doctor did so only after he took a dose of it to prove its harmlessness.[18]

To Joseph's people the coming of spring aroused no desire to

[14] Chapman to the Assistant Adjutant General, February 11, 1888. Colville Agency Records, Letterbox 20.

[15] Lewis to Hardy, February 24, 1888. Colville Agency Records, Letterbox 20.

[16] McAdoo to Gwydir, April 10, 1888. Colville Agency Records, Letterbox 20.

[17] Unsigned (probably Hutchinson) to W. Lewis, Acting Colville Agent, March (no date), 1888. Colville Agency Records, Letterbox 20.

[18] *Northwest Tribune*, April 13, 1888.

engage in spring work. On April 4, Hutchinson walked down to the leader's camp to ask for eight of his men to repair the flood-damaged mill. Joseph refused to help except on orders from Agent Gwydir.[19] Hutchinson must have turned away in disgust. If so, he had company in the Indian Office, which by this time was also quite irritated at Moses and Joseph. Commissioner Atkins, in following through on the Chief's complaints to Chapman in December, asked Gwydir to check into the matters. Wrote Atkins: "This office is of the opinion that both Moses and Joseph have been petted and humored until it has become a very difficult job to satisfy them."[20]

Moses' men, however, seemed to have caught the spirit of the season as they busily repaired the corrals for the spring roundup. A little later, led by Kulalikiyu, riding on "Papone" ("Buckskin"), they surrounded cavorting clusters of horseflesh, sleek-coated now, and funneled them into the corrals, where they marked ears and tied stallion cords with fine horse hair. (Only a few native horsemen used the white man's method for gelding their cayuses.) Finally, they raised their irons from the fire and sent curls of smoke rising from singed yearling hides to bear the double-arrow brand of their Chief's horse herds.

He had an assortment of horses to thrill the heart of an Indian! The very best native and American stock. He could thank Sarsopkin for that. Sometime earlier, the Okanogan chief had given him a good stallion acquired from Judge John Haynes at Osoyoos. He had shiny blacks, bay-and-white pintos, sorrels and whites, iron grays, blue roans with sorrel tails, strawberry roans with black manes and tails, dappled and blue roans with sorrel tails, grays, buckskins, some with striped legs, palominos, and Appaloosas. His favorite, the sorrel "Papaylekin" ("Spread Foot"), could compete with the best of them. It was unshod—its one spreading front hoof required frequent trimmings—but it was a good animal.[21] The horse was still the measure of an

---

19 Hutchinson to Gwydir, April 6, 1888. Coiville Agency Records, Letterbox 20.
20 Atkins to Gwydir, March 30, 1888. Colville Agency Records, Letterbox 20.
21 Billy Curlew Interview, Coulee Dam, Washington, January 3, 1958.

Indian's wealth and position, and Moses was not averse to accepting one more to erase the donor's responsibility for some "crime."

That spring the farmer Hardy traveled up the Valley, where he saw the women making butter and the men cutting and stacking hay. Then, finding only three plows not broken, he hurried back home to order more. Moses was absent at the time of Hardy's visit, so in June the Chief went down to see him. The farmer praised him for the fine vegetables his people were growing, but Moses had other things to talk about and to complain about—especially the Blackrobe; he asked Hardy to inform Gwydir that both he and Joseph would like a Protestant preacher.[22]

Moses continued to fret about the "Bearded One." Unable to stand it any longer, he prevailed on Streamer in mid-August to write the Indian Office about the priest.[23] Good News! The Blackrobe was leaving—but not for good; he would be gone a year to obtain funds to build a house and a church to replace the tiny log cabin he used, an indication that he had been unable to finance his projects with Indian wheat.[24]

Moses also worried about the apathy of the Nez Percés towards mill repairs and other jobs. He talked the problem over with Hutchinson, who threatened them with imprisonment if they were not more co-operative. Joseph was responsible for a literal log jam at the mill when he forced Hutchinson to pull a pile of abandoned Nez Percé logs out of the way with his oxen before Moses' people could deliver theirs to be sawed.[25] The mill needed repairs because of faulty construction (Tonasket's mill and school showed the same defects[26]); but even so, in the preceding twelve months, it had produced fifty thousand feet of lumber, most of which went into twenty-two dwellings for Moses' people.[27] With

22 Hardy to Gwydir, June 11, 1888. Colville Agency Records, Letterbox 20.

23 Streamer to the United States Indian Service, August 21, 1888. Streamer, Miscellaneous Notebooks, Folder No. 3.

24 *Yakima Daily Republic* (Yakima, Washington), September 25, 1961, p. 20.

25 Hutchinson to Gwydir, July 21, 1888. Colville Agency Records, Letterbox 20.

26 Bupshaw to Gwydir, August 20, 1888. Colville Agency Records, Letterbox 20.

27 Secretary of the Interior, *Annual Report*, 1888 (50 Cong., 2 sess., *House Exec. Doc. No. 1, Pt. 5*), II, 222.

co-operation more logs could have been cut. The government had originally intended that each Indian provide his own logs for Hutchinson to saw, and then each was to stack his lumber; but this procedure had not been followed. Thus stymied at getting the timber to saw, Hutchinson received authorization to employ Indian labor. He hired Ed McQuarrie from Moses' camp to cut logs at $1.00 per thousand, and Owhi, a Yakima who had gone through the Nez Percé war, from Joseph's camp, for $1.50 a day to haul them with a horse to the mill.[28]

Whenever the natives got little done, Gwydir surmised the chief bottleneck to be the neck of a whisky bottle. Then he admonished Hardy for his laxity and failure to prevent "agents" for whisky smugglers (who traded their wares at one gallon for one horse or cow[29]) from coming among the Indians pretending to sell notions. Hardy's reply was always the same: Hire tee-totalers for police. He named likely candidates for the force—Moses' brother, Louie, and Ed McQuarrie from Moses' tribe; and from Joseph's tribe, Sam John, George Sponen, and John Hill.[30] Finding little real support from the farmer, Gwydir sought to attack the illicit traffic by establishing a border patrol of undercover policemen along the reservation boundaries to learn the identity of peddlers, and by bribing witnesses to testify against them. Moses approved this plan, provided the police were not of his band. However, Acting Commissioner A. Bupshaw vetoed the idea for lack of money to hire and arm the policemen.[31]

Hutchinson decided to do a little sleuthing of his own. On August 14, he heard that Puckmiakin was riding naked through the camps. He arrested the Indian, who apparently was more fully dressed than rumor had it. Hutchinson then took four Nez Percés and went looking for a white peddler rumored to have

[28] Hutchinson to Gwydir, October (no date), 1888. Colville Agency Records, Letterbox 20.

[29] Secretary of the Interior, *Annual Report*, 1888, II, 222.

[30] Hardy to Gwydir, July 26, 1888. Colville Agency Records, Letterbox 20.

[31] Bupshaw to Gwydir, July 31, 1888, and September 17, 1888. Colville Agency Records, Letterbox 5.

been in a camp five miles upriver, but did not find him.[32] On his return he attempted to tie up Puckmiakin, but with little success, and Dr. McAdoo, who was visiting in the miller's home, had to run out and hold a gun on the renegade. Mrs. Hutchinson also arrived on the scene. The doctor and the miller laid their weapons down to search and tie their prisoner, who all the while spat out abusive language against the Hutchinsons. Before the men could secure him, the struggling Indian jumped up and ran off into the darkness.[33]

The whisky traffic was only one of the problems discussed when Moses walked down for his frequent visits with Hutchinson. There was, of course, the perennial grievance of the tardy annuity check. The agency still owed the Indians for seed potatoes, hay for the oxen, and wages for the laborers in the mill and in the woods. Hardy had quit his job. Since no replacement for him had come, Hutchinson, in addition to his own duties, was doing the former farmer's work, which he described as "disagreeable and nothing in it."[34]

There were some new wild Indians to guide into the ways of "civilization"—the Umatillas, whom Moses had befriended. They had remained on the upper San Poil, aloof, and had nothing to do with the government. They slaughtered deer for the hides and wasted the carcasses, a practice that aroused the wrath of Skolaskin and his San Poils. Eventually the two tribes clashed, and then Moses invited the Umatillas to join his Columbias in the Nespelem. They accordingly moved over to live with Moses' people and became permanent members of the band.

The winter of 1888–89 was milder than usual—so mild that in the latter part of February both tribes held Sunday races, and

[32] Hutchinson to Gwydir, August 15, 1888. Colville Agency Records, Letterbox 20. The name Puckmiakin has been interpreted to mean "The Wild Coyote." Another interpretation is "Puck-puck-mika," or "I fight." *Okanogan Independent, Glimpses of Pioneer Life,* 85–87.

[33] Hutchinson writing of the incident years later varied the details only slightly with those of the original reports. William Hart, Scrapbooks, Cage 85, box 1, Holland Library Collection.

[34] Hutchinson to James L. Gibson, Acting Agent, December 7, 1888. Colville Agency Records, Letterbox 20.

some of the men talked of plowing the fields. But not one of the original cast iron plows was usable. Hutchinson had to give Moses' people several unused plows, previously issued to Joseph, and twenty new plows stored in a recently built warehouse. Horrible memories of the previous winter's sickness haunted the camp as soon as some came down with coughs, fevers, and rashes. A rumor of smallpox sent some of Moses' people running to Hutchinson for vaccination. An impromptu journey was made to the doctor in the Okanogan for vaccine. When it came, some of the natives backed off from the needle, while others asked for it.[35]

In response to a call from Acting Agent James L. Gibson, Moses and Joseph left the valley on February 26, 1889, for a proposed powwow at the agency. Arriving there just as Gwydir was returning from several weeks' absence, the chiefs were treated courteously by the agent and probably were invited to dine with the officials. Gwydir wrote of such an occasion when his clerk had invited Moses and Joseph to breakfast one morning. Moses reached out over the snowy white tablecloth to a big platter of steak, tore off a chunk of the meat, and wolfed it down. Holding up his greasy hands, he exclaimed to his host, "You haven't any napkin!" Gwydir could not help laughing.[36] On such visits Moses interpreted for Joseph by rendering the Nez Percé tongue into his own Salish, which the agency interpreter could translate into English.[37]

In the main agency building Gwydir opened the council on March 4 with Chiefs Moses, Lot, Skolaskin, Barnaby of the Lakes, Oropaughn, and Kinkinochin of the Colvilles in attendance. He explained the purpose of calling them together—Washington's desire to strengthen the tribes by uniting them into one government, to have them abandon their old practice of exercising unlimited power, and to substitute an Indian court for their tradi-

---

35 Hutchinson to Gwydir, January 20, 1889. Colville Agency Records, Letterbox 20.

36 *Spokesman-Review*, October 17, 1906, p. 6.

37 *Spokesman-Review*, March 26, 1899, p. 6.

tional means of law enforcement. The agent asked each chief to give his view.

Skolaskin asked the agent to designate the first speaker. It is possible the lame chief felt that much of what the agent had said was directed towards him.

Lot rose to speak. He said that he remembered back fifty years when there were no whites and a chief was sole lawmaker and judge. Even then, he said, his people wanted a school to learn the white man's ways, and they still did. He thought the suggestion of an intertribal court a step in the right direction, and he endorsed it.

Barnaby, Oropaughn, and Kinkinochin pledged their support to the plan.

Moses spoke, confessing that his hands had been dipped in blood to the elbow, but since Washington had cleaned them, he was willing to unite; but he did not want whites coming onto his land, leveling the hills and breaking open the mountains.

Joseph said his people had dwindled to a mere handful. He would consent to join the proposed court.

Skolaskin had interrupted the proceedings at intervals, talking to Gwydir. He had "sharp words" with Moses and then said: "He and his people were all alone—they were outside of the others—had nothing in common. If the others wanted to accept aid from the government well and good; he and his people wanted no aid from any source. He didn't like the proposed court, nor wished to join it." When pressed whether or not he would join, he answered "decidedly," "No."

Before adjourning the council, Gwydir told the chiefs that Washington would not allow one man to be a hindrance and an obstacle to the civilization of the other tribes.

Skolaskin left the building in a huff, gathered his people, and shouted a dire prophecy that if the agent put him in jail he would bring a wind and blow open the doors of the cells and destroy the building; and, if the agent put him on a train, God would stop the wheels when he told him to stop running the cars. Gwydir sent the police to apprehend Skolaskin and give him a chance to fulfill his boasting, but the prophet had crossed the Columbia River.[38] At Whitestone he probably looked at his own strong arm—his own jail, a hole in the ground with a windowless log shack over it. No one could tell *him* about the law.[39]

On March 23, Moses rode down the valley to visit Hutchinson who was busy milling flour. He visited Joseph and his men, who spent many of their days lying around camp exhausted from a night of gambling and complaining of getting nothing from the government. What they possibly wanted was their next quarter's clothing issue to use as gambling stakes—items like boots, shoes, stockings, lined duck-overalls, coats, and shirts.

Moses told them that they had played long enough—that they should first put in crops and fence their land as his people had done who had been at their work eight to ten days; then they could play. When some of the Nez Percés made the excuse that they had no seed, Moses told them to plow some ground and he would supply each of them two sacks of wheat and oats for seed. He returned the next day, perhaps to test the impact of his words. True to his promise, he brought seed grain to those who had prepared the ground for planting.

Moses, proud of his philanthropy, told the miller of his gift and asked him to tell the agent of it. This reminded the miller that there were no garden seeds for the Indians in the valley, except those which his wife had raised the year before.[40]

It seemed almost impossible to get anything from the agency. Teamsters Owhi and John Hill made an attempt by constantly pestering Hutchinson for their long overdue checks. Hutchinson himself knew how slow the agency was; his own quarterly report blanks had just arrived after a long delay, and he still needed paper and ink.

38 *Morning Review* (Spokane Falls, Washington Territory), March 12, 1889, p. 4, and March 17, 1889, p. 1.

39 Mary Ann Swawilla Quiltenenock Interview, Nespelem, Washington, November 21, 1959; William Thornburg Interview, Lincoln, Washington, May 7, 1960; Jim James Interview, Soap Lake, Washington, July 28, 1960; Alice Nicholson Cleveland Interview, Monse, Washington, July 22, 1961.

40 Hutchinson to Gwydir, April 2, 1889. Colville Agency Records, Letterbox 20.

Some of Moses' complaints against the government were unfounded; he always backed out just when it arranged to protect his people through the appointment of agency police from the Valley. Partly because of this non-co-operation, the desperado, Puckmiakin, gloating over his recent escape, dared return to peddle his wares. This time, Hutchinson was ready for him and had him jailed and chained at the agency. Puckmiakin laughed defiance in the miller's face, because quite unknown to the official, he had an emissary dickering with Moses for his escape. Hutchinson paid scant attention to the boast, because he believed that since Moses had lost his son-in-law to the renegade, he would pay little heed to the proposal.

The dickering continued—just a few horses at first—then more. The offer increased until Puckmiakin contracted to deliver twenty horses to Moses for his freedom. Moses weakened; and the guard "accidentally" allowed Puckmiakin to escape.[41] In justice to Moses, it is possible that his action was not so much the compounding of a felony as it was a reversion to the Indian practice of assessing damages in lieu of punishment.

Moses glowed over the acquisition to his horse bands, but glowered at the hesitancy of the government to take responsibility in criminal matters. (Had it done so, it might have uncovered his recent deal.) By this time a step had been taken to bridge the legal hiatus that had prevented the prosecution of Indians' crimes against Indians. A recent act of Congress had provided that when such cases were tried in the local courts, the cost would be borne by the federal government.[42]

In the meantime, like a wealthy man watching his bank account, Moses watched his horses run through their paces for the upcoming Fourth of July races, enjoying every minute of it. Then he got word that Father DeRouge had returned to Omak Lake to build his mission to prepare the Indians to go to heaven. A reporter talked to Moses about not going to Mass or to confession.

[41] William Hart, Scrapbooks, Cage 85, box 2, Holland Library Collection.
[42] Public Law No. 155, Sec. 11, March 2, 1889; Acting Commissioner Bell to Gwydir, May 14, 1889 (Colville Agency Records, Letterbox 6).

Didn't he want to go to heaven? Moses replied that he wanted only to stay in the Nespelem.[43] He could have added, "or any place else where I can have a good time,"—like the Fourth of July celebration at Wilbur, the frontier town springing up on "Wild Goose Bill" Condon's ranch.

Bill Condon had worked out a favorable deal with the officials of the Central Washington Railroad, which was building through the area and had platted the townsite in April. Now the railway construction crews were approaching the place, and the boom was on. Five new buildings were erected in one week, and six were under construction; a lot that sold for $450 on Saturday was resold for $650 the following Tuesday, and an offer of $800 for the same lot was turned down the succeeding Friday. All this called for a celebration. Bill sent a special invitation to his old friend Moses; and Moses replied that he would be only too glad to attend with his wives, "children," and horses.[44]

One week before the Fourth, Moses and his party, including a newly discovered racer named "Pinto," filed off with a jig and a trot across the Big Bend. When they arrived at Wilbur, they pitched their tipis on the creek at the western edge of town. Moses with several of his band left camp to take in the sights. When they appeared in town, mothers hustled their children off the streets and men reached for their guns. Word was going around that Puckmiakin and his partner, Kemelakin, were planning to leave the trail of death they had been carving between the mouth of the Okanogan and their hiding place behind the Canadian border and head straight to Wilbur to join Moses in a slaughter of whites. Old-timers tried to assure the newcomers that there was no danger from the Indians, as they were all Bill's friends. When Bill came up from his ferry for the celebration, he saw prim ladies of the community cast dour glances at his Indian wife and overheard men talking of fighting pesky redskins. His old ranch had changed more during the year than he had realized.[45]

---

43 *Yakima Herald* (Yakima, Washington Territory), June 13, 1889.
44 Steele, *An Illustrated History of the Big Bend*, 145–51.
45 *Wilbur Register*, June 28, 1889, p. 3.

The Fourth began with a dawn-shattering blast from every gun Wilbur's able-bodied men could muster, and the din of fireworks kept up the noise all day. A program of music, speeches, and the reading of the Declaration of Independence carried the celebration through the morning. The big event planned for the afternoon was the race between a local horse named "Keneway" and Moses' favorite "Pinto." Everyone, Indian and white, had been laying bets on the outcome.

During the noon hour the white families went down by Goose Creek to eat lunch and drink lemonade. Some male members of the community, finding that too tame, remained in town to quench their thirst in the saloons. Just as the picnickers were finishing their meal, Moses rode by on his way to the race track at Reeves' field just north of Goose Creek. He was in good spirits in happy anticipation of the race and was resplendent in his trappings. One observer at the picnic said, "He had the most beautiful saddle I had ever seen, finished in silver on the horn, studded with silver stars on the side, and with fancy tapaderos hanging down from the stirrups."[46] He was well fortified with firewater; as a reservation Indian, he could not buy it at the saloons, but there were plenty of white men ready to smuggle it out to him.

The crowd gathered at the track. "Keneway" and "Pinto" were brought up. Tension mounted. Whites and Indians crowded so close to the post that there was hardly room for the horses to get through. Moses rode along the line as he did at all Indian races and urged the crowd to move back. He pointed his gun at the sky and motioned toward it with his left hand, saying, "By-and-by puff, puff," meaning, "In a little while when we get the track cleared, the starter's gun will begin the race," but to the whites it meant, "In a little while, I'm going to lead my men in an attack." Instantly, John Turner, a sort of brother-in-law of "Wild Goose Bill," loaded with holiday spirits, ran over, grabbed the Chief, and jerked him off his horse. A man appointed to act as policeman for the celebration tried to step between the two, but to no avail.

[46] George Bandy Interview, Wilbur, Washington, August 10, 1961.

Then Bill and one of Moses' subchiefs moved in, broke up the fracas, and ordered Turner to find his Indian wife and get out of town. All the pent-up fears of the whites and Indians seemed on the verge of exploding like a giant firecracker. Moses' braves reportedly stationed themselves on the bluff north of Wilbur and prepared for battle, while below in town, businessmen closed their stores. Mothers gathered up their children and hustled them out of sight, some to the willows down by the creek, where they hid all afternoon.[47]

At the race track the storm passed as quickly as a Big Bend thunderstorm. The judges called the race to begin come war or not. The jockeys brought "Keneway" and "Pinto" to the post, and they were off on the half-mile straightaway between lines of spectators, yelling their favorite to victory. In the first half of the race, the straining steeds pounded neck and neck over the saltgrass course, but Moses' piebald pony tired and "Keneway" won going away. Bets were collected and the crowd dispersed. It had been a bad afternoon for Moses.

Back home more fireworks!

Moses had a San Poil nephew, Ginnamonteesah, whose mother was the offspring of one of Sulktalthscosum's far-flung marriages. Skolaskin had put this nephew in jail, but, lacking enough horses to pay his fine, he escaped in mid-July. He had gone only a short distance when he was shot down in cold blood by Kunnumsahwickssa, one of Skolaskin's private police.[48] Moses was already nearing the boiling point because the San Poils had been stealing his cattle. Now he exploded; Ginnamonteesah had fallen in the San Poil country of his grandmother, but his ebbing lifeblood had also come from his grandfather, the great Sulktalthscosum, the Half-Sun of the Columbias.[49]

47 Accounts of the wild Wilbur Fourth of July may be found in the *Wilbur Register*, July 5, 1889, p. 3; J. P. Tamiesie, Oregon Historical Scrapbooks (Oregon Historical Society), LXXIII, 109; letter written for Viggo Jurgensen to the authors, June 4, 1960.

48 Clara Hughes Moore Interview, Belvedere, Washington, November 22, 1959; Secretary of the Interior, *Annual Report*, 1889 (51 Cong., 1 sess., *House Exec. Doc. No. 1, Pt. 5*), II, 282–84.

49 Ginnamonteesah had a sister who was later to live briefly with Skolaskin.

This was a time of transition in the white man's governments, national and local. The Republican Benjamin Harrison had succeeded the Democrat Grover Cleveland the preceding March, with a resulting change in Indian Service personnel; and the territory of Washington was feverishly preparing for statehood in November. Moses could expect little satisfaction from Hutchinson, who was in process of moving from the Valley. (Soon he would be elected to the state senate.) He went to C. E. Brooks, the Okanogan farmer who had been sent temporarily to hold things together in the Nespelem,[50] but he found no help there. Then he rode to the agency to demand Skolaskin's prosecution by the new agent, Hal Cole, on duty since May 27.

Cole had been warned that Moses was a troublemaker, but to his surprise he saw standing before him a man of profound judgment and marked intellectual capacity. The agent asked about various renegades reported to be hiding in his camps. He had received a letter from the Yakima agent at Simcoe telling of a discontent-breeding and discipline-impairing report among the Indians on the Yakima that if any of them did wrong, they should go to Moses' agency where they would be free from prosecution. Because of it, Watson Homer, an Indian from the Yakima, had deserted his family, and it was said that he had taken Gracie, an unmarried girl, to the Colville. Moses denied encouraging the escape of wrongdoers to his camp. He wanted to see such people punished, he told the agent.[51]

Agent Cole did indeed act on the murder of Ginnamonteesah. He had the backing of Commissioner T. J. Morgan and official assurance that Skolaskin had no authority to run his own style of law and order, that he would be held accountable for the death of Moses' nephew, and that he would be tried for the crime in a proper territorial court. Morgan suggested that Indian police arrest Skolaskin and hold him in jail until the territorial officers could take over. Cole then had his police hustle the Prophet off to jail.

50 Brooks to Cole, July 24, 1889. Colville Agency Records, Letterbox 20.
51 Agent, Fort Simcoe, to Cole, July 22, 1889. Colville Agency Records, Letterbox 20.

General Gibbon, on a tour of inspection on the upper river, set up temporary headquarters at Lake Chelan in September. Moses, with Joseph, hurried off to confer with the General and poured out his heart as was his practice when conferring with the military.[52] Skolaskin, he said, should be kept in jail not only for murdering other Indians, but for interfering with constructive work among his people and the Nez Percés. The Indian Office and the agency, he said, were also doing wrong in not freeing Sarsopkin's horses for potlatch. Gibbon penned a note to the probate judge of Okanogan County expressing his belief that no disposition should be made of Sarsopkin's estate until a ruling on such matters was made in Washington, D. C. That seems to have ended the matter so far as Moses was concerned. County probate court or departmental ruling was all the same to him. Indian habit and custom had come up against white legal concepts, and he was puzzled as well as aggrieved.

Gibbon also wrote to Agent Cole stating, "I think it wise to banish him [Skolaskin] from the Colville Reservation. If this plan meets with your approval I request that you will act in the matter and send him to Fort Spokane. I will see that he is taken to some distant point where he can no longer exercise his pernicious influence over his followers in interfering with the design of the Government."[53]

Cole obtained permission to follow the military's suggestion,[54] and Skolaskin was sent to Alcatraz in San Francisco Bay, a military detention facility for "troublesome" Indians.[55] Moses naturally agreed with many other tribal leaders that the "Rock,"

52 Secretary of War to Secretary of the Interior, December 16, 1889, Selected Documents Relating to Skolaskin, NA, RG 75.

53 Gibbon to Cole, September 29, 1889. Selected Documents Relating to Skolaskin, NA, RG 75.

54 Cole to Commissioner of Indian Affairs, October 10, 1889; and Acting Secretary of the Interior to Commissioner of Indian Affairs, October 30, 1889. Selected Documents Relating to Skolaskin, NA, RG 75.

55 Secretary of War to Secretary of the Interior, December 16, 1889. Selected Documents Relating to Skolaskin, NA, RG 75; Clara Hughes Moore Interview Belvedere, Washington, June 30, 1961; Joe Monoghan Interview, Soap Lake, Washington, July 28, 1961; Henry Covington Interview, Colville Reservation, May 18, 1958; Harry Nanamkin Interview, Nespelem, Washington, March 4, 1961.

which he must have seen when he was in San Francisco, was a good place for their common enemy; but the San Poils to this day blame Moses for the jailing of Skolaskin without a trial.

Six days before Skolaskin was hustled off to Alcatraz, a blizzard began blowing its Arctic breath down the reservation and across the Big Bend. Never had the natives felt such a cold wind. Was this the wind the Prophet had promised to send? If so—too late now to call him back. Activity jelled. No mail reached the valley between December 28 and February 13. Yet some new employees arrived with the storm. Joseph Bouska, the new sawyer and miller, tried valiantly to bring the mail from the Barry post office, but was stopped by the ice. Alexander Campbell, the new farmer, looked at the slowly starving cattle and permitted Joseph to kill a number for his people.[56]

White men whose cattle were dying were calling the winter the "Equalizer"; it struck everyone and his stock equally. To the natives it was an "Equalizer" because it froze the advance of white civilization in its tracks, checking squads of miners, settlers, and opportunity-seekers from sweeping onto the reservation.[57]

In mid-February there was a letup, but it was brief. The Chinook dancers danced in vain; temperatures dropped. Starving stock fell dead in huddled bundles like stacks of boards at the mill. When the snow finally receded, the carcasses lay as gruesome monuments to the winter of 1889–90, the coldest on record.[58]

Soon enough, the thawing earth would signal the end of the "Equalizer." Then, white pressures would come to life where they had frozen.

[56] Alex Campbell to Cole, January 10, 1890. Colville Agency Records, Letterbox 20.
[57] Fries, *From Copenhagen to Okanogan*, 255.
[58] Steele, *An Illustrated History of the Big Bend*, 90–91.

XIV. Reading, Writing, and Wrangling

"We wish neither for a school or for a prayer."
—Moses to Agent of Forest Grove, Oregon Indian School,
Autumn, 1880

THERE WAS ONE WHITE MAN whom winter could not stop in his tracks—the bearded Father DeRouge, whose missionary efforts were making ever deepening inroads into Moses' tribe. Tribesman Homas complained to his chief that the Blackrobe was holding his wife and two children at the mission and was threatening other Indian families when they did not bring their children in for baptism. The angry Chief hurried down to Farmer Campbell on Valentine's Day, 1890, with anything but love in his heart to unload his grievances on the official.

He asked Campbell to write the agent immediately to tell him that the priest was building a church on the reservation side of the Okanogan River and that he was urging the Indians to settle around him. He complained that the Blackrobe had men raising grain for him against their will. When they objected, saying that Moses did not want them to, he told them, "Not to mind Moses that he [DeRouge] is their Sachala Tyee [Big Chief]." If any of the Indians wanted to attend a Roman Catholic church, said Moses, they could do so on the other side of the Okanogan River. Had he not told them in Washington that he did not want a priest? The farmer obediently wrote a letter for him to Cole.[1]

The next day he rode down to have the miller also write Cole a letter. He wanted the priest removed from Omak Lake, because of the disturbance he was causing by forcing women and children to accept his creed while husbands and men were "brewing trouble over the affair."[2]

1 Campbell to Cole, February 14, 1890. Colville Agency Records, Letterbox 20.
2 Bouska to Cole, February 15, 1890. Colville Agency Records, Letterbox 20.

Agent Cole set out for Omak Lake to remove the Blackrobe. When he arrived in the Nespelem on his way west, he inquired of Moses (at the request of the Nez Percé Agent W. D. Robbins) about Potlatch Fannie, a woman who had once shared the Chief's lodge, but was now living in Montana and implicated in a crime.[3] Also, the Simcoe agent, Thomas Priestly, believed Moses could give information on one Toosehammen, who had stolen some horses.[4] Cole decided not to travel the mountainous snowdrifts blocking the trail between the Nespelem and Omak Lake; but he assured the Chief that it would be best to move the mission west of the Okanogan River and delegated to Campbell the unpleasant task of informing the priest.[5]

Continuing snows and then spring responsibilities prevented Campbell from going to the mission. Finally, with better weather during mid-March, Moses visited the area himself. He found some Indian families in the vicinity disturbed at DeRouge's assumption of increasing authority and with his appointment of Indian policemen. Meanwhile John Pecard, who lived at Omak Lake, came over to the Nespelem, and Campbell sent him back with a note to the priest ordering him to leave the area immediately.

Campbell told Pecard to have men ready at the cabins in the Kartar, for he would be there Monday of the following week with Moses and one Asa Doll. In the meantime Moses returned from the neighborhood of the mission. The next day Pecard came in again with a reply from the priest, stating he would visit the agency. Pecard told the farmer that DeRouge would resist a move. Take his building down and haul it across the river, Campbell replied. Then he wrote a report to the agent and decided not to remove the priest until he should receive an answer.[6]

Campbell must have relayed to Moses the priest's plan to talk

3 Robbins to Cole, February 10, 1890. Colville Agency Records, Letterbox 6.
4 Priestly to Colville agent, January 17, 1890. Colville Agency Records, Letterbox 20.
5 Campbell to Cole, March 29, 1890. Colville Agency Records, Letterbox 20.
6 Campbell to Cole, March 29 and March (no date), 1890. Colville Agency Records, Letterbox 20.

things over with Cole, because Moses and Joseph hastened out of the Valley to see the agent. The record of conferences that Cole had with DeRouge, Moses, or Joseph at this time is not available. Moses must have lost out in the talks, because DeRouge did not move his building from Omak Lake.

Moses was not alone in his objections to the priest. Moses had been back in the Valley only briefly when Twislikin, living in the Okanogan, was assaulted on March 26, by his own brother, Sam Pierre, and five of the priest's Indian policemen. Twislikin was taken to the mission and held there two days while Sam Pierre tried to persuade him to give the church certain properties he had inherited from his father eight years before. Robert Flett, Okanogan Agency interpreter and acting farmer, heard of the situation and ordered Twislikin not to dispose of his property.[7]

At the same time Moses found himself in another fracas resulting from his ill-feeling for the Nespelems. It began the previous month when Nespelem Frank cut some fine trees for rails from land adjoining Joseph's and belonging to a fellow Nez Percé, George Sponen. Moses, hearing the ring of Frank's ax, hurried to inform Joseph, who in turn left to ask Farmer Campbell to stop the Nespelem woodchopper. (The agent suspected Moses wanted to stir up trouble between Joseph and the Nespelems.) Believing Joseph had gone to tattle, Frank came to the mill. Moses and Joseph with their interpreters met for a showdown parley. Frank claimed through his interpreter that Sponen had given him permission to take the rails. Joseph disagreed. In the heat of the argument nobody thought to send for Sponen. Finally, at Campbell's suggestion, Sponen was brought in; and he smothered the fire by assuring Joseph he had indeed allowed Frank to cut the trees. The farmer now suspected that Joseph also wanted the rails, since he had been trying to obtain possession of Sponen's land.[8]

Now the tribes squabbled over what the Nez Percés called

[7] Indian Cowlislikin [*sic*] to Cole, April 4, 1890. Colville Agency Records, Letterbox 20.

[8] Campbell to Cole, March (no date), 1890. Colville Agency Records, Letterbox 20.

thefts of their timber and what the Nespelems called thefts of their lands. Meschelle, for example, took poles from land which former agent Gwydir had authorized David Williams to settle— lands originally claimed by a Nespelem, Quilquiltakin, who had given Meschelle permission to take the timber. The agent asked Campbell for his recommendations in the matter, whereupon the miller answered that since Moses and Joseph had been located in the Nespelem Valley, the Nespelems should be sent to the San Poil. He added that the ground they occupied was near the school building. Plans were afoot to begin instruction there, but these irreconcilables refused to send their children without paying for the service, thereby forcing Moses' and Joseph's people away.[9] Their reason for refusing free schooling was logical, and they followed it consistently in all their dealings with the government: their land had been "stolen" for the use of other Indians, and if they accepted any gratuity, it would be construed as consent, and the theft would become a sale.

School would start Monday, April 21. Its opening was made possible by a fresh breath of spring blowing into the Valley on April 15, in the person of Miss Sabina Page, the new day-school teacher. She set up housekeeping in the tiny apartment next to the school building east of the creek, attracting much interest, not because she was a school mistress, but because she was the first white woman to be employed in the Valley.

Campbell immediately called Moses and Joseph to bring their ninety school-age children to classes. Bright and trim, Miss Page opened the school doors. Not a single child appeared the first day. Perhaps tomorrow.[10] On that day, again no youngsters. Day after day she faced an empty schoolroom, patiently marking time. The first Indian response was only a grumble from Moses, who complained that the school was not a boarding school. On the first of May, Joseph took off with many of his people for the camas fields around Lapwai.[11] Campbell attempted to help Miss Page with the problem of truancy, and Moses weakly promised to have his

9 Campbell to Cole, April 20, 1890. Colville Agency Records, Letterbox 20.
10 Sabina Page to Cole, May 12, 1890. Colville Agency Records, Letterbox 20.
11 *Ibid.*

youngsters in school before the end of the first week of May. Again Miss Page hopefully awaited the government's little wards to impart to them the white man's knowledge. Again none appeared. Moses then promised that some of his families would move camp near the school when grain-planting was over.[12] Day after day slipped by and still no children appeared. Finally, on May 12, Miss Page wrote Agent Cole that she would like to have police come to the Valley to enforce school attendance. She did not blame the Indians for objecting to a day school, for the children had little to eat and little clothing. Like the Chief, she thought a boarding school, where clothes and food were provided for children, would benefit them.[13] Soon a few soiled youngsters of the Moses clan showed up to take their places with anything but shining faces.

Before the month was over, some families moved their tipis down to within a quarter of a mile of the school. At that, its highest daily attendance was only nine, as one set of poorly clad youngsters after another gave it a try. When Cole came to the Valley in June to check on its progress, Moses immediately cornered him to push his own boarding-school plan. The agent, unmoved, discussed with Miss Page the various methods of getting the young truants to school with "force"—citing a government circular authorizing the withholding of rations or annuities if the families did not enroll their children.[14] In the light of the school's weak start, the agent advised the disillusioned Miss Page to close it up until fall, when, if the youngsters had not returned, sanctions would be imposed on their elders.[15]

Cole had little time to thresh out the school situation, for he had to hurry to the agency to arrange for the forcible removal of the Indians around Lake Chelan from their homes to the Colville Reservation. Indians of other tribes deciding to remain on the ceded Moses Reservation had registered their intention of staying

12 Campbell to Cole, May 9, 1890. Colville Agency Records, Letterbox 20.
13 Sabina Page to Cole, May 12, 1890. Colville Agency Records, Letterbox 20.
14 Circular No. 126, issued by the Office of Indian Affairs for United States Indian Agents, Federal Records Center, Seattle.
15 Secretary of the Interior, *Annual Report,* 1890 (51 Cong., 2 sess., *House Exec. Doc. No. 1, Pt. 5*), II, 218.

and had accepted allotments there under the provisions of the agreement.[16] The Chelans, however, still convinced that it was sacrilege to survey and sectionalize their ancestral domain, had simply remained without making any effort to comply with the agreement; and the two years allowed them to express their choice had expired.[17] Since the white community had begun to sweep them aside as so many obstacles in the path of progress, they threatened to resist the encroachment. Cole was authorized to take a company of infantry with him to Lake Chelan to aid him in removing them.[18]

While the Chelans were attempting to avoid the reservation, Moses sought to leave it—temporarily at least. (It must have seemed a dull place. The following month, on August 23, the department would ask its agents to prohibit the sale of playing cards to Indians.) The Central Washington Railroad had thrust its rails west to Coulee City,[19] and the upcoming Fourth of July promised excitement there; so Moses led his buckskin-and-blanket brigade down the Grand Coulee to the celebration. There, he spoke to a crowd and established himself as an orator of note, displaying, as Streamer mysteriously phrased it, "all the symbols known for ages in the beadwork of his coat."[20] Streamer was becoming increasingly eccentric, seeing esoteric meanings in solar symbols.

By going to Coulee City, Moses missed plenty of Fourth of July excitement at Ruby. The sheriff of the county had campaigned for office on a "Get Puckmiakin Dead or Alive" ticket. Now, at that lusty mining town, Puckmiakin, fleeing the sheriff, jumped on a race horse belonging to Nespelem George and rode it through a crowd of miners and Indians, creating bedlam. During the wild melee, Puckmiakin's horse was killed under him,

16 Kappler, *Indian Affairs: Laws and Treaties*, I, 905–15.

17 Herman J. Deutsch, "Indian and White in the Inland Empire," *Pacific Northwest Quarterly*, Vol. XLVII, No. 2 (April, 1956), p. 48.

18 War Department to the Commanding Officer of Fort Spokane, June 27, 1890, Colville Agency Records, Letterbox 20.

19 Steele, *An Illustrated History of the Big Bend*, 560.

20 Streamer, Miscellaneous Notebooks, Folder No. 2, p. 33.

and he was shot in the arm, captured, and jailed. According to a report circulated at the time, his *klooch* (wife) stripped to the waist on a hillside and danced in protest; and the applauding miners released the prisoner. The sheriff in disgust turned in his badge.[21]

Moses had hardly touched his moccasins to the reservation when he was off again, in August—this time to attend the Grand Medicine Council at the Wenatchee Flat. This big intertribal powwow coincided with the Wenatchee's later salmon runs, to give council-goers food for their bodies; their grievances gave them ample food for thought. Nearly all the Columbia River tribes were there, along with Nez Percés, Spokanes, and "King George" tribes from across the border. Streamer recorded in his diary journals that some Sioux were in attendance.[22] This, if true, gave an ominous tone to the gathering. The strange cult of the Indian Messiah, the Nevada Paiute Wovoka (Qoitze Ow), had reached that formidable tribe; and they were excitedly dancing the Ghost Dance, which they believed would miraculously destroy the whites and restore the old Indian ways.[23] If any of them were present at the council, they had surely come to spread the cult to the West.

As the council began medicine men and women keynoted the proceedings with reminders to the five hundred assembled natives of the government's failure to live up to the words of the original treaties. Moses' amanuensis, Francis Streamer, was present to record the Indians' words and to pass them along to General Howard, whom many of them believed to be their savior from the Interior Department and its Office of Indian Affairs. Several of the Chief's friends individually sought Streamer out to unburden their hearts through him to the General. Wappato John

21 *Okanogan Independent, Glimpses of Pioneer Life of Okanogan County, Washington*, 85–87.

22 Streamer kept a strict record of the council and of his correspondence pertaining to it. Streamer to Howard, August 20, September 13, and November 2, 1890. Streamer, Miscellaneous Notebooks, Folder No. 3, 37–52. A record of the "Medicine Council" is found in Streamer, Miscellaneous Notebooks, Folder No. 2.

23 James Mooney, "The Ghost Dance Religion and the Sioux Outbreak of 1890," *B. A. E., Fourteenth Annual Report* 777.

told of being cheated of one hundred dollars by James Monoghan when the latter had been sutler and purchasing agent for the quartermaster's depot at Lake Chelan Military Post. He said he had tried vainly to collect from Monoghan and had appealed to the War Department and the Office of Indian Affairs, but without result.[24] Moses complained that Monoghan had on three separate occasions charged him one hundred dollars for cashing his annuity check. He concluded: "Tell General Howard, that I, Moses, tried time and again to get this money at the post, and they pay no attention to my pleas. My people are poor, starving, and shot and killed, when on the reservation [Colville] and when they leave it, and my life is threatened. My sons are all dead. They were kind children, and were pursued by enemies of Moses as soldiers know."[25]

Chief Suiepkine echoed one of Moses' pet grievances—that priests, as he asserted, were taking his people's money to build and maintain churches on tribal lands. "Tell General Howard that I am no priestman. I am a true Indian and object to priests stealing lands for churches," he said.

Wappato John had something to say about the government's recent order to place the Chelans on the Colville:

My people are taken from their homes and carried to the Colville reserve, and they are citizens and pay taxes. The soldiers surveyed out their lands and they lived on them in accordance with the treaty. Now, some of them filed on their lands to hold them, as they were told that the Yakima land office did not know of the surveys made by the agent from Washington and the soldiers. So white men have filed on our allotted lands and great trouble I have. Tell General Howard that I paid seventy dollars taxes to Okanogan County, and that the special agent from Washington City said I should not pay my taxes, as I was a Washington City Indian by treaty of the Chief Moses reserve. Now, three of my Indian people are robbed of their farms, and I will go next, I am afraid. I wait to know from General Howard and Washington City if their treaty is a treaty or whether the Chelan

24 Streamer, Miscellaneous Notebooks, Folder No. 3, p. 125.
25 Streamer, Miscellaneous Notebooks, Folder No. 3, p. 37.

Indians must leave their old farms and obey the Colville Indian Agent—Hal Cole—or obey the treaty made at Washington City with Chief Moses, Sus-cep-kne [Sar-sop-kin], Tonasket and Lot. The whites now survey the land and they drive us away and the soldiers help them.[26]

"Virginia Bill" Covington, now running a store near the mouth of the Okanogan River across from the Colville Reservation, confirmed reports of the Chelans' bitterness at their removal to the reservation. He warned that several of them had dropped into his store threatening war. The killing of a couple of Indians on Columbia Bar by a white man did not help the already tense situation.[27]

The Wenatchee Indians asked what had become of the treaty their chief, Skamow, had signed with Colonel Wright in 1856 which promised them an eight-mile-square reservation from Mission Creek to Wenatchee Falls. They said:

> Now we are told, we must all go away to the Colville reserve and lose all of our farms, and by and by lose the Colville reserve, and forget where we belong, and who owns us; and whether we ever had a good father or mother, or whether we are only coyotes to be shot at and corralled like cayuses. Tell General Howard that we know him, and Streamer and "Sam" [Miller] and if he will make good that Col. Wright-Skamow treaty we will then know Washington is true.[28]

With perhaps less to complain about than the others, Moses gave the concluding speech of the council: "We need a good store at the Nespelem to buy our grain and sell us goods suitable for our needs of comfort, food and work on farm and stock ranges—then we would not have to go so far off our reserve to do our trading. It is our long travels to the stores in the white-man's town that costs us so much money and trouble with our pack trains,—and bad men who fence our trails, so, that our ponies cannot get grass or water, and we cannot get water for ourselves;

26 Streamer, Miscellaneous Notebooks, Folder No. 4, p. 38.
27 *Okanogan Independent, Glimpses of Pioneer Life,* 78.
28 Streamer, Miscellaneous Notebooks, Folder No. 3, p. 38.

then the whites are afraid of us and we are afraid of them. We are all blamed for the acts of one bad Indian. Now we are done talking."[29]

Leaving the Wenatchee gathering, Moses, now on better terms with the late Sarsopkin's people than he had been at the time of the reservation settlements, rode up to gamble with them and race his few remaining horses against theirs. It was Moses' custom to drink regularly. Occasionally, he showed inconsistency by remonstrating with his own celebrating Indians with a "do as I say, not as I do" attitude. This was one of those times. He braced himself, drank the contents of a whisky bottle, then preached a sermon on the virtues of sobriety, hard work, and morality.[30]

While Moses spent much of the summer out of the Valley, crickets swarmed into it and ate up the crops.[31] Agency-hired carpenters erected dwellings for several Nez Percé families from lumber cut for that purpose in the spring.[32] The Indians at first refused to live in them, as also did their chief; Joseph laughed at his tiny box building,[33] which Bouska called a "shack."

Moses returned to the Nespelem, but only long enough to catch his breath and take off again to the agency to find Hal Cole and travel with him in the latter part of October to the Northwestern Industrial Exposition at Spokane Falls. This was a big show symbolizing the rapid growth of that city of "broad streets and broad minds," with electric street lights, tramways, fire plugs, and big stores with plate glass windows revealing silks, satins, jewelry, and all the other luxuries and necessities of civilization.

The Chief's appearance in town created quite a stir. By then, many Spokanites had read Elwood Evans' *History of the Pacific Northwest* containing a pictorial and biographical sketch of the

[29] Streamer, Miscellaneous Notebooks, Folder No. 3, p. 52.

[30] Steele, *An Illustrated History of Counties*, 862. Even though Moses drank heavily, he frequently made temperance speeches (*Wenatchee Daily World*, September 28, 1934, p. 13).

[31] Secretary of the Interior, *Annual Report*, 1890 (51 Cong., 2 sess., *House Exec. Doc. No. 1, Pt. 5*), II, 220.

[32] Bouska to Cole, May 5, 1890. Colville Agency Records, Letterbox 20.

[33] Lucy Friedlander Covington Interview, Nespelem, Washington, August 25, 1962.

Chief. The inclusion of these features in the work gave Moses great publicity, but they were apparently included at the publisher's insistence against Evans' will.[34] This writer regarded all Indians as roadblocks to civilization. "Indian wars," he wrote, "are but essential concomitants of American settlement." He sacrificed accuracy to grandiloquence to portray Moses as a figure of power, mystery, and intrigue—"more admired and feared perhaps than any Indian of the coast . . . and afraid of neither God nor man." He was of Cherokee birth, Evans wrote, and as a child traveled with an uncle to Wisconsin. There he was left to wander several years before making his way across the Rockies to the Spokanes, from whence he drew to himself all the "mongrel" bands along the Columbia. As for his life there, "There are those who hint at dark and desperate deeds in the grim defiles of his *'coulee'* which have supplied him abundantly with gold and jewels. Probably no one can aver with certainty of the matter; but it is true that traders and miners have mysteriously disappeared in those rocky solitudes; and the 'king of the coulees' is not known to be in lack of whatever of gold and wine, and women his fiery passions may crave."[35]

Through an interpreter Moses had the following conversation with a reporter from the *Spokane Falls Review*:

Yes, I am glad to see Spokane again. It is splendid.

When I think of the way it looked when I was here before, it makes me feel how lonesome it must have been then.

I am not surprised at the electric cars. I have been to Washington and am no longer surprised at anything.

Yes, I would like to again go to Washington. My heart is glad whenever I think of the great city. and the way the great father treated me. I am only sorry that I did not ask for a pension for my son when I asked for my own.

The reporter asked if he remembered the Nez Percé war:

Yes, and I came very near joining them. I sometimes wanted

34 John Maceachern, "Elwood Evans, Lawyer—Historian," *Pacific Northwest Quarterly*, Vol. LII, No. 1 (January, 1961), 17.
35 Evans, *History of the Pacific Northwest: Oregon and Washington*, II, 484.

to and sometimes I did not. I had many more warriors than
Joseph, but at the time most of them were over on the Nisqually.

My children: I have about 500; are dying off rapidly; they are
sick all the time. I do not know how long they will last.

My people do not go to school, but farm some.

Long ago, before Joseph went on the warpath, I was at the
falls of the Spokane, and it was very lonesome then, although I
did not at that time think so; but I have seen so many white
men, and so many fine cities that I have forgotten quite those
days, and the white man. I only wish my people could last long
enough to learn how to build such fine cities, but I am afraid the
end of my people is not far off. I have seen sixty-two snows, and
have watched my people dwindle from many more than I could
count down to 500. Sickness seems to kill them all.[36]

Sickness at that very moment was plaguing Tonasket in a
Spokane Falls hospital. Moses told the reporter of his reunion
with the Okanogan chief and his sorrow over the removal of one
of Tonasket's eyes and the possible removal of the other. He
understood the chief's suffering, for he too was approaching the
advanced stages of conjunctivitis and was in danger of losing one
of his own eyes.[37]

The visiting Chief must have been overwhelmed by the Exposition Building, a massive structure covering an area of 60,000
feet and rising to a height of 110 feet. As he wandered around
through the exhibits, he was the center of attention in his heavily
beaded and otter-trimmed buckskin outfit, set off by a fancy
tobacco sack and beaded collar representing his symbol, "the
half-moon that never wanes." His unusual physical appearance
completed the impression. One reporter wrote of him: "Moses,
the chief of the Columbia tribe of Indians, was the most noticeable man in the city or at the exposition yesterday. He is a
rather fine-looking old fellow about six feet tall, and of generous
proportions. His head is large and set close to the shoulder, the
forehead is big but narrow and retreating, while the lower part

36 *Spokane Falls Review* (Spokane Falls), October 31, 1890, pp. 1, 6.
37 *Ibid.*

of his face is very broad. On the whole Moses is a commanding looking Indian."[38]

No one knew better than he that he made a striking picture— so he strutted over to a gallery to have a photographer with his magic box capture him in all his splendor. Somewhere in the tour he delivered an oration to visiting legislators from Olympia, the Washington state capital, and he stuffed his big frame with clams and oysters.[39]

Critics were calling the art exhibit on the third floor "the rarest and most valuable works from famous artists ever exhibited in the West." Moses showed interest only in those portraying the West. Looking at one of them, the *Coup de Grace*, he stopped, a grim smile playing across his face, his mind turning back to his youth, when he too dealt deathblows to the enemy like the brave in the picture. Someone called his attention to Frederick Remington's masterpiece, *Questionable Companionship*.[40] He confirmed what art critics have said about Remington's portrayal of the horse, only in much simpler language: "Horses, heap good." He was still in a reminiscent mood in front of another western classic, *The Last Lull in the Fight*, and commented, "That is good. That is War."[41]

Returning to the reservation, he found that a stark event there was threatening to plunge that region into war.

38 *Spokane Falls Review*, October 31, 1890, p. 7.
39 *Wilbur Register*, November 7, 1890.
40 *Spokane Falls Review*, October 31, 1890, pp. 1, 6.
41 *Spokane Falls Review*, October 31, 1890, p. 6.

XV. Double Trouble

"I have kept my rifle behind me."—Moses at Simcoe Agency
February 19, 1879

ONE NIGHT IN MID-OCTOBER, 1890, a freighter named S. S. Cole was murdered at a lonely place where he had camped on the southwest corner of the Colville Reservation. After the smoke of many rumors cleared, it was commonly accepted among the whites that the murderers were two Indians, John, aged twenty-two, and Stephen, aged fourteen. A short time later another freighter, Wilkinson, was murdered on a lonely mountain road, and his wagon was pushed over a steep bank. An Indian girl, whom John had jilted, tattled on him as Wilkinson's killer. That in popular sentiment proved that he had killed Cole also. A deputy sheriff traced him to a camp in the Chiliwist area of the Okanogan Valley and killed him, wounding an Indian woman in the process.[1] Stephen went into hiding at Omak Lake. Very possibly, Moses knew he was there and was concerned that one suspected of complicity in the crime was so near his camps.

Meanwhile excitement of another kind struck the Valley. On Christmas day, Miss Page rose early to prepare a surprise Christmas dinner for the school children. It had been quite a term. Commissioner Morgan had suggested a noon meal to increase the school's attendance, but warned that a boarding school of the type Moses demanded was out of the question.[2] Nevertheless, school was in session with a few of Moses' and fewer of Joseph's children in attendance. The first time the number reached two figures was December 11, when ten children were present. On December 17, there were fourteen in attendance and an increasing number as Christmas neared.

[1] *Wilbur Register*, October 24, 1890, January 16, 1891; Fries, *From Copenhagen to Okanogan*, 324–34; and *Okanogan Independent, Glimpses of Pioneer Life*, 75–77.
[2] Morgan to Cole, August 22, 1890. Colville Agency Records, Letterbox 6.

On Christmas morning Farmer Campbell came over to help Miss Page cook the dinner. News of the surprise had gotten out, and, well before noontime, the children flocked in. At eleven-thirty in the morning Miss Page and Campbell began to set the table. In an explosive instant the room became a bedlam of crackling flames and shrieking children. Quickly, the two shoved the children from the building just seconds before it, together with an adjoining woodshed and outdoor toilet, was consumed.[3] A defective flue had put Miss Page in the ranks of the unemployed and formal education in the Valley into the ash heap.

Shortly after the New Year, 1891, Stephen sent word from his Omak Lake hideout that he wished to give himself up. A justice of the peace from Ruby went over, took him away from a pow-wow in progress, and turned him over to the sheriff. At a hearing in Ruby's equally boisterous twin city, Conconully, the boy admitted witnessing the crime, but staunchly maintained it had been committed by a renegade Nez Percé. Bail was refused, and he was committed to the county jail. A writ of habeas corpus was immediately sworn out and the prisoner was examined before a United States commissioner. The commissioner ruled that he was entitled to bail, set at one thousand dollars. Before his sorrowing family could raise the money, twenty masked men, on the night of January 8, rode through Conconully on horses whose hoofbeats were muffled by a fresh snow. They forced the jailer at gun point to admit them to the steel cage holding the prisoner; then whisked him half a mile below town and hanged him to a tree. His friends cut his body down, put it in a coffin, and carried it across the Okanogan River to Father DeRouge's recently completed church. The priest watched over it all one night and buried it in the church cemetery the next morning.[4]

No evidence was ever produced to indicate that the boy was guilty of murder.[5] Even the *Okanogan Outlook* at Conconully

---

3 Bouska to Cole, December 19 and December 25, 1890. Colville Agency Records, Letterbox 20.

4 *Spokane Falls Review,* February 6, 1891.

5 William Compton Brown, a prominent pioneer and judge in the Okanogan (after conversations with prominent white officials who were in the Okanogan at

admitted, "It is probably a fact that, as usual the vigilantes made a mistake and hanged the wrong man."⁶ Naturally the Indians were deeply aroused. For two days following the obsequies for Stephen, they danced, but not for joy. Many swore revenge for the deed. It was reported that one potlatch of Okanogan Indians sent sixteen of their braves to the Dakotas with plenty of *chickamin* and blankets for the trip to receive "Messiah Craze" inspiration from their eastern brothers.⁷ Hiram Smith, now a member of the state legislature, in a dispatch to the *Spokane Falls Review* said that the most trouble could be expected from natives living on the Colville Reservation at the mouth of the Okanogan River. Hitherto, he said, they had taken no stock in the Messiah dances; but Moses and Joseph had as much influence among them as Sitting Bull had among the Sioux, and if they joined the hostiles, their numbers would be boosted to four hundred, and if the British Columbia Indians were to join them, there would be one thousand braves facing the helpless whites.⁸ It should be noted, however, that the desperate faith of the Sioux ghost-dancers had not protected them against army bullets; Sitting Bull had been killed, and the massacre of Wounded Knee had occurred in December.

The Indians did one of the things Smith feared they might do; on January 10, they sent runners north to alert their fellows in British Columbia. They also sent runners east to alert those along the Kettle River and Moses' and Joseph's bands. That same night, the whites sent a messenger south to Coulee City with a frantic petition to be wired to Acting Governor Charles E. Laughton at the capital, Olympia, explaining their plight and begging for arms. Coulee citizens notified Indian Agent Hal Cole at Spokane Falls of the danger, asking him to appeal to United States authori-

---

the time of the killing), maintains that there was never any proof that Stephen or John were the killers. Letter to authors, January 16, 1959.

⁶ Steele, *An Illustrated History of Counties.* 503. In what some might call retribution, Conconully would suffer floods, fire, and economic collapse, a disaster each year for three years following the hanging (*ibid.,* 540–41).

⁷ *Ibid.,* 499–500.

⁸ *Ibid.; Spokane Falls Review,* January 11, 1891, p. 3.

ties if he thought it necessary.[9] Laughton, a heavy investor in Okanogan mining properties,[10] initiated immediate state action and assured the petitioners that two hundred rifles and six thousand round-ball cartridges were ready to roll east from the coast on the Northern Pacific Railroad to Spokane Falls and back west again by way of the Central Washington Railroad to Coulee City. He delegated to Brigadier General A. P. Curry, of the National Guard, the responsibility of delivering this military aid to the Okanogan. Calls came in thick and fast from isolated white communities in the hinterland.[11]

In a gloomy letter to General Gibbon in San Francisco, Laughton included this warning from Curry:

> Coulee City,
> January 15, 1891
>
> Brigadier General O'Brien, Olympia:
>
> Latest reports from scene of trouble are, no abatement of existing excitement among settlers. Conconully is being guarded at night by citizens. At the burial of Indian Stephen, who was lynched, Indians swore revenge. Squaws who are living with white men have warned them to leave the reservation, telling them there is danger ahead. Traders have sold considerable ammunition to Indians for the past few days. Whites who have gone to the reservation have found the Indians very surly and have been ordered not to return. Lincoln and Douglas counties were each furnished fifty arms and five hundred rounds of ammunition, leaving two hundred arms for Okanogan county, which are being hurried forward under strong escort. Moses' and Joseph's people are dancing the Messiah dance and refuse to have anything to do with the whites. [signed] A. P. CURRY, *Brigadier Gen.*[12]

In the midst of the excitement, Interpreter A. J. Chapman, came to Spokane Falls from the Colville. Only the month before,

---

9 *Senate Journal of the Second Legislature of the State of Washington,* "The Okanogan Indian Troubles," 1891, p. 549 (hereafter referred to as *Senate Journal, Second Legislature*).

10 Steele, *An Illustrated History of Counties,* 527.

11 *Wilbur Register,* January 23, 1891, p. 3.

12 *Senate Journal, Second Legislature,* 549.

he had conversed with Wovoka in Nevada, and everyone was anxious to learn whether the Paiute's strange gospel had spread to the Indians of the Northwest. Chapman said he knew the Indians were dancing, but could not tell whether they were inspired by the Messiah Craze. He said, "I visited the Nespelem tribe the other day and found chiefs Moses and Joseph people dancing in a long dance house of regular tepees during the afternoon that I arrived. They were dancing a regular war dance when I rode up. When my arrival was announced, dancing stopped and Joseph came out. I said 'What does all this mean, Joseph? Are you on the war path, and having a war dance?' 'No,' said he 'this is merely for pastime, like we used to do in years agone.' "[13] The *Spokane Falls Review*, on January 13, reported more than the customary winter dancing in the Yakima to "propitiate the Good Spirit." Continued the *Review*, "Piute runners have been among them and, it is said they are combining with Chief Moses' Indians from the North."[14]

Moses assured everyone he had no aggressive intentions. Through Farmer Bouska, he requested Agency Clerk Anderson to write to the Warm Springs (Oregon) and Yakima reservations requesting their agents to order the Indians to stop talking about his wanting to go to war. Bad rumors, he said, from those quarters were published in the papers making his *tum tum* sick. He also requested Anderson "to make out a paper and sent [sic] it or have it published in Okanogan saying that Moses and all his people wishes to be left in peace; from white peoples bad talk making false reports about him and his people. He says he wants to obey Washington's Laws." And, furthermore, whenever any of his men did something wrong he would see to it that they were punished.[15]

General Curry arrived in Conconully the night of January 17, proudly wearing a heavy Spanish dirk, which one newspaper man said might "mark the dividing line between a painted topknot

13 *Spokane Falls Review*, January 11, 1891, p. 2.
14 *Spokane Falls Review*, January 13, 1891, p. 2.
15 Bouska to Anderson, January 15, 1891. Colville Agency Records, Letterbox 21.

and an Okanogan Indian's skull."[16] Of more practical use were the 3,000 rounds of ammunition and 180 guns he brought. The following Monday, accompanied by Agent Cole and Clerk Anderson, he traveled to the Colville Reservation to hold council with several chiefs, in the course of which he exacted promises from them to stop their dancing, carrying arms except when hunting, and making threats against the whites who they believed had taken part in Stephen's hanging. He also got them to promise to ferret out whisky peddlers, the source of much disorder. The meeting was surprisingly peaceful. Even the renegade Puckmiakin was there making glowing promises of friendship for the white man. In his official report Curry praised Father DeRouge especially for bringing the tribes together and calming them down.[17]

Curry made no mention of Francis Streamer's role in the Okanogan crisis. Streamer by then believed himself to be no longer only an amanuensis for Moses and the other natives, but of a higher power. With the Okanogan outbreaks, certain ethereal powers, which he termed "Solar Command and Eye Vision," ordered him to keep Moses and other chieftains from recriminations against the whites. Some years before in their frequent correspondence, Howard had become aware of Streamer's strange obsession and, fearing for his sanity, wrote in his scripture-quoting manner, "It is a curious idea that you have formed that you are an amanuensis of a higher power. . . . Seek peace and pursue it. Lie down beside the still waters. Gather rest and refreshment from the sweetest of fountains. Otherwise your mind will lose its balance and the brittle pitcher be broken at the source."[18]

Streamer kept Howard informed of his peace-making in the Okanogan, linking, as he always did, his own welfare with that of the Indians in asking the General to secure him government aid for his good offices in the trouble. His rapidly failing mind could

---

[16] *Spokane Falls Review,* January 15, 1891.

[17] *Senate Journal, Second Legislature,* 547.

[18] Howard to Streamer, August 18, 1887. Streamer, Miscellaneous Notebooks, Folder No. 3.

neither see the illogical nature of the request nor that the embarrassed Howard was in no position to help. Yet Howard charitably continued to answer his letters. After things quieted down in the Okanogan, he sent a "Fall Coat" to Streamer, who in turn gave it to Chief Suiepkine as a "memento of the General's esteem of our respective services in restoring peace and preventing the Indians of Washington State from joining the Dakota Sioux on the war path."[19]

Later, Streamer would write a requiem for the red man, followers of evil white men rather than of beneficent solar leadings: "So long as the Indian race conformed to their aboriginal traits of kindness, they honored the Sun, and enjoyed its vizor and view. But alas! creed, greed, and whisky of a lewd race sent down their high aspirations to a common level with the square that a money-worshipping sect, sexed them with. They forgot God, and God wept over them—and called them home to answer."[20]

Upon Anderson's return from accompanying General Curry and his party, he assured reporters at Spokane Falls that no more trouble was expected. Cole said that he had seen Moses, and that Moses asked him to have something put in the papers telling the white people that he was peaceable. The Chief regretted the feeling of anxiety on the part of both Indians and whites and wanted them to have confidence in each other. Cole implied that the coincidence of winter dancing with the scare was unfortunate, that the Indians had danced less than the winter before so as not to alarm the whites.[21]

Moses held his breath, fearful that the frontier might flame up again and burn him in its fire. At the very height of the crisis, there came a period of mild weather between freezes of this "double winter," enticing his followers from their winter houses to the scene of the recent troubles. Double winter—double trouble! Two of his men, leaving the reservation, drifted over to the Ruby area to their deaths at the hands of Puckmiakin and

19 Streamer, Miscellaneous Notebooks, Folder No. 3, p. 55.
20 Streamer, Miscellaneous Notebooks, Folder (Okanogan Smith's Store Journals), 251.
21 *Spokane Falls Review*, January 11, 1891, p. 3.

Kemelakin. Because of the strained relations, Moses visited Bouska on January 19 and asked him to write Cole that he was sick of lawless whites in the Okanogan stirring up bad feeling among Indians; he wanted the whites to stop telling lies; some of his people were afraid of the whites for the way they acted towards Indians; travel on the Wild Goose Bill road was abandoned by both whites and Indians because each was afraid of the other; he wanted it understood that he and his people wanted respect from the whites, toward whom they bore no ill will. He wanted the lawless punished, and wanted the agent to "write out" a warrant for the arrest of Puckmiakin and Kemelakin for killing the two men from his tribe. Gwydir had promised time and again to arrest them, but never did. Moses even instructed the agent concerning the method of capturing the renegades: he could "easily get them" by writing to the sheriff at Ruby to arrest and hold them to be picked up. Once that was done, all the Moses people would be on good behavior and peaceful again.[22] (Moses often took the miller's little son on his lap during such meetings.)[23]

Could Moses have so soon forgotten that he too was responsible for Puckmiakin's freedom when he traded the renegade's incarceration for a band of horses?

Indians traveling the well-beaten path between the Colville and the Nez Percé agencies with their stock and their occasional drunken forays, continued to keep the white population on edge. A militia company was formed at Cortland Academy northeast of Wilbur near the Columbia as a first line of defense for the white community, and every day its cadets could be seen in the hills practicing the tactics of Indian fighting.[24] The only reassuring note in the crisis came from Rebecca Steveson, the defenseless postmistress living on the Columbia at Barry but a war whoop away from the reservation. In a letter of January 30 to the *Wilbur Register* she wrote:

22 Bouska to Cole, January 19, 1891. Colville Agency Records, Letterbox 21.
23 Mrs. Edward Neils Interview, Klickitat, Washington, April 2, 1962. Mrs. Neils is the daughter of the lad Moses often held on his lap.
24 *Wilbur Register*, January 30, 1891, p. 2. Cortland was an "undenominational" institution, but "distinctively Christian" (*Wilbur Register*, June 26, 1891, p. 3).

I see by your paper that the people along the river are considerably excited with fear that Indians will break out. I am acquainted with Chiefs Moses and Joseph and feel perfectly satisfied that there is no danger from this source, otherwise I would not keep my family here over night. The most danger is to be feared from drunken Indians coming direct from Wilbur and Coulee City. The officers of both places should use more vigilance and see that the Indians do not obtain liquor, or some of these days, some innocent person or family will have to suffer. We live at the Moses crossing, and have an opportunity to learn of all their movements and can safely assure the people that at present there is no danger to be feared.[25]

Mrs. Steveson's letter did much to put everyone at ease. The week after it was published, the Indians felt safe enough to come over to Wilbur with the agency clerk to pick up thirty wagons, seventy-four spring beds, an organ, and other articles to freight back to the reservation.[26]

Another anxiety gripping Moses in the backwash of the Okanogan troubles must have been the rapid rise of Father DeRouge in the estimation of the natives. The Blackrobe's tender care for the body and soul of Stephen and his other kindnesses did much to draw the Messiah-dazed ones to his Omak Lake mission. Even die-hard pagans at the mouth of the Okanogan, sworn to have nothing to do with the Church, were among those making their way there over trails which might as well have been sprinkled with sawdust. Worse yet, for Moses, were those of his own people caught up in the Blackrobe fever.[27] What could he do with the priest? He could not attack him physically—that would destroy his own image as a man of peace. He did not seem to be getting anywhere with the government to oust him. About all he could do was wait and worry.

Another trouble that winter was an influenza epidemic so devastating that Bouska reported that there were not enough able-bodied men to bring in logs for lumber to build a new

[25] *Wilbur Register*, January 30, 1891, p. 2.
[26] *Wilbur Register*, February 6, 1891, p. 3.
[27] *Spokane Falls Review*, February 15, 1891, p. 2.

school. This time there was an Indian Service doctor present. Dr. E. H. Latham, formerly of Spokane Falls, had come to the Valley on January 17; his arrival about the time the disease struck caused many natives to blame him for bringing it. He had hoped a small office erected for him might serve as a dispensary to which the natives would eagerly flock for medical care. It did not work out that way. Then he carried medicine to the camps. Joseph's people, encamped below the office, did not welcome him to their winter lodges. The second cold wave of the "double winter" struck in March, lowering the Indians' already weakened resistance to disease. Moses' daughter lay ill with influenza in the "white house." She seemed to rally at times; so her father bundled up some furs and took them over to Wilbur to trade and to consult Dr. J. P. Tamiesie, in whom he had considerable faith. On his return, the girl worsened in spite of Dr. Latham's care. Yet Moses did not lose his faith in "white medicine men." Of course, he still believed in his own native shaman, Tompasque. Tamiesie or Tompasque—it did not much matter which. When the girl died, he seems to have blamed neither.[28]

When Latham made his rounds on March 13, he found twenty-five natives sick in the lodges of Snawtonic; twenty in those of Blind Louie; and four, in Owhi's up at Owhi Lake.[29] Moses came down with the disease himself, but recovered rather rapidly. He would, however, never recover from the inflammation of his eyes. The pterygium, the result of catarrhal conjunctivitis, was moving closer to the center of one eye. In conditions such as this, Dr. Latham used hydrochlorate of cocaine to soothe the burning sting. Poor Tonasket died the first week of April after returning from a trip to Spokane (the new name of Spokane Falls) to check on the sight of his remaining eye.[30]

The influenza left with the arrival of good weather. Winter's toll in the Valley: twenty-seven deaths, thirteen of them Moses' people, fewer Nez Percés and Nespelems. There were only four-

28 Campbell to Cole, March 12, 1891. Colville Agency Records, Letterbox 21.
29 Latham to Cole, March 14, 1891. Colville Agency Records, Letterbox 21.
30 Secretary of the Interior, *Annual Report*, 1891 (52 Cong., 1 sess., *House Exec. Doc. No. 1, Pt. 5*), II, 444.

teen births in the Valley this year, the first year for a long time in which there were fewer births than deaths.

Perhaps at the very least, death at the hands of Puckmiakin and Kemelakin might be prevented. After Moses had appealed to Cole, the agent sent word to the Okanogan farmer to have the sheriff arrest the pair. With their arrest, Moses began, through his Indian friend Smitkin, to promote the idea at home and in the Okanogan that the killers had been brought to justice through his efforts. (Actually, he had always wanted the Office of Indian Affairs to handle the job.) But what if the two renegades should be freed! He would lose all the credit he had been claiming. And this was a strong possibility considering the shrewd Puckmiakin's cleverness in getting out of tight places. One day Moses apparently heard that the two had been set free, for on April 29 he hurried to Bouska and asked the miller to write the agent that he wanted to know whether this had happened and that, if so, why. "Moses has a very sick *tum tum* if they are let go free; as he says all of his people will make fun of him and laugh to his face." The Okanogan tribe would also make fun of him.[31] Alas, for Moses, the two outlaws had indeed been turned loose.

More trouble! The Great Father had decided to take back part of the Colville Reservation and had appointed three commissioners—Mark A. Fullerton, W. H. H. Dufer, and J. F. Payne— to negotiate with the Indians. After a briefing session at the agency, this commission accompanied by Agent Cole and Interpreter Chapman arrived in the Valley.[32] The Indians had been notified, and the chiefs and their subchiefs were there to meet them: Moses and Joseph representing 406 Indians of the Valley; Antwine, the Okanogans now that Tonasket was dead; Meschelle, 59 Nespelems; and Posahli, nearly 300 San Poils and Nespelems now that Skolaskin was away.

The council convened on May 1. Payne opened the meeting and moved directly to the point—the government wanted to buy the north half of the reservation for $1,500,000 (about $1.00 an

31 Bouska to Cole, April 29, 1891. Colville Agency Records, Letterbox 21.
32 Secretary of the Interior, *Annual Report*, 1891, II, 443.

acre). Indians living and owning improvements in the tract could remain and receive 80-acre allotments there. The suddenness of the proposal immobilized most of the natives, but the San Poils and Nespelems immediately voiced their opposition. Collecting their wits, some of the chiefs argued for half-section (320-acre) allotments.

Moses consulted with Cole privately about the offer and was advised that the deal was fair.[33] Antwine was not so sure. He wanted each tribal head with no annuity to receive a cash award. On considering this proposal, the commissioners agreed to suggest to the department that each chief receive $1,000, except Moses, who should be paid $1,500. This plan infuriated Antwine, who was trying to exclude the "drinking" Columbia from any more money.

One San Poil and Nespelem after another made long-winded, time-killing speeches, as their martyr leader, now languishing in prison, would have done. Finally, Moses spoke. The once powerful man, still large in stature, told the commission that they were making a mistake: "You are acting like a lot of fools. Don't you know that Washington is right on top of you and if they want the land, they are going to take it, whether we are willing or not?" He illustrated his point by placing one hand above the other.[34]

The council wore on for three days. The Indians, with the exception of the San Poils and Nespelems, agreed to cede on the following terms: the money offered, to be paid in five annual installments; the allotment of 80-acre tracts of land to Indians wanting to reside on the north half; and an annuity for each chief of $1,000, except for Moses, who would have his present annuity raised to $1,500. The Okanogans signed first, then Moses, and finally Joseph. The San Poils and Nespelems refused to sign.[35] To seal the transaction, Moses gave Commissioner Dufer a fine pipe which Sarsopkin had given him years before.[36]

33 Secretary of the Interior, *Annual Report*, 1892 (52 Cong., 2 sess., *House Exec. Doc. No. 1, Pt. 5*), II, 488.

34 *Spokesman-Review*, March 26, 1899.

35 Secretary of the Interior, *Annual Report*, 1891, II, 443.

36 *Spokane Review*, June 16, 1891.

Moses anticipated a brief respite from his troubles as he joined Joseph and other Indians for a trip to Coulee City. The enthusiastic builders of that place were planning a big celebration for May 8, with a special excursion train filled with business and professional men from Spokane; and they invited the Indians to bring their fastest cayuses to entertain them. Moses and Joseph with their combined people arrived on May 7 and camped at the edge of town near a band of Umatillas. On the morning of the big day, the tribal rivalry always lying beneath the surface erupted into a firewater-charged fracas, and the two chiefs had to step in and march their Indians out of town and up the Coulee to cool off before the law could catch up with them. By race time they had quieted down enough to put on a good show, but one lacking the spontaneity of the morning's unscheduled performance.[37]

Meanwhile the commissioners, with their work at the agency completed, went on to Marcus to negotiate with the Colvilles and Lakes, whose chiefs, Oropaughn and Barnaby, signed the same agreement on May 23 for the ceding of the north half.[38] Two weeks later, Payne delivered the papers to the Secretary of the Interior. The San Poils were so angry at the sell out of their land that, in the absence of Skolaskin's counsel, they sought advice from Spokane attorneys, George Turner and Frank H. Graves.[39] In answer to a query about the advisability of returning Skolaskin from Alcatraz, Colonel F. Mears, commandant at Fort Spokane, replied on June 15 that such a move would be extremely unwise in the light of his followers' extreme agitation.[40]

Trouble dogged Moses into the summer. Crickets chewed through the Valley again this season, destroying crops; late spring root trips were not very productive; and the salmon fishing was

37 *Spokane Review*, May 2, 1891, p. 3, and May 7, 1891, p. 5; *Big Bend Empire* (Waterville), May 14, 1891.
38 Secretary of the Interior, *Annual Report*, 1891, II, 442–46.
39 Lieutenant George K. French, Post Adjutant from Spokane, to Commanding Officer, Fort Spokane, April 14, 1892. Selected Documents Relating to Skolaskin, NA, RG 75.
40 Mears to Assistant Adjutant General, Headquarters Division of the Pacific, June 15, 1891. Selected Documents Relating to Skolaskin, NA, RG 75.

poor. Plenty of lumber was sawn, and a blacksmith shop and a slaughterhouse were under construction, but school plans were inconclusive. Moses would have worried if he had known that the Department of the Columbia had plans to consolidate the army posts in the region and locate them on railroad lines, a policy which would soon transfer Fort Spokane's buildings and grounds to the Interior Department to be used as an Indian school.[41]

Moses had more trouble. Two young men met him with news that his nephew, Yayoskin, was on the Nez Percé wanted list. But why Yayoskin? Moses rode immediately to the Nez Percé camp and asked Joseph. Because, said Joseph, he had gone to Ruby, traded his horse for whisky, returned, and in a drunken fit killed a Nez Percé horse. Now there was bad talk and bad blood between the two camps. Charlie Wilpaukin threatened to shoot Kiakia. The two chiefs had sick *tum tums*, with Joseph blaming the Moses Indians for the whisky trade and Moses blaming the non-working Nez Percés for the general lethargy of the Valley. The two compromised on a jail for offenders. Moses went with their plan to W. F. Leslie, who had succeeded Campbell as farmer. Leslie thought it a good idea.[42] That fall he built a small flimsy single-padlocked-door "skookum house" on the bank next to the foot bridge that crossed the river between the mill and the barn.[43]

Rumors of the Messiah Craze had died down considerably by fall, but echoes of it were heard in Portland, where officials of the Industrial Exposition asked Agent Cole that Moses, Joseph, and Lot be permitted to come to their city to perform the Ghost Dance as an entertainment feature. At that time the Commissioner of Indian Affairs was taking a dim view of Indian participation in itinerant wild west shows,[44] but he authorized Cole to consent, since the Portland show was to be held in one place and

41 *Wilbur Register*, October 9, 1891.

42 Leslie to Cole, August 13, 1891. Colville Agency Records, Letterbox 21.

43 Leslie to Cole, September 4, 1891 (Colville Agency Records, Letterbox 21); Madeline Covington Interview, Nespelem, Washington, May 29, 1961.

44 On March 8, Commissioner Morgan had sent a directive to his agents listing the evils of such participation. An editorial in the *Spokane Falls Review*, October 9, 1890, p. 4, condemned the government's policy.

but for a short period of time. He also gave permission to a band of Umatillas from their reservation to attend. The Umatilla agent, Colonel John W. Crawford, urged Moses and Joseph to join them, promising Joseph that his friends, Yatinawiz, No-shirt, and Young Chief would be there, as well as his "Boston" friend, Olin Warner, the sculptor.[45]

The first leg of their journey took Moses and Joseph to Wilbur in late September, when the Wilbur *Register*, observed "the two old murdering rascals . . . strutting around as only becomes men of rank."[46] Sauntering down the dusty main street of Wilbur, they had their minds on goals less heavenly, or hellish, than those of the Messiah Dance. Then, accompanied by Chief Lot and Agent Cole, they came into Camp George Wright near Spokane. There they saw cavalry troops riding up and down practicing maneuvers in an atmosphere of tension; they learned that there was an alert on account of reported troubles between settlers and natives in the Kalispell country to the east.[47]

At Spokane the party met another traveling companion, their interpreter of Washington, D.C., days, S. F. Sherwood, who held their passes for the Northern Pacific Railroad.[48] They bade fare-well to Agent Cole, who continued to the Kalispell country to find no trouble there. On the afternoon of September 30, they reached Portland. Lot must have remembered the time he rode horseback from the Spokane country to Portland to board General Howard's boat as it was preparing to sail for San Francisco. Taking the commander into his huge arms, he had tearfully begged him not to go away. Howard, touched by the gesture, said that in all of his experiences in the West only two other Indians—Cochise of the Apaches and Moses of the Columbias—had ever shown him similar affection.[49]

A reception committee was on hand at the station to escort the train-weary travelers on a brief tour of the Exposition Building.

45 Wood to Cole, September 23, 1891. Colville Agency Records, Letterbox 21.
46 *Wilbur Register*, October 2, 1891, p. 5.
47 *Spokane Review*, September 30, 1891, p. 5.
48 Sherwood to Cole, September 3, 1891. Colville Agency Records, Letterbox 21.
49 Howard, *My Life*, 435–42.

There the crowds hemmed them in, trying to get a glimpse of these "typical specimens of their race, large of frame with strong faces," especially Moses, who showed "great strength of character in the lines of his countenance." They were then escorted to their hotel, where they shook hands with their hosts and retired for the night.[50]

The chiefs saw in the trip a chance to put in a good word for their people. In an interview the next morning, a reporter described them as having "sinews of steel and leathern lungs," but they confessed that their childrens' sinews and lungs were not strong, as they were dying from consumption. Lot complained that his children went to the Chemawa Indian School (formerly the Indian school at Forest Grove), recently moved to Salem, Oregon, where some of them had died.[51] The following day, the editor of the *Oregonian* blasted the idea of sending Plateau children there, where the "low altitude and poor diet" were sapping their strength. Why not, he suggested, send them to industrial schools in higher country like Colorado or New Mexico?[52] Actually, the Chemawa school was plagued with health problems until nearby Lake Labish and the adjacent sloughs were drained.[53]

One of the party's first contacts in Portland was with Joseph's old friend, the sculptor, Olin Warner. Two years earlier he had sculptured a life-size likeness of Joseph and was pleased to meet Moses and Lot to have them as subjects in his continuing project of creating portrait busts of great Americans. General Howard's former aide-de-camp, Lieutenant Wood, then residing in Portland, described the chieftains' reactions as Warner fashioned their likenesses: "One of the most noticeable traits of Mr. Warner's subjects was their personal indifference to his work. They obliged him by posing as an act of courtesy or hospitality, but it was evidently a great bore, and when they were notified that the work was done, they quietly walked away without even looking

50 *Oregonian*, October 1, 1891, p. 3.

51 Marion County Historical Society, *Marion County History*, V, 37; Larsell, *The Doctor in Oregon: A Medical History*, 32.

52 *Oregonian*, October 3, 1891, p. 4.

53 Larsell, *The Doctor in Oregon: A Medical History*, 32.

at it. Whether they really saw everything out of the corners of their eyes, as an Indian has a habit of doing, and whether this lack of interest in themselves was affected or not, I cannot say; but I am inclined to think it was genuine, for when they were to inspect the medallions and to give an opinion, they did so pleasantly and simply."[54]

One day, between sittings, the Indian party went to Wood's home for a midday dinner. Moses was happy to meet the one-armed general's right-hand man, and Joseph felt no embarrassment or bitterness in the presence of the aide of his former adversary and gladly assented to have Wood's young son, Erskine, visit him at Nespelem. While they were chatting, Moses, known for his bizarre eating—and drinking—habits, gulped down the glass of wine set before him, then turned and downed the contents of Joseph's glass because his friend did not imbibe.[55]

Friday, October 2, was pioneer day at the exposition. One can imagine what a stir the chieftains created among the old-timers. Civil War veterans engaged them in discussing the fine points of military strategy, asking many questions of Joseph, the "strategist" of the Nez Percé retreat. Some observed that Moses had not fought the whites since becoming chieftain, and that Lot, the "Indian Solomon," had never fought them at all. During the day, the Umatilla delegation arrived. That evening the Indians were scheduled for a performance in the Music Hall of the Exposition Building. Exposition-goers flocked to the place. "Crowds! Crowds! Crowds!" wrote the *Oregonian*. "How they surged and swayed and rocked in the exposition building. They filled every nook and corner of the huge edifice standing in the balconies, chairs, and benches, hanging to the beams, blocking up the doorways leading to the gallery of the music hall and packing the galleries and floor of the hall to its fullest capacity."[56]

Before the performance, Agent Crawford introduced Joseph. The Nez Percé veteran remarked, "I am very glad to see you. I

54 Wood, "Famous Indians; Portraits of Some Indian Chiefs," *Century Magazine*, n.s., Vol. XXIV (1893), No. 1, p. 436.
55 Erskine Wood Interview, Portland, Oregon, April 3, 1962.
56 *Oregonian*, October 3, 1891, p. 5.

enjoy seeing this large crowd here tonight. You see me I stand here tonight very happy. I am glad to live in heaven and earth. Now the dances will begin." A fire in a tripod surrounded by a red curtain had been placed in the center of the stage, and the Indians in colorful cloaks and feathers gyrated around it, war whooping in rhythm to a pounding drum. The crowd whooped their applause. They did not seem to know or care that only a few miles upriver in the hinterland white men were not applauding Indians' dances. The management then announced that the real Ghost Dances would be held the following night.[57]

On Saturday night the crowd was bigger than the night before (one might wonder how it could be); in fact, it was the largest crowd at any event of the Exposition since it began on September 17. The Zapadores Band from Mexico City beat out the somber tones of the "Funeral March" from *Ione* to put the Ghost Dances on key. Again the audience was wild with enthusiasm. The Indians were "the hit of this year's exposition," said the director.[58] But what did he or any white man know of the hidden feelings of these "entertainers"? A question comes to mind: How had they learned the Ghost Dance? Surely the cult had spread through the camps to a greater extent than the outside world ever knew.

Word of the performance spread. The following fall, a promoter wrote to Agent Cole requesting that Moses and Joseph and two lodges of their braves and families be permitted to come to the World's Columbian Exposition in Chicago to help portray the progress of America since its discovery.[59] Unfortunately for the cause of culture, the Indians were discouraged from attending.

Meanwhile, Moses returned from Portland to find trouble brewing four miles up the Little Nespelem. Quemat, his brother Louie's wife, had taken off to work in the Yakima hop fields after a fight with her husband. She had traveled to Sprague and Cheney with Louie's belongings and their three children and had not

---

57 *Ibid.*
58 *Oregonian,* October 4, 1891, p. 16.
59 Miles to Cole, November 28, 1892. Colville Agency Records, Letterbox 21.

returned.[60] Moses sent word for her to come back, but she had already decided to come home by the time she received the order.[61]

There was ferment on the other side of the continent which would have been far more important to Moses if he had been aware of it. According to John L. Wilson, member of Congress from Washington State, the Indian Office was displeased with the agreement made between the commission and the Indians for the sale of the north half of the reservation. It was not willing to recommend more than two cash payments of $300,000 each, with the remainder of the $1,500,000 to be held in trust for the Indians, the interest from which would be applied to their needs. Furthermore, it saw little need to increase Moses' annuity or to give one to any other chief.[62] However, what it really felt was that the reservation need not have been negotiated since it was not a treaty reservation.

Hiram Smith had a conversation with Moses in November concerning the sale of the north half, but how much he knew of the changes being considered in the agreement or to what extent he informed the Chief is not known. He must have told Moses and Joseph that the Commissioner favored neither increasing Moses' annuity nor giving Joseph one; for he reported that they did not want to open the reservation. Apparently, they did not want to sell the land now if they would not receive the anticipated money. Smith said he told Moses that if he had the increased annuity, he would only spend it for whisky and on horse racing and gambling. To this Moses replied that he knew it; that is what he wanted it for; he was getting old and wanted to have a little fun before he died.[63]

His search for fun would soon embroil him in a very unfunny situation.

60 Leslie to Anderson, October 5, 1891. Colville Agency Records, Letterbox 21.

61 Madeline Covington Interview, Nespelem, Washington, May 29, 1961.

62 *Spokane Review*, November 27, 1891, p. 2. The Secretary of the Interior submitted the agreement to Congress early in January, apparently without the suggested changes. *Wilbur Register*, January 15, 1892, p. 1.

63 *Spokane Review*, November 25, 1891, p. 8.

XVI. Tempest in a Tipi

"The white man is the cause of our sorrow."—Moses to
Indian agent, Okanogan River, June 30, 1870

ON OR ABOUT OCTOBER 1, 1891, at Port Columbia, according to
the sworn statement of a deputy, C. William Brown, one Peter J.
Scott violated Section 2139 of the Revised Statutes of the United
States and did unlawfully "sell, exchange and dispose of spiritous
liquor to-wit: whisky to an Indian under the charge of an Indian
agent." That Indian was none other than Chief Moses.

On November 5, the case of the *United States* vs. *Peter J. Scott*
was heard before United States Commissioner D. K. Pendergast
in the Big Bend town of Waterville. On that site Moses had held
court many times in the past; now he was in the white man's court
and no longer on his own grounds. Platt Corbaley was sworn in
as interpreter and Moses as first witness. After answering the
usual preliminary questions about his name and place of abode,
Moses confessed he had bought whisky about three weeks before.

"Of whom did you buy?" asked the prosecution.

"I bought it from this man," he said, pointing at defendant
Scott. "I never saw him before the day on which I bought the
whisky." Then he went on to explain how he had come with one
Timentowah and another Indian from the Nespelem to Scott's
house above the mouth of the Okanogan River to buy one bottle
for two dollars.

"What was the size of this bottle of whisky?"

"About eight inches long, a black bottle it was round."

"Are you under an Indian agent?"

"Yes."

"Who is that agent?"

"I don't know his name. He has lost one hand."

"Have you always been under the charge of an Indian agent?"

Who could have known more than did Moses about that? Nevertheless, he answered, "I don't know how many years."

"Have you within the last three weeks bought any other whisky from the defendant?"

The defense objected. Pendergast overruled.

Moses then answered, "I have not bought any more." The defense, hoping perhaps to show that Scott had been framed, began to cross-examine. Moses answered its questions. He explained that he had ridden homeward after purchasing the whisky and had broken the long day's journey by sleeping on the road; and that he had not given Timentowah any whisky—but had drunk it all himself, some that night and the rest the next morning.

"To whom did you communicate the fact of your buying whisky in the neighborhood of the defendant?"

"I told Clay Mauntell three days ago. I never told him anything till three days ago."

Under further examination Moses was asked to tell of his conversation with Mauntell:

"He asked me if I bought a bottle of whisky and if the Indian that was with me bought two bottles from defendant. I told him that he did."

"What did you do with the whisky and tell us what effect did it have."

"I drank half of it that night before going to bed and the other half in the morning after getting up and threw the bottle away and felt first rate."

After several questions about the other Indian involved in the drinking, the defense asked, "During the whole of the day that you bought this whisky did you retain your senses?"

"I did."

"Are you fully cognizant to this day of all that occurred that day?"

"I remember everything that occurred that day."

After further questioning, the defense asked, "Is it not a fact that you have been told to saddle this matter off on Scott to shield yourself from your own devilment?"

"No one told me to."

"Is it not your purpose to try in this proceeding to cloak yourself?"

"That is not the purpose."

"Do you understand the nature of an oath?"

"Yes I do."

"What would be the consequence of false swearing?"

"If I tell the truth I am all right upon oath, but if he lies when he dies he is lost."[1]

On this note of judgment from a Higher Court, Pendergast adjourned proceedings until the next day. Then Moses was re-called by the defense, which attempted to discredit his answers before it called Timentowah and Clay Mauntell to testify. On the stand, Timentowah said he had seen defendant Scott sell Moses the whisky. When questioned whether Moses had been drunk, he answered in the negative. He said he had told the marshal and Mauntell that Scott had sold the whisky to Moses.

After further questioning of Timentowah, Mauntell was called to the stand. It did not come out in the proceedings, but sometime earlier Mauntell had been shot in the leg and face in a scrape over land and had been forced to post a two-hundred-dollar bond to insure his being a law-abiding citizen for a period of one year.[2] His time being up, the defense sought to plant the suspicion that he had instigated the prosecution so that during Scott's incarceration he could purchase Scott's ferry through a third party, a Mr. John J. Reed. During the proceedings, Mauntell in so many words admitted that he had wanted to buy the ferry. Pendergast gave Scott a continuance until December 1 to secure witnesses on his behalf, and court was adjourned.

Court reconvened on that day with neither Moses nor Timen-

---

1 At this point in the official transcript the recorder changed to the third person, a common practice when the answer came through an interpreter. It seems also probable that Moses indicated the size of the bottle by a gesture, rather than by the words "eight inches."

2 *Big Bend Empire*, May 16, 1889, p. 1.

towah present for the prosecution. The first witness, a Mr. Antillon, testified that Timentowah had told him that Mauntell had promised him money to enter a complaint against defendant Scott, and further that one old Indian whom Mauntell had approached would not take the ten-dollar offer because he knew nothing of the case and did not want to "steal the money." "As for Moses," said Antillon, "he is a liar." A Mr. Grenaway, testifying further in Scott's defense, said Mauntell had been on the outs with Scott, and that Mauntell once had Timentowah buy whisky of another white man so "he could get the court on him." Then Reed testified that Mauntell was Scott's enemy and that after Scott's arrest, Mauntell had asked him (Reed) to buy the ferry for eight hundred dollars.

Scott swore that Moses had not been at his place on the day of the alleged sale, and, for that matter, that he had never seen Moses before in his life. This, of course, made Scott either a perjurer or the victim of a big frame up in which Moses was playing a leading part. The Commissioner attached enough importance to Moses' and Timentowah's testimony to bind Scott over to the United States District Court in Spokane, fixing bail at five hundred dollars. Bail was furnished and Scott went home. Moses would have a respite from court until Scott's case came up in the spring.[3]

After the Scott hearing, he found Joseph most uncommunicative, in fact acting like a spoiled child. Maybe that was his way of showing disapproval of Moses' actions, which had landed him in court; or maybe he was sulking at the Columbia's recent interference in Nez Percé affairs. It seems that in early December when Joseph and his followers were in Wilbur spending the remains of their hop-picking money on fancy food to add frosting to their Christmas rations, their cattle wandered off to the San Poil. The new farmer, W. H. Burmaster, wrangled them back and admonished Joseph to take better care of them next time. Two days

---

3 Proceedings in the case of the *United States* vs. *Peter J. Scott* may be found in the Circuit Court File, Group 21, Federal Records Container 3670, Federal Records Center, Seattle (hereafter referred to as *United States* vs. *Peter J. Scott*).

Chief Moses in a coat made by his wife, Mary. Note the two beaver-tail epaulets bearing his family insignia—the half-moon with a star and four lozenges beneath.

Courtesy of Rev. Joseph Obersinner, S. J. St. Mary's Mission

Father Stephen deRouge, S. J., who established St. Mary's Mission on the Colville Reservation, was a comfort to some Indians but a thorn to Chief Moses.

later, during Nez Percé preoccupation with Christmas planning, they wandered off again. Immediately, Moses hurried to inform Burmaster that the cattle had again strayed and that Joseph had not attended to business. Such lassitude! It appears two chieftains were straying also—from their bonds of friendship.[4]

During the Christmas holidays, the Nez Percé camps were the scene of much festivity continuing well into the New Year, and Joseph was hard pressed to control the celebrants. On one occasion as he moved in to stop an argument between two drunks, one Tocarnemoick grasped a pick and lunged for him. Joseph dodged. Quickly others rushed in to subdue the attacker and secure him with ropes. Burmaster rushed down to the camp and was warned to stay clear of Tocarnemoick.[5] The Nez Percés, who had always agitated for agency help in such emergencies, now said they could handle the rebellious tribesman themselves.

On Monday evening, January 4, 1892, Moses heard that two Umatillas, Umapine and Tahasamkin, representing Young Chief, had ridden into Joseph's camp for a meeting that appeared to be more than just a social call. He learned that the envoys had come to get Joseph to go to Washington. Why? That was a secret even to the Nez Percés. It was no secret, however, that Joseph intended to ask Cole for money to make the trip. Moses hurried down the Valley the next day to ask Bouska to inform the agent of what was going on. They were discussing, wrote Bouska,

> some matter which was not known to Moses and the rest of Joseph's or Moses' people and Moses feels very offended that they should hide all their conversation from him. Moses says that it is no more than right to send you this news as he says he has no secret to make to anyone and that you are his superior chief and you should know all about what is going on here. Moses says it might be some mischief in it. . . . And further more he heard that Young Chief wants Chief Joseph to go to Washington with him and Joseph said that he has no money to go with unless you would lend him some money. Moses said that you should not lend him any money as he would not pay you back. Further Moses

4 Burmaster to Cole, December 20, 1891. Colville Agency Records, Letterbox 21.
5 Burmaster to Cole, January (no date), 1892. Colville Agency Records, Letterbox 21.

said that if there would be anything good in their conversation they would not keep it secret to themselves but this way it makes Moses and his people as well as Joseph's own people feel very much dissatisfied to be blind-folded by Joseph in this way of doing.[6]

Bouska at least would know Joseph's secret the next day when the Nez Percé Chief requested him to write the agent that he wanted to borrow money to make a trip to Washington, D. C., to get permission to move to the Umatilla Reservation. The Umatillas had brought a letter from their agent, John W. Crawford, which apparently stated that the Nez Percé chief would be welcome there if he could obtain the necessary permission. After quizzing Joseph to determine if he were lying, Bouska was convinced that he truly wanted to leave; and the miller himself thought he would be more satisfied on the Umatilla. He wrote the agent that "a great deal of jealousy exist[s] between Chief Moses and Joseph. Joseph keeps all the news as well as him. Being [his being] dissatisfied here [,] all to himself and that don't please Moses, neither does it please Moses people."

With hopes of exchanging the annoyances of the Colville for the beauties of his beloved Wallowas on the Umatilla, Joseph decided to carry the letter to the agency himself. When he left the miller's house to prepare for the ride, Johnson (Kolkolleksanim), a Nez Percé married to Moses' daughter Tomquinwit, came in and assured Bouska that Joseph was not lying, that he merely wanted to return to the Wallowas, and that for some time Young Chief had been urging him to come. He pointed out, however, that many of the Nez Percés did not want to go with Joseph.[7]

Things in Moses' camp were going along as usual. There were nine births and seven deaths of Columbias that year. The beds of confinement were off limits to the white doctor. In cases of illness the shaman was still king, although Tompasque sometimes advised families to consult with Dr. Latham at his office or as he made his rounds with Bouska. Several of Moses' families, now

6 Bouska to Cole, January 5, 1892. Colville Agency Records, Letterbox 21.
7 Bouska to Cole, January 6, 1892. Colville Agency Records, Letterbox 21.

settled in small frame houses, had adopted citizens' dress, but many Nez Percés still wrapped themselves in blankets.

When spring came, Moses and Timentowah were subpoenaed to appear before the federal court at Spokane.[8] Moses took the train at Wilbur[9] and reached Spokane on April 5, where a huge crowd gathered and gazed at him as he stood on the steps of the Traders National Bank talking with Constable William Nolan.[10] On April 8, Moses and Clay Mauntell were sworn in and examined before the grand jury. On May 27, on application of the United States attorney, a bench warrant was issued for Scott and bail fixed by Judge C. H. Hanford at two thousand dollars, but Scott forfeited his bail when he apparently left the country.[11]

When Moses returned home, summer was approaching with its usual problems. The forebay on the mill dam had washed out on May 18, and Joseph refused to let his people repair it. His liaison officers to keep the Nez Percés from working were Yellow Chief, Red Curley, Henry Curley, and Loaspus.[12] In June, Moses managed to evade giving the count of his people in the agency census.[13]

On June 20, Congress passed the bill restoring the north half of the Colville Reservation to the public domain. It went far beyond the recommendations of the Indian Office in changing the agreement made with the Indians the previous year. While the legislation was pending, the argument was advanced that the Indians had no legal title to the land, and apparently this reasoning prevailed in shaping its provisions. It gave the land-hungry frontiersmen what they wanted, the north half; and it retained one provision for the Indians who lived there, the option of selecting 80-acre allotments and remaining in their old homes. Nothing was said about annuities to the chiefs, and the $1,500,000 payment was eliminated.

8 *United States* vs. *Peter J. Scott.*
9 *Wilbur Register*, April 8, 1892, p. 3.
10 *Spokane Review*, April 6, 1892, p. 3.
11 *United States* vs. *Peter J. Scott.*
12 Bouska to Cole, May 18, 1892. Colville Agency Records, Letterbox 2.
13 Burmaster to Cole, June 18, 1892. Colville Agency Records, Letterbox 2.

When the land should be opened for homesteading, the settlers would be required to pay $1.50 an acre before receiving patents. As this money would slowly accumulate in the United States treasury, some of it might conceivably benefit the Indians. The white man's claims came first: it would be used to reimburse the government for the expense of making the allotments and surveying the land in preparation for white settlement, and it would be "subject to such future appropriation for public use as Congress may make." Then, as a gesture to the Indians, "until so otherwise appropriated" it might be expended by the secretary of the interior for schools, the payment of local taxes on allotments, "or in such other ways as he may deem proper for the promotion of education, civilization and self-support among said Indians." Finally, "nothing herein contained shall be construed as recognizing title or ownership of said Indians to any part of the said Colville Reservation, whether that hereby restored to the public domain or that still reserved by the Government for their use and occupancy."

President Benjamin Harrison did not veto this iniquitous bill, but he did have the grace to withhold his signature: it became law without his signature on July 1.[14] Agent Cole was furious at this betrayal of Indian interests, which he attributed to the influence of congressmen from Washington. He said that it made the original agreement "nothing more than a farce" and that the work of the commission negotiating it "was labor and money thrown away." In what would seem to be the understatement of the year, he concluded that it "in no way increased the confidence of the Indians in the government."[15]

Would the south half suffer the same fate? Feeling the pinch of diminishing free pasture in the Big Bend, men like John Turner, married to Simoneeta, a San Poil woman,[16] used their marriages to usurp reservation land for their livestock. When ordered to

14 Jessie A. Bloodworth, *Human Resources Survey of the Colville Confederated Tribes*, 44–45; Kappler, *Indian Affairs: Laws and Treaties*, I, 441–43.

15 Secretary of the Interior, *Annual Report*, 1892 (52 Cong., 2 sess., *House Exec. Doc. No. 1, Pt. 5*), II, 488.

16 Henry Covington Interview, Keller, Washington, November 22, 1959.

remove their herds, they claimed the stock belonged to their wives.[17] Fortunately, the Indians' crops would be good this year, and there would be no cricket scourge.

One white person who was welcomed to the reservation was Erskine Wood, Lieutenant C. E. S. Wood's twelve-year-old son, who came to spend six months in Joseph's tipi as a playmate to Cool-Cool Smool-Mool (Red Star), an orphaned Nez Percé youngster living with Joseph.[18]

Earlier, Yellow Bull and his band had given up the Colville for Cottonwood Creek on the Nez Percé (Lapwai) Reservation. Now he came back briefly to check on the interests of his son, Red Leggins, who was back in Lapwai haying.[19]

Although the reservation lost Yellow Bull, it was about to gain a former resident—Skolaskin, now back at Fort Spokane (on July 22) after a stopover in Vancouver, where he had signed a pledge not to interfere in the operation of the agency.[20] On discovering that the north half had been sold while he was gone, he angrily disavowed his pledge and sent runners to the Okanogan to order its Indians to resist the opening of the tract. He visited his daughter, Alice, and other natives in the Okanogan, and while there demonstrated that the past months of confinement had not crushed his fiery spirit. He whiplashed comments about Moses and the whites who had stolen their lands with the opium of bribes. Many families, some of them Roman Catholic, responded to his appeal, to the dismay of Father DeRouge, who from his Omak Lake mission penned the following note to Agent Cole: "Skolaskin wants to show that he gets the best of all the others. His reservation will not be open, etc. If you could hear all the talk going you would not like it. I wish you could stop the gentle-

17 Burmaster to Cole, May 3, 1892. Colville Agency Records, Letterbox 21.

18 Bruce A. Wilson, *From Where the Sun Now Stands*, 29–30.

19 W. D. Robbins, agent of the Nez Percé Agency, to agent, Colville Reservation, July 19, 1892. Colville Agency Records, Letterbox 21.

20 Enclosure with communication of Thomas Ward, Assistant Adjutant General, Vancouver Barracks, to Brigadier General T. H. Ruger, Commanding Department of the Columbia, July 23, 1892. Selected Documents Relating to Skolaskin, NA, RG 75.

man, tell him to mind his own business, and no more excite our Indians as he used to do in former years."[21]

Moses and his brother, Louie (now "off the wagon"), commiserated over the loss of their old haunts and habits and especially over the younger generation's loss of contact with old tribal ideals.[22] The Chief spent as much time this summer bending an elbow with a whisky dipper as he did shaking the hand of Burmaster's replacement, John S. Mires. The new farmer occasionally found himself confused with arguments over horseflesh and had to call the Chief to help untangle them. In one of these Moses informed Mires, as did Owhi, that since Ahchy had received her share of horses on the death of her father, Poyockon, his horses in the Valley did not belong to her, as she claimed, but to her sisters. Mires could feel a little easier now that the jail was completed and Indian Charles Kladus had been sent in as a policeman.[23]

The agency, which had once moved closer to Moses because he had taken most of its administrative time, now diverted its attention from problems in the Nespelem to those in two other troughs, the Okanogan and Colville valleys. In the Okanogan, Antwine demanded that the doctor be removed. Cullycullewy (Coxit George) was particularly disturbed that Okanogan County was taxing some Indians on their personal property. Writing a letter to the agency in his behalf was Clay Mauntell, the witness in the Scott liquor trial.[24] In the Colville Valley, near Kettle Falls, there was much conflict between Indians and white men. One day through the latter's ingenuity and engineering there would be no more Kettle Falls, a favorite fishery in the Columbia. When Moses was in Wilbur in late October on his way to collect his annuity, townsfolk were talking about a story in the Spokane *Spokesman*[25] of a fantastic plan to use the Columbia River at

21 DeRouge to Cole, September 1, 1892. Colville Agency Records, Letterbox 21.

22 Mires to Cole, October 29, 1892. Colville Agency Records, Letterbox 21.

23 Mires to Cole, August 4, 1892. Colville Agency Records, Letterbox 21.

24 Mauntell to Colville Agency, October 17, 1892. Colville Agency Records, Letterbox 21.

25 *Spokesman* (Spokane, Washington), September 28, 1892, p. 5.

the Grand Coulee by diverting its waters into its ancient channel to irrigate the Plateau before flowing back into the Columbia below Priest Rapids. Moses had heard much about dams when he was in the East and had reconciled himself to their use in the West; he appeared no more surprised at the scheme than did some of his white friends.[26]

When winter came, the Columbias and Nez Percés returned from the hunt. Two boys made news in Joseph's tipi camp below the mill this winter: one, tragic news—Little Joseph, the Nez Percé chief's nephew, died; the other, good news—Erskine Wood was given permission to stay with Joseph until Christmas. The boy's father had not let him go completely native, but kept him informed of happenings in the outside world, some of which concerned reports that Joseph was going on the warpath over the projected opening of the north half of the reservation. Erskine assured his father such was not the case.[27] Had not Erskine's father copied Joseph's words when he told General Howard at the time of his surrender, "From where the sun now stands, I will fight no more forever." As was their custom, the Nez Percés congregated in winter lodges below the mill. Look Down and his family lived with Joseph in his lodge this winter.[28] The winter of 1892–93 was very severe. On February 8 the temperature dropped to twenty-two degrees below zero. The natives suffered great losses of their livestock as inadequate stacks of hay and sacks of grain dwindled rapidly in the north-wind-whipped snow.

This winter the Chelans were living on the Colville, having been removed there over their angry protests that they had had no part in the 1879 and 1883 Moses agreements. Innomoseecha Jim (Long Jim) was embroiled in a battle with a white man who wanted to homestead his farm along the Columbia. The Secretary of the Interior reviewed the argument and decided in favor of the Indian since the signature of his father, Innomoseecha Bill, did not appear on the 1879 treaty. The white claimant then vainly

26 Robert G. Virgin, "The Saga of Chief Moses," MS 23.
27 Erskine Wood Interview, Portland, Oregon, April 3, 1962.
28 *Ibid.*

attempted to prove by Moses that Jim's father had been a part of Moses' coalition and that Jim was, therefore, bound by his actions.[29] There is a story of a confrontation between Long Jim and Moses at the turbulent settlement of Ives at the mouth of the Methow River. There, it is said, Moses offered the hand of friendship to the son of his old lieutenant, only to have the younger man refuse it because he believed that Moses had given away land belonging to the Chelans when he surrendered the Columbia Reservation.[30]

When winter broke, Moses was moved at the sight of his and Joseph's dead cattle dotting the reservation, but was more shaken by piles of their dead horses lying about.[31] Spring roundup, 1893, held little excitement for him with only thirty-four horses left from a band of three hundred. An Indian's wealth was in his horses; he was now a poor man. Few Indians could harness together a team or find horses strong enough to pack supplies in from Wilbur. People around that town observed with just a little irony that the great horseman Moses would have to travel afoot.[32] There was also irony in the arrival of the new blacksmith, J. C. Norris.

The perennial seed shortage bothered Moses again this spring. In a letter to Cole he lamented, "We are all out of grain for seed, it has been such a hard winter we have fed it all out to the stock and now most of our stock has perished. And if it is your will and in your power we appeal to you for aid."[33] Spring floods had washed out the ditch leading to the mill, and thawing ground undermined the dam. The new miller, Edward Glasgow, wanted to replace the ditch from the dam to the mill with a flume, but what would be the good of it all if there was no grain to mill?[34]

29 LaChappele to Cole, March 1, 1893. Colville Agency Records, Letterbox 23.

30 *Wenatchee Daily World*, April 7, 1925, p. 10.

31 *Northwest Tribune*, April 14, 1893.

32 *Chelan Leader* (Chelan, Washington), March 23, 1893. Moses' loss of horses this year would not deter him from joining Chief Lot and his people in the Fourth of July festivities on the Spokane Reservation (*Wilbur Register*, July 7, 1893, p. 1).

33 Moses to Cole, March 18, 1893. Colville Agency Records, Letterbox 22.

34 Glasgow to Cole, March 29, 1893. Colville Agency Records, Letterbox 22.

Perhaps there would be grain; word came in from the agency that the department had authorized Cole to spend $1,650 for seed on the open market.[35]

Now that the seed situation looked better, Moses undertook to recoup his horse bands by trading, gambling, and betting with visiting tribesmen at the races. These contests attracted many visitors, particularly the Nez Percés from Lapwai. Among them were two women: Itstsulkt, a thirty-four-year-old with willowy form; and Tamatsatsamy, her companion, slightly older, yet equally attractive. Joseph took Itstsulkt to live in his household, and Tamatsatsamy changed her name to Peotsenmy and moved in with Moses.[36]

Peotsenmy's presence seems not to have disturbed Moses' favorite, Mary, who was accustomed to women entering and leaving her lodge. Her husband still came to her for counsel—and money—and help in keeping newspaper clippings of his visits to Washington, D. C., and other big cities. The women shared a division of labor: the younger Peotsenmy performed many menial chores, and Mary sewed and made beaded articles for her master; and while Mary shared her husband's confidence, Peotsenmy shared his intimate pleasures.[37]

Moses was still annoyed at Joseph's lack of concern over his people's indolence, but after a while, Joseph began to stir a little, and under his and Moses' supervision their men expended fifty-seven days of uninspired labor on thirty miles of reservation roads badly rutted from thaws of the heavy winter snows. The wagon road from Moses Crossing had been entirely destroyed in places.[38]

Moses saw to it that there was no road work on Sundays. Those days were set aside for races, when excitement ran high at the track near his camps. On August 6, the annual Sun Races were held. Early that morning, criers on horseback circled the camps as was their custom forecasting the day's events and lamenting

[35] Secretary of the Interior, *Annual Report*, 1893 (53 Cong., 2 sess., *House Exec. Doc. No. 1, Pt. 5*), II, 321.
[36] Sadie Moses Williams Interview, Nespelem, Washington, January 3, 1958.
[37] Peone Interviews.
[38] Secretary of the Interior, *Annual Report*, 1893, II, 323.

the dead. Despite this sad remembrance, spirits were high once the contests began. Betting was fast and furious. The Columbias reserved their best horses until the visitors' horses tired; then they trotted their fresh horses onto the track to increase their winnings.

Full steaming kettles of food melted rapidly from appetites swelled by fun and entertainment. After dinner, women sat in groups gambling while their men reveled at the track.

Whispered voices passed the word, "Puckmiakin is here!" Soon the renegade's merchandise spread "joy" and noise at the track and around the evening campfires as the cacaphony of whisky-loosened tongues pervaded the air. Agency help never supervised the gatherings, and there was no policeman in the Valley, for Dr. Charles (Carlos) Montezuma, who had replaced Latham, had temporarily retired Kladus for illness.[39]

Two hours after dark, Yayoskin, Moses' "successor," numbed with whisky, became increasingly irritable and argumentative with his younger, shorter, coarser brother, Sam Staaclo, with whom he shared the bottle. When the whisky, obtained from Puckmiakin for horses and blankets, was about exhausted, the two became involved in a quarrel.

Some distance away, Moses enjoyed his barreled spirits, unaware of the commotion. A hush spread from camp to camp, and then a scurrying about. Excited voices broke out again. Yayoskin had knocked down, choked, then beat the brains from his brother with a rock.

Moses shared his overwhelming grief with Shimtel, his sister who was the mother of the principals in the tragic affair. Yayoskin passed the night, unmolested, in a drunken stupor.

On sobering, Yayoskin wept bitterly when told of his deed, of which he had no memory. No one tried to apprehend him; the

39 Dr. Montezuma, on records with his given name as being Charles, appears as Carlos in *Who Was Who in America*, I, 855. He was born in Arizona in 1867 of Apache Indian parents, was captured by the Pima Indians, and sold for $30.00 to the whites. He received an M.D. degree in 1889. He was the author of *The Indian of Today and of Tomorrow* (1900), *Let My People Go* (1914), and *Abolish the Indian Bureau* (1919).

whites believed it would take too much red tape and expense to bring the Indian to justice. Why should Mires bother? He had tendered his resignation effective August 20. Dr. Montezuma had resigned July 9 (Dr. Latham would be returning), and the agency clerk, Anderson, was resigning, as was Agent Cole. It was apparent there was a new White Father in Washington City. One of Mires' last official acts was to give the sorrowing Yayoskin a box in which to bury his brother.[40]

Moses was too grief-stricken to attend the burial ceremony. His grief was increased on learning that Indian Jim had just disemboweled Peter Sarsopkin at Omak Lake.[41] Less than two weeks later, came better, yet gruesome, news—an Indian had killed Puckmiakin a short distance from the mouth of the Okanogan, ridding the whisky trade of one of its most evil merchants.[42]

With no farmer in the Valley to help the Indians use their equipment, there was danger of a crop shortage. Glasgow, the miller, would not go out of his way to substitute as a farmer without making a big fuss. He did condescend to take the reaper to the Valley and set it up for Moses, but refused to do the same with the thresher with the excuse that he was too busy sawing lumber.[43] Moses was to experience many impatient moments waiting for the new farmer, Henry Steele, to come and help his people thresh their grain.

Glasgow could not have been milling very much flour; Steele went to Moses Crossing to supervise the ferrying of ten thousand pounds of it across the river and onto the reservation. As soon as the Indian freighters' wagons were safely loaded, Steele hurried

40 Secretary of the Interior, *Annual Report*, 1894 (53 Cong., 3 sess., *House Exec. Doc. No. 1, Pt. 5*), II, 312; Madeline Covington Interview, Nespelem, Washington, May 29, 1961; Mires to Cole, August 10, 1893 (Colville Agency Records, Letterbox 21); *Spokane Review*, August 13, 1893. The reader will remember that in March the Democrat Grover Cleveland had succeeded the Republican Benjamin Harrison.

41 *Spokane Weekly Review*, August 24, 1893.

42 Arthur Strahl to Agent John W. Bubb, August 31, 1893. Colville Agency Records, Letterbox 21.

43 J. C. Norris, the new blacksmith for the Nespelem, to Bubb, September 2, 1893. Colville Agency Records, Letterbox 22.

off to inspect Moses' homes and farms and get the thresher operating. The new farmer pitched into his job with the same eagerness to help the Indians and with the same intolerance of their
improvidence that Moses had seen over and over in new agency
personnel. Like all the rest of them, Steele vowed to do something about the unmended fences, littered camps, and unused
implements lying around—shovels, plows, broken hoes, whipple-
trees, and wagons.[44]

One white man did not try to remake the broken things or the
Indians in the white man's image. On October 16, Francis
Streamer visited Moses. Joseph joined them, and the three went
into their usual philosophical discussions.[45] Joseph had a white
visitor also; Erskine Wood had returned again this fall, but the
Nez Percé Chief did not bring him to visit Streamer.[46] At sunset
Moses and Streamer stood together. Moses remarked, "Oh!
Streamer, I am getting old and poor—too much snow and ice.
No salmon, no mat, no money. Why is it that we all are lost in
feeling and have no hope of a better cheer?"[47]

Dr. Latham, lured back to the Valley, laid in winter supplies—
castile soap, muriate of ammonia, solution of ammonia, chloro-
form, camphor gum, glycerine, turpentine, and oils to make
liniments. Hoping to discourage burglaries by thirsty natives, he
did not order alcohol to mix in liniments.[48] Nevertheless, the
Nez Percés obtained a large supply of alcohol for their annual
Christmas feast and celebration, an affair attracting many of
Moses' people. Steele contributed to the festivities with an extra
issue to Joseph's band of 45 pounds of beans, 5 pounds of baking
powder, 60 pounds of coffee, 3,000 pounds of flour, and 105
pounds of sugar, and seven beeves slaughtered on December 22.

44 Henry Steele to Bubb, September 26 and 29, 1893. Colville Agency Records,
Letterbox 22.
45 Streamer, Miscellaneous Notebooks, Folder No. 2, pp. 354, 356, 358.
46 Erskine Wood, "Diary of a Fourteen Year Old Boy's Days with Chief Joseph,"
Oregon Historical Quarterly, Vol. LI, No. 2 (June, 1950), 71–92. Wood informed the
authors that he was twelve years old when he first went to stay with Joseph
(Erskine Wood Interview, Portland, Oregon, April 3, 1962).
47 Streamer, Miscellaneous Notebooks, Folder No. 2, pp. 354, 356, and 358.
48 Latham to Bubb, December 28, 1893. Colville Agency Records, Letterbox 22.

Regretting the practice of extra Christmas issue, he decided to discontinue it in the future.[49] He regretted the practice even more when he caught a drunk with whisky on his person. The next morning he escorted the offender from the jail across the footbridge, and with the bottled spirits poised above the sad-eyed "siwash," he christened the new flume as though it were a battleship.[50] It was evident that Steele was living up to his name for toughness.

Smallpox hit the Colville this winter, mildly, but enough to make vaccination necessary. Captain John W. Bubb, new acting agent (thanks to Secretary of the Interior Hoke Smith's new congressionally approved policy of appointing military men as agents), sent Steele a letter on January 8, 1894, asking him to notify Moses of the deaths of two of his people of smallpox on the Spokane.[51] Moses was probably pleased that the Captain had taken this personal interest in him and looked forward to the same favored treatment the military had extended him in the past. Dr. Latham urged the Indians to be vaccinated; but Joseph's people, never forgetting the deaths of many of their number in the Indian Territory following vaccination, refused to submit to the practice. Owhi told Latham that he had nearly died after taking cowpox crust. Moses agreed to the vaccinations, provided they were carried out after warm weather began, when he thought they would be safer.[52]

The Moses and Joseph people were becoming cool to each other in their casual daytime encounters as were their chiefs. Agency personnel observed their petty behavior and even reckoned with it in their plans for the Indians. Steele proposed to move Latham and Norris to the east side of the river, where there was more area for the buildings. Latham thought the proposition should wait since any change of buildings might be looked upon by one chief as bestowing a special favor on the other. Latham wrote to the acting agent: "There seems to be consider-

49 Steele to Bubb, January 20, 1894. Colville Agency Records, Letterbox 22.
50 Latham to Bubb, December 28, 1893. Colville Agency Records, Letterbox 22.
51 Bubb to Steele, January 8, 1894. Colville Agency Records, Letterbox 6.
52 Latham to Bubb, March 1, 1894. Colville Agency Records, Letterbox 22.

able hard feeling existing between the Moses and Joseph Indians. I do not think it will amount to anything and am in no way uneasy but I think you should know. Both sides are holding secret meetings and doing a great deal of talking, what it is about I cannot find out, some of the Moses meetings have lasted the entire night. Moses has got it into his head that he is going to get a lot of money for the reservation and he says that when the money comes he will not give Joseph any. I think they are just talking over their imaginary grievances."[53]

The problem rested for a while with Joseph's departure for Lapwai on March 9. Some natives wondered if, perhaps, he intended to go elsewhere or, perhaps, not to return at all.[54] A few weeks later, on Sunday, April 22, he was back at the regular horse races west of the river beyond the blacksmith shop and slaughterhouse. He was wearing a pea-green shirt and was bareheaded with a yellow ribbon securing his plaited queue of hair. Moses was there, strikingly attired in white shirt and large hat studded with four silver stars which sent his newly arrived friend, Streamer, into solar ecstasies.

Streamer and Moses spent the next two days resting in the "thousand dollar house" and sharing each other's views on work —a subject about which they knew little.[55] Streamer had on occasions such as this said he did not believe man was created from clay to make a "mud-sill out of himself by doing heavy work." Moses agreed.[56] From Moses' papers, Streamer copied into a book the agreement which set up the Columbia Reservation in 1879, because "solar Command and Eye Vision" had ordered him to faithfully record their every word.[57]

They finally came down to earth with a long discussion of the poverty of Moses' people. As was his custom after such meetings, Streamer wrote of their plight to General Howard in the East. (Howard answered on May 25, sending a photograph of himself

53 Latham to Bubb, March 10, 1894. Colville Agency Records, Letterbox 22.
54 *Ibid.*
55 Streamer, Miscellaneous Notebooks, Folder No. 3, pp. 227, 255.
56 Streamer, Miscellaneous Notebooks, Folder No. 2, p. 266.
57 Streamer, Miscellaneous Notebooks, Folder No. 3, p. 203.

taken at Key West, Florida.[58]) Streamer bade his friend farewell and returned to Osoyoos by way of Omak Lake, where he had dinner with Father DeRouge.[59]

Soon reports came to Moses of increased activity of DeRouge's six policemen, who were enforcing the priest's orders on non-Catholics. At the Chief's request, Steele went to Omak Lake to investigate. To his surprise he found no disorder among the Blackrobe's happy children in citizens' dress and short hair, bustling about like white people. The disturbance in that area had been caused by a number of white men secretly running cattle onto the southwestern part of the reservation.

The priest told Steele his conduct was open to the most rigid inspection. The six policemen? They were hand-picked watchmen to protect the peace and property of the congregation.[60]

This spring the Columbia River went on a rampage and pushed its shore line back farther than the Indians had ever seen before.[61] On the south shore at Moses Crossing, freight waiting to be hauled to the reservation—including doors intended for the Indians' houses—was scattered by violent winds and swept away in the flood. The agency had started to construct a ferry there, but the two gunwales to be used in building it were carried downriver along with driftwood and twisted buildings. The ferry was eventually completed after the water receded.[62]

By the Fourth of July, the river was low enough to permit the Indians to flock to celebrations over the area. The holiday gambling luck of the revelers was not so good. Many returned two to a horse. Shimtil, Moses' sister, was one of those who came safely back with her mount. Her horse was gentle, easy to catch, and never needed hobbling. Minnie Iyutotum, the beautiful Nez Percé wife of Yayoskin, frequently asked her mother-in-law if she might borrow it, not wanting to wrangle her own horse,

58 Howard to Streamer, May 25, 1894. Streamer, Miscellaneous Notebooks, Folder No. 2, p.46.

59 Streamer, Miscellaneous Notebooks, Folder No. 3, p. 227.

60 Steele to Bubb, May 31, 1894. Colville Agency Records, Letterbox 22.

61 The floodwaters of 1894 were the highest ever recorded for the Columbia River.

62 Steele to Bubb, June 4, 1894. Colville Agency Records, Letterbox 22.

which was hard to catch. Many times she rode off on Shimtil's without permission. One day, shortly past mid-July, Minnie, wishing to ride toward the mountains for berries, asked her mother-in-law for the horse. Shimtil, tired of the practice, scolded her daughter-in-law and refused to lend it. This angered Minnie.

Late that evening, Yayoskin returned to find Minnie still upset and complaining that her mother-in-law was mean. Yayoskin listened awhile. Then suddenly, with drink-fired emotions, he grabbed up a club and went looking for his mother. Finding her sitting alone mending inside Moses' tipi next to the "thousand dollar house," he drove the club into her head. Then he returned to his wife and told her what he had done. Shimtil slumped down dead, her blood running onto the tipi floor. Jim Jack, Yayoskin's small son, found his grandmother lying there and spread the alarm.[63]

Minnie revealed that her husband was the murderer. She confessed that he had also threatened to kill Moses or to burn Moses' house and steal his horses if he continued to run his life. On learning what had happened, the Chief ordered the murderer, said to be armed with a gun and a knife, to be shot on sight.[64] At one time he had groomed Yayoskin to be his successor, but now there was no one.

Not until the next morning did Moses discover that Yayoskin had fled in the night to Poker Joe's lodge, a mile up the Valley, where he took one of Joe's hobbled horses and the customary bag of food for travel from Joe's woman and then rode off in a hurry. This time the agency seemed to be interested in the case. Okanogan farmer, Arthur Strahl, on July 28 rode out with Steele to find Yayoskin, and the next day Steele asked Captain Bubb to dispatch three of his best policemen to aid in the search.[65] They failed in their quest simply because the hunted one had fled across the Canadian border for good. (He would return only once, in the early 1940's, when his son Jim Jack was ill.[66])

63 Isabel Arcasa Interview, Nespelem, Washington, January 3, 1958.
64 Steele to Bubb, July 29, 1894. Colville Agency Records, Letterbox 22.
65 Ibid.
66 Yayoskin was referred to as Jack O'Socken.

Although Steele had co-operated with Moses' request to track down the murderer, apparently Moses did not co-operate with the farmer in his request for information on Indian marriages. Neither would Joseph give marriage information, nor would the Nespelems.[67] It should be said in their defense that these unions, easily consummated and dissolved, were difficult to enumerate.

C. M. Hinman, the new blacksmith, made large sleds for the Indians' teams to pull. The harvest had been better this year, and so there was plenty of wheat and oats to haul across the snow-covered terrain. Winter delighted the youngsters, frolicking between the new barn, the corral, and the dam, or whip-spinning egg-shaped rocks on the glassy ice of the millpond.

On January 21, 1895, Moses' friend, "Wild Goose Bill" Condon, died in a blaze of gunfire over a woman. His death caused a great stir in the Big Bend country: he had been the region's first settler, when his freighting had tied the ends of Moses' old domain together; and he had established the town of Wilbur on his old ranch. He had had two Indian wives at different times. His wife at the time of his death was Mary Ann of Moses' band, who had borne him a crippled son. A prolonged legal battle ensued between her and the citizens of Wilbur over the disposition of his holdings there; but the state supreme court in 1901 ruled in favor of the widow.[68]

After the cold weather broke in early February, Umatilla chief Peo came to visit Joseph. One morning Joseph became ill with pneumonia. Doctor Latham, making his rounds, was refused admission to his tipi; the Nez Percé leader had never consulted with other than his own shaman. He became weaker and might have died had not Peo persuaded him to let the white doctor enter his lodge. Latham discovered that he had pneumonia and was worsening. He called on him every day for two weeks until he

---

[67] Steele to Bubb, August 13 and 15, 1895. Colville Agency Records, Letterbox 22. Letterbox 22.

[68] C. S. Kingston, "Samuel Wilbur Condit: Frontiersman," *Pacific Northwest Quarterly*, Vol. XXXVII, No. 2 (April, 1946), 136–37.

was out of danger.[69] Perhaps Joseph credited Peo with saving his life.

Another of Peo's ideas set well with Joseph, but not with Moses —that of bringing two hundred horses to summer pasture on the Colville without asking the Columbia Chief's permission. Moses hurried to Steele to complain that the Colville ranges, in spite of horse losses of recent years, were too scant to pasture Peo's horses. Under Moses' pressure, Steele wrote a letter by way of Bubb to the Umatilla to inform its agent of Peo's plan and personally to discourage Peo from bringing his horses.[70] The incident must have left Joseph unhappier than ever with Moses, who was blocking his relations with his Umatilla friends. While Moses himself was laid up with pneumonia, Peo left the reservation.

Many visitors dropped in to see the convalescent. Streamer came in mid-March. Another visitor was Louie Pecard, a brother of John. Louie had been a Valley resident for three years at Moses' request to act as the Chief's special interpreter and informant of the latest news and gossip. When Pecard first came to the Valley, Moses had called a council of tribesmen to vote whether or not he should be accepted into their ranks. The majority voted in the affirmative, but a staunch minority questioned his claim to Indian blood and stipulated that if he were allowed to remain, his children must marry Indians. Pecard agreed, giving Moses a good interpreter in Chinook to deal with stern white men like the new miller, J. S. Scribner.[71]

The tiring old Chief, now in his sixty-fifth year, stayed on the reservation this spring rather than join those going to camas, the one event best uniting the families. He had probably come through the cold winter as did some of his people, sitting around stoves discussing Scribner, the toughest fellow sent by the government thus far. Owhi had brought tales that Scribner was abusing him and Tomeo Kamiakin as they went about assisting at numer-

[69] Latham to Bubb, June 30, 1895. Colville Agency Records, Letterbox 23.

[70] Steele to United States Indian agent Pendleton, March 1, 1895; Steele to Bubb, March 1, 1895 (Colville Agency Records, Letterbox 23).

[71] Madeline Covington Interview, Nespelem, Washington, November 25, 1961.

ous jobs—repairing the dam, patching the flume, calking the cracks, hauling lumber across the Nespelem for a new machine shed under construction, and hauling battens to the blacksmith shop. It was as clear to Moses as the whisky in his barrel that Scribner and Steele were not working well together; someone was going to get hurt in the clash of personalities, and most likely it would be the Indians.

With his people away, he spent much time at the mill, talking with Steele, who pounced on any unfavorable comment about the miller, and listening to the complaints of Owhi, who objected to working around the mill, especially to stacking lumber. Owhi insisted that it was his job to haul logs, but Scribner expected each Indian to haul his own logs for Tomeo to saw into lumber and stack. On Thursday, June 6, Scribner sent word to Moses to have his logs brought in so that he could saw for him on Friday and Saturday. The next day Owhi set out to snake in Moses' logs. The miller ordered him to pile lumber until Moses' men came to do that. Owhi turned to Steele and addressed him in Chinook, which Scribner did not fully understand, but guessed that Owhi complained about being ordered to work at too many tasks. Scribner asked Steele what Owhi had told him, but the farmer said only that the Indian wanted to haul logs.

Owhi did turn to stacking lumber, but Scribner observed that he was "defiant and pouty all day," working "as slow as possible" and stopping to talk to every Indian that came along. Twice during the afternoon he quit his work and went over to talk to Steele. Moses' men did not bring in the Chief's logs, but Moses came in that afternoon and told the miller the size and style of house he wanted to build.[72] (He wanted it for his daughter and his son-in-law Johnson.[73])

The next morning Owhi went under the mill to do some digging. Scribner told him when he went down to take certain measurements, but the Indian would not respond. Later in the morning when a carpenter wanted some lumber, he called Owhi

[72] Scribner to Bubb, June 9, 1895. Colville Agency Records, Letterbox 23.
[73] Sadie Moses Williams Interview, Nespelem, Washington, January 3, 1958.

to help him handle it. Owhi laid down his shovel, took out his pipe, sat down, and began smoking.

"Come! Hurry up!" urged Scribner.

Owhi stood and commenced shoveling again very deliberately.

"Aren't you going to come? I am waiting for you," Scribner called.

"You don't pay me any money for my work. I am working for Washington, not for you."

The miller told him *he* was working for Washington also, and that it was Captain Bubb's orders that Owhi help with anything around the mill.

Picking up his coat, Owhi said, "You can hunt somebody to help. I don't work any more. I stop right now." He walked over and told Steele that the miller worked him too hard and did not let him take Saturday afternoon off as the other workers did.

That evening Scribner and Steele had quite an argument over Owhi. Scribner said that it was necessary to work six days out of the seven. Then, as the miller reported it, Steele "went off in a long line of excuses for Owhi, said . . . that Moses and his people did not like me because I worked Owhi too hard. . . . He said we could not hire any of Moses' people to work with me for they all knew about the trouble between me and Owhi."[74] But Owhi's "resignation" did not hold back progress for long; Charlie Wilpaukin, his replacement, and A. E. Parsons, started to build a small toolhouse for Joseph.[75]

In evaluating the Owhi episode, the Chief may have thought that much could have been argued in favor of an Indian's opposition to work. Had not Streamer said that man was not created to be a mudsill, but to live life to the full? Like "Old Bob," the ox, who repeatedly crashed out of his corral into the Valley gardens that summer, Moses prepared to kick up his heels in the green pastures "across the fence" from his own reservation corral.

74 Scribner to Bubb, June 9, 1895. Colville Agency Records, Letterbox 23.

75 Steele to Bubb, June 11 and July 1, 1895. Colville Agency Records, Letterbox 23.

XVII. Vanity and the Fair

"I want to have a little fun before I die."—Moses to Hiram
Smith, November, 1891

TOWARDS THE END OF JUNE, 1895, Moses came down to the new
miners' outfitting towns that had sprung up on the Columbia
just below the reservation. He decided on Virginia City for his
Fourth of July horse racing. Born in 1893 when a ferry began
operating across the Columbia at its site, Virginia City would die
the following year when the steamboats plying the river moved
upstream to a better landing. However, the prospect of a gloomy
future cast no shadow on this year's celebration.[1]

A sorrel named "Roy" owned by "Buck" Buchanan, a Kentucky "colonel," had been winning all the races. Moses had
known about the horse since the time of the Scott trial and was
anxious to match one of his favorites against him. It would be a
race between mounts of two of America's renowned horseman
types—a Kentuckian and a Plateau Indian. The course was carefully paced off. (A long-legged white man would sometimes step
off a distance too long for an Indian.) The horses were brought
onto the track and wagers laid—Indian blankets and lariats
against the white man's money. Suddenly, for some unknown
reason, Moses stepped up and scratched his horse from the race.
This entitled Buchanan to the "sack"; but before he had time to
collect, he found himself surrounded by a host of semi-inebriated
"savages." Fearing that they were closing in to scalp him, he
quickly mounted his horse and rode home—leaving the pile to
the "redskins."[2]

In September, Moses took another trip off the reservation—

1 *Chelan Leader*, June 7 and 21, 1895, p. 4; *Big Bend Empire*, July 4, 1895, p. 2.
2 *Big Bend Empire*, July 7, 1892, p. 2.

this time to the Yakima Valley. He had already sent his women down to the big hop-picking *klatawa* in mid-August to earn a little *chickamin*. Since the first hops had been planted in the Yakima country in 1872, hop raising had become an important industry, thanks to good soil, a favorable climate, and the Milwaukee market. No hop-picking for him, though—that was work for women. He and his men would join them in town after harvest and help them spend their *chickamin* at an annual celebration called the Jubilee held in conjunction with the fair. The Yakima Fair had been designated the official state fair.[3] It promised to be exciting.

About mid-September, Moses set out with his men through his old home grounds in the Big Bend and Moses Coulee. Breaking into the Coulee, he passed sun-bleached tipi poles, old storage holes, blackened firepits, and littered campsites, sad reminders that this had once been his home. His anticipation of Jubilee must have been dampened by the sight of other monuments of his former tenure—his children's graves, on which the windswept ryegrass etched tragic epitaphs. He held no resentment against the new inhabitants. He felt real friendship for James Christiansen, the first white man to move there in 1884.

He always looked forward to swapping tales and talismans with the Christiansens even through the cramped media of the sign language and the Chinook jargon. On one occasion, while wandering through Mrs. Christiansen's garden and examining leaves and bushes, he remarked that she made big root medicine. On one trip through the Coulee, he spotted some unusually large potatoes. He knew all about big potatoes; his people once raised them at the same spot. Nevertheless, he traded Christiansen a stone ornament from his hatband for three bushels.

On one of his trips, he discovered little Grace Christiansen caught between the boards of a calf shed trying to hide from his braves. This evoked a little story, for he always had a soft spot in his heart for children: "I got stuck between rocks once in a deep pothole, when I was so big. I was there until they found me and

3 Lyman, *History of the Yakima Valley*, I, 487-88.

helped me out."[4] Moses now saw other kinds of holes in Moses Coulee. Discussing hell one time, he is said to have remarked, "It's not hot down in the ground because in Moses Coulee I see white men dig holes. The deeper he digs, the colder it gets. No hot places down below."[5]

On the 1895 trip, as was their practice, the Yakima-bound travelers rose early, broke camp, gathered their horses, and bade good-by to their hosts. Down toward the Coulee mouth they passed two rocks. Christiansen said to Moses one time that the rocks looked like him and Mary. "All same, Lot's wife to salt," was the Chief's reply. Crossing the Columbia, they rode west up the Colockum past the two-hundred-pound stone medicine balls, which supposedly rained down from the sky many years before to test the power of a brave. In earlier times Moses' men had often challenged him to lift one of them, and he had accomplished the feat. Now, in these later years, they laughed when he sprawled to the ground after trying unsuccessfully to gather the ball into his nearly three-hundred-pound frame.[6]

Traversing the Colockum, they descended to Ellensburg. Here the merchants were very hospitable to their Indian guests; before long they would be back with hop-picking *chickamin* to help replenish the town's coffers. It was observed that Moses' usual sunny humor was shadowed by pessimism. "Powwow in Yakima," he predicted, "will be last one Indians have."[7]

In Yakima he sought out Mary and the other women in a sea

---

[4] Stories of Moses in Moses Coulee are found in Grace Christiansen Gardner's "Life Among North Central Washington First Families," *Wenatchee Daily World,* May 31–December 20, 1935. See also Grace Christiansen Gardner's "Chief Moses as I Knew Him," *Wenatchee Daily World,* December 20, 1935, pp. 6, 10, and other stories appearing in the same publication, March 24, 1928, p. 12, and April 28, 1937, p. 10.

[5] Gardner, "Chief Moses as I Knew Him," *Wenatchee Daily World,* December 20, 1935, pp. 6, 10.

[6] *Ibid.*

[7] *Wilbur Register,* September 27, 1895, p. 8. The San Poils, who also went to the Yakima hop harvest, usually pastured their horses at Ellensburg. On returning from Yakima, they often traveled by train to the Puyallup Valley hop harvest on the coast. After that harvest they returned to Ellensburg, gathered their horses, and rode home to the Colville.

of tipis pitched under the cottonwoods near the hop fields on the edge of town. Sometimes he condescended to go to the fields to watch them nimbly gather the cone-shaped seed catkins into their baskets and dump them into large coffin-shaped boxes, which were hauled on hearse-like wagons to the kilns. It was their custom to eat a quick noon lunch and hurry back to work until dark. Then everybody would feast on salmon, other meat, and bread hauled by wagons from town.[8]

Early fall rains hampered the harvest that week, sending the pickers into town to brighten the scene with their varicolored blankets, shawls, and handkerchiefs. No less varied were their people, ranging from week-old infants to grandparents nearing death and the grave. Moses led the parade, wearing a light-colored Stetson hat with soft crown and flaring rim and a long bombazine duster, and looking, as one spectator wrote, "as vigorous and hearty as though old Father Time had knocked a third off his years."

Mary ran out of coins while shopping, but Moses' credit was good. He was always welcome at the outsized store of the three Coffin brothers, who did not mind spreading Indian butter on their daily bread. When one of them was married in Portland on September 18 that year, the other two and the store personnel wired congratulations. At the bottom of the telegram was Chief Moses' name as well.[9]

The committee of the Commercial Club in charge of planning the Jubilee seems to have invited Moses to work with it in arranging the Indian horse races, for which the merchants promised sizable purses.[10] The merchants, growers, and Indians all realized they had a good thing in Jubilee. It swelled the merchants' coffers with *chickamin*; it gave the hop-growers a means of rewarding their labor supply and thus enticing them to return another year;

8 *Yakima Herald* (Yakima, Washington), October 3, 1895, p. 1, tells of the delivery of bread in carts to the hop fields. An old-time Yakima resident, Walt Purdin, told the authors that regular meat deliveries from town were made to the Indian encampments near the hop fields.

9 *Yakima Herald*, September 19, 1895, p. 3.

10 *Spokesman-Review*, September 15, 1895, p. 1.

and it gave the Indians a whopping good time, something to talk about in their tipis all winter long.

The rapport between Moses and the Yakima business community was evidenced by the Commercial Club's inviting him to one of its meetings to share the platform with Gardiner Hubbard of Washington, D.C., founder of the National Geographic Society. When Hubbard finished a scholarly lecture on China, Moses gave a short, poorly interpreted speech in which he told how he had once been on the wrong road, but now had found the right one. Concluding, he said, "I am very glad to meet you folks here tonight and I heard there was a man from Washington city here, and one time I got in a very bad fix. I wish that man from Washington would make a report when he goes back and I am well and healthy tonight. That's all." When the meeting was over, several club members came up to greet him, expecting to shake an age-roughened hand, but to their surprise, it was soft from lack of work.[11]

On Sunday, September 26, many of Moses' camp moved closer to town and pitched their tents along the Shanno Ditch west of the track. There, hundreds of braves of the Columbias and other bands settled down to play Spanish monte, and a number of white men joined them. This was an easier way of making *chickamin* than their women found picking hops. One white loser described their method of "shuffling, dealing and slipping out the card they most desired at the opportune time."[12]

The "red horde" was quite orderly—more so, as one Yakiman described them, than the town's "wild, wooly and beer-bedraggled cowboys." They flocked to the Coffin store, buying mountains of watermelon, stacks of chewing gum, and blankets— each with a couple of gaudy handkerchiefs thrown in. Moses told a newspaperman who came to see him there, "Heap snow; the cayuses are taking on an extra coat of hair; salmon are leaving early for the Big River; geese and ducks have not gone as far north

11 *Daily Journal* (Freeport, Illinois), October 27, 1897; *Yakima Herald*, September 19, 1895, p. 3.

12 *Yakima Herald*, September 26, 1895, p. 1.

as usual; doves and larks are going south; Indians wants lots of blankets."[13]

Still obsessed with the fear that this Jubilee would be his last, he dropped into the office of an attorney, H. J. Snively, to make a will. While there, he was asked to give a brief autobiography. Through an interpreter, he told of fighting Blackfeet on the Plains, his role in the Indian wars, and his peaceful intent since then. While reviewing his life, he was asked about his relations with Joseph. With perhaps a touch of envy over his friend's growing fame, he told how he had rescued the Nez Percé from degradation and ignominy by taking him into "my arms just like a child" and establishing him on the Colville. When asked if Joseph was coming down to the Jubilee, he replied that he was coming down later with some of his people, but added, "He is not very good to ride now and it will take him as long to come down here as an old woman."

He said he had sent runners to urge all the old-timers of his band to come and reminisce with veterans of other bands, many of whom they had not seen since buffalo days. As to the disposition of his means, he said, "When I die I want my property to go to my wife and children. I have a little money every year, but I give it to the poor people among my people and the old people that can't see any more and that can't walk any more. I give it to them first. When I am dead some one who I pick out will be chief, just as I have been, but he will not have the bullet marks and tomahawk marks on him that Moses Half-Sun has."[14]

On Monday, October 7, when the fair opened, Moses was on the grounds with his people, all primed for the Jubilee scheduled for the next three days. Jubilee was the highlight of any fair, and the highlight of any Jubilee was the races. The horses sped over two-, three-, and four-mile courses, and the betting seemingly involved half the merchandise of the Yakima stores. After the races were over and the track was cleared of horseflesh, Moses and the

13 *Ibid.*

14 Moses "Autobiography." The will received considerable publicity, e.g., *Spokesman-Review*, October 5, 1895, p. 8.

other Indians were permitted to move in somewhat anticlimactically to dance and make speeches pledging perpetual good will.[15]

The good will broke down quite suddenly on Thursday when A. B. Weed, president of the fair commission, ordered the Indians to break camp on the fair grounds. He said unscrupulous persons were selling them whisky, and since the state fair buildings were uninsured, his action was a necessary precaution to protect the property. The lid blew off Moses' usual complacency. A reporter quoted him as saying he would see the people of Yakima in the "hot place" before he would come to Yakima again. The next morning he huffily gathered up his band and left town.[16]

On Monday morning, with about forty of his people, he rode into Wenatchee to visit old Indian and white friends before continuing to the Nespelem. While in that mid-Columbia town, he helped its citizens celebrate the third anniversary of the coming of the Great Northern Railroad.[17] His visit there set off a mild controversy in the press. A reporter for the Seattle *Post Intelligencer* covering his arrival described him as the most prominent and influential Indian in the Northwest. A week later, the Yakima *Herald* took exception to this evaluation, claiming that Moses, the man of "scalping, murdering and ravishing characteristics" could not hold a candle to Chief Joseph.[18]

Moses returned home to prepare for winter. He collected his annuity and bought his supplies. Joseph's people depended on rations as always. In addition to the regular supplies there was a special Christmas issue of beef, axle grease, matches, laundry starch, shoelaces, lampwicks, mineral oil, lard, and coal oil. Young Chief of the Umatillas came early to join in the Nez Percé festivities and to hold talks with Joseph.[19]

On Sunday evening, February 9, 1896, Moses received word that his Nez Percé son-in-law, Johnson, had drowned at Moses

15 *Daily Journal*, October 27, 1897.   16 *Yakima Herald*, October 17, 1895.
17 *Wenatchee Daily World*, November 11, 1920, p. 8.
18 *Seattle Post Intelligencer*, October 23, 1895, p. 2; *Yakima Herald*, October 31, 1895.
19 *Wilbur Register*, December 13, 1895, p. 1.

Crossing. He gathered his daughter, Tomquinwit, Joseph, and others and hurried to the Columbia. The Indians milled around the river until dark waiting for it to give up the body. As they waited, Moses pieced together the story of the tragedy: In company with a friend and his wife, Johnson was returning from Lapwai, where he had obtained some government money from his relatives. In Wilbur he bought whisky and rented a rig to carry him and his friends to Barry. At that point, he searched for a canoe or the agency ferry, and, not finding either, he disrobed, left his valise with the money and whisky on the shore, and swam the river to the other side. There he found a canoe and paddled back to pick up his friends and his money. The woman refused to board it, so the two started rowing across without her. In midstream, it capsized, spilling them into the icy water. The friend clung to the overturned craft, but Johnson, wearing heavy boots and fatigued from his previous crossings, was sucked under and swept away. The friend paddled as hard as he could to the reservation shore, jumped on the ferry, and cast it adrift, thinking he could rescue the drowning man. Failing, he floated down to a landing on the opposite side.

The next morning little groups of natives formed along the Columbia between the ferry landing and several points downstream. As Joseph waited nearby with some of his people, Moses comforted Tomquinwit, restraining his own sorrow. The river had given up Chillileetsah's body near this same spot. Steele came down to oversee searching operations, which halted abruptly at noon with a report that the body had been found.[20] The natives hurried to the location with Steele, who in the presence of Moses, Joseph, and Tomquinwit, found six dollars and a few trinkets in the soggy clothes of the stiff body and turned them over to the grieving widow.[21]

She would weather the tragedy; her father had given her his spirit of Wolf—the power of fierceness.[22]

[20] Steele to Bubb, February 10, 1896. Colville Agency Records, Letterbox 23.
[21] Steele to Bubb, February 11, 1896. Colville Agency Records, Letterbox 23.
[22] Peone Interviews.

Moses and Joseph blamed Kaakin, the ferry tender, for the drowning. He should have been at his ferry, they said, when Johnson and his friends came to the south shore. This was really an unwarranted charge, as the natives had been in the habit of taking the agency ferry for their personal use any time they pleased, thus making it very hard for him to tend it. He maintained that had the two chiefs supervised their people more closely the tragedy would never have occurred.[23]

Just six days before Johnson drowned, John M. Butchart, the new school teacher, and his wife came to the Valley, but only to revive the day school. Butchart invited the chiefs to send their children, and then vainly waited for the patter of childish moccasins on the doorstep. Both Moses and Joseph continued to favor a boarding school.[24] Moses seems to have been the stronger pusher of the idea. How much he may have urged Joseph to oppose the day school is not known, but Joseph was probably less seriously concerned than Moses about a school of any kind. After the March beef issue, a number of Nez Percés struck off for the camas fields near Lapwai.

Meanwhile, the north half of the reservation was opened for mining on February 23. The usual stampede followed, with miners, town builders, gamblers, and liquor peddlers running across the south half on their way to the El Dorado. A new technique for obtaining possession of mining claims and land holdings was to "marry" Indian women living there. In the next few years the Indians whose homes were in the ceded tract would receive allotments as provided in the agreement of 1891. When the work was completed, 660 tribesmen received a total of 51,653 acres; this left 1,449,268 acres for white settlement. The north half was then opened for homesteading in 1900. Eventually, a belated restitution would be made for the acquisition of this land without compensation under a Congressional act of 1892. In

23 Steele to Bubb, February 11, 1896. Colville Agency Records, Letterbox 23.

24 Secretary of the Interior, *Annual Report*, 1896 (54 Cong., 2 sess., *House Exec. Doc. No. 5*), II, 309–11.

1905, Congress provided for payment to the Indians of the $1,500,000 stipulated in the original agreement.[25]

These were events of the future. For the present, on the Colville the Indians probably knew that something was wrong in agency matters during the winter of 1895–96. Serious charges had been brought against Agent Bubb; and Scribner and Steele, always antagonistic towards each other, jumped into the middle of the controversy, with Scribner defending and Steele doubting the Captain's integrity.[26] The Indian Office sent special investigators, and after the smoke cleared, Bubb was replaced by George B. Newman, who took over the agency in June.

It was Newman's task to smooth out employer-employee relationships, to reach some understanding with the Indians on the use of the ferry, and to check on the poor attendance at the school. He considered keeping school open during summer and closed for vacation during hop-picking time. Before the end of June, however, the teacher informed him that attendance was only four or five.[27] School was accordingly closed. In September he wrote, "Prospects are not very favorable for school this month, as nearly all the Indians are away picking hops."[28] Newman considered discontinuing the school entirely and transferring Butchart. This plan must have been unknown to the lord of the Colville, who had washed his hands of the day school, agency, reservation— everything—, had gathered his people, and had headed to

25 Bloodworth, *Human Resources Survey of the Colville Confederated Tribes*, 44 (Colville Agency Records, Historical Correspondence File). Lawyers contended that the terms of the Act of 1892 opening the north half of the reservation included the mineral location. A test case, *Charles N. Collins* vs. *John W. Bubb*, to locate a lode claim within the limits of the north half was tried in the United States District Court of Washington State before Judge Hanford. Hanford decided that the locations were valid (*Spokesman-Review*, April 8, 1896, p. 5). To eliminate doubt, Senator Wilson submitted a bill to Congress to extend the mineral laws of the United States to all lands embraced within the Colville Indian Reservation (*Spokesman-Review*, February 24, 1896, p. 5).

26 *Wilbur Register*, December 28, 1894, p. 6, August 2, 1895, p. 1, August 28, 1895, p. 6, and December 6, 1895, p. 6. See also Bubb to Steele, September 28, 1895 (Colville Agency Records, Letterbox 23).

27 Butchart to Newman, June (no date), 1896. Colville Agency Records, Letterbox 23.

28 Secretary of the Interior, *Annual Report*, 1897 (55 Cong., 2 sess., *House Exec. Doc. No. 5*), XIII 290.

Yakima, apparently having forgiven its breach of hospitality the year before.

Arriving at Simcoe, he became involved in a serious difficulty on the Yakima Reservation. The trouble had begun in March, 1895, when Yakima Agent L. T. Erwin, the "Little Father," as the natives called him, and the Assistant Commissioner of Indian Affairs convened a large council at Simcoe and persuaded the tribesmen to spend twenty-thousand dollars for an irrigation ditch. (The tribe had received this money from the recent sale of their Wenatchee Fisheries, which the government had set aside for them in the Yakima Treaty of 1855.[29]) Now, after the preliminary work on the ditch was completed, the Indians met Erwin in a stormy powwow, declaring that they did not want irrigation, but their old ways of life instead. Erwin said they were too late; most of the money had already been spent for the project. The young Indians, believing that he had stolen their money, shook their fists at him crying, "Thief! Thief!" The sensitive agent left the gathering with tears in his eyes. A few evenings later, as he returned from the ditch, someone fired at him from behind a clump of sagebrush. Soon he heard rumors that the Indians were going to burn the agency.

Moses had visited Erwin and his natives at Simcoe and had almost resolved to stay out of the trouble; but one day he rode in with six of his men to lend the distraught agent a hand. Why did he involve himself in a problem which would appear to have been none of his business? Probably he decided on intervention because he agreed with Erwin that the Indians were making a big mistake by not accepting the irrigation project; then, too, he seems to have felt a strange sense of obligation to Erwin, which deepened each time he sat on the agency steps feasting on the "Little Father's" watermelons and listening to his exciting stories of the Kentucky Derby.

Moses and Erwin believed that the Indians were bluffing, but,

---

29 The sale of the Wenatchee Fisheries caused much bitterness among the Wenatchee bands. See John Hermilt and Louis Judge, "Wenatchee Indians Ask Justice," *Washington Historical Quarterly*, Vol. XVI, No. 1 (January, 1925), 20–28.

to be on the safe side, the Chief offered to have his men sleep days and patrol the grounds at night. Several times they caught Indians skulking behind the barn and found leaves piled against the building, but apparently it *was* a bluff, for no fire was ever started. Moses also took stern charge when disaffected Indians came to the agency to frighten Erwin into giving them gratuities.

One day, some agency children climbed the big back-yard board fence to play in the grove. Three hideously painted Indians sprang from behind the bushes, snatched the children, and rode off with them as their screams of bloody murder rent the Simcoe air. Erwin ran out of his office firing his pistol skyward. The Indians rode behind a blockhouse with their wriggling captives. Suddenly the screams stopped. "Oh, my God! my God!" cried Erwin as he ran to the building. There he discovered the reason for the silence—the Indians had given each of their little "victims" a stick of peppermint candy. That afternoon Moses unsuccessfully scouted the reservation for the pranksters. About that time, White Swan, the Yakima chief, returned from Washington, D.C., where he had pleaded with the Great Father for the return of his people's money. White Swan was now more kindly disposed to the project since the Secretary of the Interior had explained to him the purpose of the irrigation ditch; and he asked Erwin's forgiveness for his people's mischief, particularly the frightening of the children. Erwin said he too was grieved, but would make no official report of it; as far as he was concerned, the issue was closed. (Erwin never forgot Moses' role in the crisis. Years later, after he died, his ashes were scattered on the waters of what he believed to have been the greatest accomplishment of his life, the "Erwin Ditch.")[30]

When Moses left the excitement of Simcoe for that of the Yakima Fair, he learned that Governor John McGraw, who had come with several hundred excursionists from the coast, wished to meet him. The two faced each other, the chief of state in high

[30] Information on Moses' visits to Agent Erwin and Fort Simcoe is from an interview with his daughter (Mrs. Suzanne Erwin Bartholet Interview, Yakima, Washington, April 8, 1961) and from a story she wrote for the Fort Simcoe Centennial, 1956.

Mary, Chief Moses' wife, confidante, and counselor, survived her husband nearly forty years. After the Chief's death, she kept two treasures—the memory of her husband and the companionship of his other wife, Peotsenmy.

Chief Moses, warrior, diplomat, and protector of his
people, in the clothes of the white man, 1897.

silk hat, ascot tie, and cutaway coat, and the tribal chief, in knee-length buckskin coat trimmed with otter and weasel fur, orange and blue ribbons, and long fringes of buckskin at the seams. Moses reminded the Governor that his honor was standing on what was once Indian land; and concluded, "I have traveled much and have seen more pale faces than leaves on the trees. We must follow the ways of the white man or perish like bunchgrass before the plow."[31]

All too soon the good times came to an end, and the weary travelers rode homeward across the sagebrush plains and recently stubbled fields of the Big Bend. At Wilbur, Moses cashed his annuity check for gold coins and spent them on winter staples— pastries, canned goods, and whisky. Back at Nespelem he had barely unloaded his purchases when he learned of the loss of the school. It would be closed on November 1.

The worried chief went to Joseph, and together they went to Butchart and requested him to reinstate the classes. The teacher surmised that the Chief had boycotted the day school only to jar the government into establishing a boarding school, but now having lost, he agreed to send his children. Joseph perhaps wondered if he had made a mistake in following his friend's advice. Early the following Monday, he brought a number of Nez Percé youngsters to the school and promised to bring more when their families returned from the fall hunt. He told the teacher he would have a sick *tum tum* if school were closed. Butchart was so encouraged by the response of the Indians to the prospect of losing their school that he wrote to Newman, "We have now an attendance of eighteen with good prospects of reaching thirty this month. I write now hoping that you may be able to prevent the school closing if it is not already too late."[32] However, his hopes were not realized. The school was closed November 1, and the teacher was transferred to the day school on the Spokane Reservation.[33]

31 *Daily Journal,* October 27, 1897.
32 Butchart to Newman, October 14, 1896. Colville Agency Records, Letterbox 23.
33 Secretary of the Interior, *Annual Report,* 1897, 290.

On December 3, Tonasket's boarding school burned to the ground.

It is apparent that Moses was deeply worried that winter over the white encroachment that followed the opening of the north half of the reservation for mining. He would have liked to talk it over with the agent, but Newman was too busy with the increasing scope of these same problems to spend much time in the Valley. Moses felt resentful over this neglect. He knew that a new Great Father, the Republican William McKinley, would soon take office; and he seems to have understood the shake-up in the Indian Service that invariably came with a political change. He decided to appeal directly to the new White Chief. On inauguration day he called his interpreter, Pecard, to write for him the following:

> Dear Fried this day I understand you are going to take your position. I know that you folks have don more for me than any other kind of people in Washington. My reservation is rich with gold and the white are try to take it away from me without pay me for it and I had an understanding with the department that I would lette them have a part of my reservation for cash money and today they want it all and I haven't received a cent yet. Please tell what you are going to do. About twenty years ago when I agreed to give my home to come her I also promest you to cause no more trouble so I will not do so but I wish for you to see that the whites do not robe me my people are very poor. If you want my land and gold please give me something for it. This is all I have to support my people for a life time. The republican is my fried they have dun justes with me always. Please send me the exactly law so I will know wright. I remaine respectfully Chief Moses

Wait! Moses wanted to add a "P.S."

"Please send us a new agent at once."[34]

Moses took the letter to the Barry Post Office. He must have chuckled at the thought that he had gone to the Great Father over the head of the agent.

[34] Moses to President McKinley, March 4, 1897. Colville Agency Records, Letterbox 10.

A few days after this, R. D. Shutt, teacher in the ill-fated Tonasket School, arrived with his wife in the Valley. It was apparent that the agency had done an about-face on its threat to abandon the Nespelem school, partly at least to provide employment for Shutt.[35] Despite the fact that many of his families were off the reservation, Moses saw to it that a number of his children were in school the day Shutt opened it, April 1.[36] He seems to have decided that he had better co-operate in order to hasten the boarding school. He did not know that reservation children would soon be sent to a boarding school at Fort Spokane with the transfer of that post from the War Department to the Interior Department.

Joseph left for Lapwai on March 22 without having made an effort to get his youngsters to attend school. He returned April 3, with interpreter Wilkinson, and immediately went into a three-day-and-night clandestine council with his subchiefs. When the powwow finally broke up at dawn, Joseph rode away from the Valley. Moses hurried to the Nez Percés and learned that their chief was on his way to Washington, D.C., with Wilkinson as interpreter, to ask permission to move to the Umatilla Reservation. Not all of his people wanted to go with him. Rose Bush told Moses he wanted to stay on the Colville. Isaac said that he, too, was content to stay in the Valley. David Williams felt the same way—this was home now. William Pole was willing to have Moses ask the agent to let him stay in the Nespelem; Cayuse was, too. Two Moons did not want to move either.

Moses asked Shutt to write the agent about Joseph's too secretive plans. Since Joseph's people did not want to move, would the agent see that they remain on the Colville? He signed his "X," then asked Shutt to add a line, "Moses wishes me to add that there is none of them mad at Joseph."[37]

Joseph returned to the Valley from his Washington trip on Thursday, May 6. Wilkinson let it leak out that while at the capi-

---

35 Shutt to Newman, March 22, 1897. Colville Agency Records, Letterbox 24.

36 Secretary of the Interior, *Annual Report*, 1897, 290.

37 Moses to Newman, April 6, 1897. Colville Agency Records, Letterbox 24.

tal the Nez Percé Chief had asked permission to move to the Umatilla with a big annuity. Actually, the only tangible remuneration offered him came in New York with an invitation to join Buffalo Bill's Wild West Show. In that city he had ridden alongside General Howard (from whom he brought greetings to Moses) in a parade to the dedication of General Grant's tomb.[38]

Also in May, Moses, not caring whether school kept or not, set out with his people for their ancestral root grounds. When he passed through Coulee City, his friends there observed that "the past year had left its finger marks on his once stalwart frame."[39] He hobbled on a cane to a store for liniment to ease the pain in his big frame, and then headed west to Badger Mountain. He stationed himself there on the south side of the mountain on a large rock now known as Moses' Stool, sunning the soreness from his bones while his women scratched *house* from the scab rock with iron forked diggers. From his stool he looked down on his old homeland, and no doubt back on his past to the times Karneetsa had brought him there as a child. How long would his people be able to dig roots? He would have been comforted to know that things did not remain the same for the white man either; the council in near-by Waterville decreed that milk cows could no longer use its streets for an open range.[40]

Sundays were play days on the root grounds, and then the horses raced in a big circle above camp reminding one of the olden days. One Sunday a sudden snow squall broke up the races and drove the crowd into the circus-like tent pitched among the convulsing willows and quivering aspens. Moses and his subchiefs took their places before a sprinkling of curious white settlers and some two hundred natives bulging the tent at its seams. To drive away the snow so they could resume the races and root-gathering, the Chief ordered a Chinook dancer to gyrate in the old manner with legs together and knees slightly bent and to chant, "Ki! yi! yi! yi!" to the rhythm of the tinkling bells tied to his ankles. Faster and faster he whirled until he dropped from fatigue. Moses

[38] *Wilbur Register*, May 7, 1897, p. 1.   [39] *Wilbur Register*, May 28, 1897, p. 1.
[40] *Big Bend Empire*, May 27, 1897, p. 4.

ordered his men to carry him out, and the dance broke up. Outside, the sun had come out, and the landscape lay bare save for the trees glistening with snow on top of Badger Mountain. The old Chinook magic still worked![41]

Moses returned to the Valley, revived but little in spirit and less in body. His bones rebelled increasingly at the jarring pace of the bouncing cayuse beneath him. Why not give one of the new two-seated hacks a try? He bought one in Wilbur right after the annual Fourth of July festivities.[42] After his women had harnessed and hitched the horses to the vehicle, he climbed into the back seat and ordered them to drive home. White friends chided him for letting his women drive. "I can't drive because I get dizzy with the horses in front of me instead of under me," he explained.[43] Even Skolaskin's people were acquiring the white man's gadgets. When Steele toured the reservation in June to take the agency census, he found the old conservative very angry with the San Poils and Nespelems for emulating their Columbia neighbors by purchasing stoves and harness. He exhorted them all the harder not to accept farm implements from the agency. In this, they adhered to the wishes of their leader. Present-day San Poils boast that their people never received handouts from the government.[44]

Meanwhile, Moses learned that the letter he had expected to land on President McKinley's desk like a bomb had fluttered harmlessly to earth like a feather. It was of course sent back to Newman; Newman referred it to Steele, and Steele called Moses and Pecard in to inquire whether Moses really had dictated the request for a new agent. Moses accepted the responsibility, but the agent suspected Pecard as the instigator. Steele wrote Newman: "Mr. Picard's conduct, I assure you, is important, haughty

---

41 Amil Norman Interview, East Wenatchee, Washington, August 25, 1961. Mr. Norman was a visitor at the tent.

42 *Wilbur Register,* July 16, 1897, p. 5.

43 Lucy Friedlander Covington Interview, Elmer City, Washington, November 25, 1961.

44 Henry Covington Interview, Keller, Washington, November 22, 1959; Clara Hughes Moore Interview, Belvedere, Washington, May 28, 1961.

and arrogant and his air of independence and defiance I would say demands severe censure." The interpreter found himself in such trouble that eventually he left the reservation for a time.[45]

With approaching fall, Moses again prepared to enjoy the Jubilee. In early September, having sent his people before him, he told Peotsenmy to keep the home fires burning, and Mary to hitch up the team. Together in the new carriage they bumped toward Yakima. At Ellensburg he abandoned the vehicle to stretch his legs on the streets. After resting his bones for a day or two, he had Mary purchase two tickets from a twenty-dollar gold piece for the much more comfortable ride to Yakima on the Northern Pacific.[46]

Near Yakima, Mary again went to work with hundreds of other Indian women from all over the Northwest in the hundred-thousand-box hop harvest, which netted them as many of the white man's dollars. While she toiled in the fields, Moses visited old friends and dropped over to the fairgrounds for the usual festivities. After the races on Friday, October 1, he rode onto the track wearing a red hood crowned with horns and decorated with feathers and ribbons. His coat had two beaver-tail epaulets dropping over the front of his shoulders to form a sort of tab. Each of these bore the insignia of his family: at the top a half-moon, below it a star, and underneath the star, four lozenges. The half-moon, said the proud wearer, represented his grandfather, who like the moon stood next to the sun as the greatest power in the universe. The star, the only one in the firmament, as he explained it, which never moved, represented his father. The four lozenges completed the coat of arms of the family of chiefs. His solar-conscious friend, Streamer, would have been proud of him at that moment.

In deerskin moccasins and gaily decorated leggings and straddling a black horse with red hood headdress reaching to the animal's shoulders in imitation of the headdress of its rider, the Chief waved an eagle feather fan, encouraging his people to dance

45 Steele to Newman, August 11, 1897. Colville Agency Records, Letterbox 10.
46 *Ellensburg Capital*, September 11, 1897.

to the rhythm of his horse's tinkling martingale bells and the rumbling of a big bass drum. After the dances, he turned to the grandstand explaining with equal nostalgia and dramatics, "That's the way we used to do a long time ago when we went to war." Then he figuratively beat his own drum with this little speech: "I am glad to be with you today. I am the great chief[,] this country is mine; it belongs to me and my children. These are my children (pointing to the assembled siwashes)[,] I am a friend of the whites. My heart is in the right place. The whites look down on the Indian and the same way the Indian looks down on the whites."[47]

On the next day, Saturday, the Indians were treated to a farewell feast. They filed by large tables at which twelve men dispensed bread and meat. There, they consumed four thousand loaves of bread and three beeves—perhaps not quite that much since some of them cached their food to eat on the way home.[48]

Moses and company bought few supplies at Yakima to take home. They reserved their purchases until they reached Ellensburg, where a local newspaper hopefully estimated that each Indian carried about forty dollars. Here a photographer wanted to take a picture of Moses in his beaded buckskin suit, but the Chief demanded five dollars to pose. The photographer would not pay the price and snapped him in the white man's clothes instead.[49] Thus, Moses prevented posterity from seeing his latest likeness as a red man—or did he purposely wish to be remembered in the white man's clothes? As he turned homeward, only he knew.

Soon after Moses returned, Agent Newman was replaced by A. M. Anderson, the former agency clerk. Moses liked Anderson, regarding him as a welcome change from the cross, abrupt Newman. Perhaps he thought his letter to the President had been effective after all. But Anderson, like his predecessor, had so many big problems supervising the rapidly changing reservation that he could devote but little attention to the Valley. Among

---

47 *Daily Journal*, October 27, 1897; *Yakima Herald*, October 7, 1897, p. 1.
48 *Daily Journal*, October 27, 1897.   49 *Ellensburg Capital*, October 23, 1897.

other things a ring rustling Indian cattle was selling its purloined product in and around Marcus and Kettle Falls and was getting away with it because the sheriff of Okanogan County would not arrest the brains of the outfit, who lived on the Columbia outside the reservation. The county attorney declared that the cattle thefts constituted a federal offense and that the government would have to stand the expense of prosecuting the thieves.[50]

During the winter of 1897–98, the Yakima Reservation was being allotted. Moses became concerned lest Kamiakin's people, who were living with him, would be compelled to return to the Fort Simcoe agency and take allotments there. He had Steele write Anderson that he did not want them to leave. "If they desire to remain with me, can they not remain on this reservation?" he asked. Anderson wrote to Yakima Agent J. Lynch and Special Allotting Agent William E. Casson. They replied from Fort Simcoe that although these Yakimas had been invited to return, they were under no compulsion, but might remain on the Nespelem. Moses was "pleased" at this assurance.[51]

The Nez Percé Reservation in Idaho was also being allotted, with the usual sale of the surplus to the government and the distribution of the proceeds among the tribesmen. Thus, it became necessary for the Nez Percés living with Moses to decide whether to remain where they were or to accept allotments with their tribe. Tomquinwit, Johnson's widow, visited her in-laws at Lapwai, but could not decide whether or not to take an allotment there.[52] She eventually married Owhi and remained on the Colville.[53] Among others who went to Lapwai to protect their interests were Itstsulkt and Peotsenmy. Itstsulkt, no longer a bedmate for Joseph, but living with another man in the Valley, signed a document releasing any rights on the Nez Percé. Peotsenmy, on the other hand, decided to retain her rights there, to

50 D. W. Reid, sheriff of Okanogan County to agent, December 6, 1897. Colville Agency Records, Letterbox 24.

51 Steele to Colville agent, February 2, 1898; Casson to Anderson, February 22, 1898; Steele to Anderson, March 9, 1898 (Colville Agency Records, Letterbox 24).

52 Steele to Newman, May (no date), 1896. Colville Agency Records, Letterbook No. 9.

53 Sadie Moses Williams Interview, Nespelem, Washington, January 3, 1958.

collect her pro rata share of funds due from the sale of the surplus land, and to sign a statement relinquishing any claim on the Colville.[54] She would, however, happily return to the waiting Moses.

Not all of his people could return so happily. Those who had gone down to the camas root grounds in the Moses Lake area returned driving loose horses, trailing pack horses, and smarting from the inhospitable actions of Thomas S. Blythe. "Lord" Blythe, a monacled Englishman owning thirty sections and leasing over thirty more of the best camas grounds around the lake, objected to the Indians' flocking there each year on his grazing land with nearly a thousand cayuses. This time he went to the county seat at Waterville to get the sheriff to eject them. The sheriff refused to act on the grounds that this was the responsibility of the government agents.[55] It was evident, however, that the Indians would not long have the run of their old camas grounds.

At the same time the white man's fences were detouring the Indians from familiar trails. They could no longer ride freely even on the reservation, and it would be worse when five thousand pounds of barbed wire that Steele had recently ordered was added to that already strung around a thousand reservation acres. But Moses could understand the need of fences. The fences on the reservation kept out roving stock and enabled the Indians under his supervision to go through their fields with scythes harvesting a good crop.

Sometimes he left the workers in the fields for the shade of his "thousand dollar" house to tell stories to the children. As his great-granddaughter remembers it, they went somewhat like this:

"When I was riding a stage back to see the President, the driver suddenly halted and told the passengers we were being held-up by bandits. We had to get our guns ready. 'But I don't have one,' I told the stage driver. He handed me a gun," Moses told the youngsters, who occasionally interrupted to ask questions.

---

54 S. G. Fisher to Anderson, June 16, 1898. Colville Agency Records, Letterbox 24.
55 Blythe to Anderson, April 26–27, 29, 1898. Colville Agency Records, Letterbox 24.

"Just as he handed me the gun the speeding stage overturned. As it toppled over, I sprang to my feet with the gun in my hand and held off the bandits." The children sat motionless, listening to the story of his daring feat.

He continued, "The driver told me that he would not be afraid for the rest of the trip as long as I was along."[56]

More and more, his storytelling included episodes from his trips to Washington, D. C., the pinnacle of his leadership. There were stories of climbing long staircases of the capital buildings, and even one of a wealthy white widow who proposed to him.

Had he accepted the proposal, the wife could never have matched the work of Mary and Peotsenmy, whose efforts in the face of his increasing debility became more important each day. Mary often laid aside her craft work to join Peotsenmy in cutting wood, carrying water, and preparing food for the people always gathering around their chief. Their chores finished, they rested in the midafternoon shade and sipped "refined" liquor from small flasks their husband bought them—he did not allow them to drink from his kegs.[57] Peotsenmy combed hair and performed other services for Quiltlay (Dusty), her small daughter by Moses. She was assisted in the care of the child by Moses' orphaned granddaughter Nellie. Nellie was growing up, and Moses thought that Louie Friedlander, the son of Elizabeth, a Chelan, and Herman Friedlander, a Jewish trader, was paying too much attention to her. When Nellie asked him why he objected to Louie, his only answer was that the young man was a "breed."[58] Eventually, however, Nellie married him.[59]

Moses was giving his Swan power to Nellie in degrees, training

[56] The story of the stage holdup which Moses related to the children was given in detail by his great-granddaughter (Lucy Friedlander Covington Interview, Elmer City, Washington, November 25, 1961). The authors have failed to find a contemporary newspaper account of this particular holdup, but there is no reason to discredit his story. The stage passed through robber-infested territory, and such incidents were frequent at the time.

[57] Peone Interviews.

[58] Lucy Friedlander Covington Interview, Elmer City, Washington, November 25, 1961.

[59] Nellie Moses Friedlander Interview, Palisades, Washington, June 2, 1957.

her before many gatherings. Mary scolded and warned him not to do so. She was sure that his gifts of Sun power to their first son and of various other powers to their young daughters had caused their early deaths. (Her six children had all died before puberty. Of Peotsenmy's children, only Quiltlay survived, but she would die at age ten. Moses' grandchildren of Tomquinwit's marriage with Johnson all died.)[60]

Moses' people were being crowded in their final refuge during this year of 1898. Their diminished reservation (the south half of the original Colville Reservation) was opened for mineral entry by act of Congress, July 1. The legal justification of this light-hearted gift of the Indians' landed property seems to have been that the Colville Reservation had been established by executive order—"set apart as a reservation" for them in 1872.[61] Future acts of Congress and Indian Office regulations would eventually recognize tribal ownership of minerals and other natural resources on executive order reservations; but in 1898 the Indians were presumed to be living there on sufferance like so many animals on a wildlife refuge.

Even before the actual opening of the Colville for mineral exploration, "sooners" sneaked in to prospect; and now with the opening, miners covered the area like swarming termites seeking a place to burrow.[62] Their blasting interfered with the San Poil fishing;[63] and they took cattle and women and made agreements with the Indians which they had no intention of keeping.[64] Ironically, their efforts would turn out to be fruitless, and nearly all their claims were eventually abandoned, but the rush was disturbing while it lasted.

Whisky sellers followed close on the heels of the miners. Agent

60 Peone Interviews.

61 Kappler, *Indian Affairs: Laws and Treaties*, I, 667, 916.

62 Steele to Anderson. June 2, 1898. Colville Agency Records, Letterbox 24.

63 Frank Hughes (a half blood living near Keller) to agent, October (no date), 1898. Colville Agency Records, Letterbox 24.

64 J. F. Cholson (a prospector) to Anderson, June 6 and July 27, 1898; S. Sogel (Okanogan Valley resident) to Anderson, January 24, 1898; Martena Pingston to Anderson, August 10, 1899; J. L. Peel (Superintendent of Rogers Bar Mining Company) to agent, April 24, 1899 (Colville Agency Records, Letterbox 25).

Anderson had attempted to protect the Indians living in the north half of the reservation against this traffic, but the United States attorney at Seattle had ruled that since that tract had been restored to public domain, liquor sales were legal there. Now, the traders interpreted this to mean that since the south half had been opened for mineral entry, the ruling applied there also. The federal court in Seattle ruled against this contention; the south half was not a part of the public domain. Agent Anderson tried valiantly to clear the reservation of the liquor peddlers. He confiscated a large quantity of liquor on August 10 from a saloon which had been opened at Keller, a new miners' outfitting town that had sprung up on the San Poil.[65] A bigger problem was to find and arrest bootleggers who operated without a store.

Ferryboats now laced the Columbia like thongs on a cradleboard. The government favored Indians over whites when handing out permits to operate them; but white men often hired natives to run their boats and pose as the owners.[66]

Moses celebrated the Fourth of July that year in Wilbur. It was an exciting occasion, with the crowd stirred to a fever of patriotism by the Spanish-American War. The years had all but erased from Moses' memory the unpleasant Fourth he had spent there nearly a decade before. This time he had been a hit with everyone—almost—except Judge Harbison, who objected to marching in the big parade behind a siwash. That did not matter much to Moses. His horses ran well. On the platform of the specially built pavilion, in finery crowned by a headpiece of horns (not of Plains buffalo, but of Badger Mountain steer), he

65 Gay to Anderson, February 4 and August 3, 1898; list enumerating confiscated bottles (Colville Agency Records, Letterbox 24).

66 Wirt W. Saunders (justice of peace in Spokane) to Long Alex (Indian living at Curlew Lake) July 7, 1898; Saunders to DeRouge, July 7, 1898; DeRouge to Anderson, October 22, 1898; Reid Crowell (citizen of Bossburg, Washington) to Anderson, July 27, August 18, and August 19, 1898; Charles E. Claypool (assistant United States attorney, Seattle, Washington) to Anderson, October 5, 1899; S. L. Magee (merchant, Daisy, Washington) to Anderson, August 25, 1899; E. D. Morrison (citizen, Daisy, Washington) to agent, September (no date), 1899; C. F. Ledgerwood (Kettle Falls, Washington) to Anderson, September 16, 1899 (Colville Agency Records, Letterbox 25).

"jargoned" to the crowd through an interpreter: "I am not a Democrat, nor a Republican, or a Populist, but an American and I would like to take my men down and lick the Spaniards." The crowd loved it; Moses was no threat to them now; he had become a good American. Leaning heavily on his cane, he puffed his big frame into Marion E. Hay's store and deposited it on the nearest chair to rest his tired bones.[67]

Moses awaited the call of Jubilee for the last time that same year. He should have stayed at home, for one day he found himself in Yakima's "skookum house." Twenty years earlier he had languished in a Yakima jail, a victim of suspicion; now, he was there a victim perhaps of sorrow. "Failure to carry his liquor with his former grace," one reporter put it,[68] but his incarceration was probably not the result of a mere Jubilee jag. He had shown a remarkable adaptability to the changes that had destroyed his former way of life, but so many things had happened to destroy his hopes. Now, on top of all his other troubles, an Okanogan Indian stole his fine saddle while he was in Yakima.[69]

It was apparent that his days of power and influence were over. At one time his authority had been felt in all directions; now no one seemed to hear him any more. With the agency his problems had been obscured by larger ones, which turned the spotlight on others. Even the military, once his comfort, was preparing this fall of 1898 to abandon Fort Spokane to move to Fort George Wright (formerly Camp George Wright) near the city of Spokane.[70]

He still kept his humor. An old friend, Tom Seaton, was establishing a new ferry four miles above the mouth of the Grand Coulee, on the old Indian route linking Nespelem and Wilbur, and was moving his store from Hesseltine, fifteen miles northwest

67 *Wilbur Register*, July 8, 1898, p. 1.

68 *Ellensburg Capital*, October 8, 1898.

69 Anderson to Steele, November 4, 1898. Colville Agency Records, Letterbox 13.

70 The Fort Spokane equipment was disposed of in May, 1899, and the buildings transferred to the Interior Department the next month. Sergeant Bartholomew Coughlin (or Conghlin?), of the closing detail, to Anderson, May 2 and June 23, 1899 (Colville Agency Records, Letterbox 25).

of Wilbur to the south ferry-landing.[71] Having recovered sufficiently from an illness of the previous month, Moses set out with two wagons on a day in mid-November and crossed at Seaton's ferry.[72] It may have been on this trip that he discussed fares with Tom. He said, "My people own half the river, so they should cross it for half fare."

"All right," said Seaton, "I will take you half way across and then you and your women can just get off and walk the rest of the way." Then relenting, "It's a deal." Moses laughed heartily at the concession.[73]

Across the river, he visited Seaton's store. He may have been reminded of the times when he and Joseph used to stop at the Hesseltine store or of the times he and his wives stopped there, and how the women used to alight nimbly from their carriage and beat him to the store on a calico quest, fumbling in their bright handkerchiefs for coins. No doubt he remembered, too, how he used to go straight to a bucket of eggs on a counter in the back and begin sucking one right after another. Now he raided the eggs again. Seaton interrupted his feast, demanding, "All right, Moses, pay for the eggs."

The old Chief replied, "One half the eggs [like the Columbia River] belong to me." Then, after a pause to let Seaton feel the impact of his humor, he asked, "How much eggs?"

"Twelve and a half cents a dozen," answered Seaton, "but I never was much good at figurin' half cents. You can have 'em for twelve."[74]

Moses drove on to Wilbur, but, too exhausted for an extended visit, he returned to what comfort there was left in his tipi. Sitting on a tattered buffalo-hide mat, one of the few remaining symbols of his earlier bravery and wealth, he awaited one more spring.

71 Thomas B. Seaton (Hesseltine) to Anderson, November 2, 1898. Colville Agency Records, Letterbox 24.

72 *Wilbur Register*, October 28, 1898, p. 4; and November 18, 1898, p. 4.

73 Community Development Study, *History of Grand Coulee Dam Area: From Pioneers to Power*, 13.

74 Bessie Seaton Dumas Interview, Wenatchee, Washington, June 19, 1961.

XVIII. One Wide River

"My mind is not to die by violence and war, but to die when I get sick or old like other people."—Moses' letter, December 25, 1878, from Yakima City to General Howard

SLOWLY THE WINTER OF 1898–99, piled on top of seventy others like successive layers of snow, crushed the life from Moses. He bled frequently from the nose and mouth, and noises bothered him. Never again would he have strength to seek relief in the joys of Jubilee, the magic of the bitterroot grounds, or the bitters of a frontier drugstore. Most of his native friends were gone— Sarsopkin, Tonasket, Innomoseecha Bill—even some of their sons were dead. Francis Streamer, his "friend," had been carried away to an insane asylum, the "brittle pitcher," as General Howard had feared, "broken at its source." Nearing the end, the tired old Chief drew his wives to his side, but with the keen wit marking his speech throughout his life, he said, "You do not have to live with any of my brothers. Of course, I am the homeliest of my family," he laughed feebly. He begged them to return to their people—Mary to the Yakimas and Peotsenmy to the Nez Percés—but the two vowed before him never to leave each other. Mustering his remaining strength, he gave them specific instructions for his burial and the disposal of his possessions.[1] His hopes of perpetuating the Half-Sun chieftaincy through Chillileetsah and Yayoskin had failed.

Agent Anderson hurried to Spokane on Saturday, March 25, to tell the outside world the Chief was dying. He died that same day, where bud-bursting trees overhung the swelling Nespelem. At his side were his faithful wives and several of his "children" who always flocked to the hospitality of his house. Official diagnosis of death was given as Bright's disease, severe exposure, and

1 Peone Interviews.

347

advanced years.[2] One of his people gave a simpler diagnosis: "He was made an old man too soon and too sad."[3] In eulogy, Anderson wrote: "His judgment was rarely misplaced. He was a suave, pleasant man of sunny disposition and jovial nature; exerted a powerful influence over his people, and his wishes were never disregarded by them. Though stern in governing, he was kind to the weak and generous to those in want, caring for the old and indigent, supplying them with provisions from his own larder, and often gave them money to purchase necessaries of life. In his death the tribe loses a faithful friend, and the Government a good citizen."[4]

His wives kept a lonely vigil over his body and a close watch on his effects to keep them from friends and relatives wishing to jump the gun on the potlatch. They buried him a few days later on a low bluff overlooking the Little Nespelem near where it flows into the Nespelem not far from where that stream tumbles to the Columbia, the stream of his early life. On the sixth and seventh of June, more than one thousand of his friends flocked to his house on the Nespelem to attend a potlatch said to have been the "largest and most splendid of its kind ever known or likely to be known in the Northwest Country." The guests began the observance in an atmosphere of Jubilee and feasted on nearly a dozen beeves. Then came a period of grieving; simulated mourning, said some skeptical white men, but who were white men to say? Gifts included Moses' horses, some of them valuable racing stock, horse trappings, rare furs, clothing of richest description, other articles of fine workmanship, and gifts from government officials.

The most prized possession of the potlatch, the insigne of the late Chief's leadership, a buckskin suit and a war bonnet, said to have been given him by Sitting Bull, was received by Chief Joseph with a moving speech amid chanting and weeping.[5] Not

2 Secretary of the Interior, *Annual Report*, 1899 (56 Cong., 1 sess., *House Exec. Doc. No. 5, Pt. 1*), XVIII 353–54.

3 *Wenatchee Daily World*, September 28, 1934, p. 13.

4 Secretary of the Interior, *Annual Report*, 1899, pp. 353–54.

5 *Spokesman-Review*, June 14, 1899, p. 5. For a more complete account of the

all of his possessions were given away at the potlatch; Mary padlocked in his room many of the fine clothes and trappings her clever hands had made for him. Over the years, she yielded to relatives trophies like the buffalo head flanked with human hands, the symbol of her husband's bravery, but in her thinking no one was worthy of his treasures, so in the old tribal way, she took many of them out and buried them.[6]

Mary kept two treasures—the memory of her husband and the companionship of his other wife, Peotsenmy. Death severed this companionship when a plague swept the frail Nez Percé to her grave in 1902, some thirty-five years before Mary herself succumbed. Mary kept the memory of her husband alive in long walks and in nighttime stories of the olden days. Some time after Moses' death, M. E. Hay, Wilbur storekeeper, later governor of the state, showed her a plate with her husband's likeness painted on it. "Moses!" she gasped, and broke into tears.[7]

He had no more rest in death than in life. In 1904, the year his friend Joseph was buried, white grave robbers rudely tipped over his monument, exhumed his body, snatched his gold watch and ring and his medal from Washington, D. C., and ripped the precious beadwork from his decaying clothes. In their haste to leave the violated grave, they dropped his pipe; and some little boys found and smoked it, and became ill. Mary took from his room a fine fur-trimmed coat valued by white men at five hundred dollars and laid it as a shroud on his remains as a final token of her love.[8]

Soon after his death a new century would burst into the Valley, which now had a store and a post office. Change![9]

His people would follow the paths he blazed to the Great

potlatch, see Eugene B. Chase, "A Grand Aboriginal Function," *Northwest Magazine*, Vol. XVII, No. 8 (August, 1899), 20–21.

6 Peone Interviews.

7 *Spokesman-Review*, November 12, 1916.

8 "Chief Moses," Biography Folder, Spokane Public Library. One of the possessions that Moses gave away some years before his death was a watchcase—to a Ahna L. Hansen who often interpreted for him.

9 The town of Nespelem was established in the fall of 1899 when a post office was located there.

Father to redress old grievances, and restless white men would crowd his old trails. A decade from his passing, they would ride the iron horse up a steel path in Moses Coulee (Beulah Land the white man called it) to fetch grains from the Big Bend where once the bunchgrass grew. Two decades later, they would throw up the first concrete barrier on the Columbia near the Coulee mouth at Rock Island; and a decade from that, the giant barrier at the head of the ancestral trail, Grand Coulee. At mid-century, they would turn the vast heartland at its mouth into a garden whose vastness its first gardener, Sulktalthscosum, could have imagined only in his wildest dreams.

The bones of Sulktalthscosum's most illustrious son were scarcely at rest when white men began stirring the bones of controversy over his greatness. In 1917, Jack Splawn wrote in his book, *Ka-Mi-akin*, a chapter entitled, "Chief Moses as I Knew Him," a belated thank-you to the Chief for saving his life when he was a young towheaded drover on the Columbia. One writer attacking Splawn's characterization of Moses as "the Bismarck of the red men of the Pacific Northwest," said he was "under the surface . . . merely a composition of malignancy and cowardice—Mr. Splawn calls it diplomacy."[10] Unfortunately, many of Moses' critics compared him with Joseph, stirring about the two a controversy more bitter than any while they lived.

Thus, many have seen Moses, the Half-Sun in death, as in life, a man of shadow rather than of light. Perhaps, some day, a greater number freed from the prejudices of the past will see the eclipse of time pass from his orb. Then they will behold it in its true light—from which has been removed the shadow of doubt.

[10] *Wenatchee Daily World*, November 11, 1920, p. 8.

Bibliography

Manuscript Materials

Brown, William Compton. Papers. Manuscripts, Holland Library, Washington State University, Pullman, Washington.

"Chief Moses." Biography Folder. Spokane Public Library.

DeRouge, Etienne, S. J. "Indians of the Northwest." Manuscript, Crosby Library, Gonzaga University, Spokane.

Doty, James. "A True Copy of the Record of the Official Proceedings at the Council in the Walla Walla Valley, 1855." Typescript copy, Holland Library, Washington State University, Pullman, Washington.

Eells, Cushing. "Reminiscences." Typescript copy, Holland Library, Washington State University, Pullman, Washington.

Ferry, E. P., secretary of state. Indian War Cannister, Washington State Archives, Olympia.

———. State Documents 1876–80, Indian Affairs, Washington State Archives, Olympia.

Fort Dalles Papers. Huntington Library, San Marino.

Grassi, Urban, S. J. Letters to Father Superior 1874–1876. Manuscripts, Crosby Library, Spokane.

Griva, Edward, S. J. "History of the Fifty Years of My Missionary Life Among Indians and Whites from July, 1894 Until the End of September, 1944." Manuscript, Crosby Library, Gonzaga University, Spokane.

Haller, Granville Owen. Diaries, Letters, Papers, and Military Documents, 1839–97. University of Washington Library, Seattle, Washington.

Hart, William. Scrapbooks. Holland Library Collection, Washington State University, Pullman, Washington.

Howard, Oliver Otis. "Diary—Bannock Indian Campaign." Manuscript, Huntington Library, San Marino.

Lewis, Philip H. "Coal Discoveries in Washington Territory." Typescript copy, Bancroft Library, Berkeley.

McClellan, George B. "Papers—Engineering Notebook and Memoranda 1853 *et al.*, Journal, May 20–December 16." Library of Congress microcopy in possession of authors.

McWhorter, L. V. Papers, manuscripts. Holland Library, Washington State University, Pullman, Washington.

Moses, Chief. "Autobiography," 1895. Typescript copy in possession of Mrs. E. S. West, Yakima, Washington.

Moses Reservation. United States Department of the Interior, Special Case # 65, 1879–1907. National Archives, Department of the Interior. Photostatic copies in possession of authors.

Oregon Historical Scrapbooks. Oregon Historical Society, Portland, Oregon.

Pambrun, Andrew D. "The Story of His Life as He Tells It." Manuscript, Hargreaves Library, Eastern Washington State College, Cheney, Washington.

Parker, J. C. "Puget Sound." Typescript copy, Bancroft Library, Berkeley.

Selected Documents from Among the Records of the Bureau of Indian Affairs Relating to Skolaskin, Chief of the San Puel Indians, and Removal of the Nez Percé under Chief Joseph from Indian Territory to the Colville Reserve in 1885. National Archives, Bureau of Indian Affairs, Record Group No. 75, 1885–92. Photostatic copies in possession of authors.

Selected Documents Relating to Chief Moses. National Archives, Record Group 94. Photostatic copies in possession of authors.

Senate Journal of the Second Legislature of the State of Washington, with *Senate Journal of the Extraordinary Session, First Legislature*. Olympia, 1891.

Simms, John A. Papers. Holland Library, Washington State University, Pullman, Washington.

Spalding, Henry Harmon. "Letters and Papers." Copies and originals, Holland Library, Washington State University, Pullman, Washington.

Spalding, Mrs. Henry Harmon. "Diary 1836–1840." Typescript copy, Oregon Historical Society, Portland, Oregon.

Streamer, Francis. Miscellaneous Notebooks. Washington State Historical Society, Tacoma.

United States Army Commands. Camp Chelan and Camp Spokane, Washington Territory, Letters Sent, August, 1879–December, 1880. National Archives, Record Group 98. Photostatic copies in possession of Mr. James Lindston, Chelan, Washington.

United States Bureau of Indian Affairs. Correspondence of agents of the Colville and Simcoe Agencies. Federal Records Center, Seattle.

United States Circuit Court. File Group 21, Federal Records Container 3670, Federal Records Center, Seattle.

Virgin, Robert G. "The Saga of Chief Moses." Typescript copy, North Central Washington Museum, Wenatchee, Washington.

Walker, Elkanah. "Diary." Typescript copy, Oregon Historical Society, Portland, Oregon.

Washington Superintendency Records, 1853–74, No. 5, Roll 20; 1853–80, No. 234, Roll 918. Microcopies, University of Washington, Seattle.

Weaver, Harold. "A Tour of the Old Indian Camp Grounds of Central Washington." Mimeographed copy (no date) in possession of authors.

Washington Questionnaires. Typescript copies, Bancroft Library, Berkeley.

Winans, W. P. Collection. Holland Library, Washington State University, Pullman, Washington.

Yakima Indian Agency. Miscellaneous Files and Letter Record Books, 1878–79. Copies of excerpts in possession of Mr. Click Relander, Yakima, Washington.

Federal Documents

Annual Reports of the Commissioner of Indian Affairs, 1858–1900.

Annual Reports of the Secretary of War, 1856, 1857, 1877, 1878, 1879, and 1883.

Bloodworth, Jessie A. *Human Resources Survey of the Colville Confederated Tribes,* Portland, Oregon, 1959.

Ferry, E. P. *Report of the Governor of Washington Territory Made to the Secretary of the Interior,* 1878.

Holden, Edward S. "A Catalogue of Earthquakes on the Pacific Coast 1769 to 1879," *Smithsonian Miscellaneous Collections,* No. 1087, 1898.

Kappler, Charles J., ed. *Indian Affairs: Laws and Treaties,* 58 Cong., 2 sess., *Sen. Exec. Doc. No. 310.* 2 vols. Washington, Government Printing Office, 1904.

Mooney, James. "The Aboriginal Populations of America North of Mexico," *Smithsonian Miscellaneous Collections,* Vol. LXXX, No. 7, Washington, 1928.

————. "The Ghost Dance Religion and the Sioux Outbreak of 1890," *Fourteenth Annual Report of the Bureau of American Ethnology,* 1892–93, Part 2, 1890.

Selected Documents Relating to Chief Moses, Photostatic Copies of Records of the National Archives, Department of War, Record Group No. 94, 1879–83.

Selected Documents Relating to Skolaskin, Photostatic Copies of Records of the National Archives, Record Group No. 94, A. G. 5377 of 1889.

Stevens, Isaac I. "Narrative of 1853–1855," *Pacific Railroad Report of Explorations and Surveys,* XII, 1860.

Symons, Thomas W. *Report of an Examination of the Upper Columbia River and the Territory in its Vicinity in September and October, 1881, to Determine its Navigability and Adaptability to Steamboat Transportation,* 47 Cong., 1 sess., *Sen. Exec. Docs. No. 186 and 188.*

Teit, James H. "The Salishan Tribes of the Western Plateaus," ed. by Franz Boas, *Forty-fifth Annual Report of the Bureau of American Ethnology,* 1930.

United States Bureau of the Census. *Report of Indians Taxed and Not Taxed, Eleventh Census Report, 1894.*

United States General Land Office. *United States Mining Laws and Regulations Thereunder,* Section 2319, October 31, 1881.

NEWSPAPERS

Big Bend Empire. Waterville, Washington Territory-State, 1888–89, 1891, 1892, and 1897.

Chelan Leader. Chelan, Washington, 1893 and 1895.

Daily Bee. Portland, Oregon, 1878–79.

Daily Evening Bulletin. San Francisco, 1879.

Daily Intelligencer. Seattle, 1879–81.

Daily Journal. Freeport, Illinois, 1897.

Dalles Times-Mountaineer. The Dalles, Oregon, 1882.

Ellensburg Capital. Ellensburg, Washington, 1897–98.

Evening Star. Washington, D. C., 1879, 1883.

Herald. Tacoma, Washington Territory, 1879.

Morning Call. San Francisco, 1879.

Morning Review. Spokane Falls, Washington Territory, 1889.

Northwest Tribune. Cheney, Washington Territory, 1880–84; Spokane Falls, Washington Territory, 1888; Spokane, 1893.

Okanogan Independent. Okanogan, Washington, 1924, 1930.

Olympia Transcript. Olympia, 1879.

Omaha Weekly Herald. Omaha, 1878.

Omak Chronicle. Omak, Washington, 1960.

Oregonian. Portland, Oregon, 1873–91.

Pacific Christian Advocate. Portland, Oregon, 1879.

Pioneer Press. St. Paul and Minneapolis, 1883.

Portland Daily Standard. Portland, Oregon, 1879.

Puget Sound Weekly Courier. Olympia, Washington Territory, 1877 and 1881.

Republic. Wenatchee, Washington, 1906.

San Francisco Chronicle. San Francisco, 1879.

Seattle Post Intelligencer. Seattle, 1895.

Spirit of the West. Walla Walla, Washington Territory, 1874.

Spokane Daily Chronicle. Spokane, 1917.

Spokane Evening Review. Spokane Falls, Washington Territory, 1885.

Spokane Falls Review. Spokane Falls, Washington, 1890–91.

Spokane Review. Spokane, Washington, 1891–93.

Spokane Weekly Review. Spokane, 1891–93.

Spokesman. Spokane, 1892.

Spokesman-Review. Spokane, 1895, 1899, 1906, and 1916.

Tacoma Herald. Tacoma, Washington Territory, 1879.

Waitsburg Times. Waitsburg, Washington Territory, 1879.

Walla Walla Statesman. Walla Walla, Washington Territory, 1877–79, 1880, 1881.

Walla Walla Union. Walla Walla, Washington Territory, 1873, 1877, and 1883.

Washington Post. Washington, D. C., 1879 and 1883.

Weekly Pacific Tribune. Seattle, Washington Territory, 1877–79.

Weekly Standard. Portland, Oregon, 1878–79.

Wenatchee Daily World. Wenatchee, Washington, 1920, 1922, 1925, 1927, 1934–35, 1937–38.

Wilbur Register. Wilbur, Washington Territory, 1888; Wilbur, Washington, 1889–98, 1914.

Yakima Daily Republic. Yakima, Washington, 1961.

Yakima Herald. Yakima, Washington Territory, 1889; Yakima, Washington, 1895.

Yakima Morning Herald. Yakima, Washington, 1898 and 1961.

Yakima Weekly Record. Yakima City, Washington Territory, 1883.

BOOKS AND PAMPHLETS

Ballou, Robert. *Early Klickitat Valley Days.* Goldendale, Washington, 1928.

Brimlow, George F. *The Bannock Indian War of 1878.* Caldwell, 1938.

Brown, William Compton. *The Indian Side of the Story.* Spokane, 1961.

Community Development Study. *History of Grand Coulee Dam Area: From Pioneers to Power.* Grand Coulee, 1958.

Cox, Ross. *Adventures on the Columbia River.* 2 vols. London, 1831.

Crook, General George. *General George Crook: His Autobiography.* Ed. by Martin F. Schmitt, Norman, 1946.

Curtis, Edward. *The North American Indian.* 20 vols. Norwood, Massachusetts, 1911.

Debo, Angie. *And Still the Waters Run.* Princeton, 1940.

DeSmet, Pierre Jean. *Life, Letters, and Travels of Father Pierre-Jean DeSmet, S. J., 1801–1873.* 4 vols. Ed. by H. M. Chittenden and A. T. Richardson. New York, 1905.

Dow, Edson. *Passes to the North.* Wenatchee, Washington, 1963.

Drury, Clifford M. *Henry Harmon Spalding.* Caldwell, 1936.

———. *Tepee in His Front Yard.* Portland, Oregon, 1949.

Eells, Myron. *History of Indian Missions on the Pacific Coast.* Philadelphia, 1882.

Evans, Elwood. *History of the Pacific Northwest: Oregon and Washington.* 2 vols. Portland, Oregon, 1889.

Ewers, John C. *The Blackfeet: Raiders on the Northwestern Plains.* Norman, 1958.

Fargo, Lucile Foster. *Spokane Story.* New York, 1950.

Field, Virgil F., ed. *The Official History of the Washington National Guard.* 5 vols. Tacoma, 1961.

Foreman, Grant. *Indian Removal: The Emigration of the Five Civilized Tribes of Indians.* Norman, 1932.

———. *The Last Trek of the Indians.* Chicago, 1946.

France, George W. *The Struggles for Life and Home in the North-West.* New York, 1890.

Franchère, Gabriel. *Narrative of a Voyage to the Northwest Coast of America in the Years 1811, 1812, 1813, and 1814.* Ed. by J. V. Huntington. New York, 1854.

Fries, U. E. *From Copenhagen to Okanogan.* Caldwell, 1949.

Fuller, George W. *A History of the Pacific Northwest.* New York, 1948.

Gates, Charles M., ed. *Messages of the Governors of the Territory of Washington to the Legislative Assembly, 1854–1889.* University of Washington *Publications in the Social Sciences,* 12 vols. Seattle, 1940.

Green, Constance M. *Washington, Capital City, 1879–1950,* 5 vols. Princeton, 1963.

Haines, Francis. *The Nez Percés.* Norman, 1955.

Hodges, L. K., ed. *Mining in the Pacific Northwest*. Seattle, 1897.

Howard, Oliver Otis. *Famous Indian Chiefs I Have Known.* New York, 1908.

———. *My Life and Experiences Among Our Hostile Indians.* Hartford, 1907.

———. *Nez Percé Joseph: An Account of His Ancestors, His Lands, His Confederates, His Murders, His War, His Pursuit and Capture*. Boston, 1881.

Hull, Lindley. *A History of Central Washington*. Spokane, 1929.

Illustrated Guide and Catalogue of Woodward's Garden. San Francisco, 1880.

Jessett, Thomas E. *Chief Spokan Garry, 1811–1892*. Minneapolis, 1960.

Keyes, E. D. *Fifty Years' Observation of Men and Events Civil and Military*. New York, 1884.

Kimmel, Thelma. *The Fort Simcoe Story*. Toppenish, Washington, 1954.

Kip, Lawrence. *Army Life on the Pacific: A Journal of the Expedition Against the Northern Indians, the Tribes of the Coeur D'Alenes, Spokanes and Pelouzes, in the Summer of 1858*. New York, 1859.

Larsell, Olof. *The Doctor in Oregon: A Medical History*. Portland, Oregon, 1947.

Lyman, William Denison. *History of the Yakima Valley*. 2 vols. Spokane, 1919.

Manring, Benjamin. *The Conquest of the Coeur D'Alenes, Spokanes and Palouses*. Spokane, 1912.

Marion County Historical Society. *Marion County History*. 5 vols. Salem, Oregon, 1959.

Mengarini, Gregory. *Mengarini's Narrative of the Rockies*. Ed. by Albert J. Partoll. Montana State University. *Sources of Northwest History*, No. 25. Missoula, 1938.

McKee, Ruth Karr. *Mary Richardson Walker: Her Book*. Caldwell, 1945.

McKenney, L. M. *McKenney's District Directory for 1879–80*. San Francisco, 1880.

Bibliography

McWhorter, L. V. *Tragedy of the Wah-shum*. Yakima, Washington, 1937.

Miles, Nelson A. *Personal Recollections and Observations of General Nelson A. Miles*. Chicago, 1897.

Okanogan Independent. Glimpses of Pioneer Life of Okanogan County, Washington. Okanogan, Washington, 1924.

Oliphant, J. Orin, ed. *The Early History of Spokane Washington Told by Contemporaries*. Cheney, Washington, 1927.

Oregon Historical Society. *Notices & Voyages of the Famed Quebec Mission to the Pacific Northwest*. Portland, 1956.

Parker, Samuel. *Journal of an Exploring Tour Beyond the Rocky Mountains*. Ithaca, New York, 1838.

Ray, Verne F. *The Sanpoil and Nespelem: Salishan Peoples of Northeastern Washington*. University of Washington *Publications in Anthropology*, No. 5. Seattle, 1933.

Reinhart, Herman Francis. *The Golden Frontier: The Recollections of Herman Francis Reinhart 1851–1869*. Ed. by Doyce B. Nunis, Jr. Austin, 1962.

Relander, Click. *Drummers and Dreamers*. Caldwell, 1956.

Roe, Frank Gilbert. *The Indian and the Horse*. Norman, 1955.

Ross, Alexander. *Adventures of the First Settlers on the Oregon or Columbia River*. London, 1849.

———. *The Fur Hunters of the Far West*. Ed. by Kenneth A. Spaulding. Norman, 1956.

Shiak, William Sidney. *An Illustrated History of Klickitat, Yakima, and Kittitas Counties, Washington*. Spokane, 1904.

Shields, G. O. *The Blanket Indian of the Northwest*. New York, 1921.

Smith, Clareta Olmstead. *The Trail Leads West*. Philadelphia, 1946.

Spalding, Henry H., and Asa B. Smith. *The Diaries and Letters of Henry H. Spalding and Asa Bowen Smith Relating to the Nez Percé Mission*. Ed. by Clifford Merrill Drury. Glendale, 1958.

Spalding, Henry H., and Marcus A. Whitman. *A True Copy of the Records of the First Presbyterian Church in the Territory of Oregon, Organized in 1838* (Minutes of the Synod of Washington for the Year 1903). 1903.

Spier, Leslie, ed. *The Sinkaietk or Southern Okanogan of Washington*. Written by Walter Cline and others. *General Series in Anthropology No. 6, Contributions from the Laboratory of Anthropology, II*. Menasha, 1938.

Splawn, A. J. *Ka-Mi-akin, The Last Hero of the Yakimas*. Caldwell, Idaho, 1917.

Steele, Richard F. *An Illustrated History of Stevens, Ferry, Okanogan, and Chelan Counties State of Washington*. Spokane, 1904.

———. *An Illustrated History of the Big Bend*. Spokane, 1904.

Stevens, Hazard. *The Life of Isaac Ingalls Stevens*. 2 vols. Boston, 1900.

Victor, Frances Fuller. *The Early Indian Wars of Oregon*. Salem, Oregon, 1894.

White, Dr. E. *Ten Years in Oregon: Travels and Adventures of Doctor E. White and Lady West of the Rocky Mountains*. Ed. by A. J. Allen. Ithaca, 1848.

Wilkes, Charles, U.S.N. *Narrative of the United States Exploring Expedition During the Years 1838, 1839, 1840, 1841, 1842*. 5 vols. Philadelphia, 1845.

Wilson, Bruce A. *From Where the Sun Now Stands*. Omak, Washington, 1960.

Winthrop, Theodore. *The Canoe and the Saddle*. Ed. by John H. Williams. Tacoma, 1913.

ARTICLES

American Board of Commissioners for Foreign Missions. *Annual Reports* 1839, 1841.

Army and Navy Journal, Vol. XXI (August, 1883).

Bingham, Edwin R. "Oregon's Romantic Rebels, John Reed and Charles Erskine Scott Wood," *Pacific Northwest Quarterly*, Vol. L, No. 3 (July, 1959).

Board of Foreign Missions. "Mr. Deffenbaugh's Visit to Indian

Chief Moses," *The Presbyterian Monthly Record,* Vol. XXXII, No. 11 (November, 1881).

Bland, T. A., and M. C. Bland, eds. *Council Fire and Arbitrator,* May, 1879 and May–July, 1883.

Briley, Ann. "Hiram F. Smith, First Settler of Okanogan County," *Pacific Northwest Quarterly,* Vol. XLIII, No. 3 (July, 1952).

Chase, Eugene B. "A Grand Aboriginal Function," *The Northwest Magazine,* Vol. XVII, No. 8 (August, 1899).

Deutsch, Herman J. "Indian and White in the Inland Empire," *Pacific Northwest Quarterly,* Vol. XLVII, No. 2 (April, 1956).

Esvelt, John P. "Chief Moses of the Spokanes," *Pacific Northwesterner,* Vol. IX, No. 1 (Winter, 1965).

Gardner, Grace Christiansen. "Life Among North Central Washington First Families," *Wenatchee Daily World* (Wenatchee, Washington), May 31–December 20, 1935; "Chief Moses as I Knew Him," *Wenatchee Daily World,* December 20, 1935.

Gwydir, Rickard D. "A Record of the San Poil Indians," *Washington Historical Quarterly,* Vol. VIII, No. 4 (October, 1917).

Hermilt, John, and Louis Judge. "The Wenatchee Indians Ask Justice," *Washington Historical Quarterly,* Vol. XVI, No. 1 (January, 1925).

Huggins, E. L. "Smohalla, the Prophet of Priest Rapids," *Overland Monthly,* Vol. XVII, Second Series (January–June, 1891).

"The Indian," *The West Shore,* Vol. IV, No. 1 (September, 1878).

Kingston, C. S. "Samuel Wilbur Condit: Frontiersman," *Pacific Northwest Quarterly,* Vol. XXXVII, No. 2 (April, 1946).

"The Land of Moses," *The West Shore,* Vol. XI, No. 3 (March, 1885).

Lanham, Mrs. Z. A. "History of Chelan County," *Wenatchee Daily World* (Wenatchee, Washington), May 31, 1910.

———. "The Real Life of Sam Miller," *Republic* (Wenatchee, Washington), December 13, 1906.

Linsley, D. C. "Pioneering in the Cascade Country," *Civil Engineering,* Vol. II, No. 6 (June, 1932).

Maceachern, John. "Elwood Evans, Lawyer-Historian," *Pacific Northwest Quarterly,* Vol. LII, No. 1 (January, 1961).

Nelson, Elias. "Reminiscences of R. B. Milroy," *Yakima Morning Herald* (Yakima, Washington), January–February, 1937.

Oliphant, J. Orin. "Encroachments of Cattlemen on Indian Reservations in the Pacific Northwest 1870–1890," reprinted from *Agricultural History,* Vol. XXIV (January, 1950).

Presbyterian Historical Society. *The Spalding-Lowrie Correspondence, Journal of the Department of History, The Presbyterian Historical Society of the Presbyterian Church in the U.S.A.,* Vol. XX, Nos. 1, 2, 3 (March, June, September, 1942).

Randolph, June. "Witness of Indian Religion," *Pacific Northwest Quarterly,* Vol. XLVIII, No. 4 (October, 1957).

Ray, Verne F. "The Bluejay Character in the Plateau Spirit Dance," *American Anthropologist,* Vol. XXXIX, No. 4 (October–December, 1937).

Sherwood, S. F. "The Cunning of Chief Moses," *The Washington Historian,* Vol. I, No. 4 (July, 1900).

Strong, Thomas Nelson. "The Indians of the Northwest," *Pacific Monthly Magazine,* Vol. XVI, No. 2 (August, 1906).

Teit, James H. "The Middle Columbia Salish," University of Washington *Publications in Anthropology,* II (1928).

Whitner, Robert L. "Grant's Indian Peace Policy on the Yakima Reservation," *Pacific Northwest Quarterly,* Vol. L, No. 4 (October, 1959).

Wood, C. E. S. "Famous Indians; Portraits of Some Indian Chiefs," *Century Magazine,* n.s., Vol. XXIV, No. 1, p. 436 (1893).

———. "An Indian Horse Race," *Century Magazine, n.s.,* Vol. XI, p. 447 (1887).

Wood, Erskine. "Diary of a Fourteen Year Old Boy's Days with Chief Joseph," *Oregon Historical Quarterly,* Vol. LI, No. 2 (June, 1950).

INTERVIEWS

Andrews, Alice Moiese. Nespelem, Washington, March 4, 1961.

Arcasa, Isabelle. Nespelem, Washington, January 3, 1958.

Bandy, George. Wilbur, Washington, August 10, 1961.

Bartholet, Suzanne Erwin. Yakima, Washington, April 8, 1961.

Cleveland, Alice Nicholson. Monse, Washington, July 22, 1961.

Condon, Dan. Nespelem, Washington, November 25, 1961.

Covington, Alex. Soap Lake, Washington, July 28, 1961.

Covington, Henry. Colville Reservation, January 18, 1958, and May 18, 1958; Keller, Washington, November 22, 1959, and July 1, 1960.

Covington, Lucy Friedlander. Elmer City, Washington, November 25, 1961; Nespelem, Washington, August 25, 1962, and September 10, 1962.

Covington, Madeline. Nespelem, Washington, May 29, 1961, and November 25, 1961.

Curlew, Billy. Ephrata, Washington, October 7, 1956; Coulee Dam, Washington, January 3, 1958, and December 3, 1958.

Davis, James. Nespelem, Washington, November 11, 1961.

Dumas, Bess Seaton. Wenatchee, Washington, June 19, 1961.

Friedlander, George. Nespelem, Washington, July 16, 1961, and August 25, 1962.

Friedlander, Herman. Coulee Dam, Washington, May 4, 1964.

Friedlander, Nellie Moses. Palisades, Washington, June 2, 1957.

George, Moses. Wenatchee, Washington, June 8, 1963.

Graham, Frank. Spokane, Washington, February 7, 1958.

James, Jim. Soap Lake, Washington, July 28, 1960.

Kamiakin, Cleveland. Ephrata, Washington, October 8, 1956.

Lewis, Jess. Coulee Dam, Washington, August 2, 1961.

Monoghan, Joe. Soap Lake, Washington, July 28, 1961.

Moore, Clara Hughes. Belvedere, Washington, February 5, 1958, November 22, 1959, March 4, 1961, May 28, 1961, June 30, 1961, and July 26, 1961.

Moses, Peter Dan. Soap Lake, Washington, July 30, 1961; Nespelem, Washington, November 24, 1961.

Nanamkin, George. Nespelem, Washington, November 25, 1962.

Nanamkin, Harry. Nespelem, Washington, March 4, 1961.

Neils, Mrs. Edward. Klickitat, Washington, April 2, 1962.

Norman, Amil. East Wenatchee, Washington, August 22, 1961, and August 25, 1961.

Peone, Emily. Auburn, Washington, May 1, 1962, May 6, 1962, May 4, 1963; Soap Lake, Washington, July 27, 1963.

Quiltenenock, Mary Ann Swawilla. Nespelem, Washington, November 21, 1959.

Red Star, Hattie. Nespelem, Washington, August 25, 1962.

Red Wolf, Josiah. Lapwai, Idaho, August 8, 1963.

Someday, Joe. Curlew, Washington, August 8, 1961.

Thornburg, William. Lincoln, Washington, November 21, 1959, and May 7, 1960.

Toulou, Helen. Kewa, Washington, August 9, 1961.

Wheeler, Peter. Wenatchee, Washington, October 9, 1961.

White, Cull. Nespelem, Washington, March 10, 1957, and Moses Lake, Washington, January 2, 1958.

Williams, Sadie Moses. Nespelem, Washington, January 3, 1958.

Wine, Grace. Ephrata, Washington, July 28, 1961.

Wood, Erskine. Portland, Oregon, April 3, 1962.

LETTERS

Brown, William Compton. January 16, 1959.

Jurgensen, Viggo. June 4, 1960.

Relander, Click. November 7, 1961.

Reynolds, R. A. secretary to the governor and committee of the Hudson's Bay Company, January 15, 1962.

Index

Abercrombie, Lieut. W. R.: 193–94, 196, 200
Abraham, Charles: 223
Agency: Simcoe, 51, 57, 61, 65–68, 70, 74, 100–104, 106, 112–13, 123–31, 136–37, 140, 144, 156, 160, 188, 198, 262; Colville, 51, 180, 184, 215; Lapwai, 68, 285, 328–29, 335; Umatilla, 102, 248, 318, 336
Agreement: first Moses' reservation, 152–54; second, 208; approval, 213; ratified, 214
Agriculture: machinery for, 224–25; cricket scourge, 274, 290
Ahchy: 306
Ahtanum: 30, 34, 82, 87, 104
Ainsworth, Washington Territory: 192
Albert, Joe: 220
Alcatraz: 263–64, 290
Alice (Skolaskin's daughter): 305
Allotment: General Act, 188, 239; Okanogans, 227; others, 239; selection on North Half, 303–304; Yakimas, 340; Nez Percés, 340
American Board of Commissioners for Foreign Missions: 15, 17, 18, 23
Ancon (ship): 158
Anderson, A. M. (Colville agent): 339–40, 344, 347–48; as clerk, 282, 284, 311
Annie Faxon (ship): 141
Antillon, Mr. (trial witness): 300
Antwine (Okanogan chief): 288–89, 306
Archer, Capt. James: 42
Armstrong, F. C. (special inspector): 236
Armstrong, Len: 219
Arthur, Chester A. (President): 200
Atkins, J. D. C. (commissioner of Indian affairs): 232, 239, 251

Badger Mountain: 11, 61, 106, 164, 174, 201, 246, 336, 337
Baldwin, Capt. Frank D.: 202–205, 210, 212, 214, 217–19
Baldwin Theater: 148

Ballard, D. P.: 112–14, 121, 127, 139, 141–42, 156–57
Bannister, Mr. (Indian inspector): 232
Bannock Indians: 81–83, 96, 101–102, 107, 130, 144
Barnaby (Lake chief): 255–56, 290
Barry, Washington: 245–46, 285, 328, 334; post office, 264
Beecher, Henry Ward: 149
Big Bend: 40, 166, 201, 224, 240, 245, 259, 264, 297, 304, 317, 322, 333, 350
Big Jim: 100
Big Star (Spokane chief): 32, 40
Bitter Root Valley: 7, 8, 24, 81
Blackfeet Indians: 4, 7, 9, 15, 18–25, 28, 326
Black Hills: 190
Bland, Drs. T. A. & M. C.: 150, 204, 206 & n., 207
Blind Louis: 287
Blinn, Marshall: 174
Blythe, Thomas S.: 341
Bolon, A. J. (Indian agent): 29, 33, 41
Bonaparte Creek: 196, 211, 218
Bouska, Joseph (sawyer and miller): 264, 282, 285, 288, 301, 302
Boyle, Capt. W. H.: 145, 199, 202
Boyle, E. P. (secretary of anti-Moses campaign): 121
Brents, Thomas H. (Washington Territory delegate): 128, 176, 178, 197, 202
Brewster, Washington: 46
British Columbia: 44n., 112, 136; tribes of, 93
Brooks, C. E.: 262
Brown, Charlie: 173
Brown, C. William (deputy): 297
Bubb, Capt. John W. (Colville acting agent): 313, 316, 318, 320, 330
Buchanan, "Buck": 321
Buffalo Hunt: 5, 7, 8, 10, 18, 19, 23, 25, 64
Bupshaw, A. (acting commissioner of Indian affairs): 233, 247

Burbank, Mr. (stockman): 88
Burke, Mr. (squawman): 238
Burmaster, W. H. (farmer): 300, 301
Butchart, John M. (teacher): 329–30, 333

Cain, Judge A. J.: 90, 91, 93, 101
Calkin (Moses' subchief): 69n.
Calwash (Columbia River chief): 65, 66
Camp Chelan: 160, 174–76; on Foster Creek, 172
Camp Clark: 227
Camp Coeur d'Alene: 128
Camp George Wright: 292
Camp Harney: 130
Camp Spokane: 176, 179–81, 188–89
Campbell, Alexander (farmer): 264–65, 267–68, 279
Canada: 24, 30, 37, 39, 40, 43n., 45, 112, 141, 158
Canadian border: 35, 43n., 56, 77, 89, 136, 152, 157, 168, 178, 180, 259, 316
Canadian Indians: 40, 107, 271, 280
Captain Jack (Modoc chief): 59, 150
Carey, Louise Heiler: 109n.
Cascade Mountains: 4ff., 43n., 47, 54, 70, 75, 76, 91, 138, 182
Casson, William E. (special alloting agent): 340
Catley, Capt. Henry: 223
Cattle Raising: 5, 168ff., 193ff.; stealing, 340
Cayuse Indians: 3n., 4, 23, 132, 137
Cayuse (Nez Percé Indian): 335
Celilo: see fisheries
Census: 53, 184, 194
Ceremonies: 62
Chapman, Arthur J. (interpreter): 182, 188–89, 190, 248, 254, 281–82
Charlie (Moses' nephew): 137
Chelan Indians: 10, 71, 107, 159, 218, 229; forcible removal, 269–70, 272–73, 307, 308
Chelan Lake: see Lake Chelan
Chelan-Methow Ridge: 30
Chelan River: 47
Chelan Valley: 38
Chelohan (root grounds): 4, 11, 94
Chemawa (Indian school): 177, 184, 223, 293
Cheney, Washington: 178, 295

Chewelah, Washington: 215, 217, 229, 232, 235, 239
Chiliwist Valley: 278
Chillileetsah (Moses' nephew): 25, 90, 137–38, 140–41, 144–45, 147–48, 179, 181, 186, 222, 347; drowning, 223–26
Chinese: 46, 47, 76, 79, 187, 245
Christiansen, Grace: 322
Christiansen, James: 322
Chuckchuck (Perkins' murderer): 86, 176; see also murder
Clark Fork River: 7, 56
Clearwater River: 15
Cleveland (Kamiakin's son): 227
Cleveland, Grover (President): 262
Cleveland, Ohio: 210
Cochise (Apache chief): 292
Cody, William "Buffalo Bill": 149, 336
Coeur d'Alene Indians: 7, 40, 52, 72, 112, 128, 215n.
Coeur d'Alene Lake: 41
Coffin Brothers: 324–25
Cole, Hal (Colville agent): 262–63, 265–67, 269–70, 273–74, 280, 283–85, 288–89, 291–92, 295, 301, 305, 309, 311
Cole, S. S. (freighter): 278
Colfax, Washington: 69
Colockum Creek: 323
Columbia Indians: other names, 3n.; subchiefs, 51; removal to Yakima, 99, 107; reservation for, 154; drunken, 165
Columbia Plateau: 3ff., 56, 71, 96, 98, 180, 191–92
Columbia River: 3ff., 100ff., 161, 172, 196ff., 250, 254, 307, 310, 321, 337; bar, 157; flood, 315
Colville Indians: 52, 72, 73, 159–60, 189, 222, 290
Colville Valley: 31, 43, 143, 189, 191, 221, 306
Commercial Club (Yakima, Washington): 324–25
Conconully, Washington: 279, 281, 282
Condon, William "Wild Goose Bill": 65, 259, 261, 317
Continental Divide: 7
Contractors: Davis and Todd, 216–17, 246; Jones, M. M., 220; Todd, 225
Cook, Capt. W. C. (commandant of Fort Colville): 78, 175, 178

Index

Cool-Cool Smool-Mool: 305
Corbaley, Platt: 297
Cornoyer, N. A. (Umatilla agent): 128, 131–32, 140, 144–45
Cottonwood Creek: 305
Coulee City, Washington: 270, 280–81, 286, 290, 336
Councils: Sulktalthscosum, 21; Grande Ronde, 30; Walla Walla, 30, 64; Simcoe, 70; Spokane Falls, 74, 80; Grand Medicine, 75; Priest Rapids, 91ff., 137; Wenatchee, 162–63, 271
Courtland Academy: 285
Covington, John C. "Virginia Bill": 176, 181, 273
Covington, Madeline: 216
Covington, Nettie: 181, 186
Cowiche Valley: 82
Cowley, Rev. Henry T.: 62, 70, 183
Cox, Ross: 14, 49
Crab Creek: 48, 49, 56, 69, 71, 87, 100ff., 133, 161, 172, 179
Crab Creek Valley: 89
Crawford, Col. John W. (Umatilla agent): 292, 294, 302
Crook, General George: 39, 158
Crow Indians: 239
Cultus Jim (Methow Indian): 54
Curlew, Billy: 211, 216, 251
Curlew Lake: 204
Curley, Henry: 303
Curley, Red: 303
Curry, Gen. A. P.: 281–84
Custer, Gen. George Armstrong: 190

Dance: winter, 11, 284; thanksgiving, 14; buffalo, 19; *kaseesum*, 19; *washat*, 51, 58; chinook, 230, 264, 336–37
Daughters of the American Revolution: 34n.
Davis and Todd: see contractors
Deffenbaugh, Rev. George L.: 183–84
Demers, Rev. Modeste: 18
Denison, E. W.: 205
Department of the Columbia: 64; see Fort Vancouver (U.S. Army)
DeRouge, Rev. Stephen: 235–36, 244–46, 252, 258, 265–66, 279, 283, 286, 305, 315; private police, 266–67
Dickson, Charles H. (special Indian agent): 214, 216–18, 223, 227

District of the Clearwater: 90
Division of the Pacific: 78, 80, 90
Doll, Asa: 266
Douglas County, Washington: 281
Downing, A. (topographical engineer): 211
Dry Falls: 10
Dufer, W. H. H.: 288–89
Duff, Mr.: (Moses' friend): 151
Duluth, Minnesota: 210
Dwellings: pit houses, 10, 58; canvas, 215; hide, 215; mat, 215

Eagen (Paiute chief): 148
Earthquake: 57ff., 165
Eells, Rev. Cushing: 23
Elder (ship): 146–47
Ellensburg, Washington: 77, 81, 142, 167, 179, 245, 323, 338–39
Eneas (Indian policeman): 100–101, 107–10, 116, 118, 120, 124, 144
Entiat Indians: 107, 159, 227
Ephrata, Washington: 10
Epidemics: smallpox, 6, 27, 29, 53, 194, 234–35, 255, 286–87, 313; intermittent fever, 7; measles, 7, 22, 248; consumption, 293; pneumonia, 318
Erwin, L. T. (Yakima agent): 331–32
Erwin Ditch: 332
Evans, Elwood (writer): 72, 274
Expositions: see fairs
Eytinge, Rose (actress): 148

Fairs: Buffalo Bill's Wild West show, 149, 336; Northwestern Industrial Exposition (Spokane), 274–77; Industrial Exposition (Portland), 295; Washington State (Yakima), 322–27, 332–33
Ferry, Gov. E. P.: 69, 87, 113, 122, 139, 140–41, 143, 156, 159, 160–61, 163–65, 169
Ferry Boats: *bundles*, 8; Condon, 224, 240, 259; Scott, 299; Barry, 315, 329; Virginia City, 321; along Columbia River, 344; Seaton, 346
Festivities: Christmas, 301, 312
Fires: forest, 210; schools, 279, 334
Fishel and Roberts (merchants): 143
Fisheries: Wenatchee, 11, 31, 35, 168, 273, 331n.; Kettle Falls, 11, 306; Priest Rapids, 59; Yakima, 94; San Poil, 179

Fish Lake: 246
Flathead Indians: 7, 8, 21
Fletcher, Col. J. S. (commandant of Fort Spokane): 229, 232
Flett, Robert (interpreter): 267
Flint, P. J.: 121
Food: roots and berries, 4, 9, 10–14, 59; duck eggs, 192; see also buffalo
Forest Grove: see Chemawa (Indian school)
Forsyth, Col. James W.: 161, 164, 166
Fort Coeur d'Alene (U.S. Army): 165, 193, 196, 222
Fort Colville (Hudson's Bay Company): 18, 32, 189
Fort Colville (U.S. Army): 43, 49, 55, 56, 58, 72, 136–39, 157, 172
Fort George Wright (U.S. Army): 345
Fort Lapwai (U.S. Army): 81, 166
Fort Nisqually (Hudson's Bay Company): 5, 25, 27n.
Fort Okanogan (Hudson's Bay Company): 18, 29, 38, 43n., 53
Fort Simcoe (U.S. Army): 36, 39
Fort Spokane (U.S. Army): 196, 197–98, 201–202, 204, 210, 212, 214–15, 217–19, 222, 226, 228, 263, 305, 335, 345
Fort Vancouver (Hudson's Bay Company): 4
Fort Vancouver (U.S. Army): 64, 73, 88, 89, 99, 104, 121–22, 125–26, 128, 131, 143, 146, 159, 174, 182
Fort Walla Walla (Hudson's Bay Company): 18
Fort Walla Walla (U.S. Army): 74, 78, 83, 119
Foster Creek: 165, 210, 224
Four Lakes: 40
Fourth of July: 207, 258–59 & n., 260, 270, 308 & n., 344–45
Frank (Nespelem Indian): 234, 267
Fraser River: 37, 38, 166
Friedlander, Elizabeth: 342
Friedlander, Herman: 342
Friedlander, Louie: 342
Fullerton, Mark A.: 288

Galler, John: 162
Gardner, Robert S. (inspector): 193, 195, 197, 201
Garnett, Maj. Robert: 36, 39, 40, 42, 65

Garry (Spokane chief): 15, 40, 72, 128, 165, 205; accuses Moses of murder, 166
Gearvis, P. G.: 139
Geary, Edward R. (superintendent of Indian affairs): 44
George (Indian): 131, 234
George, Coxit: 306
George, Nespelem: 270
Ghost Dance: see Messiah Craze
Gibbon, Gen. John (commandant, Department of the Columbia): 248–49, 263, 281
Gibson, James L. (acting agent): 255
Gilbert, P.: 128
Ginnamonteesah: 261–62
Glasgow, Edward (sawyer and miller): 308, 311
Goethals, Lieut. George W.: 211
Golden Gate: 147
Goodwin, George (posseman): 113–14
Goodwin, J. W.: 121
Gracie (kidnapped girl): 262
Grand Coulee: 9, 10, 40, 61, 112, 166, 174, 247, 345, 350
Grand Coulee Dam: 306–307
Grand Ronde River: 30
Granger, William (cattleman): 193, 196
Grant, Ulysses S. (President): 66, 158
Grant County, Wash., PUD: 51n.
Grassi, Rev. Urban: 177–78
Graves, Frank H. (attorney): 290
Gray, William: 43n.
Great Lakes: 210
Great Plains, the: 5, 7–9, 18, 19, 21, 23–24, 47, 64, 128n., 326
Great Republic (ship): 146
Great Spirit: 14, 28
Green, Maj. John: 156
Greenwood, A. B. (commissioner of Indian affairs): 44
Grenaway, Mr. (court witness): 300
Guns: Hudson's Bay rifles, 38, 39; Sharps, 40, 186; request during Nez Percé troubles, 69; Yakima citizens request, 82, 87; needle, 111; Moses' confiscated, 116; Moses asks for his, 133; Moses' returned, 160–61; Winchester, 186; Okanogan citizens request, 283
Gwydir, Rickard R.: 237–39, 241–44, 247, 249, 251, 253, 255–56, 268, 285

Half-Sun family: 35, 39, 41, 42, 50, 225
Haller, Maj. Granville O.: 33, 35
Hamilton, J. W.: 170
Hamilton, Capt. Samuel Todd: 227
Hampton, Virginia: 157; Negro school at, 158
Hanford, Judge C. H.: 303, 330n.
Hangman Creek: *see* Latah Creek
Harbison (judge): 344
Hardy, H. E. (farmer): 231–33, 235, 248–49, 252–54
Harmelt (Wenatchee chief): 163, 173
Harrison, Benjamin (President): 262, 304
Harvey, George W. (farmer): 51, 52, 53, 175
Hawk Creek: 176, 181
Hay, M. E.: 345, 349
Hayes, Rutherford B. (President): 151–52, 154, 158–59, 176, 198
Haynes, Judge John: 251
Hayt, E. A. (commissioner of Indian affairs): 99, 101, 109, 114, 123–25, 128–30, 140, 150, 152, 169
Helena, Montana: 205
Hell Gate (Missoula, Montana): 7
Hell Gate River: 8
Herring, George (interpreter): 52, 60, 204, 206n., 210
Hesseltine, Washington: 345–46
Hiachenie (Cayuse chief): 132, 134, 141, 144–45, 148
Hill, John (Nez Percé Indian): 253–57
Hinman, C. M. (blacksmith): 317
Holmes, T.: 237
Homas: 234, 265
Homer, Watson: 262
Homily (Walla Walla chief): 90–92, 128, 134, 141, 147–48
Honsan Canyon: 161
Hop Picking: 295, 322, 331–32, 338
Hoppin, Lieut.: 243
Hoptowit: 100
Horse: stealing, 4, 266; Appaloosa, 16, 18; racing, 29, 164, 254, 261, 274, 290, 309–10; roundup, 251; gelding, 251; branding, 251
Horse Heaven Hills: 82
Howard, Gen. Oliver Otis: 64ff., 72ff., 81ff., 90ff., 100ff., 113ff., 120ff., 131ff.,
140–42, 144–45, 156, 158–66, 170, 174–75, 231–32, 248, 271–72, 283–84, 292–93, 307, 314
Hubbard, Gardiner: 325
Hudson's Bay Company: 4, 5, 19, 43n.
Huggins, Edward (manager of Fort Nisqually post): 27n., 43n.
Huntington, J. B.: 142
Hutchinson, Mrs. Richard: 254
Hutchinson, Richard (sawyer and miller): 224, 231, 233, 238, 248, 250–53, 257–58, 262

Idaho Territory: 221
Indians Affairs Office: 77, 80, 89, 126, 143, 149, 154, 158, 181, 201, 211–12, 224, 230, 248, 251–52, 263, 271–72, 288, 296, 303, 330
Indian Jim (murderer): 311
Indian police: 110n., 104, 106, 118, 121, 258, 262
Indian Territory: 220–29, 232, 248
Innomoseecha Bill (Chelan chief): 38, 54, 71, 83, 110–11, 122, 156, 165, 347
Innomoseecha Jim: *see* Long Jim
Isaac: 335
Isles de Pierres: 3n., 55
Itstsulkt: 309, 340
Ives, Washington: 308
Iyattooweanetenmy (Joseph's wife): 234
Iyutotum, Minnie: 230, 315–16

Jack, Jim: 316
Jacob: 183
Jatoiah (Columbia chief): 65
Jocko River: 8
Johawahliwicks: 234
John (Cole murderer): 278
John, Sam (Nez Percé Indian): 253
Johnson (Moses' son-in-law): 302; drowns, 327–28
Joseph (Nez Percé chief): 64, 71, 72, 75, 78, 89, 102, 124, 132, 135, 149–50, 158, 190, 220–21, 226, 229, 230–31, 234–36, 238ff., 300ff.
Joset, Rev. Joseph: 72 & n.
Josiskin (army scout): 42
Jubilee: 323–24, 326, 338–39, 345

Kaakin (ferry tender): 329

Kachhachtaskin: 91
Kalispell Indians: 7, 23, 49, 52, 72, 215n.
Kalispell Valley: 292
Kamiah: 16, 18, 59
Kamiakin (Yakima chief): 29, 30, 32–36, 51, 227, 340
Karneetsa (Moses' mother): 5, 8, 9, 23, 25, 48
Kartar Valley: 172, 192, 225, 266
Keelpucken (Moses' half brother): 42
Keller, Washington: 344
Keller Mountain: 42
Kemelakin: 259, 288
Kent, Col. J. Ford (commandant of Fort Spokane): 240
Kettle Falls: 11
Kettle Falls, Washington: 340
Kettle River: 187, 203
Kiakia: 291
Killsmoolah (in Moses' lodge): 216
Kinkinochin: 255, 256
Kiotanie (Kamiakin's daughter): 227
Kist (in Moses' lodge): 216
Kittitas Indians: 22, 227
Kittitas Valley: 4, 28, 35, 42, 69, 74, 77, 80, 82, 87, 94, 98, 114–15, 120, 138, 161, 164, 167, 171, 185, 193–94, 245–46
Kiyuyu (David): 36, 65
Kladus, Indian Charles: 306, 310
Klickitat County, Washington: 104
Klickitat Valley: 114
Komellakaka: 186, 216, 179–80
Komotelakia (San Poil subchief): 179
Kootenay Valley: 89
Kunnumsahwickssa: 261
Kuykendall, Dr. Chester Benson (agency physician): 104, 131, 134
Kype (Perkins' murderer): 86, 170–71; see also murder

Labrie, Joseph: 184–85
Lahoom (Entiat chief): 30
Lake Chelan: 10, 54, 58, 157, 159, 161, 164–65, 167, 171, 173, 192–93, 220, 223, 263, 269–70
Lake Indians: 52, 72–73, 189–90
Lake Labish: 293
Lake Osoyoos: 78, 189, 247
Lancaster, Joe: 123–24
Language: Shahaptian, 11, 92, 255;

Salish, 11, 92, 255; Chinook, 25–26, 172, 318, 322
Lapeetheshentooks: 234
Lapwai, Ida: 221
Latah Creek: 41, 60, 128
Latham, Dr. E. H. (agency physician): 287, 302, 310, 312–13, 317
Laughton, Act. Gov. Charles E.: 280–81
Lava Beds: 59
Legends: coyote, 10–11; gray squirrel, 10; coming of Indians, 61
Leslie, W. F. (farmer): 291
Lewis, W. (acting agent of Colville): 250
Lewiston, Ida: 87
Lincoln, Abe (interpreter): 131, 141, 144–45, 147–48, 154, 171
Lincoln County, Washington: 281
Linsley, D. C. (surveyor): 56
Liquor: 49, 61, 165, 173, 219, 236, 260, 253, 274, 280–91, 294, 310, 312, 343–44; Moses, a trial witness, 297–300
Little Blackfeet River: 8
Little Joseph (Joseph's nephew): 238, 307
Little Nespelem River: 216, 295, 348
Loaspus (Nez Percé Indian): 303
Lockwood and Breyman (stockmen): 95
Locos (Kamiakin's son): 227
Lokout (Upper Yakima Indian): 28n., 40
Long Jim: 193, 218, 220, 223, 307–308
Look Down: 307
Looking Glass (Nez Percé chief): 75
Loolowkin: see Moses
Lot (Spokane chief): 203, 209, 223, 241, 255–56, 273, 291–92, 294, 308n.
Lot The Elder: see Big Star
Louis (Moses' brother): 177, 216, 253, 295, 306
Louis: see Quiltenenock
Luganbeel, Major Pinkney: 44, 49

McAdoo, Dr. R. M. (agency physician): 250, 254
McBean, John (interpreter): 162, 198
McCauley, Alexander "Slick" (cattleman): 71–72, 175
McClellan, Capt. George B.: 27–29, 149
McDowell, Gen. Irvin (commandant, Div. of the Pacific): 130, 137, 171, 182
McGraw, Gov. John: 332–33
McKay, Charles: 83, 84

McKenny, Gen. T. J. (superintendent of Indian affairs): 52
McKenzie, Patrick: 195
McKinley, William (President): 334, 337
McLoughlin Canyon: fight at, 38, 39
McMicken, Gen. W. (surveyor general, Washington Territory): 185
McQuarrie, Ed.: 253
Maginnis, Martin (Congressional delegate): 212
Marcus, Washington: 340
Mary (Kamiakin's daughter): 227
Mary (Moses' wife): 25, 40, 43, 60, 84, 225, 231, 309, 323, 338, 342–43, 347, 349
Mary Ann (Condon's wife): 317
Masons: 212n.
Mauntell, Clay: 298–300, 303, 306
Mayer, Louis (freighter): 237
Mears, Col. F. (commandant of Fort Spokane): 290
Medicine man: 49, 62, 234, 250; for Moses' people, 193
Merriam, Col. Henry C.: commandant, Camp Coeur d'Alene, 128; commandant, Camp Chelan, 172–76; commandant, Fort Spokane, 196–98, 202, 214, 217, 220
Merriam, Dr. C. N. (acting assistant surg.): 218, 223
Meschelle: 234, 248, 268, 288
Messiah Craze: 271, 280–86, 291
Methow Indians: 52, 65, 107, 159, 187, 218, 229
Methow River: 47, 308
Middleton, Frank (correspondent): 101, 124–26
Miles, Capt. William: 198
Miles, Gen. Nelson A. (commandant, Department of the Columbia): 182, 184, 188–89, 190–93, 197–202, 214, 312
Miller, Sam (trader): 58, 61, 71, 81–82, 88, 91–95, 142, 162, 164, 273
Milligan J. K. (sheriff): See Mullican
Mills: saw and flour for Moses, 216, 217; saw and flour for Tonasket, 247; trouble at, 319–20
Milroy, R. H. (superintendent of Indian affairs): 60–61
Minerals and mining: 29, 168ff., 192ff., 281; north half of Colville opened

for, 329; court decision regarding, 33n.; south half of Colville opened for, 343
Mires, John S. (farmer): 306, 311
Mission: Lapwai, 15; Waiilatpu, 23; see St. Regis; see Omak Lake
Missoula, Montana: 205
Missouri River: 4, 7–8, 23, 81
Mizner, Maj. Henry: 89
Monoghan, James (trader): 215, 229, 231, 235, 248, 272
Montana (state of): 239, 266
Montezuma, Dr. Charles (agency physician): 310 & n.
Moore, Benjamin (Colville agent): 228–30, 232–34, 236–37, 239
Moostonic (Perkins' murderer): 86, 111, 170; see also murder
Morgan, T. J. (commissioner of Indian affairs): 262, 278
Mormon: country, 63
Morris, George (Lapwai agent): 239
Moses: birth, 3; power spirits, 14, 342; kills enemy, 20; murders, 32, 38, 129, 166; in Indian wars, 33ff.; takes father's name, 43; nickname, 60; health, 66, 276, 287; requests reserve, 73, 94; threatens war, 78; confronts militia, 82; meets with General Howard, 91–96; meets Yakima citizens, 104ff.; captured, 116ff.; jailed, 119; placed in Simcoe guardhouse, 124; embarks on first Washington, D.C., trip, 146; confers with Indian affairs personnel, 152–54; before grand jury, 170; second trip to Washington, D.C., 205–10; accepts issues for people 223ff.; settles Nez Percé on Colville, 241–43; liquor trial witness, 297–300; Jubilee, 322–27, 332–33, 345; death, 347–48; potlatch, 348–49
Moses, Joe (Moses' nephew): 216
Moses, Peter Dan: 216
Moses Coulee: 3, 6n., 10–11, 38, 47, 53, 60–62, 70, 78, 82–83, 123, 172, 180, 322–23, 350
Moses Crossing: 179, 186, 193–94, 217, 223–25, 245, 286, 309, 311, 315
Moses Lair: 18n.
Moses Lake: 10, 50, 161, 175, 192, 341
Mount Baker: 29

Mount Chopaca and Similkameen Mining District: 168
Mullican J. K. (sheriff): 136
Murder: Perkins' murderers, 86, 103, 105, 121, 127, 136–37, 157, 170; Locos, 227 & n.; Staaclo, 310; Sarsopkin, 311; Shimtel, 316

Naches Pass: 43n.
Naches River: 36, 82
Naches Valley: 35
Nahanoomed (in Moses' lodge): 216
Nanamkin (Entiat Indian): 45–46
Nanum Creek: 35, 167
Nellie (Moses' granddaughter): 227, 342
Nespelem Indians: 159, 179, 232, 237, 239, 267–68, 317, 337
Nespelem River: 58, 157, 186, 211, 216–18, 225, 230, 241, 250, 297, 319, 347
Nespelem Valley: 179, 186ff., 193ff., 215ff., 310, 333, 345, 349
Netsaspooshus: 172, 180
Newell, Gov. William A.: 187
Newman, George B. (Colville agent): 330, 333–34, 337, 339
Nez Percé Indians: 6, 24, 36, 49, 57, 65, 68–71, 89, 128, 176, 220, 222, 229, 230, 232ff., 303, 307, 314, 325
Nichols, Thomas M., (acting commissioner of Indian affairs): 180
Nisqually River: 70, 276
Nolon, William (constable): 303
Nontreaty Indians: 44
Norris, J. C. (blacksmith): 308, 313
Northwest (ship): 159–61
Noshirt: 292

O'Brien, Gen.: 281
Okanogan County, Washington: 233, 263, 272, 281, 306, 340
Okanogan Indians: 38, 44, 65, 71–73, 77–78, 92, 107, 159, 189, 202, 229, 246, 288–89
Okanogan River: 29, 38–39, 42, 43n., 44n., 47, 53, 56, 89, 152, 168, 177, 187, 192–93, 196, 201, 259, 265–66, 273, 279–80, 286, 297, 311
Okanogan Valley: 43, 72, 156, 158, 161, 191, 198, 202ff., 305–306, 340; outbreak in, 279–83, 285, 288
Olmstead, Sam (storekeeper): 167

Olympia, Washington: 82
Omaha, Nebraska: 158
Omak Lake: 172, 177, 193, 218, 258, 265–67, 278–79, 286, 315
Omak Lake Mission: 286, 305
One-Eyed John: 65, 66
Oppenheimer, Joseph: 142–43, 150
Oppenheimer, Marcus: (merchant): 142
Oregon Territory: 30; state, 122
Oropaughn (Colville chief): 203, 255–56, 290
O'Shea, Ed: 215, 230
Osoyoos Lake: 43n., 194, 315
Otski: 220
Owhi (Upper Yakima chief): 22, 25, 26, 27n., 28–30, 32–33, 35, 40–42
Owhi (Yakima Indian): 253, 257, 287, 306, 313, 318–20, 340
Owhi Lake: 287

Pacific Ocean: 6, 56, 147, 158
Page, Sabina (teacher): 268–69, 278–79
Paiute Indians: 82, 130, 148, 282
Palmer, Joel: 43n.
Palouse Hills: 69, 87
Palouse Indians: 35–36, 38, 40, 49, 72, 144
Palouse River: 31
Pambrun, Andrew D.: 65, 67–68, 70, 90–93, 145
Parsons, A. E.: 320
Patoi: 58
Patshewyah (Moses' brother): 15, 24–25, 28
Paul (Moses' brother): 107, 137, 141
Payette Lake: 137
Payne, J. F.: 288, 290
Pecard, John: 266, 318, 334, 337
Pecard, Louis: 318
Pee-el: 115–16
Pendergast, D. K. (U.S. commissioner): 297–99
Pendleton, Oregon: 125
Pend Oreille Indians: 7, 215n.
Peo (Umatilla chief): 317–18
Peotsenmy (Moses' wife): 309, 338, 340, 342–43, 347, 349
Perkins, Mr. and Mrs. Lorenzo: 86–88, 102
Peter Dan Creek: 186
Petty, Joseph: 80

Peu Peu Mox Mox (Walla Walla chief): 147

Phelps, E. D. "Ed": 70, 74–75, 80, 92, 168, 173, 177

Pierce, Lieut. Henry: 192

Pierre (Okanogan chief): 38

Pierre (Spokane subchief): 128

Pierre, Sam: 267

Pike, Col. Enoch: 82–83, 123–24

Pine Grove: 59–60, 151

P'na Village: 50, 58, 62

Poker, Joe: 316

Poker Jim: 248

Pole, William: 335

Port Columbia, Washington: 297

Portland, Oregon: 43n., 44, 47–48, 54, 77, 85, 104, 121, 142–43, 145–46, 156, 159, 292

Posahli (San Poil chief): 288

Posse, Yakima: 105ff.

Post Chelan: 272

Potlatch: 246–47, 263, 280; Moses', 348–49

Potlatch Fannie: 266

Power Spirit: 14, 26, 34, 37, 41–42, 342; theft of, 52; dance, 284

Poyockon: 306

Price, Hal (commissioner of Indian affairs): 193, 197, 204, 207, 210

Priestly, Thomas (Yakima agent): 266

Priest Rapids: 36, 44n., 50, 60, 62, 65, 80, 89–90, 96, 99, 109, 120, 124, 126, 134, 161, 307

Prophets: 57–58, 256, 271

Puckheim (Moses' brother): 216

Puckmiakin: 227–28, 253–54, 258–59, 270, 283–85, 288, 310, 311

Puget Sound: 28, 56, 70, 104, 192

Puget Sound Agricultural Company: 43n.

Pukakheen: 53

Qualchan (Upper Yakima chief): 27n., 30, 35, 37, 40–42

Quanspeetsah (Moses' niece): 216

Quemat (Louie's wife): 216

Quemollah (Moses' wife): 22, 25, 42–43

Quequetas (Nespelem chief): 172, 175, 179

Quetalican: *see* Moses

Quiltenenock (Moses' brother): 15, 28–32, 35–37

Quiltlay (Moses' daughter): 342–43

Quintolah (Moses' brother): 216

Railroads: Great Northern, 29, 327; Northern Pacific, 56, 152, 192, 205, 281, 292, 338; Pennsylvania, 149; forty-mile limit of Northern Pacific, 153–54, 159; Chicago, Milwaukee and St. Paul, 205; Central Washington, 259, 270, 281

Rains, Maj. G. J.: 33–35

Rattlesnake Hills: 94, 97

Red Jacket (Palouse chief): 38

Red Leggins (Nez Percé Indian): 305

Reed, Charles B.: 115

Reed, John B.: 299–300

Remington, Frederick: 277

Reservations: Yakima, 31, 44, 47, 57, 70, 73, 77, 79, 80, 84, 96, 122–23, 126, 130, 132, 146, 331, 340; Colville, 56, 60, 73, 77, 122, 142–43, 150, 158–59, 160, 172, 174–75, 203–204, 207–10, 218, 224, 232, 263, 269, 272, 278, 280, 304–307, 341; Nez Percé, 64, 314, 340; Moses' request, 73, 91–96; Columbia, 162, 169, 202, 207–10, 218–19, 233, 308, 314; Neah Bay proposed, 122; Umatilla, 128, 148, 302, 335; Ten-mile strip, 178, 180; Fifteen-mile strip, 203; Coeur d'Alene, 232; Standing Rock, 239; Warm Springs, 282; commission for purchase of Colville, 288–89; cession of North Half, 289; North Half opened for mineral entry, 329; South Half opened for mineral entry, 343

Rheem, Lieut. E. B.: 121–22, 128

Ritzville, Washington: 222

Road ("Wild Goose Bill" ferry): 285

Robbins, W. D. (Lapwai agent): 266

Rock Creek (British Columbia): 189

Rock Creek (Spokane root ground): 11, 51, 53, 73

Rock Island: 11, 33, 45–46, 73, 350

Rocky Ford: 10, 49

Rocky Mountains: 4–5, 8, 14, 19, 25, 70

Roman Catholics: 18, 24, 126, 184, 226, 265, 305

Rose Bush (Nez Percé Indian): 335

Ross, Alexander (fur trader): 14, 48

Ross, Col. Samuel (superintendent of Indian affairs): 53
Ruby, Washington: 223, 246, 270, 279, 284–85
Runnels, George W. "Tenas George": 175
Russ Hotel: 147, 158

Saddle Mountain Gap: 108
Sahmesahpan: 42
St. Paul, Minnesota: 205
St. Regis Mission: 177
Salishan people: 7, 8, 11, 19–21, 23, 92
Salmon City, Idaho: 138n.
Salmon River: 168, 233
Saluskin (Perkins' murderer): 86, 136, 139, 157, 170–71; see also murder
Sam (Moses' nephew): 216
San Francisco, California: 146–47, 158, 172, 196, 205, 264
San Poil Indians: 52, 69, 71, 73, 92, 159, 172, 175, 193, 203, 218, 239ff., 261, 264, 289–90, 337, 343
San Poil River: 6, 53, 58, 94, 165, 185, 196
San Poil Valley: 11, 42, 203, 268
Sarsopkin (Okanogan chief): 38, 112, 122, 173, 187, 192–93, 197, 200ff., 246–47, 251, 263, 273–74, 289, 347
Sarsopkin, Peter: 246, 311
Satus Pass: 141
Schnebly, F. D.: 115, 136, 138, 156, 171
Schofield, Gen. J. M.: 196
Schofield, Nicholas: 146, 152
Schools: Tonasket's, 216, 236, 246, 334; Spokane Reservation boarding school, 246; Moses', 268; Nespelem school burns, 279; revival of, 329–30, 334–35
Schurz, Carl (secretary of the interior): 113, 122, 129, 131, 149, 152, 155, 156–58, 160, 169, 175, 182
Schwatka, Lieut. Frederick: 91
Scott, Peter J.: 297–300, 303
Scribner, J. S. (sawyer and miller): 318–20, 330
Seaton, Tom: 345
Seattle, Washington: 104, 177
Selah: 33
Shahaptian people: 11, 21, 92
Shanno Ditch: 325
Shannon, Alex (farmer): 240
Shantlahow: see Mary (Moses' wife)

Sherman, Gen. W. T.: 73, 80, 176, 178, 210n.
Sherwood, S. F. (interpreter): 73, 181, 193–95, 206n., 208, 210, 292; district court clerk, 78
Shimtil (Moses' sister): 216, 310, 315–16
Shomak (Great Spirit): 14
Shoudy, John (trader): 77, 80, 92, 142
Shows: see fairs
Shuluskin (Kittitas chief): 50
Shutt, R. D. (teacher): 335
Sibin, Mr. (repairman): 237, 239
Silpe (Moses' wife): 21–22
Similkameen River: 168, 174
Simms, John (Colville agent): 60, 71–72, 159–60, 167, 180, 185, 189, 195, 207, 211
Simoneeta: 304
Sinkiuse: see Columbia Indians
Sinsinqt (Moses' daughter): 186, 227–28
Sinsinqt (Moses' sister): 25, 90
Sioux Indians: 158, 190, 271, 280, 284
Sitting Bull: 136, 150, 158, 239, 280
Skagit River: 87, 137, 193
Skamow (Wenatchee chief): 37, 273
Skloom (Yakima chief): 30
Sklumskin (Kamiakin's son): 227, 233
Skolaskin (San Poil chief): 69, 165, 172, 179, 185, 193, 203, 219, 238, 243, 261, 290, 305, 337; jailed, 257; private police, 261–64
Sladen, Lieut. Joseph A.: 89
Smith, Dr. Randolph: 198
Smith, Hiram F.: 78, 168–69, 174, 186, 194, 247, 280, 296
Smith, Hoke (sec. of the interior): 313
Smith, Rev. A. B.: 16–18
Smitkin: 288
Smohalla (Wanapum prophet): 50ff., 62ff., 70ff., 111, 124–25, 185
Snake Indians: see Bannocks
Snake River: 15, 30–31, 44n., 89, 192
Snawtonic: 234, 287
Snively, H. J. (Moses' lawyer): 326
Societies: 20, 21
So-happy: 141
Sokula (in Moses' lodge): 216, 234
Spalding, Mrs. Henry H.: 16
Spalding, Rev. Henry H.: 15, 18, 57, 59–60, 62, 149–50, 236
Splawn, Jack: 45, 47, 50, 70, 350

Splawn, William: 108, 110 & n., 111–12, 114, 116, 118–19
Spokane (ship): 35, 40, 59, 62, 68, 87, 129
Spokane, Washington: 41, 290, 292, 347
Spokane Falls: 41, 68, 72, 128, 165, 195, 214, 276
Spokane Falls, Washington: 87, 129, 205, 210, 217, 221, 227–28, 233, 244, 275, 280–81, 284
Spokane Indians: 7, 15, 23, 40, 49, 52, 72–73, 77, 92, 107, 112, 166, 176, 215n., 238, 271
Spokane Plains: 35, 40, 59, 62, 87, 129
Spokane River: 6, 31, 40–42, 44, 51, 55, 68–70, 73, 92, 142, 183, 240, 313
Sponen, George: 253, 267
Sprague, Washington: 194, 196, 201, 295
Staaclo, Sam (Moses' nephew): 310
Stair, D. W.: 121, 139
Steamboat Rock: 11
Steel, Henry (farmer): 311–13, 315–20, 330, 337, 340–41
Stephen (Cole murderer): 278–79, 280–81, 283
Steptoe, Col. E. J.: 36
Stevens, Isaac I.: 28–30, 32, 34, 65
Stevens County, Washington: 53
Steveson, Rebecca: 285–86
Strahl, Arthur (farmer): 316
Streamer, Francis: 74–75, 77, 81, 142, 168, 176, 197–98, 200, 226, 246, 252, 270–71, 273, 283–84, 312, 314–15, 318, 338, 347
Suiepkine (Okanogan chief): 178, 193, 246, 272, 284
Sulktalthscosum (Moses' father): 3ff., 216, 261, 350
Sunacka Creek: 193
Sutherland, Tom (reporter): 144
Symons, Lieut. Thomas W.: 176, 195

Tahasamkin: 301
Tamatsatsamy: *see* Peotsenmy
Tamiesie, Dr. J. P.: 287
Tatahala (Moses' agent): 112
Tecolekun (Wenatchee chief): 28, 30, 37 & n.
Teias (Upper Yakima chief): 22, 40
Teller, Henry M. (secretary of the interior): 197, 201, 204, 208, 214

Tes Palouse (Kamiakin's son): 227, 233
The Dalles: 11, 25–27, 33–37, 43n., 46, 64, 85, 113, 121, 125, 140–42
Thomas (Columbia River chief): 65, 78
Thompson River: 44n.
Thorp, Maj. John: 45, 46
Thorp, Willis (sheriff): 156
Timentowah: 297, 299–300, 303
Toats Coulee: 194, 200, 218, 227
Tocarnemoick: 301
Tolemiat: 234
Tomehoptowne (Perkins' murderer): 86, 170, 171; *see also* murder
Tomeo (Kamiakin's son): 227, 233, 318–19
Tompasque (Moses' shaman): 93–94, 234, 287, 302
Tomquinwit (Moses' daughter): 186
Tonasket (Okanogan chief): 77–78, 107, 173, 187, 194, 202–203, 207, 209–11, 217, 234, 241, 247, 347; illness, 276; death, 287
Toohulhulsote (Nez Percé chief): 65
Toosehammen: 266
Toppenish Creek: 33
Trails: Columbia Plateau, 11; Walla Walla, 51; Silver Creek, 218; Fort, 218, 237, 240; Nanum, 245
Treaty: Walla Walla, 44, 331; Col. Wright-Skamow, 273
Tremont House: 149, 205, 206
Turner, George (attorney): 290
Turner, John (squawman): 260–61, 304
Twenty-One Mile Creek: 217
Tweonne (Perkins' murderer): 86, 170–71; *see also* murder
Twislikin: 267
Two Moons (Joseph's shaman): 233–34, 335
Twotownahhnee: 34n.

Umapine (Umatilla chief): 147–48
Umatilla Indians: 36, 49, 85, 112, 120, 151, 154, 170, 176, 290, 292, 294; flee Oregon, 186, 211, 217, 254
Umatilla River: 63, 141
Umatilla Valley: 6
Umtanum Ridge: 82, 94
Union Gap: 34
Utz, John "Buckskin" (cattleman): 193, 196

Vancouver, Washington: 85, 142, 144, 152, 200
Vancouver Barracks: 198, 202, 305
Vantage: 48
Vigilantes (Okanogan): 279
Volunteers: Palouse rangers, 69; Klickitat rangers, 82–83, 88; Yakima posse, 105ff.

Wadleigh, W. I.: 70, 168, 177
Waitsburg, Washington: 90, 101
Walla Walla, Washington: 58–59, 68–69, 114, 129, 139, 170, 222
Walla Walla Indians: 36, 107, 154
Walla Walla River: 38, 221
Walla Walla Valley: 29, 36
Wallowas: 64, 302
Wallula, Washington: 44n., 79, 85, 89–90, 159–60
Wallula Junction: 221
Wanapum Indians: 49–50, 65, 70, 107, 189, 229
Wappato, John: 54, 91, 271–72
War Department: 80, 83, 88–89, 131, 137, 190, 199, 201, 203–206, 232, 240
Waring, Lieut. John K.: 226
Warner, Olin: 292–93
Wars: Yakima, 30, 65, 147; Wenatchee, 38; McLoughlin Canyon, 39; Civil, 44, 66; Modoc, 59; Apache, 66; Nez Percé, 67ff., 82, 95, 98, 163, 221, 231, 253, 275; Bannock-Paiute, 81ff., 95, 98ff., 130ff., 144, 163
Washington, D.C.: 49ff., 97, 99, 103, 129, 137ff., 149–55, 167, 175, 183, 191, 198ff., 210, 214, 219, 224, 242, 256, 263ff., 272ff., 282, 289ff., 309, 311, 325, 332ff., 342, 349
Washington Territory: 28
Waters, Sidney (Colville agent): 211–12, 214–15, 217, 219, 220
Waterville, Washington: 336, 341
Watkins, Col. E. C.: 64–67, 70, 72, 80, 166
Weather: severe winter, 264ff., 307ff.
Weattatatum (Moses' runner): 101
Webb, C. F. (agency physician): 234
Weed, A. B.: 327
Welch, E. R. (chairman, anti-Moses campaign): 121
Wenamsnoot (Umatilla chief): 147, 148

Wenas Valley: 27, 33, 82, 104
Wenatchee, Washington: 327
Wenatchee Flat: 4–6, 28, 45, 49, 56, 58, 71, 81, 91, 164
Wenatchee Indians: 28, 35, 107, 158–59, 229, 273
Wenatchee Mountains: 28, 35, 81, 94
Wenatchee River: 4, 6n., 11, 29, 37, 42, 46, 58, 70, 87, 91, 144, 161, 172
Wenatchee Valley: 82
Weowikt family: 35, 39, 41, 42, 50
Wheaton, Col. Frank: 72; commandant, Fort Walla, 83–85; commandant, District of Clearwater, 90; charge of Department of Columbia, 203
Whipple, Capt. (Gen. Howard's aide): 91
Whisky: see liquor
White Bird (Nez Percé chief): 75
White Bluffs: 43, 86, 94, 97, 107, 112–15, 118–19, 121, 174
Whitestone: 257
White Swan (Yakima chief): 332
Whitman, Marcus: 23
Whitson, Edward (Moses' attorney): 170
Wilbur, Rev. James (Yakima agent): 57, 61, 65–67, 70, 78–80, 84, 99–105, 112–14, 119, 122–23, 126–34, 136, 138, 140, 160, 171
Wilbur, Washington: 259–61, 285–86, 292, 306, 308, 317, 333, 344–46
Wilkes, Commodore Charles (U.S. Navy): 29
Wilkinson (interpreter): 335
Wilkinson, Lieut. M. C.: 64, 73, 77, 80, 85, 165–66, 178
Wilkinson, Mr. (freighter): 278
Willamette Valley: 28
Winwintipyalatalecotsot: 234
Williams, David: 268, 335
Williams, Richard (Oregon congressman): 128, 143
Williams, Robert: 183
Wilpaukin, Charlie: 291, 320
Wilson, John L. (Washington congressman): 296
Wilson Creek: 49
Winans, W. P. "Park" (Colville agent): 52–53, 55–56
Winecat (Perkins' murderer): 86, 137, 170–71; see also murder

Winters, Capt. W. H.: 130–31, 134, 136, 138, 141, 156, 160, 169
Winthrop, Theodore: 25–26
Wold, Francis (trader): 38
Wood, Erskine: 294, 305, 307, 312
Wood, Lieut. Charles Erskine Scott: 89, 123, 126, 129, 131–32, 136, 139, 159, 161, 164, 175, 293, 294
Woodward's Gardens: 148
Wovoka: 271, 282
Wright, Colonel George: 34ff
Yakima, Washington: 323, 331, 338
Yakima City, Washington Territory: 29, 82ff., 104ff., 156ff., 169–70, 172
Yakima County, Washington: 87, 114, 136, 157

Yakima Falls: 94, 97
Yakima Indians: 4, 34–36, 39, 49–50, 87, 107, 227
Yakima River: 21–22, 33–35, 68, 106, 138
Yakima Valley: 27, 32–33, 69–70, 74, 82, 87, 98–99, 107, 138, 322
Yantis, Ben F.: 44
Yatinawiz: 292
Yayoskin (Moses' nephew): 216, 225, 230, 291, 310–11, 315–16, 347
Yellow Bull (Nez Percé chief): 230, 305
Yellow Chief: 303
Yellowstone Valley: 8
Young Chief (Cayuse chief): 65, 147–48
Youngt, Dr. B. F.: 250
Yow, Sam: 47